Cyberwar and Information Warfare

Cyberwar
and
Information Warfare

Edited by
Daniel Ventre

First published 2011 in Great Britain and the United States by ISTE Ltd and John Wiley & Sons, Inc.

ISTE Ltd
27-37 St George's Road
London SW19 4EU
UK

www.iste.co.uk

John Wiley & Sons, Inc.
111 River Street
Hoboken, NJ 07030
USA

www.wiley.com

© ISTE Ltd 2011

Library of Congress Cataloging-in-Publication Data

Cyberwar and information warfare / edited by Daniel Ventre.
     p. cm.
  Includes bibliographical references and index.
  ISBN 978-1-84821-304-3
  1. Information warfare. 2. Psychological warfare. 3. Computer crimes. I. Ventre, Daniel.
  U163.C937 2011
  355.3'43--dc23
                                                                                                                    2011024020

British Library Cataloguing-in-Publication Data
A CIP record for this book is available from the British Library
ISBN 978-1-84821-304-3

Printed and bound in Great Britain by CPI Antony Rowe, Chippenham and Eastbourne.

Table of Contents

Introduction

Through a range of articles which suggest different and additional approaches, and following in the footsteps of the French experts in this domain, this book takes us into the concepts of information warfare and cyberwar.

Information warfare above all expresses the concept of conflict and the position of information in this context, and it brings conflict into the perspectives of technology and the information society. It is both a war in cyberspace, and a war of ideas. In *Ecran/Ennemi*, François-Bernard Huyghe[1] defines information warfare as "any activity intended to get data and knowledge (and to deprive the enemy from it) for strategic means, either by systems (vectors and means of processing the information), or by content, by ensuring informational domination. Under its offensive perspective, it refers to any operation resorting to rumor, propaganda, computer viruses which corrupt or hijack an opponent's information or data flow, whether this is a State, an army, or a political or economic entity"[2]. It may also be understood as the aggressive/defensive use of components of informational space (information and information systems) in order to hit/protect the sovereignty of a State, by action taken in times of peace, crisis, or conflict [VEN 09].

Cyberwar, a technical dimension of information warfare, may be defined as the recourse to cybernetic capabilities to lead aggressive operations in cyberspace, against military targets, against a State or its society. It will also be defined as "a classic war, where at least one of the components, in execution, its motivations and tools (weapons in the broadest sense) is based on the computerized or digital field"[3].

Introduction written by Daniel VENTRE.
1 François-Bernard Huyghe, see Chapter 1.
2 [HUY 02].
3 Eric Filiol, see Chapter 4.

It is certainly a matter of "war" here, even if we understand that the term may raise problems due its metaphorical use for forms of confrontation which do not use lethal weapons, and do not result in "declarations of war" or "peace treaties". But, moreover, this may be due to the difficulty of making the distinction between a military operation, an act of war, a criminal act, and between a politically, ideologically, criminal or playfully motivated action. Even when it has a negative effect on the balance in our society (and even marginally if the State uses its methods and activists punctually), cybercriminality will not be included in our research here, and will be removed from the field of information warfare and cyberwar definitively. We will focus on more threatening forms of action taken in informational space, which are either destabilizing or destructive, and which target the most vulnerable, important components of our society: our sovereignty, our culture.

At the time when the important, but also the most modest, nations of this world seem confronted with the whole range of cyberattacks, the questions asked by those working for security and defense concern aggressive as much as defensive potentials offered by their own information systems, and of course, those of their competitors or opponents, or even their partners.

The French White Paper on Defense and National Security [GOU 08], and the report by Senator Roger Romani on cyberdefense [ROM 08] have clearly placed the issue of information system security on the same rank as defence and national security.

In 2005, the Labordes report [LAS 05] adopted the same perspective, by considering information system security (ISS) as "an issue on a national scale […] For the State, national sovereignty is at stake. In fact, it is responsible for ensuring the security of its own information systems, the operational continuity of vital institutions and infrastructures for the country's socio-economic activity and protecting companies and citizens".

Armed with this knowledge and political will, the country is therefore not so sheltered from risks, especially when they are difficult to apprehend, and when their production is unpredictable.

In this way, and in the same way as all industrialized countries which are developing a relatively high level of independence in relation to cyberspace, in recent years France has been caught up in the ever growing waves of what we call cyberattacks (attacks against the French Atomic and Alternative Energies Commission in 2006: French diplomats suffering hacked emails, Rafale fighter planes "nailed to the ground", victims of the Conficker impact, etc.).

According to the Romani report, these incidents would have "materialized a still badly identified threat to our continent in a very concrete way, particularly in France". The report proposes a brief list of possible reasons for these flaws in security which are common to all modern States: system interconnections, their relation to the Internet, the contaminating nature of the Internet (everything which comes into contact with it becomes fallible), society's dependence on information systems, the permeability of informational space due to portable equipment (threat to network integrity), flaws in Internet protocol, use of applications (off-the-shelf software) which add to the complexity and flaws in security, contamination of the most solid software by the weakest, etc.

If the positive aspects of the technological revolution of information build the structure of our modern society, then threats of deconstruction are just as high. At the turn of the 1990s, the USA expressed its approaches to information warfare, revealing their ambitions for exploiting and dominating informational space, followed by other large nations. Today, all those intent on getting themselves a place in the mix of nations are considering the possibilities offered by cyberspace as a platform for confrontation and expressing their power. But alongside these groups, we also find those who pay little regard to the doctrines of those in power, and who endeavor to be on a par with them, turning around their traditional forces and challenging them in informational space. This is the combined action of legitimate and illegitimate forces, bred by the instability and insecurity in cyberspace. This is without even mentioning actions of ordinary cybercriminality. All these parties exploit technical flaws, the weaknesses in architecture and its components, and use these weaknesses as their means of force and capacities.

Of course, vulnerability to risk is not exclusive to French systems. With several billions of dollars, the USA is (in pursuit of their quest to dominate cyberspace) also under strain to secure their technological scaffolding, under stresses of alarming discussions on security: "If the nation went to war today in a cyberwar, we would lose. We are the most vulnerable. We are the most connected. We have the most to lose", spoke out Michael McConnell, executive vice-president of American National Security business Booz Allen Hamilton, in February 2010[4].

This type of catastrophic address is, of course, often dictated by direct mercenary interests. But it is also part of an older line of thinking, which sees certain sources of weakness, and societal or civilizational vulnerability in technological power.

This is an interesting question. Has the technological information revolution, which shaped our civilization during the second half of the 20th Century, really changed our vision of the world?

---

4 www.zdnetasia.com/news/security/0,39044215,62061413,00.htm?scid=nl_z_ntnd.

The new world. This is the world in the aftermath of the Cold War, scarred by the attacks of 9/11. It is globalization which creates a world "[...] neither better nor more dangerous" yet "clearly more unstable" (the proof is in the financial crisis of Fall 2008). It is a world which remains dominated by the USA's power but which has a rebalancing effect, to the advantage of Asia, and with:

– new threats (terrorism, ballistic missiles, attacks on information systems, espionage, organized crime networks);

– the gradual disappearance of the distinction between internal and external security;

– a necessary global approach to problems;

– more complexity and uncertainty which make our environment and its threats difficult to apprehend;

– an increase in military spending throughout the world;

– a fragile system of collective security.

This new world also confirms cyberspace as a vital system, a nervous system, of our model of society. Information is more widely spread and much more quickly in cyberspace, with a resultant sped-up action, more media power (The White Paper refers to the "CNN effect"), an uncontrolled flow of ideas, particularly those concerning ideological, religious, and radical contestations, a power gained for non-State groups and a reduced expression of the capacity to control, and State sovereignty. "The staggering acceleration of the circulation of information...makes the States' capacity for autonomous intervention fragile", is written in the White Paper from 2008. This is also a new world which creates a new space out of nothing (cyberspace) and which puts all its hopes into it (economy, a more open, fairer, more equal society). But it also transforms its power and therefore its violence, its crises, its conflicts, as it is a matter of finding the limitations of its sovereignty within it, and defending them.

For all this, if technologies are new, if the global context evolves, we cannot help but notice that constant factors exists in the way mankind may represent technological power and the associated fears (risk, threat, violence, war).

> "Wireless telegraphy and telephony were being used right across Europe, and were so easy to use that even the poorest of men could speak to a man located at any point on the globe, how he wanted, when he wanted [...] This was the abolition of borders. A critical time for all! [...] The French Republic, The German Republic [...], the Swiss Republic and Belgium (sic), all expressed by unanimous vote in parliament and in several meetings, the solemn resolution to defend

national territory and industry against any foreign aggression. Forceful laws were promulgated [...], ruling out the use of wireless telegraphy [...]. Our borders are defended by electricity. A fire zone reigns supreme around the federation. A small, bespectacled man sitting somewhere, anywhere, in front of a keyboard. This is our only soldier. He just has to lay his finger on one button to pulverize an army of 500,000 men".

This article seems extremely modern. However, it is signed by Anatole France and dates back to 1905. In this writing, entitled *Sur la Pierre Blanche* (On the White Stone) [FRA 05], we may recognize very contemporary themes from the start of our 21st Century. They include threats to national defence and security, the negative equivalent (in the eyes of leaders) of the new freedom of communication offered to the people, the threat of foreign attack born out of using these communication technologies, authoritarian and lawful reactions when aware of this threat, and the cooperation of European powers when faced with informational threats. Moreover, we recognize the theme of absolute power which can be found concentrated in the hands of a single man (the hacker sitting in front of his keyboard who became the soldier), as powerful on his own as a whole army (concept of asymmetry). In one single move he is capable of destroying an opponent (the utopia of all technological powers, the will to defeat without confrontation, the war of networks). This is an apocalyptic discourse, reminding us of the catastrophic predictions of an electronic Pearl Harbor (discourse on major threats, collapse of a model society, fatal strategic surprise).

The article writers' relationship with electronic space greatly resembles the relationship that our peers have with cyberspace. Is this wrong, or right?

Faced with this knowledge, and aiming to pull itself away from sometimes exaggerated representations of the role and capacities of informational space and information technologies (apocalyptic and utopic discourse), this collective work by a few French experts having put a vast amount of effort into the themes of information warfare, cyberwar, information and communication, and security and defence, wish to propose a tool for understanding the mechanisms, logic, and modalities which characterize the power struggles within informational space. This is (space of ideas and cyberspace) one of these places where State power and influence will manifest itself. It is a space to be conquered. But States are being challenged by real heavy threats in these spaces with evasive borders. Therefore, in order to respond to the expectations written into the White Paper, as far as the security of our information systems and our sovereignty are concerned, we must measure up the stakes, the capacities and the modes of action which could be used by an aggressor, so that they may defend themselves better, by themselves.

The authors of this collection propose a reflection on key concepts which are: information (in terms of data, messages, knowledge, programs), war, attack, strategic surprise, (military) information warfare, cyberwar, the nature of "cyberwars" or "information warfare", the position of cyberwars in warfare, of cyberspace in conflict, dimensions (of conflict, of cyberspace and information warfare), borders, the enemy (difficulty of identifying, locating, and defining it), power struggles between cybernetic conflict activists, interaction between knowledge and violence, between the real world and cyberspace, the transfer of conflict into cyberspace, the role of politicians when confronted with cyberwars, the victim's political attitude, the strategy (offensive and defensive), the consequences of applying the term "war" to cybernetic attacks, the relationship between the West and non-Western world, the relationship that Western democracies could or must have with the war of meaning and cyberwar in order to retain their vision of the world and their power.

On the other hand, this book proposes an insight into the technical, operational, and strategic dimensions of a cyberattack. This includes the accompanying role played by cyberwar (in relation to classic military operations), the importance of combining old strategies with technology, the imputability of attacks, the limits imposed by the impossibility of a backlash (where the aggressor cannot be identified), the difficulty of defining and understanding the rules to be applied in the absence of direct combat, the essential characteristics of cyberwar; obliterating space (ignoring distances and borders), time (surprise), proof (the attacker operates with complete impunity), the attacker's advantage gained on the target, the aggressor's power, the position of human beings in cyberattacks and in cyberspace.

Individuals are the major cogs in important infrastructures, and they make up the easy and favored targets that we can hit via cyberspace (rumors, misinformation, and personal data exploitation). This book will also include the manipulation of reality, the major importance of strategic and tactical frameworks and methods which are capable of giving an aim to cyberwar, and to cyberattacks which are capable of putting together operations in the pursuit of well defined aims. It also includes the vital role of information, the exploitation of paralysis brought on by a strategic surprise cyberattack, the choice of targets, the extent of the attack's impacts when carried out electronically, the real effects on organizations which have been attacked, identification of the manifestations of reciprocal interactions between humans and systems, between the "real" and the "virtual".

The first four chapters compose the theoretical and conceptual part of the book:

– *Cyberwar and its Borders* (François-Bernard Huyghe) which is an interrogative and mediological chapter;

– *War of Meaning, Cyberwar and Democracies* (François Chauvancy), dealing with the historical-cultural factors of a new polemology;

– *Intelligence, the first Defence? Information Warfare and Strategic Surprise* (Joseph Henrotin), a strategy analysis;

– *Cyberconflict: Stakes Of Power* (Daniel Ventre), on the geopolitical dimension of cyberconflict.

The last three chapters offer a more practical, empirical, and operational approach:

– *Operational Aspects of a Cyberattack, Information, Planning and Conduct* (Eric Filiol), thus analyzes the connection between the attack and general strategies;

– *Riots in Xinjiang and Chinese Information Warfare* (Daniel Ventre) analyzes the Chinese strategy when confronted with an internal crisis;

– *Special Territories* (Daniel Ventre) deals with information warfare and cyberwar in North Korea and Hong Kong.

Bibliography

[FRA 05] FRANCE A., *Sur la Pierre blanche*, fr.wikisource.org/wiki/Sur_la_pierre_blanche, Paris, France, 1905.

[HUY 01] HUYGHE F.B., *L'ennemi à l'ère numérique*, PUF, Paris, France, 2001.

[HUY 02] HUYGHE F.B., *Ecran/Ennemi. Terrorismes et guerres de l'information*, www.huyghe.fr/dyndoc_actu/424eb3aed503a.pdf, Editions 00h00, Paris, France, 2002.

[LAS 05] LASBORDES P., *La sécurité des systèmes d'information, un enjeu majeur pour la France*, www.mag-securs.com/IMG/pdf/rapport_Pierre_Lasbordes.pdf, Paris, 26 November 2005.

[GOU 08] GOUVERNEMENT FRANÇAIS, Le livre blanc sur la défense et la sécurité nationale, Odile Jacob, Paris, France, 2008.

[ROM 08] ROMANI R., Rapport d'information fait au nom de la Commission des Affaires étrangères, de la défense et des forces armées sur la cyberdéfense, Sénat, www.senat.fr/rap/r07-449/r07-4491.pdf, Paris, France, 8 July 2008.

[VEN 09] VENTRE D., *Information Warfare*, ISTE Ltd, London and John Wiley & Sons, New York, 2009.

List of Acronyms

AFCYBER	Air Force Cyber Command
ANSSI	*Agence nationale de la sécurité des systèmes d'information* (National Security Agency Information Systems)
APCERT	Asia Pacific Computer Emergency Response Team
ARCYBER	Army Cyber Command
ASAT	Anti-Satellite Technologies
ASIO	Australian Security Intelligence Organisation
AusCERT	Australia Computer Emergency Response Team
BCS	Baltic Cyber Shield
BPC	Bipartisan Policy Center
C2	Command & Control
C4ISR	Command, Control, Communications, Computers, Intelligence, Surveillance and Reconnaissance
CAHK	Communication Association of Hong Kong
CARIS	Chemical Accident Response Information System
CCDCOE	Cooperative Cyber Defence Centre of Excellence
CC-IN2P3	*Centre de calcul de l'IN2P3* (A computing center in Villeurbanne, France)
CDX	Cyber Defense Exercise
CEPA	Closer Economic Partnership Agreement

CERN	European Laboratory for Particle Physics
CERT	Computer Emergency Readiness Team
CIA	Central Intelligence Agency
CID	Confrontations in the Information Dimension
CNN	Cable News Network
CND	Campaign for Nuclear Disarmament
CNO	Chief of Naval Operations
CNRS	*Centre National de la Recherche Scientifique* (National Center for Scientific Research)
CSOC	Cyber Security Operations Centre
CSS	Central Security Service
CyberOps	Cyber Operations
CyberSA	Cyber Situational Awareness
CyberSpt	Cyber Support
CyNetOps	Cyber Network Operations
DDoS	Distributed Denial of Service
DHS	Department of Homeland Security
DNI	Director of National Intelligence
DoD	Department of Defense
DPRK	Democratic People's Republic of Korea
ENISA	European Network and Information Security Agency
FEMA	Federal Emergency Management Agency
GCHQ	Government Communication Headquarters
HKCERT	Hong Kong CERT
HUMINT	HUMan INTelligence
IC3	Internet Crime Complaint Center
ICT	Information and Communication Technologies
IP	Internet Protocol
KAIST	Korea Advanced Institute of Science and Technology

LID	*Lutte Informatique Défensive* (Defensive Computing)
LIO	*Lutte Informatique Offensive* (Offensive Computing)
MyCERT	Malaysian Computer Emergency Response Team
NASA	National Aeronautics and Space Administration
NATO	North Atlantic Treaty Organization
NCSC	National Cyber Security Center
NIS	National Intelligence Service
NSA	National Security Agency
ONI	Office of Naval Intelligence
OODA	Observe, Orient, Decide, Act
OOTW	Operation Other Than War
RFID	Radio Frequency Identification
RMA	Revolution in Military Affairs
SCADA	Supervisory Control and Data Acquisition
SGDSN	*Secrétariat général de la défense et de la sécurité nationale* (Secretary General for National Defence and Security)
SIGINT	SIGnal INTelligence
SingCERT	Singapore Computer Emergency Response Team
SNDC	Swedish National Defense College
UN	United Nations

Chapter 1

Cyberwar and its Borders

In recent decades, military ideology has produced a plethora of concepts, each time indicating a "new war" or a never-before-seen method of war. These are all supposed to reflect evolutions in technology and emerging political factors (and all of them must be sent to the dusty shelves of history, as a "classic" or "Clauswitzian" war[1]).

The non-initiated person struggles to find his place between asymmetric warfare and fourth generation warfare (4GW), and image warfare and information warfare. He will find it difficult to grasp the slight difference between the *PSYOPS* (psychological operations) and public diplomacy, and a computer network exploitation (CNE), *infodominance*, electronic warfare, or *I-War*[2].

Yet, in this flowery if not conceptual language, at least one term follows a media criterion: *cyberwar*. The term is contested by those who, much like the author, believe that it is not truly a war. Businesses selling security products often use the term for indicating facts which unmask simple, self-interested criminality, and by no means, a real conflict... But *cyberwar* is upon us, and we must pay homage to a success which it is not forbidden to question or even explain.

Chapter written by François-Bernard HUYGHE.
1 See the interesting review by S. Colin [GRA 05], [GRA 07].
2 We pointed out this strategic prolixity in [HUY 01] and it has only become more apparent since.

1.1. The seduction of cyberwar

Can we lead a conflict with, by, and against computers and networks? This hypothesis is indeed attractive, because several factors are involved:

Everybody has, at least once, been subjected to a computer attack, often a relatively benign form of malware (viruses, "malicious" software, which has made him/her lose time in repairs or adjustments). Even if the damage only seems minor (a few hours where the machine has stopped working, the time and energy needed to get anti-virus software or find a solution for the breakdown), each person has had the feeling that a hostile force was attacking them from the interfering machine (and after all, if just a few lost hours are irritating for one person, it may have dramatic consequences for services, a large organization or a country).

An Internet user, John Doe, was a victim, or almost, of phishing (who has not received a request from a mysterious person promising a percentage of an enormous money transfer?). For most of us, these cons or attempts at information theft have hardly led to much damage (except for a few unfortunate people who had personal data, and sometimes money, stolen, or even more seriously, had their identity hacked by con artists pretending to be them). But more still, the average citizen may be faced with the intrinsic dangerous nature of the computer + network combination, even if it is in a toned down way: falsification, bait files, paralysis, invisible and remote intrusion, destruction or substitution. There are as many new situations as attacks on the goodwill or security of the internet user who may start to suspect the system's intrinsic danger. He can easily grasp that cyber security is a major issue and involves enormous budgets. He may also imagine the chaos that might be let loose for a Nation which depends on electronic networks, if acts such as these were to multiply, or if State services could do with their royal finances what hackers manage to do with their limited resources. This mainly consists of intruding on someone's privacy, their secrets for example, or looking for a way to disrupt them (disorder, breakdown, etc.). As the citizen was able to feel the vulnerability of their own machines (after all, if they had been properly armed with sufficiently resistant cryptology systems, useful security procedures, good anti-virus software, good firewalls, etc., meaning if they had been more careful then nothing would have happened), then they may comprehend the flaws in general informational systems and take from it that the seriousness of the attack would indeed be decreased.

The idea that the weapon of knowledge – a way of producing algorithms, of revealing *secrets*, of discovering flaws which allow the weak and cunning to send a whole country into chaos – is like something from a novel, if not intellectually stimulating. It has managed to fuel an entire literary and cinematographic movement.

A science fiction novel, *The Shockwave Rider* [BRU 75], described a *cyberpunk,* the hero who was already fighting the authorities by sending worms into computer networks with an oppressive power. The imagination (pirates, chaos and electrons) preceded the effective spreading of cyberattacks.

From *Softwar*, a science fiction novel published in 1984 by Thierry Breton [BRE 84] to the latest video games, including *Digital Fortress* [BRO 98] (author of Da Vinci Code), the figure of the scientist when discovering with dismay that the computer (which the whole country depends on) has been compromised has become a stereotype. We can add to this the infinite number of films or series whose plots include an electronic virus put into the computer by demon intelligence.

In a more academic listing, nearly twenty years ago, think-tanks greatly increased studies on cyberwar and developed increasingly more worrying scenarios. In 1993, with a ground breaking article by Arquilla and Rondfelt, we too knew that *Cyberwar is coming* [ARQ 93][3].

Ever since, the reports, plans and cries of panic have multiplied, whether addressed to the President of the USA or to the latest Davos Forum[4]. These are often doubly classified as either apocalyptic or utopic.

In the first case, the world is warned against a technological catastrophe: the collapse of great nations which, through a lack of solid defense systems, could be brought to their knees by disorganizing digital attacks. To give just one example, in February 2010 a few weeks after the Obama administration named a *cyber czar* who was responsible for all these matters, it was followed up by an exercise known as the *cybershockwave* which simulated a computer attack on the USA[5]. Michael McConnell, who was Head of National Intelligence from 2007 to 2009, declared in front of the American Senate Committee, "If we went to war today in a cyberwar, we would lose"[6].

In the second case, 21st Century policy makers plead (or rather *pleaded*, because inspiration somewhat dried up after September 11th), for a high-tech, newly considered, resolutely post-modern war, where information superiority would practically stop resorting to force.

---

3 This concept is taken up again and developed in [ARQ 97].
4 "Prevent 'cyber war' by a treaty", recommended by a UN agent, in *Libération*, 30th January 2010.
5 "CybershockWave: quand les Etats-Unis simulent une cyberattaque" by Gueric Poncet describing this exercise organized by the *Bipartisan Policy Center*, Le Point, 15th February 2010.
6 "US would lose cyberwar: former Intel chief" by Chris Lefkow, AFP, 23rd February 2010.

The terminology of cyberwar spreads via acts which range from economic espionage to computer sabotage. The media's interest in the matter (and in cybersecurity discourses, which are not always objective, and which wrongly use terms of war or terrorism) have made the idea popular. It is not lacking in foundations, seeing as every four to six months Western information systems go under attack. They are often said to come from Russia or China and considered as being serious enough to constitute as acts of war, at least enough to create diplomatic problems. As for political and international governmental organization heads, they are referring more and more to a hypothesis of cyberterrorist danger, without always clearly distinguishing communicational facilities – terrorists use the Internet to express themselves, to recruit, to spread messages, to get information, to instruct, exactly like every other user – and the harmful capacities that they could lead to in cyberattacks. For the moment these hypotheses remain theoretical.

The image of *cyberspace* is rather eloquent. Why does the human desire to fight and destroy not take place in *this* space? The vision of the Internet is naturally becoming "a new battle ground" or offering a new "dimension" (the fifth dimension after the earth, sea, air, and stratosphere) to conflict that which is established by the power of metaphors.

1.2. Desirable, vulnerable and frightening information

In short, we are getting used to the idea that cyberwar (above all virtual, for the time being) is inevitably going to break out on a large scale. Moreover, our future vulnerability will be proportionate to our present dependency, with regard to our prostheses which are supposed to compute, monitor and memorize everything for us, but also to bring us together.

Another decisive element, the notion of information warfare, in spite of or thanks to its lack of precision, has been easily established as a promising project for the strategist (saving violence by information, bringing conflict into the perspective of technology and information society), a slogan for the politician (declaring him/herself as a victim of information warfare will stigmatize the opponent and explain, sometimes at a low cost, why public opinion does not believe what we might want it to). Here, there are four kinds of information:

– data which is stored somewhere, which can be quantified, transported and reproduced;

– circulating messages and particularly the "news" which describes world events;

– knowledge or belief systems which are built into the human brain;

– programs carrying instructions (such as genetic codes or software algorithms).

Of course, without counting for the fact that, if information is immaterial, then it depends on material supports: systems, vectors, networks, memories, etc., which are all susceptible to being altered, blocked, sabotaged, violated (to seize information), hijacked – which could be subjected to conflicts and seizures of power. In today's usage, "information warfare" may have several meanings:

– "lies, propaganda, manipulation", on an international scale (according to which side of the camp we are on, we will accuse, for example, the Israelis or Palestinians of poisoning Western journalists, of inventing fake victims or mass graves, of having accomplices working in the French press which censor news which may not be in their favor, and yet may exaggerate other news). In the current context, the term "information warfare" is used by the media as a synonym for the war of images or confrontation used by propaganda. It would be more precise, in this restricted meaning, to speak of "war of information", meaning the "news" that we see, hear, or read. The definition would then be: conflicts, maneuvers, the polemics which concern the representation the public makes of military events;

– "destabilization, accusation before public opinion, starting rumors, subversion". For example, the campaigns led by NGOs against large businesses, or the rumors which go around on the Internet to do with some industrial accident, or some pollution. But the term may also be applied to operations of communication, lobbying, or other operations led by specialized organizations supporting economic interests: helping a company within a hostile tender offer (TO) framework, supporting the tobacco or weapons industry, by reassuring consumers or influencing international organizations and other manifestations of what some are calling "public relations" and what others are calling "lying industries";

– a definition which is close to industrial espionage or electronic surveillance;

– a technological definition where it is a matter involving harmful software, sabotage of vital infrastructures and taking power over the millions of "zombie" computers;

– a military definition where it is a matter of making the battle ground "transparent", of having "informational dominance" over the enemy, and of leading "psychological operations".

In more theoretical articles, information warfare is described as being a general dimension of strategies in information society. Thus, we are referring to a war *by*, *for*, *against* information, meaning moves which are illegal but still aggressive and which are intended to either:

– spread a point of view in favor of its objectives, or to weaken a rival by a discourse and/or attacks which may damage its image as well as its information systems;

– gain decisive knowledge in order to win control over a market, a technological superiority, lead a military or political operation;

– counter the enemy's or competitors' moves compared to that of public opinion or decision-makers (refuting its propaganda, its slander, its proselytism, its attempts to destabilize) but also ensuring the safety of its own information systems against an attack by being overloaded with a site, virus, or other "malware".

These alternations go from the military to the political, from the economical to the technological, from the psychological to questions of security. For the first, this means applying Sun Zi principles. For the second, it means buying good software. For the rest, it is a question of controlling the media.

1.3. Conflict and its dimensions

On the other hand, we could support the fact that there has never been a conflict without an information strategy, and that each time we must answer the questions which already preoccupied Greek Sophists and Chinese generals:

– How do we make the other believe what we desire, whether it is a matter of persuading them through reasoning, or deceiving them by a ruse?

– How can we know what he does not know? Or how do we know what he does not know, but what we *do* know?

– How do we make the other predictable and elusive? Make ourselves elusive.

Military information warfare also includes information in the sense of "data", when it is a question of computer data and communication systems. See the section on *high tech* in the *Revolution in Military Affairs*, the changes brought about by art in order to take over computers, networks, satellites, intelligent weapons, etc.

Offensive techniques are changing; they paralyze adverse communication networks, they send vital infrastructures into disorder, etc. In addition, they integrate digital technologies into the recognition of objectives, data transmission, the coordination of armed forces, the management of intelligent weapons, etc.

If we take it up a level, information warfare is also a war of information as knowledge. Having informational dominance is like having an exact and global representation of the situation, enabling a suitable and instantaneous strategic decision, whereas the opponent is thrown into the fog of ignorance. Therefore, it is a matter of a structural condition of military superiority (because this presumes, prior to everything, equipment and the belief that structures and mentalities will adapt to the information revolution).

To a certain extent, the "strong" will fight to keep their global informational domination in terms of outlets, technology and the influence of their technological, media, cultural and ethical models. But, in the spirit of the strategies which design the project, this may be confused with the passing over to the Information Society, and with the global predominance of American influence. Therefore, it is indeed legitimate to say that any war led by a hyper power is a war "for information", a war to make a certain conception of what information is predominate above all others; an ideological and Messianic war.

The global nature of conflict, spanning across the political-military, techno-economical and ideological-cultural domain is confirmed. While war activates an increasingly more important component in terms of information and communication means (including "civilianization"), the apparent "information" economy becomes ever more conflicting. This is also through the sometimes regal methods that it uses (see the espionage systems from the Cold War such as *Echelon*, reconverted into winning markets in the 1990s) and because economy, technology, culture, diplomacy, and war are included in the perspective of the same geopolitical project. "Information warfare" is, then, a label which covers all sorts of goods. For all this, it is not forbidden to try to put everything back into order.

There is a first distinction here. Information warfare mainly consists of inflicting damage on an opponent or competitor by using signs instead of force. The damage in question may be performed directly, by affecting what the other side knows or what it can be. Or it can be done indirectly, by changing the opinion of the outsider.

In the first case, it is a matter of making a decision in favor of our intentions (or, which boils down to the same thing, preventing action in want of choice). The aim is to manipulate the cognitive factors and to gain the monopoly of relevant information ("true" descriptions of the reality making it possible to act). We reach this aim by processes which may include espionage, electronic surveillance, poisoning or informational sabotage.

In the second case, the aim is to reduce the opponent's freedom to act by discrediting them, by making them lose their forces or allies – in short, by changing their image rather than their will. Therefore, by depriving them of means of action rather than means of cognition, and by making them believe rather than actually knowing (or preventing them from knowing). Here, it is a matter of making the information "efficient", of using the information whose strategic value does not depend on its truthfulness but in fact, its diffusion. It is powerful insofar as it finds takers, "believers" who adopt the point of view and desired judgment values.

Information warfare possesses both a cognitive dimension and a dimension of belief, which we will call "accreditative" (the ability to impose oneself, which presupposes the ability to attract attention as a precondition). However, the knowledge and assessment of the first case above raises technical problems. The second case inevitably causes psychological problems.

In the first case, the ever-changing nature of technology is combined with the interests of those involved (overestimating or underestimating damage, depending on the case), to render it more obscure and uncertain.

However, in other cases, our ignorance stems from our lack of knowledge for message efficiency: this is the mystery of persuasion. What is it that makes a campaign, either for publicity or propaganda, fail or not fail?

For more than 70 years now, sciences known as "information and communication" and "media studies" have been banging their heads against this brick wall (particularly concerning "mysteries of acceptance"). They have rejected the myth of an intrinsic force in the messages which would enable them to trigger emotions at will, or to produce beliefs on demand. They tend to conclude that the message "receiver" is much less easy to manipulate than we would believe, and much more capable of reinterpreting or refusing the message if it did not correspond to their own codes. A practical reflection would be to say that no information warfare campaign is certain of being a success, even if it has enormous means of broadcasting itself, and even if it is formulated by professionals, following all guides. But on the other hand, such a campaign may only succeed if it relies on its "target's" expectations, a mass of beliefs and already accepted ways of reasoning, on a general pre-established belief system; a "doxa" in the jargon of human sciences. Upon mastering the message and the media (where Western people no longer have full control), we may add the control over cultural mediums (understanding the codes of the intended message receiver and the way in which they will interpret them). Finally we will add control over mediations, organizations and communities through which new beliefs spread and stabilize.

1.4. The helm and space

Cyberwar seems to be a component of a much vaster matrix (unless the right metaphor is that which refers to Russian dolls which fit into each other).

Yet, upon a closer look, this neologism raises questions. Its etymology combines the term "war", a universal, anthropological experience (which does not necessarily mean that the term is universally fixed), with the prefix *cyber*. The latter, which comes from the Greek word *kubernein*, which means that the *helm* has become a trend by Wiener's cybernetic in the post-war world. It then ended up being coupled with all sorts of notions (like cyberculture, cybercrime, or cyberpunk), and taking on a definition which is so vast that it ends up meaning "vaguely linked to computer science". But the idea that we might have of war by or with a "helm", therefore by managing information or managing ourselves in an informational environment, does not seem any less paradoxical.

Other than frightening (see the fantasies of a digital *Armageddon*), we have been told that cyberwar will be in networks, dematerialized and without boundaries, etc., along with other notions which have become standard in the last 20 years of anticipation describing the information society. These are all negative attributes, or more exactly, those which reject point by point the supposed traits of the industrial society which is based on a hierarchical order, on the intense use of matter and energy, on the circulation of objects, time and distances, etc. In this sense, cyberwar, the obscure side of the emerging world, is doubly utopic.

Here, we use utopic in the sense adopted by today's language: imaginary production, description of a possible state to come from society (here, this would be catastrophic in relation to happy utopias), assessed according to present potential and intended to incite leaders, even citizens, to take measures for moving towards a better future and avoiding the worst.

But in its real meaning, cyberwar is deprived of *topos* (*u-topia*), and we cannot give it a location with certainty. What are the invaded, digital provinces? Where are the troops of electrons deployed? Which front for which battles? Where do the belligerents come from, and where they going?

In other words, cyberwar must be understood in its relationship to a *double border*:

– *Ontological border*: is it really a war? What are the limits between this category and others such as crime, conflict, aggression, predation, etc.?

– *Topological border*: a war has a location and in principal takes place over the territory of such or such a State; how do we transpose or reinterpret these concepts to the digital age?

Reminder: there has never been a computer war with an opening and closure of hostilities, linking of strategies and counter strategies, backlashes and offensives, deaths, occupied territories, armistice and peace, disarming, etc. (no more than an attack by an intervening electron which has caused death or unimaginable damage).

Indeed, there have been offensives and attacks (generally unilateral and discovered afterwards). Those responsible for cybersecurity periodically unmask attempts to intrude computer networks, and nobody thinks about denying that certain large, private and public organizations may suffer from it. Thus, at the precise moment in time, it is a question of flaws in Internet Explorer which may have allowed Chinese pirates to perform a high measure offensive and to seize confidential data via Google (at the same time, other sources are referring to human complicity in the firm's staff). The predation was electronic, on a large scale, and a source of economical and political complications. However, it was not a war.

References are often made to the Estonia "conflict" in 2007. That summer, watchers were able to observe the country's informational systems being blocked in public services or important infrastructures. This was attributed to a Russian neighbor and its computer pirates. The attack was interpreted as a warning to the little country of Estonia, which was guilty of a symbolic offense (moving the statue of a soldier from the Red Army).

Some attacks create undeniable damage for the operation of the State's devices, even if it were only by freezing sites by overloading them with DDOS (denial of service attack) type techniques, or by intruding computers which are, in principle, secured to protect against disturbances in normal use.

These famous examples (that others will analyze better than us here) reflect two types of aggressive action. Firstly, the aggressors try to seize confidential and precious data (in order to increase their own power, whether aimed at economic competitors or rebels). Secondly, they try to stop an informational system from working.

Thus, it is a question of weakening the other. Both methods remain on a scale of certainty and difference: more certainty for "my" side (I know the other's resources or plans); less certainty for "him" (the data to guide his action is corrupted or inaccessible and/or is no longer capable of communicating or coordinating his forces).

It might seem that the classic categories of espionage (stealing protected information to strengthen one's own offensive capacity at a later date, or such as suggested in the Chinese case, to recognize its own opponents), or sabotage (putting things into disarray, producing damage, disorder, errors, paralysis, leading the machine or the opening to make wrong decisions, etc.) are sufficient here. The predation/confusion combination seems to include most computer attacks. Indeed, the conflict is not only a matter of certainties (for example, data and knowledge, information likely to be true or useful); it also depends on beliefs and motivations which act upon our minds. This explains the existence of other methods.

In contrast to previous attacks which are "system oriented" and "given", one form of offensive seems to be "message oriented". Thus, the "defacing" of opponent sites, the use of Internet resources to overload favorable or hostile message in forums for expressing ourselves: in short, media appropriation. However, these offenses which are much more benign fall into the well-known category of propaganda, which include a battle of opinions to monopolize attention; new due to its technical forms, but old in terms of its motivations.

1.5. Between knowledge and violence

We have already written that there are four "martial arts" of information. The four ways of using this resource ("information") may also indicate, in addition to the information which is in newspapers and supposed to reflect reality, the data which is stored over time, messages which communicate with each other via vectors or media, or even programs which are produced). These are:

– the art of keeping our own secret, in order to make our intentions or abilities impenetrable for an opponent or rival;

– the art of stealing secrets from the other side, surveillance, espionage or information retrieval in order to know what the other side can be or wants, or in order to solve the old military problem of "what's over there behind that hill?";

– the art of misleading, misinforming, in short leading the opponent by a ruse, faking or setting him up to wrongly use his abilities;

– the art of "declaration", to propagate positive or negative convictions in order to liven up activists, to rise up those who are neutral against the opponent and discourage or divide his camp.

Hiding, knowing, baiting, and persuasion: these four are necessary and inherent to any conflict, and are recognized by ancient strategies. However, they may take on another dimension with the technique's capacities.

In fact, each operation responding to these four functions is deeply affected by the "computer + network" binary:

– For the most part, secret keeping becomes a matter of cryptology, algorithms, software, firewalls, passwords and other devices which are both sophisticated and dematerialized (in contrast, for example, with a secret formula recorded on paper under lock and key, or omerta, which is based on fear). The secret is protected by signs, and no longer by walls or weapons.

– *Espionage* may be practiced with this single terminology. It is useless, in order to take up the previous idea again, to send people to force locks or to slip through corridors in secret. Malware, such as Trojan Horses, not only reproduce and export confidential data, but also operate a true seizure of power. They literally give orders through algorithms, and carry out certain tasks on their new slaves. Hackers are innovators: for instance, by turning an infected computer into a "zombie" slave they practice a kind of invisible *coup d'etat*; a machine, or more often whole networks, which no longer obeys its real owner, and are manipulated remotely by the pirate. Through the "knowledge" function, the pirate then passes onto the "command" function. This is also an innovation in relation to classic war, where it is rare for someone to be skilful enough in order to take command over enemy troops.

– *Sabotage*, often by destroying the opponent's means of communication or transport, increases what Clausewitz called the "friction and fog" of war, to the detriment of the other side. Friction (inability to carry out orders, to coordinate oneself, etc.) or the fog (bad perception of the environment, impossibility of accessing reality, making risky decisions) are frightening in societies which operate in tense flows, by a continuous exchange of information and interactions. The infectious nature of chaos could, according to certain projections, culminate a society whose vital infrastructures would be thrown into disorder by surprise, anonymously and through remote manipulation. This is where the myth of a Digital Pearl Harbor or a Cybergeddon (cyber + Armageddon)[7] comes from, which feed on futuristic or even apocalyptic literature [CSI 08]. In these scenarios, the damage caused by chaos in emergency systems, airports, energy supplies, etc., would finally result in death through a chain of consequences: digital disorder, giving organizational paralysis of services and institutions, social disorders, or death.

– *Propaganda* is made easier through dematerialization. There is no longer any need for leaflets or brochures to be hidden from customs or police to make a cause known, or to symbolically humiliate an enemy. Some methods, even if they are not very elegant, may with some difficulty be described as guerrilla methods. Thus, when the Chinese authorities, which are not lacking in human resources, use millions of badly paid internet users to defend patriotic theses in forums throughout the world, this still remains under the scale of armed conflict.

The three elements may be combined. Often it has been necessary to "violate a secret" (seizing a code, crossing semantic defenses) in order to alter (infect a computer by malicious software which will execute instructions with a delayed effect), all of which will potentially aim for the opinion (i.e. zombie computers to deface a site and ridicule an institution using "tag", drawings or vengeful slogans put on its public display).

Would cyberwar, a defensive for the aggressor, when widely opening up the range of instruments of constraint and destruction in the aggressor's possession, only be a way of doing with machines and algorithms (anonymously, risk-free and remotely), what strategists have always wanted to do?

---

7 "Le FBI hanté par la menace d'une apocalypse cybernétique", *Le Monde,* 7th January 2009.

It is tempting to respond to this affirmative insofar as it is a matter of responding to secular functions by new instruments. However, digital techniques do not play a simple substitution role here, where electrons replace human beings or information replaces forces.

1.6. Space, distance and paths

If the transposition of conflict into cyberspace raises new problems, they are still of the same nature. We know that the word "cyberspace" first appeared in 1984. Then it appeared again in a science fiction novel by William Gibson, *Neuromancer*, in order to show the "graphic representation of data extracted from memories from all the computers in the human system". The space in question [LEV 98][8] is made up of interconnected information (the internet user feels as though he is moving "through" data worlds, immersing himself in information and not considering it to be collected in objects like books). As the existence of hyperlinks will symbolize, in this world, "movement" brings together signs and representations according to a perspective where any word, image, or number may lead to others, according to a code and a meaning.

The same sort of miracle is not possible so long as cyberspace is supported by another space, which is completely physical, inhabited by machines whose hard drives contain any information, cables (which may possibly be sectioned off), and antennas which cover a certain area, etc.

Everything relies on material structures. Indeed, we move in cyberspace according to a semantic logic (a certain link towards a certain page, a certain message towards an address made of symbols, etc.). But the interaction between representations covers the circulation of electrons. They come from material objects (memories, hard drives where data is stored); they circulate via physical channels and vectors (cables, machines, antennas, etc) towards objects. Cyberspace is dematerialized if we consider it to be a pure system of circulation and organization (it hardly matters to the user whether a certain information package followed a particular itinerary on the network, the concept of paths no longer seems very relevant), and greatly depends on material "things" where the said information still exists as a trace inscripted on a memory but also on material infrastructures (like a submarine cable which can be cut).

A third factor enters into the world of representations and the world of material things. Some say that it is the third dimension of cyberspace, a syntactic dimension

---

8 For more on this subject, see the analyses by Pierre Lévy who very quickly recognized the new type of conflicting dimensions in this space, particularly in Cyberculture, a report to the European Council, Odile Jacob, Paris, 1998.

opposed to physical and semantic components: standards and protocols. So that everything communicates and interacts, so that "it" circulates and is transformed, we must indeed have some rules (the Internet would not exist without the Tcp/IP protocol). Attacks could be made on each of these components, with these "things" acting as containers, vectors or channels (sabotage or destruction of the physical carrier), data (copied or altered in order to change the "message"), or codes (as when the viruses change the "game rules" and change the way in which the data is diffused or ordered).

In the cyber world, a battle unfolds by instantaneous and delayed action which may come from anywhere to reach any point in the world, even by relaying, which is physically difficult to identify. Therefore, the victim could go to "places" in cyberspace such as IP addresses, which are machines (which have an "address" but nothing can prove that the owner is aware of the use that has been made of it). Nobody moves large battalions or has a strategic position, if not in the order of knowledge. We fight from address to address, and no longer from province to province. Power is no longer evaluated in terms of missile heads, but by the millions of compromised computers. If the attack is just a nuisance or disruption (even espionage involves preventing a system intended to guarantee confidentiality from working properly and keeping its secret), it is located within the system of anomalies and exceptions, and may only be deployed where there is a flaw, shortcoming, or a vulnerability. This logic, in comparison, comes from the conflicts in the two "worlds".

In "our" real world, everything happens according to the movement of people and "projected" forces: an army or missile will go from one point to another in order to conquer or destroy. The strategy is thought out in movements: the good general will ensure the freedom of the maneuver, will move his troops like the skilled Chess or Go player, will restrain his opponent's moves and move to favorable spots. He reasons in terms of territory, "center of gravity" or "concentration of forces", etc.[9]

Space is linked to time: the winner is he who leads his troops to the right place on time; the loser is he who realizes that, to his expense, following the famous formula, all battles were lost due to being half an hour late.

As cyberwar offers an advantage to the attacker and the innovator, and since it can be summarized as – at least up till now – a single offensive, it forces us to think in terms of defensive position and *after* the surprise, without it being easy to project a rational attitude on the presumed meaning of *events*. This being so, cyberwar queries the hierarchical link between the military and the politician (the *primat* of the political aim over the military method). Once the havoc wreaked by the attack is

---

9 For an excellent summary of these concepts, see [MAI 05].

observed, the political leader (had he equipped his country with offensive means recommended by the French military doctrine) is faced with an interlocutor's problem: to whom must he address a counter message, verbal or violent, backlash or retaliation? Moreover, which threat should he shake up, in front of whom, and for which reason? The traditional way of anticipating initiatives and answers, threats, promises and compromises, had a sort of rationale which is cruelly lacking nowadays[10].

A "military capacity" which may only rely on knowledge (if a pirate may borrow other machines, he no longer even needs the machines and computing capacities that only a State may provide) has no intrinsically martial qualities. Here, "war" goes through the movement of men and weapons from the other side of a border (possibly to conquer it and push back the said line), to the movements of invisible electrons which affect computers located over a territory.

Information can be used to damage things (putting computing or communication means out of order), to change or take pieces of information, and finally, to affect people, bully them, shock them, or send them into disarray, but not by killing them directly. This takes us back to the general question on the nature of war.

One distinction separates computer offensives which accompany a classic military action (like the theft of the enemy's plans or sabotaging his communication lines which might accompany an armored tank during WWII), from those offensives which might replace them or be sufficient alone to constitute a "war".

In the first case, if we summarize the supposed cyberwar as information techniques which complete the use of armed force, there is no difficulty. It seems logical that an army would be subjected to the enemy's communication capacities, etc.

The digital army as a way of leading one's own forces (and, in the same line of thinking, to disperse and disorganize the enemy's forces) is included in the strategy's continuity. Nobody would doubt that, when combined with other weapons, those also capable of destruction, that the arsenal of computers helps to win battles, above all between two powers with a certain technological development (which is hardly the case for recent wars).

On the other hand, the description of wars applied to cybernet attacks carried out in peace time raises more problems still. This, above all, concerns an international organization or State which, before reacting, must judge whether it is an act of war

---

10 See the way in which a famous strategist and specialist in information warfare, Martin Libicki, discovers the intrinsic unpredictability of cyberwar in an article published by Rand in 2009: *Cyberdeterrence and Cyberwar* [LIB 09].

calling for punishment, retaliations, counter-attack, etc. It may also have to justify it in front of its own opinion, the media, or a legal authority.

1.7. The permanency of war

There are hardly any cultures which do not distinguish war from other types of violence, and which does give it its own sense of dignity. European tradition, for example, sets the *public enemy* opposite the *private enemy* (*hostis* against *inimicus* for the Romans, *polemos* against *extros* for the Greeks).

After the pioneers of European public law from the 16th Century, lawyers were distinguishing the "symmetrical" opponent, the sovereign over the territory, who could start a war for a just cause ("just" at least in its form, if not its cause or method), from the rebels of civil wars[11] or revolts. This may have no less important historical consequences, but not able in a lawful sense to obtain the "dignity" of a real war. "The other is the enemy, the other is the rebel", according to a legal maxim of people who confirm that war is a monopoly of the sovereign (main component of the famous "legitimate violence" which is reserved for the State) [WAL 06].

The simple reminder of these concepts raises an initial question: who is, *where* is, the enemy is the cyber world? The doubt which looms over the status of the enemy is the first clue. The difficulty stems from the haunting "imputability" of the attack. A government cannot react in the same way when faced with another State which is attacking it, or when facing militant groups who are possibly tolerated or helped by a neighboring government, or even when confronted with private parties only seeking profit such as transnational mafias who have been reconverted into cybercrime. This gets complicated insofar as the suspicious State could very well "hire" a criminal organization, the way some might take on mercenaries or hired killers. Moreover, they may manipulate "ideologically" motivated groups, the way that certain States have funded terrorists in flesh and blood, helped by guerillas, or favored activists or protestors on the other side's territory.

All the same, even if we were to assume that matter was resolved (equipped with an excellent information service, the victim State knows who the guilty parties are, for example), the political dimension of the decision made by the victim would still remain in the foreground. Recognizing the act of war (and offering alliance or assistance to a State which has been a victim of attack, within a treaty framework), deciding to continue with a plan for symmetrical retaliation, or another plan

---

11 Carl Schmitt's theory on "discriminating between the friend and the enemy", the political criterion and developing a general theory of the activist as a new figure head of conflictuality can be used here as a greatly discussed reference. See [SCH 32], [BAL 06], [MON 07], [ZAR 09].

(economic punishments, diplomatic-political action or open violence), is not a choice which carries the same consequences. Deciding whether to act publicly, or secretly and anonymously (just like the enemy's first blow) is also a politically serious choice.

Finally, and above all, this figure of the enemy emerging from the Net (like the Tatars who rose up out of the desert in Buzzati's novel) reflects the issues in the modern Western world; above all the problem of identifying the enemy in the post Cold War world. If people, above all in Europe, no longer refer to the *Justus hostis*[12] of our secular tradition (he who is both just an enemy, not an absolute criminal, but who has a fair right to carry the symmetrical status of the enemy in a public war, from his own territory, his own border, and with the assets of his *sovereignty*). In addition, the discourse of Western powers reflects a visible embarrassment with the concept of hostility. On the one hand it results in criminalizing the enemy who is considered a delinquent (thus deserving a punishment administered by armies acting in the name of mankind) and an immediate danger in terms of global vision and security.

Describing conflictuality in terms of low intensity asymmetrical wars, fourth generation, out of bounds, etc., reflects the regular armies faced with a range of insurrectionary situations, local disorders, "psychological" operations or influential on both sides, "civilian-military" relations with populations (whose "hearts and minds" need to be won over), destruction/reconstruction (*Nation Building, State Building, Peace Building*)... a wide spread range of intermediate situations between maintaining police order, political fights and battles.

The difficulty of pointing out the opponent or understanding the game rules is the same as the difficulty of locating the war. In the absence of an enemy who is likely to acknowledge his defeat over the land, the *strong* know the necessity of controlling a far away territory and having unlimited vulnerability. If the "West" is omnipresent as a principle of globalization, the "target" is also everywhere where we find its symbols and representations: in an airplane, a megalopolis, a bus, or a tourist destination. If its technique is the proof of its domination, then it is also considered as its main point of vulnerability.

This idea of disorientating the strong is not only the product of fantasies for ultimate control; it also reflects the objective strategies of the weak, "unofficially". In situations where the distinction between civil, military and political has been erased, fluid and changing conflicts intervene against a backdrop of "gray areas" and defeated States, multiple hostile parties, militia, warlords, half-mafia, half-terrorist irregular groups, guerillas, networks with international connections, etc. Therefore,

---

12 The root of this concept can be traced back to [SCH 98] and [SCH 01].

military aggression tends to melt away into the dangers and emergencies of "risk" which our societies are obsessed with. The last White Paper of Defense is symptomatic of this, which establishes the function of the territory's armed defense as a "global" concept, mixing together risks and threats likely to bring an attack on the life of the nation[13].

An attacker from the cyberworld currently remains both anonymous and unpredictable, with the confusion between economic, technical and military risks, the ambivalence of criminal guilt and political intention, the violence of the real chaos and the potential threat, and finally the difficulty of separating internal and external security. Without a doubt, this makes the "new enemies" the most emblematic, that our era likes to create [COP 10] and locate somewhere between the fatality of the accident and the perversion of moral intention. The distinctive feature of cyberwar is not limited here, and makes a much vaster use of what is called "classic" war. It is based on different conditions[14]:

– *political*: the willingness to constrain the other party ("enforcing our law on the other side" according to Clausewitz), to obtain a resolution for a dispute and the satisfaction of a "historical" demand;

– *lethality*: the possibility of human loss[15];

– *techniques*: the use of weapons, resorting to specific strategies;

– *symbolic and cultural*: war assumes beliefs, symbols, and communities which are persuaded of the legitimacy of a cause, and the need to crush the opponent's cause.

In other words, war, even when led outside of a State framework (civil war, guerilla, etc.), has always presupposed three "canonic" components:

1) *Specific tools, i.e. weapons*: they offer the possibility of administering collective death (a war where nobody risks their lives would be a tournament, a game, a threat, etc.). The concept of the enemy stems from organized death. He is led to fight, not for what he is personally or for what he has done, or for what he has in his possession, but for what he represents and to what he belongs (the other Nation, for example). The lethality of weapons (therefore the possibility of giving or

---

13 "The strategy for national security encompasses external security as well as internal security, with military means as well as civil, economical or diplomatic. It must take into account all the phenomena, risks and threats likely to bring an attack on the life of the nation", adapted from the *White Paper of Defense and National Security*, 2008 [LIB 08].

14 Alberico Gentilis, in his *De jure bellis* from 1597, was already defining war in this way. War is an armed conflict, public and fair (fair in the eyes of those who practice it). "Hostis hi sunt qui nobis aut quibus nos publice bellum devrevimus", as said Pomponius (Digeste).

15 The French expert in peace and conflict studies, G. Bouthoul, even attributes a demographic function, see *L'infanticide différé*, Hachette, 1971 [BOU 71].

receiving upon order, which is both morally approved and socially glorified) makes war the supreme form of conflict. However, there are never any cyberdeaths in cyberwar. There are obvious losses in finances, knowledge, capacities, potential spreading of disorder or panic, and above all, enormous losses of time. Sooner or later, except for exceptional cases, the damage caused by a cyberattack may be repaired, a question of computer DIY and undoubtedly a warning for the future, if we can spot the vulnerability that the attackers have used to their advantage. Even if the financial, psychological or social damage was huge, nobody will have died. Some scenarios contemplate crossing this border in a country where air traffic, emergency services (police, fire brigade and ambulances) energy or other supplies would undergo an exceptionally serious disruption. This is a simple assumption, from which doubts reduce, at least on the symbolic front, the dimension of this "war".

2) *War is a matter for organized communities*: the fighter recognizes himself as a member of a community who uses his life and orders to take the life of the enemies without counting it as a crime. War is, then, a matter of transmission, in every meaning of the word. Firstly, this involves transmission of identity (us/them). This is manifested by signs, emblems, a discourse in an exultant and sublime register, identifiers (paintings, clothing, uniforms), symbols, rituals, discipline, traditions: in short, everything which links the group together. It is also a matter of transmitting orders, instructions, in the technical meaning of circulating messages well, etc., as the exact term here is rather "communication". War is part of the duration. It could not be summarized as a single rupture of violence, or a unique battle. There is a before and an after the confrontation, a strategy, maneuvers, provisions, moves, gathering resources and managing them. War, even in its primitive form, assumes a materialized organization and a system of legitimacy or even a vision of history. More still, it is difficult to find all these components in cyberattacks as we know them, insofar as it is tricky to describe the parties involved, in terms of the attacker as much as the attackee. The victim: the State may be directly targeted when the aim of the attack is to decrease its defense capacities or to threaten it (diplomacy reinforced by the Internet): "we will continue to disorganize your information systems until you make a political decision".

But the State may also be involved more indirectly, for example when some of its businesses are victims of computer piracy with damage affecting the national economy, and with regard to the order that the politician is supposed to guarantee those working in the economic sector. We may push the argument further: in a democratic system, the authorities ensure our security; if the private life of citizens, their intellectual property or their interests are threatened by computer pirates, then this is a matter for justice and police. This internal question may become a diplomatic or military problem if the attack comes from beyond the external boundaries. The White Paper on Defense, by categorizing computer attacks amongst the main dangers for the nation's "global" security, reminds us that it is up to the State's competence to decide when a prejudice is not simply a private matter. It is up to the politician to say whether the unrest to "public order" causes a problem on an international scale.

3) *A specific aim – victory* (another way of saying that war has a political aim, modifying a power relationship for a long time): victory presupposes the possibility of peace (and everybody from Saint Augustine's time that "we make war that we may live in peace"). Both include either the enemy's physical disappearance, or his renounced demands and surrender. The latter is either through a compromise, a treaty, a form of half-victory (and therefore, he stops being an enemy). Victory changes (or comforts) power in a long-lasting way. For example, we often hear phrases such as "from now on, the Alsatians will be French", or "from now on, the right to trade in a certain port will belong to a certain authority and no longer to a certain other", etc. A power struggle is part of the duration. A political willingness has given in: leading a war consists of, in the end, convincing the other that he has lost. If the opponent is not reduced to silence and is not persuaded of his defeat, then there is not really a victory to be said. War is led and dedicated to a project which can be read, either in history books or on the front of a monument; a new power struggle sanctioned by the recognition of the conquered (and if possible, by the group of nations involved).

The preceding concepts come from the following categories:

– a soldier who fights, a politician who commands, and a civilian who is subjected to it;

– belligerents and neutral parties;

– from the front and behind;

– war time, peace time.

But there is also a towering mass of philosophic categories which define just wars (by their objective or necessity) and unjust wars, either in terms of their principle, or in their methods.

The key to this metaphorical safety box of reasoning is the same for the opponent. This is particularly important for the notion of a just enemy. He is both simply an enemy (and not an absolute criminal), but also he who has the "right" to become an enemy, because he takes delight in the very status.

This entire mental construction is badly adapted to the ambiguous nature of cyberattacks. If the *other side* (also badly identified) attacks you, still, we have to know what he wants to do or what he expects (as it happens, this does not seem to be signing a treaty or surrendering in good and due form).

Faced with an aggression of this type, the victim is reduced to assumptions (by hoping to not have been a victim of a "false flag", a deception raised by a skilled third party).

If the cybernet war mainly requires technological know-how, this knowledge may be acquired by any brain with enough perseverance and inventiveness. In theory, everybody can start an "immaterial" war based on knowledge.

The question of the attacker's status completes the question of his intention. Firstly, it is important to know what he is looking for. Since attacks in the cyberworld hardly give way to repetition or experience, as innovating as they are, they may be way below the hopes of their creators, and it may be that the targeted systems had anticipated the attack. But, it might also be the case that a virus had spread over the aimed target and that the interconnection into the virtual world had spread disorder out of the target's territory (seeing that he had hit the initiator with a counter strike). The struck land and targeted territory might differ, here, where everything is interconnected to everything.

What does the aggressor want, meaning, what is his criterion for victory? Insofar as cyberattacks have always been surrounded by secrets and deception, and as a regular army or State has never taken responsibility for it, there can be no clearly expressed "war aim" (this would be a vow). A demand from "private" groups claiming, for example, to "punish" a state, resorts to activism and to its known forms: symbolic humiliation, "we struck you because you represent a certain type of crime or injustice that we despise, and your punishment will be made public". Or rather threats: "obey our orders or we will start over". This idea could be applied perfectly to an anonymous statement after a bomb explosion, following the tradition of the 19th or 20th Century.

If a cyberattack does not necessarily shatter the opponent's political willingness, then it violates a guard's small amount of will, or even that of a legitimate owner. It consists of knowing, disorganizing, or commanding (taking control over a machine), but it is always in spite of what the legitimate owner wants.

If the aim is "pure" espionage, then the answer is in the question. The objective, like that for the information in "the real world", is not to inflict damage in the immediate surroundings, but to gather up information to increase one's own potential (economic, technical, military, etc.) or to decrease that of the opponent.

Contrary to sabotage whose effects are instant and invisible, espionage is an investment for the future.

For a "glitch attack", the message behind the havoc is not necessarily unique. It may be a form of punishment or a demonstration of power. In each case, it is a question of making the targeted authorities understand something. The political question, then, is in the foreground.

1.8. No war without borders

The question is tied around the question of real borders, but more exactly, the relationship between the place of attack and sovereignty. It also determines the difference between cyberwar and cybercrime. The latter is punishable by law and by international treaties, is part of different nomenclatures and under constant surveillance. The concept brings together crimes and offenses which could be committed in the real world, but which are facilitated and developed by computers and networks (like starting up a con plan or publishing remarks which fall under the limits of the law). On the other hand, attacks on intellectual property or a victim's security and which could only happen in cyberspace, such as violating databases or introducing malware. The political objective forms the demarcation line with self-interest or free delinquency.

In the same way, cyberterrorism, a concept which has been made popular by the media, really covers two kinds of activity. On the one hand, it deals with activists groups whose activities could be led better on the Internet: expressing themselves, recruiting, communicating (potentially coded), etc. On the other hand, they include attacks intended for, if not to, "spread terror", at least to force a constraint on opinions and decision-makers. In this hypothesis, which has not happened yet, the effect of the chaos corresponds to a symbolic and political goal. Nothing, if not the description of the attacks ("terrorist group") distinguishes them from an attack led by a State service potentially hired by mercenary services, or by manipulating ideological motivations. As a consequence, the States may include supporting dissenting groups from abroad, by providing them with technical tools for protest and expression. A large range of techniques is therefore available from giving them the tools to express themselves in a subversive way to leading a violent attack.

A vast amount of guerilla attacks are a part of espionage, as we have already mentioned. They may be for economic reasons, but also repressive reasons: the State's fight against its own opponents, meaning internal politics. This is, for example, the same as the Tsarist services which used agents and informants across Europe to counter revolutionary exiles, the way in which China pursued the Dali-Lama's and his supporters' correspondences all the way to Western servers, if we are to believe in the revelations printed in the press on "Operation Aurora"[16]. This police raid over the border and by intermediary electrons, moves us further away from the classic war scheme.

The same acts will be of criminal, terrorist, police or military matters, depending on the status of their creators and according to where they come from.

The political example (the State likely to start or be subjected to war), and the border are defined in the same way, even in cyberspace.

Let us put this knowledge into another long perspective, which will relativize the strange nature of cyberspace. The word *border* has its roots in the military, where it first appeared in 1213 in order to indicate the situation where an army made a front line, a line of defence. This invisible line (that only the progress made in the field of cartography may trace with accuracy) can be used as an isobar to make the power relationship between two monarchs who decided to stop pushing their military forces any further, more concrete. They often held onto this line because the border is recognized by two neighbor States and with good will. In this way, neither country would attack the other. Unless, without so much as acknowledging the border, neither of the two felt the need to risk moving a soldier a meter beyond the theoretical barrier which separated the hostilities in order to go from a "country of peace" to a "country of war". In a canonical schema:

– acknowledging borders is supposed to guarantee peace, or "we will always make war to have better peace";

– to start a war, we must enter the enemy's country. Consequence: violating the border, an act of war, opens up belligerence;

– the place of hostility (military operation ground) determines its nature and therefore the status of its creators: a "just" or illegitimate enemy. Borders have the privilege of causing conflicts (stake), of preventing them (so long as they are respected), and often of proving them. Their violation (the presence of armed men committing violence on the foreign territory) often marks the beginning of real wars.

Better: the border is used to qualify the war. According to its "location", it is symmetrical, "public", international, regular, "authentic" and between two monarchies. Or, the war is "internal", irregular, or even "civil" if at least one of the sides does not command a certain status (related to the authority over the territory).

Amongst these internal wars, for a long time we have hoped to be able to distinguish the ones which raise a population up against foreign occupation, from

---

16 "Opération Aurora: Pékin réplique à Washington," *Le Monde*, 22nd January 2010.

others which are often said to be revolutionary which are opposed to groups trying to seize the State, and finally separatist wars (to win borders).

Currently, some are adding a fourth category: *terrorism*, "war of the poor and powerless", a clandestine, urban, sporadic and modest version of guerilla warfare, by those who are lacking in number and not territorially stable enough to lead a "real" irregular war.

It goes without saying that the intellectual clarity of these distinctions developed by people's rights over the centuries no longer has hardly any meaning in the cyber world; no more than what the mental categories are worth when strategic tradition tends to reflect on conflict, meaning in terms of moves and maneuvers, in Earth's space.

For Clausewitz, in a large part war consists of "fog and friction", ignorance and dysfunction related to the difference between the map and the land, between the strategy and its concrete application to the real word. Therefore, we are dealing with questions of vision and movement.

Another marker for the unrest into which we are thrown by the deterritorialization of war, is the way in which it clashes with our conceptions of a rooted monarchy: the positive assets of sovereignty (where the State is the only holder), are theoretically unlimited and quasi "theological", relating to supremacy, perpetuity, lack of lawful limitation, completeness, non-transferability, etc. This would be true if it were not for one dimension: space. Since it is only exerted over a territory (which is the coincidence of a physical space and the symbolic meaning it has for the occupiers), sovereignty only exists for and within the coexistence of other monarchies, even in confrontation. The supreme form of political authority, showing the enemy and starting a time of war, can only be exerted from a land which is duly enclosed, at least in terms of law and geography.

 The many years of political philosophy have distinguished a "real" war (with a "just" enemy, another monarch who has a somewhat "skill" for being the recognized opponent), from civil, irregular, guerilla wars, etc., where one of the armed groups inside the territory fights "legitimate" forces, or those known as such. The State, then, attempts to maintain its famous, double-sided "monopoly over legitimate violence": the *jus belli* (the right to make war) and the "repressive" force dedicated to internal order. Let the fight unfold in a certain place, at so many kilometers from a line, and it will be known for being symmetrical, regular, so as not to say canonical or even irregular.

Jurists often resort to the metaphor of the "big men": the States, likened to giants fighting for their fenced off lands, on an international scale behave like citizens who might fight or make an agreement regarding their limited property.

This explains the holy nature of borders, but also their propative value. The border identifies the war's "location", and therefore its existence and nature. It inevitably unfolds from one side or from the other. They unmask the aggressor, and demonstrate a threat. Thanks to these borders, each person knows where the national haven begins, or where such a skill is exerted, where power stops and where the influence over geopolitics starts. Secular international order is connected to the closure of terrestrial space, at least in terms of law, and to the equilibrium of the forces it fixes in place.

1.9. The enemy and the sovereign

Over time, this theoretical representation is subjected to several adaptations which reflect the changes in battle ideas and techniques. It would be suitable to mention them here:

– the separation between European land which is shared and ordered, and the rest of the world which is open to colonization and, therefore, the taking of new lands by discoverers and conquerors. Thus, by the Tordesillas treaty of 1494, a North-South meridian line shared between the Spanish and Portuguese gave the right to colonize the New World, which up until then, was considered as "nobody's property" (*res nullius*);

– standards applied to the Earth and sea. With the latter being a free space, with the exception of coastal areas, this leads to obvious consequences regarding the use of war forces in the water and on the status of pirates ("enemy of the human race") who are out of the range of areas protected by States (an enemy that we all have the right to punish in virtue of a principle of universal jurisdiction);

– air warfare, which assumes acts of recognition, transport, or air fire, above the territory and against the State's wishes. Crossing the border from above extends the battle ground even further, and drastically changes laws for units of time and space, which are typical of an old perspective;

– nuclear dissuasion which is characterized by futuristic discussions (multiplication of scenarios regarding a conflict which never took place), or even by its esotericism (the plethora of speculations on the opponent's supposed reaction to a game theory model) questions war and the border:

- mutual assured destruction (MAD) with the Dulles' plan;

- the McNamara doctrine of a progressive backlash (apocalypse is no longer an automatic reaction in the case of a Soviet attack against any USA ally countries);

- nuclear strategy and nuclear tactic;

- French doctrine of sanctuarizing the national territory and dissuasion, which corresponds to a "threshold" of technical and political credibility. In short, this was a project of "flexibilization" put forward by Jacques Chirac to extend the list of vital interests (terrorist attacks by weapons of mass destruction), whose use could lead to a nuclear retaliation;

- dissuasion from the weak to the strong, or from the strong to the mad (the insane dictators ready to take the risk of a conflict where they would perish).

The common theme for all these mental constructions is the desire to establish a new relationship with the borders.

These are both sacrilized by the possibility of a punishment which is disproportionate the eventual benefit, and insignificant. The shelter which is traditionally provided by the territory becomes deceptive in the possibility of a global apocalypse.

In addition, the logic of nuclear dissuasion tends to separate the sanctuarized territory from the vital interests which, if they were threatened, could lead a state to resort to this terrifying vision of *ultima ratio regum* (the last argument of kings)[17]:

– the short life of the strategic defense initiative (SDI), aka *Star Wars*, which would project the "location" of the war onto the stratosphere and re-establish, in space, (with its anti-missile and anti-satellite weapons) the concept of an impenetrable shield. Due to nuclear war, it was hoped that it would no longer be positioned on Earth's borders. In their entirely theoretical (since such as 15 second war never actually took place), military operations would consist of the struggle between machines out of sight of humans;

– the RMA (*revolution in military affairs*) was formalized after the fall of the URSS, and for which cyberwar was a logical extension relying on the use of information technologies, whether it is a matter of getting information, of "making the battle field transparent", of striking where the force is most needed, of perfectly coordinating our own forces, of reacting instantaneously from the "sensor" which slows down the targets to the gunman, or without going through the heavy hierarchical processes of traditional military commands[18].

Technology makes it possible to destroy any conventional force, as if punishment were to fall from the sky without worrying about old concepts of front lines or borders (or battles). However, the enemy "cheats". He would put himself in

---

17 "La dernière raison des rois" (The Last Argument of Kings) was what Louis XIV had engraved on cannons.
18 See [BRA 02] and [DUR 03] in particular. For a few futurological anticipations, see [ADA 98].

an asymmetric perspective, aiming to transform his own weaknesses into strengths, in particular with relation to the media and opinions. The "strong" will have to resolve "low intensity conflicts", terrorist acts, guerrilla warfare, with civil opponents, etc., in a context which increasingly resembles the maintenance of order on a global scale.

An additional reason to unleash the multiple effects of information in conflict is: the chaos effect (reducing the other side's capacities, for example, by sabotaging his systems); ruse effect (leading the opponent to the wrong decision); *capacitating* effect (knowing more than), but also the qualitative, negative (reducing combativity, demonization, discrediting) or positive (support, moral, or even recruitment or conversion), etc.

In this *crescendo* of complexity (because these different layers are adding up and not being cancelled out), we will also find cyberspace as a supposed battle field. The metaphor of space must not be pushed to the absurd, as we have seen that the concepts of displacement, path, territory, crossing, distancing, etc., without losing all relevance, cover interactions in the "real" world with the world of signs and codes.

In truth, an attack in cyberspace means an act of aggression from the real world, by means of the media or using networks, and intends to produce effects in the same real world such as material damage, and organizational or psychological damage to humans in their flesh and blood. It includes the "non-authorized" use of technical prostheses that the legitimate owners trust in: their machines, their software, their codes, and all this is by an illegal intrusion into an informational system (there had to be one way or another of "entering" it).

From the victim's point of view, a computer attack seems to come out of nowhere. Indeed, there is a relative aspect of traceability (which most often results in discovering an IP address located in a particular country, which may very well be a bait file), but with no certainty. A war in cyberspace takes place from address to address, not from province to province.

1.10. Strengths and weaknesses

However, the notions of power and vulnerability take on a whole other meaning, in relation to maps. The "strong" are no longer essentially those who possess a large territory, which is profound and well defended. On the contrary, it may well be that this becomes a more visible target. The more a country is supposedly rich and technically advanced, the more it can depend on its digital networks, the more it is linked to the rest of the world, and then the more it offers more points of entry and targets open to attack. On the other hand, a "powerful" aggressor will not necessarily have gathered together means of communication and calculation over his territory. He may very well lead a network of corrupted computers throughout the world (like "Ghostnet" which is said to be installed in 130 countries) rather than at his own home. The question of imputability with its consequences on proof concerning opinions and international authorities (therefore backlash or retaliation may ensue) is just another aspect of topological data, i.e. the indirect and dissimulated path of the attack when it is difficult to say where it comes from, via which route, and where it aims to go (and the consequence? Instantaneous, with no preparation time or noticeable path). This spatial problem, coupled with a temporal problem, produces some worrying effects:

– its singular and unidirectional character (for the moment). If the classic war were compared to a dual where belligerents exchange blows, retaliate and perform maneuvers, then the concept of cyberattack as we know it would be a single-barreled rifle. It is launched at moment T, the attacked systems detect it or react at time T + 1. At best, after some time of resilience, they go back to normal at moment T + 2, and the "war" is over. So long as we have still not seen cyberretaliation or a linking of strategic initiatives, then the so-called war is unilateral and does not constitute this dialogue of forces over time, which it has always been;

– its relatively predictable effects. Here we still speak according to limited experience. It seems logical for an attack made once to not be repetitive (or to go through the same channels). We find it hard to imagine that the opponent will reuse the same "malware", against which the victim would hasten to defend himself again. The unknown factor concerning the effect of the attack (before or beyond the aggressor's calculations) obviously weighs down any anticipation;

– the impossibility (perhaps temporary) of establishing an implicit code for the attack, the damage, the response, the threat, means that it is still impossible to project the cyberwar perspective in the long term. Even if countries such as France and the USA wish to be well equipped with offensive capacities in this domain, the question of a use doctrine remains crucial. Its dissuasive effect (ability to convince a potential aggressor that he would have more to lose than gain in attacking a country) rests upon the question of likelihood. Damage, fear, the adverse strategy must undergo speculation. The relative anonymity of the attacker, the asymmetry of the attack (led by, for example, the "weak" with no status as a creator acting in the name of the state, against a "strong" State), and the random nature of events, do not facilitate the implementation of the measures which are likely to discourage an aggressor. Whether the offensive develops neither in the classic time dimension (system intrusion does not coincide with the havoc), nor the classic space dimension (from and towards which territory?) hardly facilitates a gradual or targeted retaliation.

Nobody thinks about denying the importance of computer science and networks in the running of war. It would indeed be surprising if it were the only aspect of human activity not to have been affected by the digital revolution. Cybernetic operations cannot *not* play an increasingly important role; they will act as components of war but by no means as its substitute.

1.11. Bibliography

[ADA 98] ADAMS J., *The Next World War*, Simon and Schuster, New York, USA, 1998.

[ARQ 93] ARQUILLA J., RONFELDT D., *Cyberwar is Coming. Comparative Strategy*, vol. 12, no. 2, p. 141-165, Spring 1993.

[ARQ 97] ARQUILLA J., RONFELDT D., In Athena's camp: preparing for conflict in the information age, *Rand Monograph Report*, Rand, Santa Monica, USA, 1997.

[BAL 06] BALAKRISHNAN G., *L'Ennemi. Un portrait intellectuel de Carl Schmitt*, Editions Amsterdam, The Netherlands, 2006.

[BOU 71] BOUTHOUL G., *L'infanticide différé*, Hachette, Paris, France, 1971.

[BRA 02] BRAILLARD P., MASPOLI G., "La Révolution dans les affaires militaires: paradigmes stratégiques, limites et illusions", *Annuaire français des Relations internationales* (AFRI), vol. 3, Paris, France, 2002.

[BRE 84] BRETON T., BENEICH D., *Soft War*, Robert Laffont, Paris, France, 1984.

[BRO 98] BROWN D., *Digital Fortress*, St Martin's Press, London, 1998.

[BRU 75] BRUNNER J., *The Shockwave Rider*, Harper & Row, New York, USA, 1975.

[COP 10] CONESA P., "La fabrication de l'ennemi, Réflexions sur un processus stratégique", *Revue internationale et stratégique*, no. 65, p. 35-44, Dalloz, Paris, France, 2010.

[CSI 08] CSIS (Center for Strategic International Studies) Cybersecurity Commission, Securing Cyberspace for the 44th Presidency, Washington, USA, December 2008.

[DUR 03] DE DURAND E., *Révolution dans les affaires militaires. Révolution ou transformation?*, Hérodote, Paris, France, 2003.

[GOU 08] GOUVERNEMENT FRANÇAIS, Le livre blanc sur la défense et la sécurité nationale, Odile Jacob, Paris, France, 2008.

[GRA 05] GRAY C.S., *Another Bloody Century: Future Warfare*, Weinfeld & Nicholson, London, 2005

[GRA 07] GRAY C.S., *La guerre au XXI siècle*, Economica, Paris, France, 2007.

[HUY 01] HUYGHE F.B., *L'ennemi à l'ère numérique*, PUF, Paris, France, 2001.

[LB 08] Livre blanc sur la défense et la sécurité nationale, French government, 2008.

[LEV 98] LEVY P., Cyberculture, report for the European Council, Odile Jacob, Paris, France, 1998.

[LIB 09] LIBICKI M., *Cyberdeterrence and Cyberwar*, www.rand.org/pubs/monographs/ 2009/RAND_MG877.pdf., Rand, Santa Monica, USA, 2009.

[MAI 05] DE LA MAISONNEUVE E., *Stratégie crise et chaos*, Economica, Paris, France, 2005.

[MON 07] MONOD J.C., *Penser l'ennemi, affronter l'exception, réflexions critiques sur l'actualité de Carl Schmitt*, col. Armillaire, La Découverte, Paris, France, 2007.

[SCH 72] SCHMITT C., *La notion de politique* (1932) and *Théorie du partisan*, Calmann Lévy, Paris, France, 1972.

[SCH 98] SCHMITT C., *Der nomos der erde*, Duncker & Humboldt, Berlin, Germany, 1998.

[SCH 01] SCHMITT C., *Le nomos de la terre dans le droit des gens du jus publicum europaeum*, PUF, Paris, France, 2001.

[WAL 06] WALZER M., *Guerres justes et injustes*, Gallimard, Paris, France, 2006.

[ZAR 09] ZARKA Y.C. (ed.), *Carl Schmitt ou le mythe du politique*, PUF, Paris, France, 2009.

Chapter 2

War of Meaning, Cyberwar and Democracies

2.1. Introduction

The world does not live in peace. The crises or conflicts experienced represent the fate encountered every day determining new power relationships or enabling new more ambitious, better armed actors to impose their power. "This new strategic reality expresses the life or death of a nation confronted with its destiny, faced with the competition and ambition of other human groups" [LAB 96]. This is all within a space restricted by culture, geography, law or the people. It leads to the war of meaning and cyberwar.

Why should we speak of the war of meaning? Our approach is based on current conflicts to which Western states are deeply committed. This is not simply a question of conquering a land, but rather bringing about peace there in the name of the international community. They are acting within a context of an information society, which allows any actor (either state-controlled or not), to dispute their conception and perception of the world, regarding their position of dominance held since the 15th Century.

The "war of meaning" is regarded as the desired direction and is reflected upon by different actors for international relations, in fact, more precisely in our discussion between Western states and non-Western actors, according to their strategic interests and the future they anticipate. The war of meaning is based on the

Chapter written by François CHAUVANCY.

values which establish the ideologies of these actors, where the confrontation of these ideologies will lead to a situation of confrontation or war. This understanding of the war of meaning can be seen in the new White Paper on Defense and National Security, published in 2008, France[1].

As for cyberwar[2], here it is considered as a support in its technical dimensions for the war of meaning. The question of defining it is raised and justifies this choice. There is no official definition of it, in France or in the USA. On the other hand, the European Security and Defence Assembly [AES 08] translates "cyberwar" as "digital war", defined as "the recourse to computers and the Internet to lead a war in cyberspace". Finally, let us underline that the American Department of Defense identifies cyberwar as: "A global domain within the information environment consisting of the interdependent network of information technology infrastructures, including the Internet, telecommunications networks, computer systems, and embedded processors and controllers."[3]

Martin Libicki[4], a Senior Management Scientist specializing in information warfare, distinguishes cyberwar at the operative level (theater of operations) from the strategic level [LIB 09][5].

Acting against military targets using non-lethal methods on an operative level, this mode of action is in support of, and therefore complementary to, other modes of military action. On the other hand, strategic cyberwar is considered as "a campaign of cyberattacks launched by one entity against a state and its society, primarily but not exclusively for the purpose of affecting the target state's behavior"[6]. The aggressor may be a State or a non-state controlled actor. The aim is to affect the behavior of a State and its society according to the objectives sought after.

Cyberwar is a vector and a method which responds to a political aim. Therefore, it raises questions on the war of meaning and the objectives sought by the aggressor. It may be understood as a concept with enables us to create, exploit, spread, and

---

1 www.defense.gouv.fr/livre_blanc. A summarized English version is also available on the website.
2 The notion of cyberwar was developed by John Arquilla from the Rand Corporation, who acted as Consultant to General Schwarzkopf during the First Gulf War.
3 American Department of Defense (DoD), Joint publication 1-02 (JP 1-02) from 30th December 2010.
4 Martin Libicki is a researcher for the Rand Corporation. He is a specialist in the application of information technologies to the benefit of national security. In 1995, he considered responding to terrorist atacks by a combination of forces attacking by remote technology, based on tools for acquiring information and employing special forces.
5 [LIB 09], p.6.
6 [LIB 09], p. 143.

influence, because it allows for an exchange or confrontation of ideas which are sometimes arranged into ideologies. However, these objectives are determined by man in light of the desired effects on individuals, whether they are part of a group or not.

In terms of strategy, the matter at hand is that of shaping the world according to a vision held by idea bearers. It underlines the deeply human nature of the set of problems here. Man is at the heart of the "war of meaning", whether it is in his knowledge or his perception of the world. This is why, through the "war of meaning", we will bring together the set of issues for a Western democratic society which may weaken or strengthen it, in the conduct of today's conflicts through this confrontation of ideologies by the "interposed" cyberwar.

War of meaning, cyberwar and democracies sets out the issues concerning Western democracies confronted with a meaning to be given to their particularly military strategies in an information society.

This war of ideas, or rather *by* ideas, is to be made during, prior to, and above all after the resolution of the conflict[7].

The war of ideas and the battle of perceptions are now essential for the military engagement of Western democracies through a comprehensive approach to conflict, i.e. a strategy which does not only call upon its military dimension, even if it represents a vital factor for power struggles.

In fact, reflections and experiments on managing international crises by Western States now include all instruments of power via an American concept from the 1990s: DIME (diplomacy, information, military, economy, sometimes extended to DIME-SC with security and culture), undoubtedly a form of doctrinal influence, which was tested in multinational experiments[8]. Today, it contributes to defining what could be a comprehensive approach to resolving crises by favoring interoperability between States (i.e. the capacity to work together, be it through institutions, doctrines or procedures) and by accompanying this common action with strategic communication.

---

7 If we refer to recent wars and political debates (such as in the UK in 2009 on its political engagement in Iraq), we may note that even if a war is considered as being *over*, democratic debates may lead to a "re-writing" of meaning even afterwards, and therefore to new justifications which had been put forward to wage that war (or a simple military intervention), both before and after the conflict itself. This can also be verified for other conflicts such as in Kosovo or Rwanda.

8 A series of MNE (multinational experiments) combining a party from European States, allies of the USA, and the USA itself. Since 2009, the MNE6 has been experimenting on strategic communication and the cultural approach through a situation of counter-insurgency.

The question of giving meaning to such an international action is relevant here. It cannot be separated from the question of "why?" and the potential ideologies which may come up against each other during these interventions when they have a military aspect, particularly in modern conflicts. In particular, if the intervention is decided on, then no force can be involved for months or even years over a foreign territory without an information – or influence – campaign on local, national and international levels. Military intervention led by a democracy must be prepared and accompanied by the formulation of the meaning to be given, and therefore by influence or communication activities.

Moreover, the often asymmetrical conflicts today are founded on a war of ideas, whether these ideas are political, social, religious, or even ethnic. However, as much as those against Western society are motivated, then to the same extent this society will seem further removed from any vague desire to defend or firmly promote its model. But, this model gives the sense of commitment chosen by the public community, possibly by its armed fist, *the soldier*. It defines the cause he will be ready to fight and even die for in a land far from his own. There can be no military commitment, even for a democracy, without strong and motivated ideas to support it. This means that the willingness to conquer must at least be the same on both sides (and even legitimately superior) in Western armed forces, and also that it cannot be gained *ex nihilo*.

After having determined the new operating space where the Western world can lead conflicts, we will discuss the factors which enable the application of an influence strategy in a military intervention.

2.2. Informational environment, a new operating space for strategy

As recalled in the White Paper, the complexity of international crises forces us to define the strategies bringing together diplomatic, financial, civil, cultural and military instruments, in stages of crisis prevention and management as well as in sequences of stabilization and reconstruction after a conflict[9]. However, a general strategy without an influence strategy will not be able to reach its objectives. It is understood, in fact, and led within a globalized society where both good and bad information circulates together, and is nearly unrestricted. Possessing and exploiting it leads to what we may call *information warfare*. The resultant strategies and those put head to head in current or future conflicts express what is at stake for new power struggles between States, and between States and non-state controlled actors. This is truly a war of meaning, interpreted as an understanding of our future by each State or civilization, if not by a non-state controlled actor. The stakes involved are the influence and the power to choose our own future without destructive and random confrontation.

---

9 [LB 08], p. 58.

2.2.1. *War and information: stakes for the West*

As a term which has been commonly used for the last several years, *information warfare* covers a range of domains to the point where no official definition as of yet has remained. Above all it expresses the concept of conflict and the role of information within this context. It concerns war in cyberspace, its technological dimension, the war of ideas transferred to cyberspace, and the human dimension. This new battlefield is, in fact, the field of information and its effects which help to construct the war of meaning. Particularly in democracy, the latter aims to make the average citizen understand and abide by the politics chosen, especially in military intervention. It also tries to avoid the use of force or moderate it during international crisis management. On the contrary, a person opposed to a war will act on this same battlefield to instill doubt and enforce his own legitimacy.

2.2.1.1. *Information society and 21st Century conflicts*

International relations intertwine and unravel in a context where excessive information changes or crystallizes perceptions through globalized communication. There are now several influence strategies in competition with each other. The French White Paper from 2008 specifies that globalization goes together, paradoxically, with a rise in nationalism, religious fanatics, or those in authority taking over [...]. Some exploit the possibilities of spreading their ideas via the Internet and other means of information and communication. Others endeavor to implement means of dividing virtual space, means of control and prohibition, or even communication manipulation. In this quest for domination, this situation amplifies the differences in representing an international society by the West and non-Western world, which we must outline here.

During the debate on reintegrating France into NATO, the French President very clearly stated on March 11, 2009, that France belonged to the Western family, saying that France is proud of being what it is; a free democracy, a European democracy, and a Western democracy. He believes that France knows who its allies are, and who its enemies are, and he is not scared of saying that France's allies and friends are first and foremost the Western family. Let us note that yesterday's Western society could be defined as European and Christian. It showed itself as powerful, all-conquering and dominating. This West, both Christian and white which is undoubtedly a cause for current tensions, more or less dominated the world, whether in terms of politics, military, culture or the economy. It proposed, or rather *imposed*, its vision of the world in the resolution of conflict, by creating the Society of Nations, then the United Nations. This was part of the promotion of individual freedom and Human Rights from the American Revolution in 1783, and the French Revolution in 1789, which was finally made universal by the Universal Declaration of Human Rights in 1948.

Today, the idea of belonging to the West could be understood by a strong historical, cultural relationship, referring in particular to Christianity and the resultant civilization, and to humanistic values. Initially European, this Western society broadened its geographic hold by becoming Euro-American with the USA and Canada, and by forming allies with Australia and New Zealand. These Western references unite these States and their people. Therefore, the West might correspond to a geographic zone of civilization which traditionally covers Western Europe, including Poland and the Baltic States. We can also add States which are mainly populated by Europeans which belong to ABCA[10] and who, with a few exceptions, are members of NATO.

This group of States and nations shares the same democratic values and the same respect for societal characteristics for those who make up the said group. In particular it is founded on the individual's bond to the political, social and cultural models of the majority. It also exists through a common understanding of its collective security. This is still possible despite a gradual weakening in its military capabilities, enabling it to retain a certain sense of unity and not see a vision of the world, which is different to the one it has built up, be imposed upon it.

However, the West[11] has a very strong image indeed, through its economic and military capabilities. But it still remains vulnerable to any opponent or challenger. Today's reality shows how the Western states of yesterday which were so powerful, are now contested, fended off, threatened and even attacked.

2.2.1.2. *Informational environment and cyberspace*

Information and the effects that we might expect from it in a strategy act in an information environment which may be defined as a virtual and physical space where information is received, exploited and spread[12]. The concept of information includes information itself, as well as information systems [OTA 07].

---

10 The American, British, Canadian, Australian and New Zealand Armies Program.
11 Huntington S., *Le choc des civilisations*, Odile Jacob, 1996 [HUN 96]. This strategist has thoroughly studied what makes the West, and has identified the issues regarding the "clash of civilizations", which has become a known expression, used according to the desired effect. For Huntington, the concept of universal civilization which is a characteristic of the West, has come from this understanding of Europe's mission to civilize. This universal civilization, however, presupposes the need that other civilizations might have to imitate Western customs and institutions. S. Huntingdon calls this the Davos culture. The concept of universal civilization also leads us to believe that non-Westerners will indeed "westernize themselves" by consuming more Western products.
12 PIA 03-253 (French Joint Publication), Joint doctrine for military influence activities operations (PSYOPS), CICDE, 2008.

These actors, whether they are individuals, groups, organizations or States, want to conquer this new battlefield in support of their objectives. They use, create, and spread information which is easily accessible, and selected with the aim of having an effect, thus influencing the decision making process for those in charge of such tasks, and putting pressure on certain players in our societies.

The cyberspace included in this information environment is defined in a military sense by the USA as "a global domain within the information environment consisting of the interdependent network of information technology infrastructures, including the Internet, telecommunications networks, computer systems, and embedded processors and controllers"[13].

A generic information environment

Figure 2.1. *Generic example of an information environment in a theater of operations*

Let us add here that there is no territory, and no physical border. This includes digital transported information as well as online service operators. It is, then, within this technical battlefield that the digital fight in the domains of protection or offensive actions is carried out.

---

13 [JP1 10], p. 141.

Whoever speaks of a battlefield is effectively speaking of war: defense and attack between States, if not between non-state controlled actors, in terms of sovereignty and rivals. This virtual space is the target for a control or influence strategy, as we can see in the laws found in different countries regarding the Internet and the information which flows in it. There are several terms which transpose traditional war terms into the realm of cyberspace: cyberwar, cyberattacks, cyberdefense, cyberagents, cyberdissenters, cyberterrorism, cyberpolice, "cyberdeterrence" or cyberdissuasion [LIB 09]. We could also add cyberinfluence to the list, why not?

We should however differentiate cyberattacks[14], in our meaning of the term, which establish the concept of cyberdefense, and thus a cyberwar. For our discussion, we will distinguish two objectives: attacks on operating systems, which are the most worrying for States, and secondly the attack on conveyed ideas. On the one hand, it is a question of preventing ideas from flowing by attacking private or state-controlled websites, and of fighting ideas with ideas.

In fact, the human aspect must be not covered up by a technically-oriented vision [ELL 90] which prevails today in reflections on information warfare. From now on, the weak point will come from humans, and therefore their values of loyalty and commitment to serving their national community will be as dominating as their technical skills in societies where the individual, and therefore his/her convictions or interests, prevail over collective interests.

Weapons, including computers, are only tools and only possess positive or negative action according to the will of the human bringing them to life. Within the framework of cyberspace, the digital fight cannot be separated from a more global vision of information warfare which we are facing head on.

2.2.1.3. *Emergence of non-state controlled actors*

Non-state controlled actors also play a part in the ruling of conflicts because they often have ways of affecting a State's decision making processes. Thus, besides cyberspace, the opening up of physical borders has enabled new actors to develop, these lobbyers defending "personal" causes. This evolution relates to a gradual weakening of the Nation-State. Individuals come together above the borders to influence the States and to come to decisions which are more in line with their objectives, in spite of a noticeable reaction from people who need landmarks.

The initial non-state controlled entities are the many NGOs, fighting for just causes through the meaning they give to their commitment, which are often altruistic and have a strong media image. Private actors whose generic title of NGO may

---

14 [LIB 09]. Also see Eric Filiol's contribution in this book.

cover other purposes such as humanitarian, economic, political, as well as armed, vocations take several forms or have many objectives which are not all humanitarian. Those influential actors, but also those who have no political legitimacy, are nonetheless capable of rallying up Western public opinions for the most popular amongst them, particularly by communicating or lobbying. They may also be the acceptable window onto a clandestine movement, following the tradition of the revolutionary wars of yesterday[15]. Other pressure groups are developed to defend more personal interest, whether lawful or not: financial parties, criminal organizations, private military societies. Finally, any private or non-state governed group has the means today to weigh down on a decision. Al-Qaeda has shown that an "armed NGO" could declare war on a State.

In this new composition of the international society, the French White Paper on Defense and National Security (2008) identifies the development of influence strategies intended to weaken our role in the world and on the international market[16]. The primary tool for these influence strategies would be digital attacks which could aim at people or groups by general misinformation spread in the media and via the Internet in particular. French communities abroad and foreign communities living in France could also be targeted by such action[17].

The White Paper's orientations take us towards the real stakes of cyberwar, far from an entirely technological approach, which is the human mind that thinks, decides, acts or reacts. The fight against misinformation must, therefore, be engaged. A part of the targeted audience is represented as much on the national territory by decision makers and the media as by foreign communities.

2.2.1.4. *The West perceived negatively by the non-western world*

As recalled in the White Paper, the contestation of Western ambitions feeds new tension and violence[18]. This well-identified situation shows that it is *not* the West's power which is being questioned here, but in fact the perception that the non-Western world has of it, either coming from good faith, or in order to create a new power relationship, exploiting the bad conscience of the West regarding its past hegemony.

---

15 *Le Monde* (daily French Newspaper), May 29th 2009. On May 27th 2009, the leader of what was the biggest Islamic NGO based in the USA was condemned to 65 years imprisonment for supporting Hamas Palestinian extremists, in the biggest terrorist financial affair in the USA ($12m).

16 [GOU 08] French Government, The White Paper on Defence and National Security, p. 52, Odile Jacob, Paris, 2008.

17 [GOU 08].

18 [GOU 08], p. 35.

Besides the new interstate relationships of a country like China or Russia with new power, the non-state governed actors contest the Western system. Finally the individual constitutional freedoms which are the very foundation of western States and which are adapted to their societal functioning, paradoxically contribute to their domestic weakening by their instrumentalization through other actors.

Western power, its obsession with security since 2001, and the way it expresses itself, are all often perceived as being aggressive[19]. It is officially contested today, if not fought against, be it by Islamic or Chinese civilizations, for example.

The tensions between the USA and China following the Chinese cyberattacks in 2009 are expressed perfectly by this comment in the Chinese press reported by *Le Monde* on the 23rd January 2010: "The USA's campaign for free flowing and uncensored information on an unrestricted Internet is a disguised attempt to impose their values on other cultures in the name of democracy", written in the editorial of the English version of the *Global Times*[20] reminding that "the vast amount of information coming from the USA and other Western countries is filled with an aggressive rhetoric against all other counties which do not follow their leadership".

2.2.1.5. *A thought to be renewed on the concept of subversion*

At this stage, we cannot overlook a reflection on subversion, a concept which has been commonly used during the Cold War, but which has been slightly abandoned to the extent where it is no longer referenced in French Military Terminology. It can, however, be found in the NATO terminology, validated by France: "Action designed to weaken the military, economic or political strength of a nation by undermining the morale, loyalty or reliability of its citizens"[21]. The USA has a similar definition[22]. However we must ask whether these definitions which have mostly come from the Cold War are still relevant.

In fact, the question of the "loyalty" of those living in the West as part of military intervention abroad is raised here. Our societies are actually gradually getting used to groups calling on civil disobedience[23] but also on public support for

---

19 [GOU 08], p. 35.
20 The Global Times, published by the Quotidien du Peuple (Chinese Newspaper) in April 2009, launched its English edition and its website www.chine-informations.com /actualite/chine-le-global-times-lance-une-edition-en-anglais.
21 AAP6, Terminology, definition from March 1st, 1981, NATO [OTA 81].
22 American Department of Defence, JP 1-02 from March 17th 2009: "Action designed to undermine the military, economic, psychological, or political strength or morale of a regime" [JP1 10].
23 Article taken from *Le Monde*, December 4th 2001, "Le Syndicat de la magistrature refuse d'appliquer certaines lois antiterrorists", (one of the Magistrate Unions refused to apply certain anti-terrorist laws) for just one example.

those spreading violence. These actions may violently block actions made by the State. They are favored in peace time legislation which gives maximum opportunities to an opposed force[24], which is not intended to reach its objectives (its victory) within an asymmetrical strategy framework. It also gives this opposed force access to the media space, and therefore to its instrumentalization in the normal game of debates and freedom of expression.

This new domestic front is therefore naturally favorable in our democratic institutions to this opposed force which takes care to remain as an opponent within the normal framework of a democracy. It is, then, vital for this force that the law is strictly applied in terms of respecting freedom, which might only be limited by an exceptional situation. It may rely on well-wishers who have every opportunity to express themselves legally, and therefore to put doubts in the supporters of these operations.

The question is therefore very important, particularly with the enemy to Western values: radical Islam. Through its various cells, particularly in France, radical Islam actors recruit their militants via charity organizations, youth movements, local associations, schools, prisons, etc. The following questions are then raised: at what moment, and to what point, is an action on national territory, by forced opposed to an external intervention, part of the democratic debate? At what point can it be considered as an act of subversion? We are at the heart of the debate on ideological warfare, on the choice of political commitment and the possible limits to be imposed there, according to general interest.

2.2.1.6. *The debate on the use of force*

With its military force displayed in both men and equipment, the power of the West could be expressed by resorting to force. But however, today one of the characteristics of Western democracies is *not* using military force, except as a last resort. An old reflection as it may be, we will quote Machiavel here: "I am far from thinking that force and weapons must never be used, but we must use them in the last resort, failing other means"[25]. Yet, expressing this limitation of resorting to force gives less demanding opposed forces the possibility of developing a more efficient alternative strategy, combining influence activities and the use of force.

General Poirier had already raised this problem in 1994: "Their society's allergies to armed violence slow down the politicians who can no longer decide on external action without laborious psychological preparation. With the operations being launched, the strategist can no longer lead them without fearing repercussions,

---

24 The term "opposed forces" will be used in the first part of this chapter to describe those opposed to military operations launched by a democracy.
25 [MAC 80], p. 212.

in the view of losses and employing exotic weaponry. Constantly under the critical eye of the media informing us in real time, the politicians and military will from now on be tied down with paralyzing restrictions"[26].

This old debate could be summarized by the discussion from Serge Tchakhotine "hating war is a *thing*, and cultivating the mind to conjure it up by speech alone, by litanies or invocations in the face of danger, is a whole other matter"[27].

Consequently, with the pressures of conforming to international law but also due to pressure of the media and non-state controlled parties, it is no longer a matter for a democracy to lead a total war, but to reduce violent situations. In particular, democracies want to protect innocent people as much as possible from a conflict when it is deemed necessary. A strategy is implemented by relying particularly on diplomatic and economic actions, with anticipation of rebuilding the States who are suffering the conflict. It also takes into account the understanding of cultural differences.

2.2.1.7. *The rejection of death in the West*

The psychological weakness of public views in democracy is indeed real in the face of death. We just need to remind ourselves of the reactions to the 15,000 body bags in France during the First Gulf War[28], the fear of ground engagement in Kosovo in 1999 and the panacea, now obsolete, of the victory of a single air army "with no apparent deaths", and also the impact of soldiers killed in Iraq or Afghanistan. The death tolls of those in combat cited by the media, the images of the dead turn into influence activities by the emotions they stir up according to public opinions. Deaths within civilian populations, and we will underline the death of women and children here, are particularly denounced when they are the direct consequences of Western military operations, without taking into account the disproportionate acts of violence caused by opposed forces.

Regarding deaths in combat, let us use the figures taken from summer 2009, broadcast by the media and let us observe their effects on public opinion [CHA 09a]. On August 16th, the death of the "200th" British soldier killed in Afghanistan was interpreted by the media as a symbolic threshold. 58% of British people considered, at that moment, that this war was destined for failure and that the soldiers should be repatriated. In the USA, 45 soldiers were killed in July, and 46 died at the end of August. A survey taken on August 21st 2009 shows that 54% of Americans were against this intervention. How can a motivated and indoctrinated enemy respect and

---

26 [POI 84], p. 47.
27 [TCH 39], p. 14.
28 [CHA 98], p. 446.

therefore *fear* an army which could be pulled out from a theater of operations following losses in combat which are, numerically, so low?

However, the growing importance of the nation's duty to recognize its soldiers has been greatly portrayed in the media, by bringing together the national community in the spirit of sacrifice. In France, the ritual of honoring soldiers who have died in combat has been reintroduced [CHA 08][29]. Thus, the Head of State is turning into the very icon of this recognition with a re-broadcasting of the ceremonies on television at *Les Invalides* (area in Paris comprised of buildings and monuments relating to France's military history), either in 2004 for the dead in the Ivory Coast, or 2008 in Afghanistan. But these exceptional losses for France since the Algerian war, and the legitimate homage made to them, must be compared with the honors given by English-speaking countries, where patriotism is clearly in demand by each citizen and not just by political authorities.

Sending the coffins home is still an important fact with regard to conflict management. The image of their repetition affects our opinions and the enemy fighters, whose objectives include killing western soldiers, which is often filmed and easily spread on the Internet. However, we might notice that we are far from the concept of "zero death", a trend of the 1990s, and that the use of professional forces in far away wars has not only contributed to trivializing the death of the soldier, but also the gradual acceptance of this fact. On the other hand, the effects of civil or military deaths are still one of the key aspects of an influence strategy in a conflict. The psychological weakness of public opinion subjected to opponent propaganda, and their fragility faced with loss in combat are now vulnerabilities which need to be overcome.

2.2.1.8. *Soldier-citizen and individual freedom of expression*

In democracies where most of their external security is entrusted to professional armed forces, the question of motivation in combats away from the national territory must be raised here. Moreover, the soldier is also a citizen, is he not? In this vein, communication or information on warfare are becoming possible influence tools, left in the hands of each individual despite all the warnings.

Raymond Aron recalled that "all real wars pit communities against each other, where each one is united and expresses itself at will. In this perspective, they are all psychological wars"[30]. The question of will is at the heart of the problems of conflict, whether they are interstate or domestic conflicts, or against non-state controlled actors. Man is at the center of gravity of conflict. Human relationships,

---

29 This article deals with the soldier's motivations, the ritual and the sacred nature of military commitment within armies.
30 [ARO 62], p. 37.

and therefore the individual or collective perception of a situation, are fundamental for decision making and getting the support of individuals and groups for the strategy or policy chosen. The moral and psychological aspects have been, are and will remain an important factor in humanity's conflicting relationships. In particular, they affect the citizen, whether he is a fighter or not.

Democracies at war are subjected to the legitimate questioning from their citizens on the meaning of the conflict and on the personal commitment of the fighter, whether he is professional or drafted. New social tools and blogs must be considered so long as they have a certain audience, even though they do not answer to any ethical rules. The difficulty is indeed real, insofar as during the operation, access to the Internet becomes a condition of morale for troops who are distant from their families. The possible influence of blogs [KDD 06] written by American soldiers in Iraq has led the Pentagon to order soldiers to record their blogs, as of 2005.

The same trend has been noticed in other Western armed forces. Thus, it was necessary in France for the army chief of staff to create a directive for "sensitizing all the members of the army to the dangers of divulging information relating to military operations"[31] on websites, blogs or forums. Even if the expansion of military blogs is nowhere near as developed as the USA, military blogs have become an alternative source of information since the war in Iraq. They are also watched by opposed forces so as to identify the effects of actions carried out, and to deduce new tactics from them. The possible consequences for operations, the safety of the soldiers and their families, are obvious. For the military, we must combine the freedom to use data, the respect for the private sphere and the necessary safety of information to the benefit of the operations, particularly against cyberattacks or misinformation.

2.2.2. Strategy in the information environment

Today, the strategy for national security as conceived in the 2008 French White Paper is above defense policies. The strategy, now a grand strategy, takes a necessary importance. It is turning into the art of combining methods into means in different domains (military, economic, diplomatic, and psychological) in order to obtain the desired political effect. Moreover, today the strategy does not aim to go to war but to avoid it, by getting the same advantages and by convincing the individual who had to be persuaded of the fairness of the aims and methods used.

---

31 *Le Monde*, August 19th 2008, "L'armée française veut « modérer » les blogs des militaires" (The French army wants to "moderate" soldier blogs).

2.2.2.1. *The global nature of the State's strategy in resolving crises*

Today, just like yesterday and tomorrow, the strategy aims to give a vision of the world and to make it accepted. The war through information is one of its components. Resolving a crisis must be achieved by an influence strategy which, then, not only aims to persuade the equity of the suggested solution but also to limit without excluding the use of force. The targets are not only State or non-state controlled actors but also individuals.

The concept of a strategy for national security combines, without confusing them, a defense policy, a policy for domestic security, a foreign policy and an economic policy. Strategists are inclined to think of war today in the framework of a comprehensive approach, which must give the meaning of commitment, its legitimacy and the objectives to be reached including the ideological dimension. We must however remember that "war is only a part of political relationships, as consequently, and by no means independent"[32].

As a working definition, NATO defines a comprehensive approach as all the action taken in a coordinated and collaborative manner by the States concerned. This includes inter-ministerial relationships, civil and military ministers, international and intergovernmental organizations, NGOs and the private sector with a view to achieve a better level of consistency in analysis, planning, management and assessing the necessary action in order to anticipate, improve, harmonize and/or resolve the conditions which could worsen or cause a crisis.

This global perception of external defense or security combines the military dimension with a civil aspect, coordinated at the inter-agencies or on the multinational levels in order to efficiently respond to the diverse threats which are weighing down our society. It breaks down into general strategies specific to diplomatic, information, military, economic, security and cultural domains. It is without a doubt an improvement on what Clausewitz was writing when he said that war is nothing other than the continuation of political relationships, with the contribution of other means[33].

2.2.2.2. *Comprehensive approach and military strategy*

The French military school of thought had already identified this comprehensive approach within a different context: colonization. In the French tradition of war overseas, in Madagascar, Gallieni therefore gave the following instructions in his directives on May 22nd 1898: "The only way to reach calm in our new colony is to use the combined action of force and politics".

---

32 [CLA 65], p. 50.
33 Ibidem, p. 453.

In 1937, Lieutenant Colonel de Monsabert, who became an army General and Deputy after WWII, recommended the "intense use of political action and the measured use of force"[34] in order to make the enemy submit. The "measured use of force" was a much different understanding to that concept of a disproportionate resort to force[35], which is instrumentalized today by politicians and the media. Colonel Trinquier underlined that victory no longer depends only on a land battle [TRI 61], [TRI 68].

D. Galula was writing within a context of counter-insurgency when he wrote that "the interactions between political and military operations are becoming so strong that we can no longer separate them. On the contrary, any military operation must be planned by considering its political effects, and vice versa"[36]. Although this was written with a perspective of a conflict considered as domestic at this period, D. Galula tackled the inter-ministerial (interagency) aspect and, finally, the "global" contemporary approach of conflict regulation, which calls upon instruments of State power potentially extended to a collective action of coalition states.

The comprehensive approach must be understood as a political war with a confrontation of ideas, because it is applied within the context of a globalized society of information which only partially encompasses operating theaters. It is conceived of, by a permanent consideration in the operating zones of the information environment, influence activities and persuasion, and therefore the field of perception. In particular, it means the construction of a coherent discourse going alongside facts, conforming to the defended values, supported by an argument which fights the ideology of the opposed forces.

2.2.2.3. About the influence strategy of Western democracies

The objective consists of ensuring the coherence of messages, both image and text, and of the actions in support of the operation's legitimacy. In times of peace and crisis, a democracy must be able to envisage an influence strategy which aims to "persuade any allied decision-maker, neutral or opposed, that the objectives and modes of action chosen to reach the military aspect of the state are legitimate, relevant, credible and efficient. Before, but also during or after a conflict, it acts in the fields of understanding and perception of individuals or entities in order to contribute to building a favorable environment, but also to anticipate a decision

---

34 [GOI 37], p. 13.
35 Article 57 from Protocol 1 from the 1997 Geneva Conventions: the principle of proportionality commands that we abstain from launching an attack which we may expect to incidentally cause death within the civil population, injuries to civilians, damage to goods belonging to civilians or a combination of deaths or damage which would be excessive in relation to the expected concrete and direct military advantage.
36 [GAL 64], p. 18.

which may not be favorable for national interest or coalition" [CHA 09b]. The influence strategy is therefore conceived of within a permanent confrontation of wills.

Democracy calls upon influence activities[37] which group together activities whose first and direct aim is to influence willingness and primarily relies on communication methods. They also act to counter adverse influence activities. They are mainly driven by functions devoted to information. They look to predispose, persuade or dissuade, and to psychological restrain the target audience. They may aim to assist, encourage and reassure, or even establish or re-establish trust. They may be accompanied by physical actions which will reinforce the delivered message.

In addition, in a comprehensive approach, military force is only one method amongst several others, as was already envisaged in the expression of "total strategy" by General Beaufre: "military war is generally no longer decisive, in the real sense of the word. The political decision, which is always necessary, can no longer only be reached by a combination of limited military action with suitable action led in psychological, economic and diplomatic domains. War strategy, governed before by the military strategy which put military heads first for a while, now comes under a total strategy led by government heads, and where the military now only plays a subordinate role"[38]. However, it is possible today to note that the distancing of conflicts and their lesser influence on a State's domestic politics leads to a larger margin of autonomy being left to the commanding officer in operation.

Conceptualizing and leading an influence strategy in order to dissuade or neutralize opposed forces is an additional approach and one which cannot be overlooked for resolving international crises. It may go alongside or gear down the effects of other State actions, whether they are diplomatic, military, or economic. The synergy of the State's capacities to influence encompasses governmental communication in all its forms, as much as a military information strategy. It is conceived of within an inter-ministerial structure which leads and adapts it according to the evolution of conflicts and crises, by liaising with the allied States for a military operation in coalition. It is adapted to the target audience. In synergy with a State's instruments of power, it calls upon diplomacy, economic power, military force, and cultural influence.

The influence strategy is indeed interesting. In fact, diplomacy and communication are intended to compensate for *not* resorting to the force of democratic armies, particularly by relying on their potential capacities for restraint.

---

37 [PIA 06], p. 12.
38 [BEA 72], p. 21.

The effects of the armed forces depend heavily on the other side's perception of their power; the more the will to use it is perceived, the greater the other side's perception will be. As R. Aron recalls, up until now, "constraint is inseparable from all politics"[39]. This does not mean using force, but the possibility of using it, "constraint between two States is expressed by the threat or use of armed forced"[40], which joins with the indirect strategy for reaching "the decision by deception and maneuvers, surprise [and] psychological activities" [LID 54].

2.2.2.4. *The return to ideologies*

However, recent conflicts show the new found importance in the confrontation of ideologies. Through the war of ideas and words, these ideologies express a vision of the world for their different supports with, however, some common ground. The dominant position of the West since the 15th Century, either European or transatlantic, is contested against in the search for a redistribution of power, whether it is political, philosophical, economic, or gradually, military. This state of international relationships therefore expresses a context of competition, or an ideological conflict between heterogeneous parties (Western states faced with non-Western states, States and non-state controlled actors, etc.), between an actor who has spread and established his own ideology and other growing or renewed ideologies throughout the world.

The Websters dictionary refers to ideology as "a set of aims and ideas, especially in politics… or a set of ideas proposed by the dominant class of a society to all members of this society". In an extreme understanding, it could also be understood as the expression of totalitarianism, imposing ideas or "a vague philosophy speculating on hollow ideas". For our subject matter here, far from a conception inherited from the Cold War, ideology will be understood as the set of ideas making up the mind or soul of the strategy led by a social group, a State or a group of States, in the attempt to reach long term objectives relating to the ideas which it can identify with and adhere to.

However, democracies accept the debate on ideas and therefore the coexistence of different systems, even totalitarian systems, so long as they do not provoke a reaction through an unreasonable attitude, in comparison with their own values. The conflicts in the 1990s (First Gulf War and the Balkan Wars) as well as conflicts in Iraq and Afghanistan at the beginning of this 21st Century highlight the fact that military success still remains within reach of the coalitions bringing together Western democracies which are acting under an international mandate, but which do not necessarily lead to peace; in other words, a certain form of victory. This does not only include re-establishing peace and the political legitimacy of the government in

---

39 [ARO 62], p. 765.
40 [ARO 62].

power, or rebuilding the State in all its forms, but also a necessary mental pacification[41] of the actors, to persuade them of the validity of this peace which is not, perhaps, what they were wishing for.

In fact, the new State is only considered legitimate depending on the criteria imposed by the international community, acting and reacting using a comprehensive approach for its action, according to standards and behavior which are more or less negotiated on with the West. Following its own objectives for peace, the West affects the way out of the crisis, notably by its own indirect strategy which calls upon diplomacy, economy, international law, assistance via aid programs for reconstruction and good governance, security system reforms (SSR), and potentially the deployment of armed forces.

Western ideology today, however, is retreating in the face of national (or nationalist), religious or ethnic ideologies. The rise in power from States such as China, and thus the supremacy of their own values and their conception of the world in the name of their history and their new instruments of power is an example of this. The Franco-Chinese or Sino-American relations show this rise in power, whether in terms of displaying Chinese influence or by means of Chinese cyberattacks which are regularly denounced. Other States are also involved in this view of ideological confrontation such as Russia, or simply in the confirmation of a new power to be respected, such as Brazil.

The religious aspect is visibly present in a Muslim world which is comprised of 57 States, grouped together within the Organization of the Islamic Conference (OIC) and which gathers minorities within a certain number of States, which are particularly Western. This religious ideology naturally puts its own values first. However, we cannot forget that Islam is political, and that this religion is written into the constitution of Muslim States as a *state religion*. It then reaches the status of "all-conquering", by its most radical components. These have, nonetheless, the full support of the Muslim community, although violence is condemned. But the ideology expressed in its values is not put into question. Finally, conflicts where people from the West are involved today are mainly the theaters of operation where Islam is exclusive, which is a far cry from the concept of secularity in countries such as France, for example.

These different ideologies identified here have, however, something in common: a desire for revenge, based on past humiliation, stemming from past relationships with the West.

---

41 [CHA 98] This reflection has been discussed in the concept of "democratic pacification".

2.2.2.5. *War of meaning and strategic communication*

Confronted with the propaganda in Iraqi and Afghan theaters of operation, the West (via NATO, its armed fist) is led to propose its narrative in order to get or maintain the support for its strategy and not to leave the influence terrain to the single opposed forces. Yet, Raymond Aron had already warned us that "rebels in bare hands are irresistible when men in power cannot, or do not, want to defend themselves"[42]. It is not just a question of proposing our own vision of the world, but, in fact, expressing the will to defend it.

We must refer to concepts of information and communication strategies, which is not simply semantic. This idea raises the question of the level of conceptualization of influence, and of the zones of action or skills, in order to identify who does what and for what use or effect. The information strategy defines the application of the strategy in the information domain for all actors – civil and military – able to contribute to resolving a crisis. The strategy acts in synergy with the use of economic, diplomatic or military tools, even social and cultural, in order to give meaning and get the desired effects in pursuit of the end-state. The communication strategy refers to government politics on communication.

However, information and communication strategies together build up the credibility of the messages, potentially by proposing changes to the general strategy adopted by considering that "the instant spread of information which characterizes the pace of the crises imposes other strategies of communication and information through its course"[43]. These strategies must also contribute to making the State or the coalition into a credible source of information. The key word in this case is "trust", that the public actors must develop in order to be heard, believed, and thus to lead a conflict, notably such as the kind in Afghanistan, by preserving their freedom of action.

2.2.2.6. *NATO and strategic communication(s) in Afghanistan*

Using the expression "strategic communications"[44] (STRAT-COM) which could ensure this synergy for responding to the synergy of Taliban movement, NATO is looking to conceptualize its own collective influence to the benefit of the Afghanistan theater of operation. STRAT-COM is defined as the coordinated and appropriate use of NATO communications activities and capabilities – public diplomacy, public affairs (PA), military public affairs, information operations (InfoOps) and psychological operations (PSYOPS), as appropriate – in support of

---

42 [ARO 62], p. 45.
43 [LB 08], p. 191.
44 Why NATO adopted the term "strategic communications" and not "strategic communication" is not clear. We will only use "strategic communications" for NATO.

Alliance policies, operations and activities, and in order to advance NATO's aims[45]. It is understood as a process which seeks to support the decisions made as of the initial stages of planning an operation. It aims to explain and persuade others of the legitimacy of the military intervention. In fact, it is at least a matter of keeping the support of State citizens committed to the conflict, or on the best to win over the population in the intervention zones. It must consider information as a weapon.

How is the STRAT-COM perceived today? The first report is that all those who may influence the information environment must contribute to synchronizing strategic communications. It is a matter of influencing, in order to convince others to adhere to NATO's objectives, in order to correctly understand these aims. It is also imperative to consider that we are no longer at war, or at peace, but in a continuum where war and peace are interwoven with no clear distinction. Information is broadcast 24/7. The opposed forces, whether this is Al-Qaeda or different Jihadist movements, have their own service for communication and propaganda. In this context, besides institutional communication and military information operations, the strategic level uses the American concept of *Public Diplomacy*, which includes *soft power* and is incorporated into NATO. It may also include cultural diplomacy which, for the long term, is addressed to the elite members, built within a framework of developing trust and a mutual understanding through dialog. This is the *to know us is to love us,* that, for example, the French White Paper (2008) may correspond to.

The country's domestic communication, and the communication which is adapted to the operations must permanently act in synergy on different levels: strategic (out of the theater), operative (over the set of theaters) and tactical (level of fighters). The messages and means are different, but must remain coherent during global action. On each level, it is a matter of destabilizing power relationships in favor of NATO. In fact, the Afghanistan conflict is also a war of communication and propaganda. In particular, this means getting the displayed support from the international community and allies on an intermediate level, to put pressure on the will of the opponents, both political and military. On a local level, it means acting on opinions, belligerents and our own troops, the best messengers to transmit our own will through their behavior and commitment.

The stake remains above all strategic, however. The objective is less that of physically destroying the opponent, and more destroying his *image* in an information environment which is global, and where the will to go till the end regarding the decided aims is expressed (or not, as the case may be). Only having a few men, the rebels shape their own information environment with low intensity operations, but ones which are remarkably portrayed in the media, to the extent

---

45 NATO Strategic Communications Policy, September 24th 2009.

where the journalists, Western in particular, interpret (due to their lack of military knowledge) these actions as a question over the superiority of the Western military, and therefore retransmit this lack of knowledge to the public view. Confronted with this action, strategic communication must become offensive and must not leave the initiative to anybody intervening, or to the belligerents, media, or pressure groups.

The State or a coalition's strategic communications presume that sources of information are unified, and assume that there is strict control over news broadcasting without it turning into propaganda.

2.2.3. *Winning the battle of legitimacies*

The West is leaking its own doubts and is struggling to define its project in order to keep its rank but also to continue to offer its vision of the future world. As a victim of non-military aggression, its certainties are shaken up by the certainties of those wanting to contradict it. In spite of a gradual and painful awakening by the return from the war or military operations, it feels the great difficulties in holding a motivating and unifying, if not ideological, discussion. The war led by those refusing to accept the values of the West aims to make it doubt their relevance. But, a military defeat leads us to re-question the ideas of those conquered, and this is a more sensitive matter in a Western democracy when it feels like it is losing a war, in particular a war of values.

2.2.3.1. *Creating legitimacy out of a military intervention*

Declaring a war to be just or unjust implies a value judgment which depends on the societies carrying this judgment. The wars of believers against infidels were, or still are, in their eyes just or unjust, such as the wars of Rome against the barbarians, and wars of defense, liberation, aggression, conquest, pacification, extermination. All the religious wars, crusades, civil and revolutionary wars, are justified in the eyes of those who start them. As a partisan, it will be difficult for the aggressor to find *unjust* motives for resorting to force. The democracies which are not aggressors but which are restrained from acting today avoid describing an armed intervention as being just.

In order to justify a war, it is therefore essential for a democracy (or a democratic coalition) to be able to demonstrate, and thus communicate, that it has used all the diplomatic channels possible in order to peacefully resolve a crisis before resorting to high military forces. In the first Gulf War, indeed using important military forces which needed time to be deployed, actually started at the end of a six month period of great diplomatic efforts. NATO hesitated for nearly three years before becoming resolutely involved in Bosnia in September 1995 by bombarding the artillery of

Bosnian Serbs around Sarajevo in order to lift the siege over the city. In Kosovo, NATO launched the *Allied Forces* operation in March 1999 after only one year.

The legitimacy of a military intervention once it has been launched is therefore permanently constructed and must respond to a certain number of criteria depending on generic situations. However, the concept of legitimacy is not universal, and everybody has their own concept of it. Its duration varies, especially as several democracies are involved. Political criteria (particularly leadership elections) or legality criteria – national or international – regarding the proportionality of resorting to force, of multi-nationality, of humanitarian need, and then the capacity to exert influence, may contribute to its support.

Constructing legitimacy leads to a war through information between those who have it, and those who do not have it, and between those who manipulate it and those who release it, in a certain way bordering objectivity. Finally, the position of communication in all its forms in modern societies forces inserting information in the State's strategy with care, so as not to put public power at peril. It aims to guarantee its freedom of action [CHA 06] which is a major principle of any strategy. Therefore, a democracy cannot ignore it, because it conditions the decision making, which is more important especially as the decisions are made within the context of an international crisis. However, when faced with information warfare, what can the freedom of action for democracies be when there are multiple limitations on their action? Thus, a new strategic reality is imposed today. The freedom of action of democracies is restrained, and the weakness of the decision makers faced with crisis is becoming more and more apparent. They must win back this freedom of action.

2.2.3.2. *The asymmetry of ethics*

Today, democracies respect a certain number of operation principles which construct and validate their political system. They are subjected to influence or destabilizing actions by those who do not share their principles or values, or who aim to redefine power relationships in their favor.

For the opposed forces, information warfare and cyberwar, the latter acting as a multiplier of IW efficiency, are similar to the tactics of the "weak" who, in order to compensate for his inferiority next to the "strong" acts on perceptions. This is notably via modern means of communication, across a world opened up by the Internet, by the instrumentalization of freedom given by democracies on the respective territories.

Whether they are acting publicly or privately, the opponents or enemies of the West mostly lead an insidious war, if not a subversive one, against our political system and our democratic values by deformed or manipulated information. This is favored by the Internet which allows access to information, the capacity to develop this information as images and to spread it, without the deontological filter of the media, such as the principle developed in our societies even if it is not perfect. Rumors are, for example, weapons which have found their youth[46].

This information warfare is a fundamental element of a kind of indirect strategy, the difference being that it is neither thought about nor coordinated as it was before by a State such as the URSS. Now it is via a multitude of partisans who adhere to this project ideologically by a convergence of interests relying on a will, or rather *hatred*, to fight that which Western civilization represents. This method of action leads governments to be put in a position of defense, as they must offer a valid answer, and then they must convince others of the truthfulness of this response. Any conflict (including conflicts of information) can, then, only be played out within a limited margin of freedom of action, due to the repercussions that its development could have on the international situation and on questions within it.

In this context, the media has a weakened role. On the other hand, they contribute, in fact, to the conflicts. As pointed out in the 1994 French White Paper, "media is no longer just a spectator, but is active in crises and conflict, which weigh down on its conduct and outcomes (…) media management is becoming one of the elements in military strategy. Information is now at the heart of all defense policies. Often referring to a "right" to information which does not exist, the media may also contribute to creating or maintaining a crisis by refusing to conform to military recommendations. This can be seen in the situation in Afghanistan with the journalists being taken hostage who were working for a French television channel in January 2010. The result of the search for them naturally triggered resentment within the populations and thus a new outbreak of violence in the zone under French liability.

2.2.3.3. *Why fight?*

The question of the legitimacy of a war has become a critical problem for the political engagement of Western democracies. In fact, we must concentrate on the

---

46 The doubts regarding the truth behind 9/11 is important, like the revival of conspiracy theory. In 2008, seven years after these attacks, a question was asked to samples of the population of 17 different countries by the site WorldPublicOpinion.org (L'Express, French weekly newspaper, September 11th 2008) "Who is behind the 9/11 attacks?", there was no consensus on the fact that they had been committed by terrorists from the vague al-Qaeda. Less than one out of two people (46% on average) answered instantly that radical Islamists had prepared and carried out these attacks. Israel and the American government came up in other answers. In Europe, important minorities (35-45%) in France, the UK, Italy, Germany or even Russia said something other than al-Qaeda. See [KRE 08], a collection of texts contributing to conspiracy theory.

question: "why fight?" We must rebuild, if not simply build, the meaning of combat and the commitment of democracies in current wars, and maintain it over time.

A democracy no longer fights, or at least no longer knows how to fight against someone or ideologies, but for values. For this reason, the engagement of the armed forces, which is becoming more and more frequent, can only be done by respecting international law. Thus, French interventions within the UN or another organization are not justified to fight against such or such dictator, but they are justified, with regard to human rights for international law, to save a civil population. This concept of fighting "for" something is fundamental. Our ideological action therefore relies on defending human rights and the application of international law, potentially against authoritarian regimes. Moreover, favoring future relations with a spared Other, and persuading him to take on our democratic principles, are two factors which determine our relationship with an opposed force, both today and tomorrow. This means in particular that victory must be discrete and partial.

On land, which is inseparable from the strategic level for today's conflicts, D. Galula pointed out that it is not enough to roughly define the aim (winning the support of the population), "we must also explain how to reach it. We must also do it in such a way that the men leading the counter insurgency, whether they are politicians, civil servants, social or military workers, have a certain initiative whilst remaining in control of the government"[47]. An armed force must, then, develop internal adherence and exemplary behavior from the ideas that it preaches. The concept of "strategic corporal" coined by General Krulak, an ex-commanding general of the Marine Corps, is fundamental today. Any individual action on the land, including that of a corporal, the lowest rank in military hierarchy, or a civilian, may have a strategic effect through its spreading.

2.2.3.4. *Necessary domestic adherence*

However, the democratic legitimacy of military engagement relies on the support of the national community, not only through its parliamentary representatives, but also through a strong national cohesion. Military commitments are naturally discussed within a democracy. It has to prove that there is a strong and determined collective will in favor of the chosen politics. Executive power must, then, permanently build up the support for its external politics by explaining the aims of the end-state or by not speaking about them at all. However, these aims are naturally contested against by democratic discussions or the propaganda spread by the opposed forces who rely on potential setbacks, deaths of civilians or in the military, taking hostages including soldiers (term used by journalists) who are no longer prisoners of war (and therefore no longer have the protected status of the Geneva Conventions).

---

47 [GAL 64], p. 125.

The absence of "borders" for information to be spread allows free expression of the opponent's propaganda, and leads to a permanent war of words and images with their emotional content. This "propaganda" allows rumors, misinformation, instilling doubt especially as the conspiracy theory is extremely present in our societies, thus making the government's discourse and its credibility more fragile, as the French White Paper highlights.

In addition, the ideological conflict led by opposed forces aims to infiltrate our societies by returning our own values back to our opposition. By playing on certain freedoms, the objectives of these opposed forces is to plant doubts in the mind of the voting citizen and to pressure the elected leader's will, i.e. he who represents the majority building itself into a democracy from a common point of view, and therefore being the instigator and a subject of compromise.

It is true that the simple belief regarding the inescapable relevance of democratic ideas is not the best of solutions, above all in war. We must, then, be committed to a long fight which incorporates the battle of ideas, ideology, and the cause or justification of a war's legitimacy for peace which is conceived of differently by each belligerent. But, also, we must be committed to the fight which refers at one point or another to national interests, even under the umbrella of a resolution from the UN's Security Council.

In the conflict state we live in today, there are two points where we must make an effort: strengthening the beliefs of our own public opinion through the legitimacy of the action and conviction brought to it; and building a constructive perception for long lasting peace, particularly by fighting against the propaganda spread by opposed forces.

2.2.3.5. *Sensitizing domestic public opinion*

Despite the non-military frame of mind inherent to the democratic system which calls upon diplomatic and economic action to resolve conflicts by sometimes excessive compromises, the use of armed forces in coalition or under the national flag still remains as the concrete expression that the ideas which are considered to be fundamental are worth being defended and fought for.

For military intervention decided on by a democracy, the action must be fully prepared, so as to quickly get a significant outcome which valorizes the resources and men involved. The nation's adherence is also conditioned by the effectiveness of the defense and security devices above all if, as history shows, victorious and quick wars are rare. Trust in the action of public power, then, is put on first rank. The chosen strategy must be preceded by an action which is supported, planned sensitively and the education of opinions in order to give the citizen the elements needed to understand the event when it happens. It also requires a collective memory, shared within society, to be able to firmly reject the ideology of the opposed forces.

Moreover, military threats are often perceived as coming from far away. The "*esprit de defense*" (accepting the defense of his/her country in mind and in acts), in the military sense of the expression, is increasingly more distanced from the worries of the Western citizen who generally entrusted his external security to professional armed forces. The reality of threats which are indeed real, as with terrorism, raise a certain incredulity which is reinforced by the opponent's potential capability to interfere with the democratic debate.

Finally, such involvements in the 21st Century are conditioned by the support of public opinions which do not necessarily correspond to national borders. Everything which takes place on the political stage in other nations is incorporated into each public space. Through this sort of *porosity*, the international public opinion is incorporated into a State's domestic debate without, however, being able to identify the reality of its effects, except through the reactions of possible diasporas. As the White Paper points out, under the influence of Al-Qaeda and those inspired by it, terrorist groups which used to act in a segmented manner prepare operations in several points of the globe, conducting cross-border ideological warfare and attempting to interconnect crises with distinct local or regional roots. Nonetheless, with the growing speed of information exchanges – both images and ideas – as we have seen in recent years in the religious domain, flare-ups can occur, creating a particularly unstable environment prone to sudden burst of violence[48]. It can lead to major crises, such as the cartoons drawn of Muhammad may show, for instance.

2.2.3.6. *What is propaganda today?*

Today, just like yesterday, propaganda exists and is verified by contemporary conflicts. NATO defined propaganda in 1970 as "any information, ideas, doctrines, or special appeals, disseminated to influence the opinions, emotions, attitudes or behavior of any specified group in order to benefit the sponsor, either directly or indirectly"[49]. Now is, without a doubt, the time to have a definition which is more adapted to a theme which has triggered several reactions, including within a military alliance such as NATO. Thus, propaganda could be understood as the *set of actions led in the information environment to alter and constrain perceptions, attitudes and behavior*. The point of these actions is, in fact, to deliberately harm the individual or collective freewill by damaging and/or falsifying information. To reach these objectives, propaganda then proposes the incorrect and partial understanding of a fact.

---

48 [GOU 08], p. 57.
49 [OTA 81], Official English definition.

However, it is characterized today by the manipulation of emotions, to the detriment of the faculties for reasoning and judgment. It may resort to threat, violence, terror, and lying by using methods which aim to subject, press-gang, and indoctrinate. In a coercive way, propaganda acts maliciously, which takes it out of the acceptable field of influence and communication. Indeed, a force opposed to one's own strategy is always accused of spreading propaganda and this reproach will be applied by the enemy to democracies at war. Yet it seems they are more credible in uttering a whole truth, if not, some truth.

By considering this new approach to propaganda, democracies are influencing and communicating. They do *not* create propaganda. The reference to the truth of facts, the credibility in the sense that they will not lie deliberately, the deontology of those who spread the information, and finally the respect for people through images or texts make up the criteria which differentiates communication from propaganda.

2.2.3.7. *The Internet: new battlefield for propaganda*

The Internet is a new battlefield for ideological combat[50]. In the absolute, it boundlessly links individuals together through information, or produced or transmitted knowledge. It disseminates and multiplies more or less reliable sources of information which shapes opinion via individuals being more informed by themselves and choosing the sources of information which suit them the best. Its control is indeed critical for an asymmetric war. This explains why the terrorist network Al-Qaeda has entirely invested in it. Its cells merge with the Net. Several thousands of Jihadist sites are popping up on the Internet today [AAR 08]. The Web gives any terrorist organization or resistance both visibility and intelligibility.

Having become this sound box which is essential for violent movements, it offers the most determined Internet users an ideological corpus from which adherence and persuasion can be triggered. As a useful vector for spreading information, the Internet also acts as a discreet and different procedure for liaison. The access to sites with satellite images and to plans published online enables a discreet aid for pinpointing objectives. It enables them to collect funds and make financial transactions. On the international stage, Afghan rebels [ELK 07] have taken to the Internet to implement strategic communication. Their main website in 5 different languages is updated every four hours. Several hundred other Jihadist sites with products, videos and magazines, radio and television relay information from the main site.

---

50 For more information, see: [BOC 08], [RON 07], [WAL 07].

2.2.3.8. Communication or propaganda

As the different conflicts today show us, the opposed forces therefore lead their own information warfare and have their own strategic communication. However, is this communication, or is it *propaganda*? Communication is based on checked information, precise figures which can be verified, and is aimed at reason, not just emotion. NATO's strategic communications in Afghanistan, for example, fulfills these criteria. However, the strategic communication in Afghan rebel groups and Al-Qaeda relates to our understanding of propaganda. Yet, this propaganda works according to an information environment which has been left for too long under the control of the Taliban and Jihadists, NATO being too confident in its *just cause*. In fact, radical Islam does not generally resort directly to force, considering Western military supremacy, but instead prefers strong propaganda which supports its ideological war. Radical groups have understood perfectly that globalized information, available 24/7, addressing an often weak audience in terms of understanding, would be their best weapon against the West, and that they could rally up others in the name of discrimination against Islam. The use of vocabulary is, then, fundamental with its references to the holy war, martyrs, and caliphates.

In Iraq and Afghanistan, moreover, information is used in rebel operations. Killing an American soldier or exploding a military vehicle by an improvised explosive device (IED), with no military value in terms of outcome, firstly aims to create propaganda images which will be broadcast across the world via the Internet, with a view to influence our public opinions and to galvanize Muslim populations. These types of attacks, or indeed others, will not always exist if the scenario planned to be filmed cannot take place. The concept of military efficiency is thus different for Westerners acting within a technically-minded vision, and for Islam rebels acting within a political and psychological vision. Information exists because the soldier has been killed. However, the question of the meaning given to this information raises a difficulty, particularly in a different cultural context, and it reiterates the problems regarding the war of meaning.

2.3. Influence strategy: defeating and limiting armed force physical involvement

Today, the various different conflicts impose a new strategic approach, in particular through the role of information and its effects in the functioning of international relations, and more particularly, in conflicts. By considering the two existing political conceptions, democracies and States not applying democratic principles as they are commonly accepted, these are confronted with each other in the reconstruction of a new international order and in the meaning which must be given to understand this future world. This is a major stake, not only in terms of power, but also in terms of the meaning of the values to be promoted.

To support the legitimacy of their action, democratic societies must, then, be in a position to express their ideology, including resorting to force. However, military interventions led by democracies must use all their powers of persuasion not resort to excessive force, but at the same time expressing their power.

2.3.1. *Describing the aggressor*

The enemy no longer exists. But, groups taking on weapons with the aim of fighting the Western world *do* exist. Must we not redefine the enemy on the one hand to be in a better position to fight, and on the other hand, to convince him to stop his aggression?

2.3.1.1. *What is an enemy?*

By defending universal values such as Human rights within a context of international law, then democracies are not fighting an enemy, but fighting for values. As a consequence, this means knowing how to identify ideas and those who support them, which could seriously endanger their own values. The enemy of yesterday inherited his fate or was appointed – he could be located. For a long time now, France has had no official enemies. In this vein, the Soviet enemy was only defined as such under the presidency of François Mitterrand.

If we believe in what official texts have us believe, today there are no enemies. On the one hand, the conflict between democracies is not very likely, at least on the military front. On the other hand, a democracy no longer fights an *enemy*, but is put in competition with a State considered, above all, to be an adversary "future economic partnership". As Liddell Hart stated in 1951, the enemy of today may be the client of tomorrow, and the ally of the day after[51].

It cannot be a social or religious group either. Western elitists cannot accept this potential demonization in contradiction with the hammering of their principles. Above all, a democracy must enable reconciliation if it is involved in an armed intervention.

Only references to risks and threats remain. The 1994 French White Paper did not use the term "enemy", but favored "adversary" (5 times), and mentioned risks 56 times, and threats 25 times. The former Joint Concept for Operations (1997), which expressed the military vision from the 1994 White Paper, did not use the words "enemy" or "adversary", but used "threat" 24 times, and "risk" 4 times.

---

51 [LID 51], p. 18.

The 2008 publication of the French White Paper does not use the word enemy, but does indeed use adversary (13 times), at the same time referring to threats 122 times, and risks 180 times. The new Joint Concept for Operations of 2010[52] uses the term "adversary" 37 times, but only uses the term enemy once: "Combat is inherent to military intervention. It is permanent in operations of war against conventional enemies, possibly in the presence of irregular adversaries which must be neutralized to reach the fixed political objective". Interestingly, the term "enemy" is used in the discussions of Volume 3 which goes with the White Paper. Politics have chosen to have no enemies, but the qualified or moral authorities do not have this restriction. This refusal to choose, which is a legitimate political choice, makes any rallying, and any commitment, extremely difficult. Nonetheless, this maintains the blurred nature which prevents any distinction between good and evil, loyalty and possibly betrayal, and between the general interest which forces involvement in the case of conflict and the particular interest, as much in terms of personal convictions as our own interests.

But, as Colonel Trinquier wrote in another context that can be adapted to many points regarding Afghanistan and Iraq, "in modern warfare, the enemy is otherwise difficult to define. There is no material border separating the two sides. The limit between friends and enemies cuts through the very heart of the nation, in the same village, sometimes in the same family. This is often an ideological boundary, which must be fixed if we want to be sure of hitting our adversary and defeating him. Guerilla warfare and terrorism are only stages of modern warfare, destined to create a favorable situation, allowing a regular army to get the feet on the ground, to be in a position to confront an enemy army on a battle field and to defeat it"[53]. Where there is military involvement, we must accept that there will be an enemy.

2.3.1.2. *Redefining the enemy*

The conditions of engagement in the 21st Century are defined by a necessary *new* definition of the enemy. Democracies must clearly identify their aggressors. Once identified, they must dare to describe those in combat boldly and without fear. Terminology is still very important, not only because it must define the meaning of the combat and those involved in the conflict, but also because it is used, before by propaganda, and today by a globalized form of communication which is for supporting or weakening a cause.

The corpus of French doctrinal publications refers to the irregular adversary[54] who, when confronting our forces, expresses the confrontation between different political, social, cultural and strategic systems. This is a partial response to the lack

---

52 [PIA 10], CICDE, 2010.
53 Colonel Trinquier, op. cit., p. 32.
54 [PIA 08].

of legal description of this type of adversary, but this concept is also mainly aimed at armed NGOs who try to seize power in an intrastate conflict. This could mean that the enemy can *only* be state-controlled, which is not satisfactory for the conflicts of today and tomorrow.

To support the legitimacy of the action, democratic societies must be in a position to clearly identify their aggressors, in order to direct their strategic choices and to accompany them by either explaining or persuading others of their fairness. However, willingly or not, democracies do not qualify the enemy as such[55]. Also, the concept of a "source of opposition" may contribute to determining this dissimulated enemy, and make it possible to lead this undeclared war. A source of opposition[56] is the generic term to name any State, force or agent, military or civil, which is likely to weigh negatively on the realization of the political goal (end-state). A source of opposition will produce effects in material and immaterial fields. It may be active or potential, because it may concern a declared or undeclared adversary, a neutral opportunist, or a friend whose interests are different.

In this framework, an adversary is above all a source of opposition which uses no violent methods to resolve a disagreement, and which accepts the ruling of a conflict through the application of democratic rules. On the other hand, the belligerent is a source of opposition which uses violence if need be to achieve its ends against another belligerent. These two approaches rely on the concept of impartiality, set ahead in the 1990s within armed forces. But there cannot be any impartiality towards an aggressor. A source of opposition which goes to war with Western armed forces is an enemy by behavior.

Consequently we may propose the following definition: "an enemy is he who, State, group or individual, crosses a threshold of hostility comprised of voluntary violent act(s) in material or immaterial fields, expressing by this a will to harm our vital strategic or power interests. Depending on the circumstances, including criteria of subversion and destabilization, the threshold of hostility is comprised of several criteria relating to a real or potential aggression, whether it is terrorist (conventional or unconventional), with the criterion determining the irreversibility of the capacity to harm". This definition broadens the tradition meaning of the enemy, where most often in the past it covered the simple antagonistic relations between States, the people, or ideological blocks. Thus, the real enemy exists today when he crosses a threshold of hostility by his behavior and acts. Still, the potentially enemy will must be diverted from this threshold of hostility and all the criteria which construct it. This can only be achieved via an information or influence strategy.

---

55 [CHA 06a], p. 47-52.
56 [PIA 06], definition amended by author.

The concept of the enemy is still complex today. Yet, such a notion seems fundamentally important for moral and material preparation of going into combat. The enemy is mainly human in terms of physical representation, which naturally leads to a respect for the other fighting for another cause. However, he is also the symbol or the representative of ideas, the political, religious, ethnic systems which go against our own. Therefore, mankind still remains as the target of a State's action strategy.

Analyzing the enemy in this manner cannot be ignored, particularly in counter-insurgency conflicts. In his thoughts on the revolutionary war, the ideological war of yesterday, General Delmas pointed out that it was a *war of militants*, the only just war, as it brings about justice; killing is necessary for truth [DEL 72]. For this militant or, from now on, this actor, there is both good and evil, as "each lie turns into the truth if it helps history to be accomplished, depending on his meaning". He fights to impose his truth. He does not discuss the legitimacy of his action. All that counts is the meaning that he gives to this action, and it is indeed this enemy that the West will encounter in Afghanistan, that it docs not demonize, where as the West itself *is* demonized.

We must note that the victory achieved by military force only, or only by destroying the source of opposition's capabilities to harm, is rarely a total victory. In fact, the victory of one side, i.e. instilling peace, must be accepted by the defeated side. However any source of opposition (and there will *always* be a source of opposition which does not accept defeat) has the means today to express through terrorism and guerilla warfare…a globalized propaganda, its resistance to a will and force perceived of as enemies. Targeting our worn down determination and the weakened legitimacy of our actions according to the populations, this source of opposition relies on information warfare and a cyberwar which are easily implemented today, enabling an easier spread of ideas.

2.3.1.3. *Understanding the adversary and its human environment*

The White Paper reminds us that the human factor remains, and will still remain, decisive[57]. In fact, adapted to the operation, the military influence strategy must shape the human environment of operations by acting upon the perception of the populations, by striving to understand local cultures. This is a matter of understanding and making the complexity of the human land understood, and not simply collecting data. The method for considering the problems regarding armed forces is based on the PMESII model (political, military, economic, social, "infrastructure", information). We now also add "physical environment" and "time" to the model, creating the acronym PMESII-TT.

---

57 [GOU 08], p. 58.

This model enables us to draw up a detailed image of the human environment, which also makes it possible to identify and analyze perceptions, local dynamics, and the effects which need to be researched or obtained. Intercultural communication has unmasked a majorly important component insofar as all civilizations are in contact with each other. In fact, receiving the message and decoding it may present an obstacle depending on the culture of the population receiving it, when the message is compared to information coming from a national background, and the presence of stereotypes.

With the wars in Iraq and Afghanistan, the USA and the West in general have realized that the human environment of a theater of operations must be known in order to understand this enemy and its ideology. In other words, we are referring to the construction and the sources of its understanding of the world according to its cultural characteristics. This cultural awareness[58] has become a major theme in military efforts. Certainly, we must know our enemy but we must also know its human environment in the operational context. In fact, in current conflicts, Western armed forces are directly in contact with people and societies with values and cultural references which are very different from their own.

It is, then, very important for the military to be acutely aware of these differences, not only to protect themselves against errors of judgment, but also to make the best use of this "gap" to achieve the operation's objectives. Knowing the "human environment of the operations"[59] also tries to identify cultural representations on the one hand, and the people in societies in the middle of which the armed forces, often on land and therefore in contact with the people, act in order to integrate favorable or unfavorable characteristics into the development of modes of action. This knowledge is vital for action in the information environment and for influence activities.

The American army doctrine underlines the need to obtain this cultural information in a tribal, ethnic and religious setting. This is why around 30 "cultural" teams have been deployed in Afghanistan since February 2007 and in Iraq in Summer 2008. Their missions are to lead a *cultural preparation of the operational environment* (CPOE), to integrate information on the human environment into the decision making process, to permanently evaluate depending on the effects of friend or enemy forces in the response zone. These teams of 5 to 9 people are deployed according to the land brigades. Mainly civilians, they call upon researchers of social sciences, including anthropologists[60], despite the reserve from a part of the scientific

---

58 Several works are currently being produced on this subject: [BED 09], [MBD 09], [KIM 09], [FIE 06], [USA 09].
59 France uses this term and not "human terrain initiative" (USA) for example.
60 Defense News, April 18th, 2008.

community. The success has been noted, because their approach has made it possible to reduce 60% of the armed confrontations in certain areas of Afghanistan, on the side of the Taliban as much as the US forces.

2.3.2. *Armed forces and the information environment*

The 2010 Joint Concept for Operations has identified new fields of action, namely cyberspace and the field of perception[61]. This has become a major stake because it has a large impact on the legitimacy of military operations, and therefore political legitimacy. In fact different parties act within the information environment in order to uphold or support the chosen strategy. In this new environment the actions of the stakeholders try to influence the different perceptions of public, local or international opinions.

2.3.2.1. *New wars*

The armies of yesterday were so prepared for "conventional" wars where using force was favored, that today Western supremacy has strongly toned down this type of involvement in order to leave room for a new theoretical model of using armed forces. Warfare uses these modes of action where influence, willingness, and moral factors have become dominant (see *supra*). Still further back than yesterday, war is not just an act of physical destruction but also *psychological*, which favors influence strategies to act on the will of both sides.

High-intensity interventions are relatively short today. However, they leave room aside for a transition phase whose duration is undetermined, with the objective of rebuilding a State of law, determined by elections and the implementation of a legal and legitimate government, often with the help of the international community. This transition phase is called "stabilization". It must be followed or accompanied by a reconstruction phase in order to allow the new State to assume its independence. The stabilization phase first supporting a political objective to the benefit of the host State. The authorities and local populations are the main beneficiaries and represent the true stake. They are supposed to adapt, and to make the processes for ending the crises "theirs".

Stabilization, then, aims to restore the foundations of these three pillars, in other words, the "social link" in the broad sense between political power, the social and economic parties, as well as the population of the State in question, at the same time fulfilling the fundamental aspirations of the individuals before engaging in the reconstruction phase of the State in question.

---

61 [PIA 10], p. 13.

It is theoretically favored by the democracies' refusal to accept the enemy's total defeat [CHA 06a], to the benefit of a discrete and limited victory which prevents, if possible, any action which could lead to its humiliation. Even the war terms, conqueror and conquered, have disappeared. Democracies support, by a suitable financing, international organizations in a post-conflict policy of domestic or external reconciliation, and of rebuilding the States having been subjected to the conflict. In the world of yesterday, a defeated country was siphoned off and war damages were paid to the conqueror. Today, democracies, and therefore their taxpayers, becoming involved in a conflict, thus pay for the reconstruction.

Nonetheless, the forces supporting the stabilization phase are foreign, and this presence may be conceived of as an "occupation", above all if this feeling is skillfully exploited by those opposed to the stabilization process. Those opposed to this process, often using irregular modes of action, generally try to turn this population into a target, a scapegoat, or even an instrument to reach their own ends.

Confirming the "three block" theory, coined by General Krulak, it turns out however that on the same theater of operations and at the same time, three military situations may arise: calm zones which accept peace, zones which undergo a lack of security which hinders reconstruction, and zones which escape all control and lead to guerilla and counter-guerilla type confrontations. This phase is favorable for armed movements which often use guerilla or terrorist type modes of action. It then requires counter insurgency operations.

This reality limits armies whose both meaning and modes of action must be defined [CHA 09c]. Insurgency is defined as "an organized, often ideologically motivated, group or movement that seeks to effect or prevent political change of a governing authority within a region, focused on persuading or coercing the population through the use of violence and subversion"[62]. NATO defines counter-insurgency as "the set of political, economic, social, military, law enforcement, civil and psychological activities required to defeat insurgency and address any core grievances"[63]. The information and the ideological context determine its success.

2.3.2.2. Understanding to influence and act

From now on, we must understand the operational environment where we act, and how to affect both the environment and the actors there. There is, then, a need for "understanding the situation in detail, however complex it is, and being able to explain it to others"[64]. In this environment, the armed forces aim to help create favorable conditions for an acceptable compromise for the parties present. Thus,

---

62 AJP 3.4.4, Doctrine on counter-insurgency, NATO working definition.
63 AJP 3.4.4.
64 General McChrystal, June 13th 2009.

military action is only *one* expression of this persuasive communication which could work along side coercive diplomacy, a theory developed by the USA at the end of the Cold War [CHA 93] and inevitably more credible than the public diplomacy in force today.

Today much more than yesterday, the matter at hand is one concerning conquering without losses, and with the least cost possible especially as these conflicts do not concern the national territory directly. The Internet has become this new battlefield where information warfare, as much as cyberwar, is controlled within an asymmetrical framework. NATO's forces, then, deploy a website in each of their theater of operations, informing the local population and trying to persuade them of the legitimacy of their actions. The stakes involved are as much persuading the populations, therefore influencing[65] the theaters of operation as maintaining the cohesion and support of the Western citizen, including fighting for actions with an unknown duration.

Influencing the decision making process and the human environment is indeed possible. Of course, this can be achieved by direct contact with the human, and also by messages transmitted to him/her. This may also be achieved, however, by operations led in cyberspace. We must act on perceptions, and therefore operate in the immaterial domain of the perception of events and forceful action. This must be coordinated, either by producing and spreading information, or by protecting information systems by a digital fight and electronic warfare, albeit by countering the destructive effects of false or manipulated information.

The importance of perception in the acceptance and appropriation of the stabilization process highlights the crucial importance of behavior, of the image given and the messages from outside parties. But it also shows, however, the importance of their ability to counter opponent propaganda. In particular this involves a real strategy for information and communication, and therefore, an influence strategy.

2.3.2.3. *Information operations*

The success of the armed forces generally depends on destroying the enemy's commanding capacities, meaning, its reorganization. This military logic must be applied today to conflicts where the concept of destruction is less suitable for information activities[66] which distort, change, and block information, to lead the

---

65 [PIA 05] "Concept for information operations". To apply influence through an information strategy by the actors of a crisis is considered as a principle (11th March 2005).

66 [OTA 09] Actions designed to affect information and/or information systems. They can be performed by any actor and include protection measures (AJP-3.10, 2009). In fact, they integrate influence activities.

other side to make a bad decision or to support a "good decision", and the resultant actions. Moreover, the enemy is not uniquely state-controlled and is tightly linked into civil societies. To respond to this new environment, the armed forces have developed the "information operations" doctrine, which must act on the decision making process as well as the population's perception, including in particular the human environment of these operations. Its effectiveness, however, is still controlled by the conviction of the armed forces in their mission and of their public opinions.

After the war on terrorism, the information operations considered to be the RMA's[67] third revolution took on their operational dimension. These are the results of the studies led, particularly in the USA, at the beginning of the 1990s by the Tofflers[68], and then by Martin Libicki amongst others. Information operations are primarily the military's response to conflicts taking place in the new information society. The organized management of information comes into the initial American concept of battlefield transparency, which was based on this freedom of action given by information superiority, defined by the US as the operational advantage derived from the ability to collect, process, and disseminate an uninterrupted flow of information while exploiting or denying an adversary's ability to do the same"[69]. Friendly forces must be able to know everything. They may, then, put all their efforts together, and therefore save their forces, or a blind enemy, lost in the fog of war, faced with surprise, controlled by errors of judgment or deception, and finally led to defeat at the lowest cost for the adversary controlling the information.

In the military domain, it is a question of shaping the battlefield by underlining that it, due to the development of information technologies, is no longer simply limited to the operations' geographical area, but can extend out of the borders on a global scale. Finally, the term information operation does not denote "operations on and by the media". "Media" communication (operational communication for armed forces, or *Military Public Affairs* in NATO) is a function in its own right which cannot be integrated into democracy in information operations. It is, however, clear that there is a strong interaction between these two functions.

2.3.2.4. *From command and control warfare to the battle of perception*

From a military view, it is in the very nature of war to harm the opponent's Commander and his technical as well as intellectual or psychological capacities. Teaching on conflict in the 1990s, and the technological bond of information techniques initially allowed the development of C2W, preceding the concept of information operations. In 1996 and 1998, the USA and NATO respectively defined

---

67 Revolution in Military Affairs.
68 [TOF 80] and [TOF 93].
69 [JP1 10], 30th December 2010.

their C2W[70] doctrine, which was the integrated use for operations in all military capacities, including coercion and actions in the information field.

Considering information in this way aims to deny the opponent command certain access to information, to influence, damage or destroy its capacities, at the same time protecting our capacities to command these types of attack. It uses functions dealing with the technical dimension (electronic warfare, computer warfare), in order to defend or attack computer systems, whether this means hardware, networks or computers, or even the information stored there. The human dimension uses influence functions (information safety, psychological operations or PSYOPS in NATO, MISO or Military Information Support Operations in the USA since June 2001, knowledge and exploitation of influence relays or Key Leader Engagement), coordinated by the information operations cell.

In order to act within the force's information environment, information operations are therefore the adaptation of a political influence strategy into a military strategy, in order to make it last longer, to adapt it to the land and to help keep coherence between action and messages. These information operations may be defined as the set of activities led by armed forces which are defined and coordinated on the highest level, and which aim to use or defend information, information systems, and the decision making processes, in permanent support of an influence strategy, and in the framework of operations, contributing to the achievement of the desired end-state, in full compliance with our values[71]. The "information operations" function is, of course, in support of an influence strategy.

By controlling the force's information environment, the operational function of information operations aims to give advice and to coordinate information actions in order to create the desired effects on will, understanding, and the capacity of the sources of information, whether they are real or potential, in line with traditional military actions. It aims to influence the adversary's decision making process, by looking to affect its information, its processes and its information-based systems. It must also guarantee the correct working order of the "friend's" decision making process. The similarity to command and control warfare is indeed real, but the field of action has broadened to the human factor.

The evolutions of these doctrines were integrated by the USA in 1998, and then by NATO and the European Union. After the USA[72], NATO renewed its doctrine in 2009 [OTA 09]. The noticeable thing today is the marked orientation towards the contact with populations, and the way of communicating with them, particularly in a counter-insurgency conflict. The soldier in contact must act and communicate

---

70 Command and Control Warfare.
71 [PIA 06], French Joint doctrine for information operations, 2006.
72 [JP3 06], US Joint doctrine for information operations, 2006.

according to what is called a strategic narrative, which is increasingly more apparent in order to convince different target audiences.

Information operations aim to guarantee freedom of action on a political-military level, and to have a positive influence either to make the action legitimate, or to discredit the adversary's action. The "battle of perception" takes on both an offensive and defensive, and strategic and tactical character.

2.3.3. *The need for moral force*

Clausewitz is still relevant here: "War is an act of violence to compel the enemy to do our will"[73]. However, to reach this outcome, the soldier must know *why* he is fighting. Just like the community he belongs to, he must be protected from activities of destabilization.

2.3.3.1. *Political action and armed forces*

The Western armed forces want to defend their political system, not start a war of aggression. Out of respect for the rules defined by the international community, a democracy is not aggressive, despite this perception which is deeply rooted in a number of non-Western States. This perception is subjected to war more than it instigates it; it sees it is a type of proof. This does not mean that it is not capable of taking it on and therefore leading a war, but it will take on this obligation reluctantly, letting the adversary reach what are considered to be acceptable limits before going into conflict. It must remain in a position to destroy the enemy's armed forces, even if this is no longer the main objective but simply a means to win. It must define victory and justify the withdrawal of military forces. It will make it possible to develop influence activities which will be all the more effective when our forces adhere to the objectives.

Reaching war objectives comprised of "victory" in some form or another depends on the political legitimacy and therefore the perception of the reached outcome by acting within the information environment. With the objective of keeping the meaning of military commitment in a bond with the action led and therefore to maintain its legitimacy [CER 08], it is a question of developing messages suitable to the action, with the (right) influence vectors, from a strategic level to the lowest tactical level. Referring to D. Galula in particular, it is vital for Western forces to be convinced of the cause they are defending, above all the societies who are reluctant to using force. This counter-cause must also respond to the operational objectives of the theater of operations in order to persuade of its justness on a local level.

---

73 [CLA 65], p. 40.

The war of counter-insurgency, which is currently the most restrictive context for the armed forces, must be based on a cause which removes all adherences and fights the enemy's ideology effectively.

In line with the objectives on a strategic level, this war must be defined by concrete and convincing action. In Afghanistan, there is a policy put into place by government forces which have formed a coalition on the land, conforming to the local political power made up as a triplet: forces targeting actions to destroy diehards, political actions including an economical dimension to the benefit of the populations, and actions of persuasion to make others understand, adhere or fight false ideas.

2.3.3.2. *Defining the counter-cause*

As a consequence, military operations are in permanent contact with the population because security does not allow for the deployment of civil workers, and the civilian tasks led by armed forces are becoming political actions, integrated into this conception of counter-cause. In fact, if we follow the words of D. Galula, the insurgent rebel justifies his action by a *good* cause that he must be deprived of. To his own ends, he questions the possible initial superiority of the ideology of insurgency, particularly through a change in attitude of the population at the heart of the conflict by "its vital need for security" which will finally support the counter-cause. The questions raised are therefore: "what is the opponent's need which offers the best protection, which is the most threatening, whose victory is the most likley?" Finally, coercion operations and the displayed determination remain essential: "the population will only join forces when it is convinced that loyalists have the willingness and the means to win", knowing that "when the lift of a man is a stake, propaganda is not enough to convince him"[74]. According to the counter-cause determined according to the chosen strategy, the governmental and allied armed forces will be the dominant vectors in the messages transmitted towards the right audience for the expected effect.

A war can only be explained in a political framework, understood on the lowest level. It must be defined and above all constructed so as to make it legitimate, in relation to its own soldiers: "the armed forces must incorporate the political dimension into their action in order to better guarantee decision autonomy which is necessary for the different levels of command"[75].

By using the least possible force, but without ignoring it within a coercive diplomacy, a civil-military force, either multinational or national, creates a trusting climate, which is sufficient to rebuild a state which has been totally or partially

---

74 [GAL 64] p. 117.
75 [PIA 10].

destroyed by war. The influence strategy is relevant here, particularly in order to confirm the legitimacy of the action taken.

When faced with an enemy who is determined and often hateful as a result of his indoctrination, the Western soldier's moral force is characterized by the "importance of the human factor over any other factor (technological, organizational (…) and the renewed need to strengthen the quality and effectiveness of armed forces by a shared ethical development"[76]. It must also understand the political dimension, i.e. understanding the goals pursued and the stakes at hand which justify risking our lives. As a consequence, the moral force of the military is directly linked to their strength, particularly their psychological strength which may ensure the quality of individual behavior in the face of difficulty, and guarantee the execution of orders which may be contested in a war led by civilian soldiers from a democracy. It is also a matter of being able to make a decision on the lowest level, according to strategic matters, because any local action may have a global effect today, especially for globalized information.

The fighter, and therefore man, is at the center of the action. He must understand the political meaning of his mission, both to shape his human environment but also to stay motivated.

2.3.3.3. *Image-emotion control, condition of the partial success of communication*

"Textual" information is drowned out by its rapid spreading. On the other hand, the image – through its emotional value and its diffusion over the Internet – is an important influence factor which must be controlled in order to prevent it from being exploited by those opposed to the intervention, at the same time respecting the deontological rules in force in Western democracies. Whether it is through propaganda or individual actions of "exteriorization", most often today the proliferation of images across the Internet and the understanding of their emotional effects represent a new challenge, particularly during conflict. The motivational effect must be controlled by the emotion held in the image which may affect military operations. In a view to look for weak signals, recent conflicts give us a certain number of exploitable facts and conclusions.

Conduction of the operations is possible till the end, so long as the images are not spread or questionable. During the recapturing of Sri Lanka in a Tamil terrorist movement in 2009, no dead bodies were seen in newspaper headlines or on television screens. All those people who could have weighed down the operation objectives by the image's emotional factors, above all on an international level, were prevented from physically entering the combat zone, except the ICRC which does not communicate on war. In Lebanon in 2007, the rare images which were spread

---

76 [CLA 65].

from the 21st June during an attack by the Lebanese army on the Nahr Al-Bared Palestinian refugee camp, in spite of 5 months of fighting, were distributed by the army's information service. No photographer, cameraman or journalist could access them[77].

During the Israeli operations from December 27th 2008 to January 19th 2009 in Gaza, the operation's center of gravity relied on the support of the Israeli population against the offensive, and not that of the international community. All the images or communications were carefully chosen in order to obtain and make this support last in an operation which was meant to be short-lived. It should be noted that no programs from Arab television channels were broadcast on Israeli channels during the conflict. The pursuit of controlling images was bound to control the emotional effect.

However, Israel created a platform on YouTube which hosted videos showing Israeli air attacks on Gaza, and the preparation of an operation, or even the journey of Israeli humanitarian aid headed towards Gaza residents. Videos showed the precision of the shots fired, and the willingness to avoid collateral damage. Some videos showed shots which were diverted at the last minute due to an uncertainty regarding the target. If the real impact is difficult to measure, it can be shown by the 2,119,492 hits on YouTube on January 27th 2009. In the end, it was a matter of "supply" for the images chosen. This action of controlling images is justified during a military operation due to the use made of them by sources of opposition which are not only the official enemy.

In addition to actions of propaganda, it is true that sources of opposition may use the image which is spread instantly and coordinate themselves to carry out their terrorist missions or combat. Thus the role of the media in this domain is under accusation, according to a report from the survey led by New Delhi on the Bombay attacks which resulted in 170 deaths in November 2008. The attackers took advantage of the approximately 100 cameras pointed at the theater of operations for 72 hours. One of the minds behind the attacks advised one of the attackers to throw grenades on the commandos via a satellite phone in Pakistan, whose arrival had just been filmed live outside the Taj Mahal City Hall[78].

In September 2008, a report in *Paris Match* containing both text and images in the September 4th-10th edition aroused indignation. The weekly magazine confirms showing members of the Taliban on August 18th who killed 10 French soldiers in Afghanistan. The rebels can be seen posing with their war takings, raised up as trophies, provoking strong reactions. On Christmas day 2009 (we cannot ignore this

---

77 *Le Monde*, September 10th 2007.
78 *Le Monde*, January 23rd 2009.

symbolic data for the Christian religion for more "effective" action), the Taliban[79] broadcasted a video showing an American soldier Bowe Bergdahl, the first Western soldier captured by rebels and detained for 6 months.

This war of images via the Internet is involved in today's conflicts. To respond to this, the ex-general secretary Jaap de Hoof Schaeffer declared on October 8th 2007, regarding NATO operations in progress: "Unfortunately, we in NATO are not doing nearly well enough at communicating in the new information environment. And we are paying a price for it, not least over Afghanistan". In October 2007, Denmark proposed launching www.natochannel.tv, a television project on the Internet. In the same vein, NATO's strategic communication videos were put up on YouTube in the same area as the Taliban clips.

In the same way, in 2008 Israel launched anti-propaganda actions against Hamas which besieged YouTube with its images. Therefore any search for Hamas gave videos stigmatizing its use of human scapegoats. Hamas retaliated by launching its own image sharing site[80], "PalTube", whose server is based in Moscow and which functions on the same principle as YouTube. The Islamist organization exposed massacres of the Hebrew state in Gaza and denounced a *Zionist holocaust*, combing strong images and provocative expressions. The videos celebrated the martyr of the Izz ad-Din al-Qassam Brigades, the Hamas affiliated army wing. The non-state controlled actors joined up with state-governed actors with this site set up by Russia.

2.3.3.4. *Vital protection of information in conflicts*

In the last ten years or so, information technologies have made it possible for everybody to express themselves or to communicate, including in a theater of operations. This means that the soldier (and his family) from a democracy is linked to communication society as much as any other citizen. However, through this access to information, today his security is put in danger through the communication of personal information, or information regarding his professional life. He must, then, be educated on the safety of information in all its forms. This obviously goes beyond the single dimension of keeping military secrets, as the various feedback from experiments on recent or current conflicts will bear witness to. This safety of information also contributes to operations of deception [CHA 07] and rehabilitates the return to deception in a certain way, going back to a time when everything seemed technologically transparent and accessible.

This concept of information safety (OPSEC in NATO) is aimed at internal military information as well as the information distributed in the information environment. Information safety could be defined as an operational function which

---

79 *Le Monde*, December 25th 2009.
80 *Le Monde*, January 12th 2009.

is written into the field of information and which helps to protect the freedom of the action of forces, by keeping the reliability of their decision making process. It tries to define and apply the active and passive, material and immaterial provisions which aim to deny any source of opposition from accessing or using essential information which contribute to the mission's success[81]. It is, then, a process which depends on the technical aspect of the information distribution and the soldier's education.

Once again, teachings from the field must enable us to identify its variety and complexity. Firstly, it is a technical matter. Over the 33 days of war in July 2006, Hezbollah used different innovative tactics, in terms of information protection. The group made itself invisible to American satellites in order to slip through surveillance and avoid air bombings. On the information systems, it concealed itself from digital codes as well as sophisticated electronic sites. It tricked Israel's most developed interception systems by using fiber optics for telephone communication. It tightened up the security on its networks. Hezbollah also succeeded in deciphering Israeli coded messages.

Secondly, information safety has a human aspect. Opponents of Western armed forces in their interventions have identified this vulnerability within an information society and personal externalization. In September 2007, 8 people who confessed to being Muslim, 6 of whom were Danish and living in Denmark, were arrested. These people had tried to intimidate families of Danish soldiers in Afghanistan. This event triggered a strong worry amongst the Danish. The families were identified by intercepting cell phone calls between soldiers in Afghanistan and their families. Email inboxes had also been hacked.

Another source of compromise on security is the use of social tools. They have they turned into a source of risk to the extent that in March 2008, Ottawa wanted to restrict the use of the Internet network for its forces in Afghanistan, where confidential information was revealed. The Ministry of Defense asked its men to stop publishing photos of them in uniform on Facebook, and not to specify their combat unit because these images were becoming a source of information on the operations. Canadian General Atkinson estimated that 80% of the information obtained by the Taliban came from the Internet. However, the warning has not been really effective especially as the soldiers' families creating Facebook profiles are not restricted in the same way[82] as the soldiers themselves.

---

81 Adaptation of the definition proposed in a doctrinal study carried out by the French War College, "Exploratory concept on information safety" (Concept exploratoire sur la sûreté de l'information), 2008, edited by Colonel Chauvancy. The expression "opsec" translated into French is not relevant and the term "information safety" will be preferred.
82 *Le Monde*, March 9th 2008.

2.3.3.5. *Preventative strategy and counter-influence actions*

A study on counter-influence activities could lead to an interesting area of research. In fact, it would make it possible to develop the concept of monitoring influence activities, in the domain of misinformation or propaganda. This also leads on to blocking the freedom of action for the sources of opposition in the influence strategy. This may consist of anticipating the different influence activities of the opponent by a counter-argument. This would also have the advantage of making it possible to apply the red team process[83], to test the solidity of the ideas being defended in a conflict, possibly to put forward changes in the action strategies to be applied. On an operative level, Colonel Lachéroy, chief PSYOPS and influence in Algeria, was already practicing this at the end of the 1950s during the briefing of the Force commander. Expressing himself after the brief, his aim was to re-frame the proposed courses of action within the information context.

In this view, we can use Israel's intervention in Gaza in 2009. The Israeli armed forces carefully studied the lessons learned on the reasons behind the failure of their intervention in Lebanon in 2006, in order to apply it to the Cast Lead operation in the Gaza strip. Aware that the Israeli and international populations were major stakes, the Israelis had chosen to "deny" them of certain information coming directly from the zone of action. In order to limit the risks of spreading information, the "need to know" basis was strictly applied within the joint staff. The official possible relays abroad were only informed afterwards and after an analysis of the decisions made and the actions carried out, despite strong pressure coming from the outside. On information safety, the analysis of the previous conflict had also demonstrated that several soldiers had been killed after their cell phone calls had been located. To avoid this risk and the spreading of sensitive information, all cell phones belonging to the deployed units were confiscated, and this was on the lowest of tactical echelons. This also led to operations of control for respecting these measures.

In terms of information warfare, the aim is to achieve the mission of convincing of the justification of the operation by explaining to its public opinion and international public opinion, the legitimacy of resorting to force by referring to law, taking into account the debate on the proportionality of military strikes and by showing a consideration for the populations concerned by the conflict. Thus during the operations in Gaza, the official Israeli communication relayed the major threat of rocket attacks against the Israeli civilian population. The Israeli media was abundant in alarmist information on the possibility of Israeli military action. In this same vein, the Israeli government had launched a diplomatic offensive to convince Western capitals that strong military response was the only solution. It organized "citizen press conferences" on Twitter, the first one taking place on December 30th 2008 with

---

83 A red team is a team responsible for acting as a source of opposition to test the modes of action considered, whether in terms of strategy or operations.

D. Saranga, diplomat at the Israeli consulate in New York. Israel summarizes its military operations into 140 characters, still on Twitter. These tools are accompanied by the use of civil societies such as "Acanchi", expert in State makeovers, having already operated in Northern Ireland and Lebanon.

On the theater of operations, information activities were engaged in order to limit deaths of civilians with two objectives: pre-warning populations and confirming the presence of Hamas leaders. Campaigns dropping leaflets from the air were carried out in order to call upon the population to denounce members of Hamas, who were accused of being those responsible for the strikes. The Israeli services led a telephone call campaign to civilians in the immediate vicinity of imminent strikes. According to *Le Point*, another French weekly, 100,000 calls were made during the campaign. The number of calls made and the effectiveness still remain difficult to assess, however.

Despite resorting to the Foreign Press Association in front of the Supreme Court, the Israelis also decided to deny the entire operation zone to all journalists, both Israeli and foreign. The images and videos selected were transmitted by the Israeli defense forces[84]. Of course, this choice left the field free to images and videos under Hamas control. However, as the only images available, they forced the international media to take precautionary measures before distributing the images, and finally to prevent them from getting involved in the conflict by restricting themselves to analyzes and *not* to exploiting the emotion of the images. The Western televised media, lacking images, tried to illustrate the information with possible misuse and therefore the risk of discrediting. The CSA[85] gave an "ultimatum" to France2[86] (the main public TV channel) following the broadcast of fake news images in a report on the Israeli-Palestine conflict in the Gaza strip in the afternoon news on January 5th 2009.

These examples clearly show the new possibility of an influence strategy via cyberwar, which is inseparable from traditional military operations, and also the confrontation of ideas through the images on the meaning to be given to the chosen action strategy. They also point out the need to educate soldiers and civilians on information safety.

---

84 During the war in 2006 in South Lebanon, the Israelis had chosen to put journalists in Israeli units. This choice proved counter-productive with the mediatization of Israeli losses.
85 The CSA, French High committee for television and radio council (official office for controlling and regulating the media with respect to the rules of a democracy) pointed out the terms of its recommendation on December 7th 2007 in relation to international conflicts and their potential repercussions in France, in particular in the example of editorial responsibility with regard to checking the truth behind information.
86 *Le Point*, January 13th 2009.

2.4. Conclusion

The war of meaning, cyberwar and democracies raises the question of the engagement of Western democracies faced with, indeed, armed threats, but also and above all ideological threats of those opposed to their values and their model of society, which is based on a certain perception of the individual and freedom, particularly in reference to Human rights. This point of reference determines the foundations of the ideological corpus.

Today Western democracies are permanently engaged in limited, distant and lengthy wars, not only in combats against rebels, but also within a framework of rebuilding a country which needs time and pacification. In other words, *the reconciliation to be reached by influence activities* such as can be seen in Bosnia and Kosovo. In spite of the progress made in human society, a step back perhaps or simply the reality of international relations, Western democracies have realized that neither negotiation nor the display of an often disregarded ceasefire are enough to resolve a conflict which is opposing personal willingness rather than interests.

New non-state controlled violent actors, state actors, and new ambitious powers to take a place in society appear and then demand the power be redistributed within the international community. The dimension that we dare to call the most *mediatized* is the digital threat and therefore cyberwar, due to the implications for dependent Western societies. The triggered cyberattacks contribute to developing a war of suspicion and thus instability, because it is indeed difficult to formally blame a cyberattack on a silent supporter. It is also a war of intimidation, and therefore it becomes psychological because it forces, in a certain perspective of survival, Western states which depend on computer networks and the Internet to involve important resources for cybernetic defense.

However, far from this technically oriented vision, the major stake in the war of meaning for Western democracies is to preserve their vision of the world and to develop a future strategy. It is not only limited to international conflicts which need to be resolved; it must identify the rank the West claims to hold in a generation, not only according to instruments of power that it will have developed but also depending on the influence that it seeks to have on its values. These values are the common framework of the nations which constitute it. In this way they give it an identity, a directional strategic line to establish new force or power relationships. Furthermore, this vision of the international society must be communicated, explained, and effective in an influence strategy. Indeed this cannot be common to all, but in fact where each State is involved depending on its own national characteristics.

However the West does not practice cyberwar as a war which should be conducted as such. On the other hand it develops a cyberdefense which is only expressed, however, in its technical dimension. It does not take into account the necessary influence strategy which aims to convince others of the validity of its choices. In fact, the problem here is with regard to its power to be maintained and thus its survival, even civilizational survival, in the development of its ideas, and its concept of international society.

This power can only be exerted and be credible if Western States are convinced of their future. The success of their military interventions is also subordinate to this conviction. We close our chapter with the words of Marshal Foch, "in knowing why and what you act with, you will know how to act"[87].

2.5. Bibliography

[AAR 08] AARON D., *In Their Own Words: Voices of Jihad,* Rand Corporation, USA, 2008.

[AES 08] ASSEMBLÉE EUROPÉENNE DE SÉCURITÉ ET DE DÉFENSE (Assemblée de l'Union de l'Europe occidentale), La guerre informatique, rapport de la commission de défense, document C/2022, November 5th 2008.

[ARO 62] ARON R., *Paix et guerre entre les nations*, Calmann Lévy, Paris, France, 1962.

[BEA 72] BEAUFRE G., *Stratégie pour demain*, Plon, Paris, France, 1972.

[BED 09] BEDAR S., BAUTZMANN A., *L'interface culturelle*, Centre d'Analyse et de Prévision des Risques Internationaux, Etude HCCEP pour le centre interarmées de concepts, de doctrines et d'expérimentations (CICDE), September 2009.

[BOC 08] BOCKSTETTE C., *Jihadist Terrorist Use of Strategic Communication Management Techniques*, George Marshall Center, December 2008.

[CER 08] CEREMS, *La légitimité des interventions militaires*, Les cahiers du CEREMS, March 2008.

[CHA 93] CHAUVANCY F., "Diplomatie coercitive et communication dans le maintien de la paix", *Le Casoar*, Paris, France, October 1993.

[CHA 98] CHAUVANCY F., L'information, arme stratégique des démocraties, PhD Thesis, Celsa, Paris, France, 1998.

[CHA 06] CHAUVANCY F., "Les principes de la guerre encore et toujours", *Défense nationale et sécurité collective*, March 2006.

[CHA 06a] CHAUVANCY F., "Conceptualiser l'ennemi", *Cahiers du CESAT* no. 6, October 2006.

---

87 [FOC 05], p. 38.

[CHA 07] CHAUVANCY F., *Les opérations de déception*, doctrinal study for the French War College, 2007.

[CHA 08] CHAUVANCY F., "La laïcité dans les armées: une contrainte, une nécessité, une liberté ou une force?", *Inflexions*, La Documentation Française, Paris, France, July 2008.

[CHA 09a] CHAUVANCY F., *Afghanistan: combattre l'idéologie islamiste*, Le Casoar, Paris, France, 2009.

[CHA 09b] CHAUVANCY F., "Livre Blanc et stratégie d'influence: une réflexion incomplète et pourtant nécessaire", *Défense nationale et sécurité collective*, February 2009.

[CHA 09c] CHAUVANCY F., "Démocratie et guerre des idées au XXIe siècle: la contre-insurrection, une nouvelle confrontation idéologique?", *Stratégies irrégulières*, edited by H. COUTAU-BÉGARIE, *Stratégiques*, April 2009.

[CLA 65] CLAUSEWITZ C., *De la guerre*, Editions 10/18, Paris, France, 1965.

[DEL 72] DELMAS C., *La guerre révolutionnaire*, Que sais-je, Paris, France, 1972.

[DOD 09] DOD, *Operational Culture for Afghanistan*, May 2009.

[ELK 07] ELKIER N.TH., *The Taliban's Information Warfare*, Royal Danish Defence College, December 2007.

[ELL 90] ELLUL J., "Propagandes", *Economica,* Paris, France, 1990.

[FIE 06] FIELD MANUEL 3.24, Doctrine terrestre de la contre-insurrection, CDEF, USA, 2006.

[FOC 05] FOCH F., *Des Principes de la guerre*, Berger-Levrault, Paris, France, 1905.

[GAL 64] GALULA D., *Contre-insurrection: théorie et pratique*, Economica, Paris, France, 1964.

[GOI 37] DE GOISLARD DE MONSABERT, *En relisant Bugeaud et Lyautey*, Charles Lavauzelle & Compagnie, Paris, France, 1937.

[GOU 08] GOUVERNEMENT FRANÇAIS, Le livre blanc sur la défense et la sécurité nationale, Odile Jacob, Paris, France, 2008.

[HUN 96] HUNTINGTON S., *Le choc des civilisations*, Odile Jacob, Paris, France, 1996.

[JP1 10] JP 1-02, DoD, December 30th 2010.

[JP3 06] JP 3-13, DoD, Joint Publication 3-13, Information operations, February 2006.

[KIM 09] KIM J., *Cultural Dimensions of Strategy and Policy*, www.StrategicStudiesInstitute.army.mil/, May 2009.

[KIN 06] KINNIBURGH J., DENNING D., *Blogs and Military Information Strategy,* Joint Special Operations University, June 2006.

[KRE 08] KREIS E., *Les puissances de l'ombre*, CNRS Editions, Paris, France, December 2008.

[LAB 96] LABOUERIE G., *Stratégie: réflexions et variations, Esprit de défense*, ADDIM, 1996.

[LB 08] Livre blanc sur la défense et la sécurité national, French Government, 2008.

[LIB 09] LIBICKI M., *Cyberdeterrence and Cyberwar*, Rand Corporation, USA, 2009.

[LID 51] LIDDELL HART B.H., *Le but de la guerre*, Forces aériennes françaises, October 1951.

[LID 54] LIDDELL HART B.H., *Strategy: the Indirect Approach*, Frederick A. Praeger Publishers, New York, USA, 1954.

[MAC 80] MACHIAVEL N., *Les discours sur la première décade de tite-live*, Berger-Levrault, 1980.

[MBD 09] British Ministry of Defence, The Significance of Culture for the Military, Joint Doctrine Note, February 2009.

[OTA 07] OTAN, MC422/3, *Politique militaire de l'OTAN en matière d'opérations d'information*, March 9th 2007.

[OTA 09] OTAN, AJP 3.10, Doctrine for Information Operations, November 2009.

[OTA 81] OTAN, AAP6, Glossaire, March 1st 1981.

[PIA 02] PIA 00.200, Doctrine interarmées d'emploi des forces, 2002.

[PIA 05] PIA 03-152, Concept interarmées des opérations d'information, 2005.

[PIA 06] PIA 03-252, CICDE, Doctrine interarmées des opérations d'information, 2006.

[PIA 07a] PIA 00-401, Glossaire interarmées, France, 2007.

[PIA 07b] PIA 3.252-1, CICDE, Doctrine interarmées de la communication opérationnelle, 2007.

[PIA 08] PIA-00.180, CICDE, Concept des opérations contre un adversaire irrégulier, 2008.

[PIA 10] PIA 00-100, CICDE, Concept d'emploi des forces (Joint Concept for Operations), 2010.

[POI 84] POIRIER L., *La crise des fondements*, Economica, Paris, France, 1994.

[RON 07] RONFELDT D., *Al-Qaeda and its Affiliates: A Global Tribe Waging Segmental Warfare*, Rand Corporation, USA, 2007.

[TCH 39] TCHAKHOTINE S., *Le viol des foules par la propagande politique,* Gallimard, Paris, France, 1939.

[TOF 80] TOFFLER A. AND H., *La Troisième vague*, Mediatons, 1980.

[TOF 93] TOFFLER A. AND H., *War and Antiwar*, Little, Brown and Co., Boston, USA, 1993.

[TRI 61] TRINQUIER R., *La guerre moderne*, La Table Ronde, Paris, France, 1961.

[TRI 68] TRINQUIER R., *Guerre, subversion, révolution*, Robert Laffont, Paris, France, 1968.

[WAL 07] WALLER M., *Fighting the War of Ideas like a Real War*, The Institute of world politics press, Washington, USA, April 4th 2007.

Chapter 3

Intelligence, the First Defense?
Information Warfare and
Strategic Surprise

One of the most spectacular aspects of mobilization in the military domain of information warfare over these last 20 years has affected the evolution of either civilian or military intelligence services. Often seen as a "first line of defense", these services may be considered as the guarantors of the impossibility of a State being the victim of a strategic surprise.

Increasingly more present in literature (yet nonetheless still hardly defined), *strategic surprise* amounts to a diplomatic or military surprise which could radically bring into question the security of the political organization subjected to it[1].

This assertion of intelligence able to guarantee that a strategic surprise will *not* take place, albeit through *intelligence as the first defense* which is often seen in literature on the revolution in military affairs (RMA), may come across in varied forms of political and doctrinal crystallization.

The most spectacular form is undoubtedly the link between the new strategic function of "intelligence/anticipation" and strategic surprise from the last French White Paper on Defense and National Security [GOU 08].

Chapter written by Joseph HENROTIN.
1 We will return to this later in the chapter, on its types and characteristics.

As the fundamental material for intelligence services, information is becoming one of the supporting pillars of the French security system[2]. However, the link between information and intelligence services, and the prevention of a surprise attack deserves to be questioned. This is not only from the standpoint of strategic studies, but also *intelligence studies* which is prolific in the USA and the UK, having gained the status of a discipline of social sciences in its own right, with its own academic journals and having generated a relatively important source of theoretical literature.

This chapter will be the basis for a solid apprehension of a set of problems which should enable us to consolidate a theory of information warfare which is still affected by real, theoretical weak points [HEN 08], [VEN 08]. These shortcomings stem from an almost anarchic proliferation of studies dating back to the 1990s, at a time when assets such as the boundlessness of information technology was still not properly understood, and yet at the same time was greatly appreciated in armies (particularly American forces), centers for research and also on a political scale[3].

At this time, a biased perception of the contribution of state-of-the-art technology in military operations (after the Desert Storm operation in particular) opened up a debate on the RMA where a certain number of technologies were bound to trigger a radical change in the conduct of conflict, enabling the person controlling the conflict to systematically win the operations he engaged in. The RMA mobilized many technological categories: first and foremost came precision strike systems (lasers, GPS, cruise missile, etc.), C4ISR (*command, control, computers, communications, intelligence, surveillance, reconnaissance*) systems[4], and more broadly, information warfare techniques and tactics – technologies inherent to stealth. Some authors only saw an initial technological "wave" in this, which was followed by an "RMA after next", led by biotechnologies, nanotechnologies and even cognitive sciences[5].

Affected by technological determinism, the historical context where the theme of information warfare emerges from is also affected by an over-simplification of the relationships between belligerents, with the RMA having to change the nature of the war by denying the adversary any possibility of hitting its target. Any threat, and on whatever level it might be (and therefore, on a strategic level) had to be systematically and immediately detected before being eliminated[6]. As a theoretical construction which hardly takes strategic models into account other than those based

2 Moreover, information is very widely considered as such elsewhere in the world, without such a degree of doctrinalization of its role necessarily being reached.
3 A classic problem in the sociolgy of innovation.
4 Particularly allowing for target acquisition and also force command and control.
5 See [BRA 93].
6 A type of situation summarized by the acronym "O3" [CRO 97].

on regular strategies[7], for a long time now the RMA has found itself being put back into question, particularly due to experiences in Iraq and Afghanistan, but also due to its own theoretical limits and the context in which it sees the light of day [WAS 06].

In this framework the chapter aims to demonstrate the limits of the link between information warfare, intelligence and two large types of military strategic surprise. The first deals with a surprise attack through conventional methods (armies) or further still by terrorist attacks (in the example of 9/11). The second goes back to the possibility of a massive surprise attack on a country's computerized infrastructures, bringing back the question of a *digital Pearl Harbor*[8]. The limits of the link between intelligence, information warfare and strategic surprise will be analyzed in turn from three different angles:

– the existing relationship between war (understood as the dialectic of opposed wills using force to resolve their differences[9]) and the different meanings of information warfare;

– the relationship between intelligence and strategic surprise (in its conventional or terrorist forms) by focusing in particular on the entire intelligence cycle which not only includes its collection, but also its processing and analysis, its exploitation and its distribution;

– the relationship between strategic surprise (this time, as a sort of *electronic Pearl Harbor*), intelligence and information warfare. Here too, it is a question of taking the entire intelligence cycle into account.

3.1. Information warfare, information and war

Before going into the heart of the subject, we must still note beforehand that the different interpretations of what constitutes information warfare are different depending on the authors. These interpretations may, for example according to Libicki [LIB 95], [LIB 09] incorporate attack and defense:

– networks and information infrastructures (*cyberwarfare, strategic information warfare*);

---

7 Through opposition to irregular strategies (terrorism, guerilla, insurgency) or even alternative forms of regular strategies. One of the main critical schools of the RMA will highlight the difficulty of defeating asymmetrical adversaries [HEN 08].
8 We may contemplate other kinds of military strategic surprise, particularly those using nuclear, biological, chemical or radiological weapons.
9 A definition that we will borrow from André Beaufre [BEA 85], pg. 16.

– mediatized and psychological operations;

– intelligence in the broadest sense (including tactical reconnaissance); the different reprisals of electronic war[10];

– the strategies and tactics aiming to eliminate opponent leaders, from the tactical front to the political front (or even their developments in nuclear or air strategies);

– paralysis or destruction of their command and control infrastructures or even deception[11] strategies and tactics, or C3D2 (*camouflage, cover, concealment, deception, denial*).

If we are not careful, defining the scope of information warfare would be similar to that for operational strategies, which could scramble the essential categories of the art of warfare[12]. Therefore information warfare and combat (and not *war* in the Beaufrian or Clauswitzian meanings) might have similar definitions but would lose all their operative range.

Information plays a vital role in the art of warfare: just like any technically-oriented system, armies and combats are fed and motivated by information. Thus, anything which may affect, both near or far, C41SR modalities is highly considered as being crucially important in practically all the world's armies, whatever their doctrines may be [VAN 87]. To a certain extent this is also the case for sub-state governed group fighters, such as Hezbollah or al-Qaeda whose strategic acts ("manual" and other information given to their fighters) show just how much attention is paid to the subject.

We must, then, "see and control", so as to be able to optimize military action, be it tactical, operative or strategic. "Knowledge" is an integral element to the art of warfare. When intelligence is not available (or not available enough), one of the commonly accepted trends of the Clauswitzian "genius" is to know where the adversary is, by a sequence of successive deductions, at the same time correctly maneuvering so as to defeat him.

---

10 Anti-radar operations (active or passive), electronic intelligence, scrambling, intrusion, etc.
11 Military deception, a loanword from the Russian *maskriovka* (literally meaning concealment/camouflage) goes back to connotations of systematization, which is an element of tactics but also part of the search for cognitive confusion in the enemy.
12 In strategic studies, traditionally we distinguish three spheres of action from military strategy: strategy of means, declarative strategy and operational strategy [COU 99].

From this perspective, we may say that the vast majority of technological artifacts produced in the wake of the RMA and then *Transformation*[13] boils down directly to "knowledge", to its prohibition or its transformation. Various sensors (air, terrestrial, naval), targeting pods, experimental stealth technology, modernizing infantries and reticulation, are examples of representations of a willingness to "know"[14]. In the same view, the concept of "network-centric warfare" (NCW), created in the wake of the RMA, is first and foremost a concept of information sharing [DEN 06]. Moreover, we must specify the range of an RMA (and its resultant transformation) which has been widely interpreted as an "information revolution"[15]. If information warfare follows in its footsteps, then it above all constitutes a new reprisal of Western operative art, which tends to reproduce old trends of the American art of warfare. Therefore, it would not count as a revolution but a radicalization of pre-existing trends [GER 00]. But it also tends, in the debauchery of the capabilities it promotes, to make the important distinction between information, intelligence and knowledge be forgotten. We notice this jamming behind the information quadrisection that Arquilla and Ronfeldt were operating, i.e. information which is thus equivalent to intelligence, knowledge, and wisdom [ARQ 96].

Whatever the approach used may be, and behind all the academic quarrels, we must understand that accumulating information does not mean very much for the analyst, or the decision maker. First of all the information has to be checked, correlated and confirmed in order to be considered as *intelligence*. It also has to be analyzed, contextualized and distributed. It will only become knowledge when it is discussed outside the circles of intelligence services and thus used by political decision makers. Faced with the probability of having to deal with rumors or information which has been manipulated by an opponent party, the distinctive feature of an intelligence service and its main quality are precisely to validate or invalidate received information and to put it in their own domains (political, military, economic). Information alone is not enough: only the analyst will give it

---

13 The concept of transformation was used for the first time by Donald Rumsfeld when he took the post of American Secretary of Defence in 2001. Transformation seeks to apply a certain number of lessons (via C4ISR and their interoperability or even concepts such as NCW in particular) to American armed forces (then NATO forces, from 2002 with the creation of the Allied Command Transformation in the Prague summit) which were quickly applied from the RMA.

14 In the American case, since 1992 and the initial works on the occurrence of an RMA, only two new types of combat platforms went into US armed forces services. The first was the F-22 Raptor, planned in the 1980s. The second was the arming of Predator drones, therefore systems intially designed as intelligence platforms.

15 A wrongly worded description, as it is also a revolution of the generalization and diversification of precision strike capabilities.

added value. The perception of intelligence services with regard to the "information revolution" has evolved considerably in this perspective.

Firstly, intelligence services have upheld a certain mistrust for new sources of information appearing by means of the Internet, but also and above all as a new source of vulnerability[16]. Therefore in several European intelligence services, analysts' computers were not linked to the Internet in the development of wordy literature on information warfare and hacking, which could have compromised the information at their disposal. Secondly the Internet has also been considered as a particularly rich and open source of information, and therefore more and more newspapers and research institutions are putting their editorial content online, notably post 2000. As such, intelligence services were considerably expanding the already outdated technique of *open source intelligence* (OSINT), offering intelligence on the political, economical or military aspects of a nation, and based on freely accessible content produced by the "7 tribes"[17]. Thus in 1949, Kent Sherman estimated that 80% of the information from US intelligence services came from open sources [SHE 49]. At the same time, certain services, depending on their legal attribution and the scope of the missions entrusted to them, launched penetration operations into the enemy's electronic networks in order to take information.

From this point of view, the dissemination of computer networks and the Internet may be considered as the cornerstone of the revolution in intelligence affairs (RIA) concept in two respects:

– on the one hand, through the organizational cultures and means of networking intelligence services whose respective cultures have led to a certain mistrust. The main aspect of the RIA would, then, be an organizational order for Barger, and would involve coordinating intelligence services depending on their specific features, but also developing a common doctrine [BAR 05]. Computers and networks are considered as the infrastructure which makes this evolution possible, particularly in a post 9/11 backdrop, having seen the blow by blow failure to prevent attacks [GOO 05] and the failure on the question of Iraq's weapons of mass destruction[18];

– on the other hand, with the generalization of the Internet and adapted software, it is composed of a "web 2.0", an application where users can collaborate and share information quickly in a few minutes or a few hours[19]. According to Samuel Wilson,

---

16 The author's various interviews with operation chiefs in security services led from 1999 to 2009.

17 Either governments, armies, security services, the business world, the civil world (citizens, unions, religious groups), the media and NGOs and the academic world [STE 07].

18 In fact considered as existing but have turned out to be practically non-operational, only representing a very limited danger.

19 In this last case in particular, when Web 2.0 is used by fighter groups.

ex-deputy director for the American Defense Agency, the status of OSINT in intelligence increased to providing 90% of the information for intelligence services in 2000. OSINT is considered to be a "vital component of NATO's future vision" [STE 07]. The RIA stems from exploiting new characteristics of information flow, here also via networks [WHE 08]. In such a context, the rate of acquiring information in an age where threats are increasing by the minute, this would become a crucial factor for national security.

The truth still remains, however, that it is a particularly complex task to make such visions go from theory to practice. Culturally, intelligence services are hesitant towards organizational evolutions, particularly those affecting the balance in their relations, more on an international scale (where multi-nationalization is one of the obligatory factors of new forms of the art of warfare) than within the intelligence community of a given country. Speaking from a technical point of view, accessing more sources of information in an OSINT does not require a through reconfiguration of the intelligence cycle [STE 07]. From this point of view, Web 2.0 has an impact on the information collection process, but causes a problem for processing and analyzing it. Therefore, the value and quality of this information is a far cry from being systematically attested. If a researcher's work appearing in a peer-review journal is probably more likely to be true than an anonymous contribution on Wikipedia, then we cannot help but notice, just like any intellectual work, that they are vulnerable to manipulation by their author, whether this is knowingly or not. By extension, the work of any analysis is also vulnerable to being, in a certain way, distorted. However the enormous volume of information washed up by the Internet operates a growing geometric, whereas the resources in terms of intelligence service analyzes are limited. If the systems for processing information and calculation have seen a wide increase in their capabilities, then this is not necessarily the case for human resources which were allocated to them, particularly in terms of analysis.

Consequently, intelligence services are confronted with the need to define strategies which will make it possible to avoid seeing themselves drown under the mass influx of information, and to remain focused on the prioritized questions which are unique to them. However the sheer volume of information available on the Internet must be put into perspective, in two aspects.

On the one hand, in 1999, this information was evaluated at 6 Terabytes, i.e. the equivalent of a library containing 450,000 books [LAW 99]. And so, NATO's *Open Source Intelligent Reader* indicates that if the information can be found quicker on the Internet, then it only represents a *fraction* of the information available in open sources [NAT 02 and STU 93]. As a prudent document, it also indicates that the growth of the Internet is exponential, and so the volume of available information is also just as exponential. In fact, the volume of available information "on the surface" (accessible via search engines) does not seem to have greatly increased. On the other hand, the *deep web* would be much more important and would see a bigger growth following Moore's law [GUO 09].

Moreover, the information available on the internet, whether it is published as news articles, academic publications or even blogs, only makes up a small portion of open sources which are more widely available, which includes publications on paper or conference proceedings.

On the other hand, the problem of the volatility of this information is raised. Some estimates indicate that the average lifetime of a page on the Internet is 75 days, whereas entire sites disappear from one day to the next [KAH 97]. If the question of the cost of storing the information makes it possible to moderate this phenomenon (over these last 10 years, it has not stopped getting smaller), a certain amount of information, particularly in the media, is frequently being renewed. As such, information in open sources must be processed quickly, requiring in return sufficient human resources.

Finally, the effective value of the resources offered to intelligence services by information warfare from day to day may be difficult to evaluate, whether it is from OSINT or even from penetrating opponent networks. Modern literature, faced with the discretionary measures around questions of intelligence, undoubtedly has not gained enough retrospect to show the decisive role that such or such information gathered by these means could have on an operation. For all this, the importance attached to OSINT compels many analysts to say that it plays a vital role in terms of the intelligence's architecture, not only allowing it to provide contextual information or to monitor the other side, but also to play a "tripwire" role. When correlated, this information would then make it possible to, taking Van Creveld's expression of the "directed telescope" [VAN 87], towards the technical and human means towards a given problem, thus making it possible to purge all the intelligence that it harbors. As appealing as this structure may seem on the theoretical front, however we cannot help but see the need for a strengthened capacity to analyze and interpret. In this respect, the OSINT on the Internet confirms the following axiom once more, one where the higher the technological intensity of the strategic action is, then the more the human factors must be evolved [HEN 08].

3.2. Intelligence and strategic surprise

This question of the link between human and technological factors and intelligence is also at the heart of the theme which is prominent in strategic studies: *strategic surprise*. A concept which is little defined and goes back to a somewhat instinctive apprehension, in truth the notion covers very different connotations. If it implies an event which could put the State's security in danger [CHE 08], then we cannot help but notice that it may take extremely different paths to reach this point: is it economical? Is it military? Is it computerized and does it aim to destroy the enemy's networks? Does it affect the energy sector? Or even the population? For Tertrais and Debouzy, it has plenty of aspects and it has become one of the permanent factors in international relations [TER 08]. As a notion which brings together perceptions and connotations around this concept, a major strategic effect occurs when the party suffering the attack has failed to predict it, or is the result of insufficient anticipation [BRU 08].

What is understood to be "strategic" is little defined in existing literature, but the territorial integrity of the targeted state *is* directly put into question. This may mean its capacity to ensure the security of the majority of its citizens, or still, the serviceability of its vital infrastructures. On the highest level, strategic surprise puts national security, or even the State's very legitimacy, into question, (forcing a decision to go to war).

3.2.1. *Strategic surprise*

However, after this positive portrayal, strategic surprise may also be characterized negatively. Strategic surprise could, then, be distinguished from operative, tactical[20] or technological surprises, and more specifically military surprises, and those inherent to the hazards of the battlefield which may naturally be considered as a characteristic of warfare [GRA 05].

In this context, the examples of strategic surprise throughout recent history are limited to the Barbarossa operation against the USSR (1941), the attack on Pearl Harbor (1941), the Korean War (1953), the Kippur War (1973) or even the 9/11 attacks in 2001. In a similar idea, the attack on Hiroshima, for example, may be understood as a technological surprise, at the very most. Still in the same schema, the 1940 German offensive on France, Belgium, Luxembourg and the Netherlands is an operative surprise. From September 1939, high magnitude operations were expected and war was declared. The only unknown factor lies in the form taken by these operations, and the place where these operations happen.

But this concept is naturally ambivalent. For example, C. Brustlein considers the surprise, for the USA, stemming from the launch of the USSR's first *Sputnik* in 1957 as being strategic [BRU 08]. However in practice, it quite rightly indicates that a strategic surprise is the result of hostile intentions. But between the launch of *Sputnik* and the start up of the first strategic Soviet nuclear charged, ballistic missiles

---

20 Tactical surprise intervenes on the battlefield; where operative surprise intervenes on the scale of a theater of operations.

capable of striking the USA, a certain time had passed. In this example, if the *Sputnik* was effectively a technological surprise, then it had above all warning value with regard to the course that Moscow could have taken by means of the vectors of its nuclear arsenal.

Even if operative, tactical or technological surprises can have strategic consequences (let us think back to the German's attack in 1940), then there was nothing strategic about the surprise in 1940. In truth, there were only a few strategic surprises in the 20th Century and more generally, the phenomenon is actually rare in terms of history. In the 19th Century, the battle of Sadowa could come under this category, along with the Mongolian invasions further on in history. The reasons behind this rarity can be quickly grasped: implementing a strategic surprise seems eminently difficult. For the attacker, his plans and the safety of his devices must be maintained, and he must act promptly.

At the same time, most strategic surprises also require that the means be concentrated, implying not only the provision of such means (generally in large quantities) but also important organizational and conceptual abilities, and therefore the concentration followed by the implementation of forces must be achieved in both time and space. These forces must also be exploited, militarily or politically, in order to be able to come entirely into operation. They do not exist on their own, as though they were disconnected from the international environment. Above all they involve a violent break in the given international order so as to try to produce an order which is more preferable to those implementing it: no one goes to war to lose it, or at the very least, not to reach the success hoped for. There are several pre-conditions needed for success.

Another one of its characteristics can be added to its rarity, which relates to the volatility of its strategic effects. As John Keegan shows, in the stead of military history, no strategic surprise has ultimately led to the defeat of the State suffering it [KEE 03]. Its value as a "decisive strike", alone capable of bringing down an enemy (by gaining clear and definitive victory) is low due to the magnitude of what it must achieve. If a decisive strategic surprise must not be excluded from a strictly theoretical point of view, then it does involve considering such a variety of factors so that its probability of materializing remains low.

To take the Soviet example from 1941, the Germans were forced to penetrate the Soviet territory, and managed to take Moscow, neutralize the Soviet political leadership at the beginning of the operation, and without a doubt, eliminate the huge capabilities in terms of defense industries before they could be transferred to the

East[21]. In modern contexts, the question of our dependence on computers and networks brings the problems of decisive strategic strike up to date: it would be possible to strike everything at the same time. We will come back to this problem further on, however we must point out that, always in theory, organizations in hierarchies are more susceptible to this type of strike than reticulated organizations [ARQ 96].

Yet, not only do computers *per se* induce reticulation, moreover the physical domains (military units, political and decision making staff, industrial capacities) are clearly defined from computer systems[22].

Furthermore, strategic surprise has fundamentally transitory effects, which are wiped out by adapting the plan belonging to the targeted State. If the surprise can suspend the fight between the opponents by radically reworking the very structure of the confrontation, as James Wirtz points out, then there never seems to be a total paralysis as the complexity of the effect to be reached is too important[23].

In terms of the combat's morphology, it generally represents the sign of a long and expensive commitment, as much in costs of human lives as it is financial, and it tends to be more strategically expensive for the instigator than for the victim.

This was the case for Japan after Pearl Harbor or for Germany after the invasion of the USSR. The Korean War led to the re-establishment of a *status quo ante*, and the 9/11 attacks, if they did *not* lead to defeating al-Qaeda, nonetheless brought the

---

21 From this point of view, we may consider that on top of a lack of means, the Germans ran up against a defective conceptualization of the action and its implications.

22 At least for the time being. The increased dependence on networks induces new forms of reticulating ergonomy, by interpenetrating humans and machines. There are also works focused on exoskeletons in the domain of infantry combat or more generally, on the omipresence of computer systems in a country like Estonia. Always theoretical, certain conceptions developed in the current post-humanist framework, forming a hybrid between man and machine, by interconnecting brains and computers, could way to such a capacity. For now, the perspective goes backs to possibilities in the long term, mainly affecting science fiction [GRA 97], [SUS 05].

23 In many aspects, the idea of a definitive suspension of the dual by surprise goes back to a wrongful interpretation of John Boyd's works on air combat and the OODA loop (observe, orient, decide, act), when he said that the operational ability of a given system was a decisive factor in its capacity to permanently surprise an adversary, and yet which is incapable of continually adapting itself. What is true on a technico-tactical level (an air combat takes place over a few minutes at most) is not true, however, on the strategic level. Not only is the magnitude of the desired effect more important, but the strategic level does not only represent the increased and homothetic projection of the tactical level, and therefore the former fulfills real constraints [COU 99].

attention of the intelligence services to the risks of Jihadist attacks, thus rearranging their devices and enabling them to anticipate a new strike[24].

In the end, the probability of *actually* suffering this type of attack, if it still exists, has decreased since 2001, whereas the number of attempts tends to increase.

3.2.2. *Perception of surprise*

These characterizations nonetheless leave several questions hanging which may relativize the very concept of strategic surprise.

Firstly, this concerns the perception of what a surprise represents by different State-controlled activists which might come to suffer it. "Surprise" may first of all be considered as a perception which may vary between political decision makers, intelligence specialists and average citizens[25]. In the attacks of 9/11, the US political, military and civil worlds were obviously surprised when faced with the magnitude of the attacks, but also with the form taken by the attacks. But the possibility of business planes being turned around to become, in fact, cruise missiles had been mentioned in US intelligence circles from the end of the 1990s, particularly by Bruce Hoffmann at the RAND Corporation.

In the current context, how should we consider the possibility of Iran being equipped with an effective military nuclear capacity? In the absolute, it could come as a technological surprise (if, for example, Tehran very quickly acquired this capacity), but would it represent a strategic surprise in the military sense, or even the diplomatic sense, in light of the thousands of publications that this question has generated since the beginning of the 1990s, without even counting the negotiations which are frequently portrayed in the media? In this, without a doubt, can be seen one of the flaws in the concept of strategic surprise, particularly such as it is referenced in the French White Paper.

In the same view, a high magnitude hypothetical military conflict, which also slots into the category of strategic surprise in the French meaning, is not lacking in raising problems from a conceptual point of view. The armies' equipment processes in major materials (combat buildings, planes, tanks and armored tanks) are currently taking place over a period of years, and preparing the forces themselves is a both

---

24 However, let us note that if the Jihadist ideology is not defeated, then al-Qaeda as an organization, has been largely reduced. It no longer possesses the same material, human means or infrastructures that it had before September 2001, whilst at the same time however keeping a certain capacity to motivate others, particularly via the Internet.

25 On this set of problems regarding the differences of perception between the categories of public opinion and the political level, see [STE 07] and [HEN 10] in particular.

complex and visible process for the observer interested in it[26]. On a more frequent basis, these preparations are processed by open sources which are or are not specialized in questions of defense. In return this raises the questions on the nature of, in terms of doctrine (and not in terms of theoretical strategy) a strategic surprise. All too often it is interpreted as a wildcard in a pallet of strategic scenarios, a sort of guarantee of abiding by reason, which demonstrates that the unforeseeable has also been taken into account. And so, strategic surprise becomes the equivalent of an *et cetera*, complementing the detailed list of the possible strategies. If the concept has its own characteristics, then strategic surprise, whether military or diplomatic, tends to be cliché.

There is also a second series of questions to be asked, this time inherent to the use and perception of intelligence (or information) by the different parties which might have to confront a strategic surprise.

3.2.3. Perception of the possibility of surprise

There is often a difference of understanding between the different parties who will have to process or exploit intelligence, insofar as several writers under the heading of "intelligence studies" are not lacking in underlining that the problem of surprise does not so much lie in the fact of possessing intelligence and making it possible to cope with it, but in the perception of an emergency by political and military decision makers.

In the Yom Kippur War (1973), for instance, the Israeli intelligence services, just like the American services, had warned the political leader of the Hebrew State that Egypt and Syria were preparing for a joint attack. Too much trust in the capabilities of Israeli forces to retort and the perception, on the political front, that Egypt would not launch into such an adventure both meant that the order to put all forces on alert was not given [RAZ 99].

Persuaded of the solidity of the German-Soviet pact, in 1941 Stalin ignored intelligence sent in by his own services. In spite of accurate information coming from Richard Sorge in particular (friend to the German ambassador of Japan regarding the USSR's preparation to invade) or Germans who were "returned" by

---

26 We will add here that these processes of rising to power are getting longer and longer due to the design time and delivery of equipment, but also due to organizational and conceptual rearrangements imposed by their integration into military institutions.

the Soviet services, Stalin clearly believed in the rumors sent to him by Hitler in their secret correspondence[27].

Still in 1941, the tense diplomatic situation between Japan and the USA left a wide space for envisaging the probability of a war, with some doubts remaining as to the whereabouts of its launching point. In spite of the fact that Japanese codes had been broken, and that the intelligence services had access to communications in Tokyo, analysts believed an attack on Pearl Harbor to be improbable (considering it too far from Japan). They imagined it to be more towards the Philippines, i.e. closer to the Japanese bases. Numerous warnings and alerts from US forces in the zone were given in vain, which led to fatigue and the alerts given by intelligence services to be discredited. However, going by the hypothesis that the Japanese were looking to operate their attack by sending in land forces, the American analysts supplanted the possibility of a surprise attack which would have been limited to reducing the US Navy's capabilities, just like at Pearl Harbor.

Furthermore, when devices are detected on the base's radars, the officer will interpret the echoes as an American bomber plane returning, and will not push his questions any further, not triggering the alarm. Yet, demonstrating that possessing information is not everything, American teams had broken Japanese codes and were then in a position to get first hand direct access to decrypted data [WHO 62].

Moreover, producing intelligence is proving to be particularly difficult, and more often that not, with a vast amount of information not being available, the analyzes finally produced are partial and of little use. In 2001, the FBI and the CIA investigated the possibility of major attacks on American soil. But the lack of collaboration between the two institutions means that they could not share their information or provide the political and military worlds with information any more accurate than that preparations for attacks were being made [HEI 04]. However, the question of knowing whether it is relevant to only have one single opinion faced with the possibility of a strategic surprise is raised. Therefore a number of States have several services at their disposal, and so they are in a position to produce different warnings. In some meanings, this multitude of advice sent to the political world would also constitute as a political guarantee. But these different opinions also put political staff in a delicate position. In fact, it is then up to the politician to mitigate the different interpretations (and to take the necessary precautionary measures), or even to decide in favor of one hypothesis over another. But the decreased aptitude for controlling strategic questions from the political world is being considered as a recurring problem in Europe, and also in the USA.

---

27 Sorge was then arrested by the Japanese. They wanted to exchange him for a Japanese officer captured by the Soviets but Stalin refused, saying that he had never laid eyes on Sorge [MUR 05].

In *intelligence studies*, one of the major problems concerned is related to the distinction between "signals" (representing utility in terms of intelligence), and "noise" (which represents no utility). However, it may hide signals and may scramble or *deceive* perceptions. Roberta Wohlstetter, analyzing the deep-rooted causes for the lack of reactivity on the USA's part in the face of a possible Japanese attack, indicates that signals which are useful for intelligence services were drowned out in the "noise" of the traffic of ordinary communication.

This being the case, she underlines a difficulty which is only worsened by the age of information: the increase in available sources may saturate the capabilities of the analyses, generating a mass of noises, such as additional, potential signals. The skill of the intelligence services is to be able to extract signals from noise; a rule which still applies in modern contexts. However, the preparation of a surprise (be it strategic, operative, tactical or technological) by a given party frequently calls for deception and dissimulation, so as by remaining hidden from the adversary for as long as possible, the surprise will increase its effects tenfold once it is materialized[28]. Thus deception brings about an increase in the amount of "noise", to the detriment of the signals.

In this vein, the problem goes far beyond accessing information. The allies had means to intercept and decipher German communications (Ultra messages) [HIN 93][29]. All the same, they were able to break through Japanese codes before Pearl Harbor. We note, then, that just having the capacity to access the adversary's secure information is not, in itself, a guarantee of lifting the "fog of war". This depends on more complex factors. However, debates on the Revolution in Military Affairs (RMA) in the 1990s clearly established a semantic shortcut (which tends to continue on[30]) between accessing the information and extracting useful intelligence.

Consequently, the problem of intelligence is raised in terms of capacity – acquiring information collection systems (human or technical) – so that the aspects inherent to analysis and exploitation were almost systematically ousted or, at least,

---

28 Suspecting (rightly so) the allies of being able to listen in, the Germans did not use their systems in the preparation for the attack on Ardennes in the winter of 1944, totally surprsing the US forces. The allied forces had just developed excessive dependence with regard to sources [AMB 89], [DEL 04].

29 "Ultra" was the codename for messages coming from German Enigma decoding machines, whose code had been broken by the Polish before the hositilities started. There were several applications of Ultra, from the knowledge of submarine mission orders to the knowledge the Germans had of ally preparations for leaving Normandy. Ultra was so secret that it was only revealed at the beginning of the 1970s [HIN 93].

30 At least, in the debates of strategists not devoted to studying intelligence, but the morphology of modern day operations [STE 09].

were undervalued[31]. Some authors, then, consider the RMA as a school of knowledge which is dominant in battle zones [JOH 96], ready to "lift the fog of war" [OWE 00].

3.3. Strategic surprise and information warfare

In each of the examples of strategic surprise given here, the surprise lies in an armed attack, an invasion or even a diplomatic surprise. But over the last few years, the mobilization of the concept has also given power to the domain of information warfare. Consequently, the idea of a *digital Pearl Harbor* became a central theme in American strategic debates in the second half of the 1990s and has been recurring since [WAL 95], [SCH 96]. Strategic surprise may come as a massive attack on networks, aiming to paralyze them, or even break down their software, eventually creating damage in the "real world". The concept of strategic surprise is systematically perceived as being catastrophic or even, in the context of a cyberwar, apocalyptic[32].

An electronic strategic surprise could also replace more classic, diplomatic forms, or those based on military action in the most extreme of interpretations. In this example, evolutions in cyberwar allow the attacker to lead a frontal and massive strategy of engagement. This would authorize a decisive strike, letting the attacker reach a new speed in strategic-political results which are disproportionate in relation to the agreed strategic investment. This would be simpler to plan and lead to a conventional strike. Moreover this type of strike could be led away from security measures and it would affect all sectors within a country. This would especially be the case when (the USA, at a time when the Internet is massively available and there is a high awareness of its possibilities), for the economic evolutions willingly rely on computerization and online business. In such conditions, can the characteristics of a "classic" strategic surprise as we have discussed here still be considered as *in use*? First of all, here the analyst must note that this *Strategic Information Warfare* (SIW) scenario has not yet happened [SCH 00] in spite of high magnitude attacks, such as those aimed at Estonia in 2007.

At the same time, however, this type of attack does not happen against institutions and infrastructures which are totally defenseless, and so a considerable

---

31 Or have been transformed, as was the case on the tactical front, into issues concerning capability. The question of bringing data together and their automatic processesing has often been discussed as the condition enabling a multitude of sensor systems to exist (drones, ground sensors, vehicle observation systems).

32 An apocalyptic theme which was reinforced by the exercises methodologies such as *The Day After… In Cyberspace*, carried out in March 1996, which made an open reference to a total nuclear war (in the wake of the TV film *The Day After*).

amount of progress has been made in network protection[33]. Furthermore, an ever increasing amount of specialized units are placed inside the armies. In information warfare as with classic operations, the dialectic of the defensive and offensive also plays a part, as it is governed by their law [MOL 96]. But if the possibility of a cyberattack on the scale of an entire country which systematically aims to disrupt its networks has already been frequently discussed in literature on strategic surprise, then analyst D. Londsdale feels that the fact that this has *not* yet happened must not be taken lightly – it is simply a question of time [LON 04].

In this view, the probability of seeing this type of attack happen could increase over time through a development in the capabilities of hardware, of new software tools and new tactics to use them. There may also be an evolution in the awareness of the possibilities offered by information warfare, just like the attention it would get from potentially hostile organizations, whether they are state or non-state governed. In this regard, some analysts have suggested that $10 million would enable a sub-state governed organization to have the capacity to launch information warfare equivalent to that on a State level [LON 04]. A certain number of these organizations actually have such means (the Lebanese Hezbollah, or the Columbian FARC, for example) and are seeing their financial capacities increase over time. In fact, it seems wise to oust any historical determinism from the analysis, according to which an electronic strategic attack has not already happened, would tell us that the threat is by no means major. On the other hand, the material and tactical evolutions which have been observed over history show that those practicing such strategies are working more and more on the possibilities of information warfare in all its aspects, from digital attacks to mediatized operations [HEC 09].

In practice, information warfare cannot be removed from classic war laws, including the dialectic between offensive and defensive. So if the offensive capabilities advance, then this will also be the case for defensive. In addition to advances in software, this is what is attempted to be shown by intervening military organizations, specialized in network security but also detecting attacks and knowing how to avoid them. In itself, the question is raised more and more in national documents which define security and defense policies. Moreover, it seems dangerous not to consider such a form of strategic surprise in terms of its capacities by focusing the analysis on the fact that it is led electronically. Taking place in the "real" world and not on a conceptual level, an electronic Pearl Harbor raises several questions:

– firstly, how can we exploit the initial attack beyond the paralysis of enemy systems? A strategic surprise is often followed by exploitation through the

---

33 In practice, the capacity to detect attacks on networks has also been put into question, particularly by conducting several exercises showing that the majority of attacks went undetected or had not been reported to higher officers by those suffering the attacks.

development of a military thrust, as the surprise is only rarely sufficient on its own. This exploitation may be direct (German thrust on the USSR after the launch of Barbarossa, North Korean thrust towards the South of the peninsula), or indirect (Japanese thrust in the Pacific but not on Hawaii after having reduced US naval forces). But, how can we exploit a massive electronic attack by a single digital channel? Except for considering that the coup is substantial enough in itself (a valid hypothesis for a terrorist scenario[34] or within a limited strategy[35]), resorting to "concrete" forces, and those capable of transforming the initial attacks into a long-lasting political victory seems necessary. In fact, the single digital attack is not sufficient in itself. When all our societies – and therefore our armies – are incapable of functioning without computers, then attack alone would not be enough to take possession over the attacked State;

– secondly, how can we assess, either before or after the attack, the consequential impacts, whether they are real or perceived? In several respects, the lack of available historical examples limits the range of the analysis, and confines it to a simple hypothesis. However, one of the major assets of strategic surprise is its ability to make an impression and be remembered, paralyzing the reactions of the victim for a certain time [BRU 08]. In such a context, the visibility of the action taken (particularly through its echoes in the media) seems like an important aspect, whereas by definition an electronic attack has much less visible consequences than a standard military attack in terms of physical destruction. This factor, then, tends to relativize the perceptual range of a digital strategic surprise[36]. Moreover, let us note here also that the Pentagon, with a relatively low amplitude and generally causing no major damage, also raises the question of what a strategic surprise should be. In such conditions, it should undoubtedly involve massive attacks on the entire

---

34 In this example, a single strike is considered to be self-sufficient. Except if it is coupled with a guerrilla strategy, terrorism essentially has a semiotic value, of expression a political position by the one implementing it. Creating a strong impression, it is considered as a poor strategy in terms of the potentiality that it offers its user and tends, in literature, to be considered more as the marker of a strategic powerlessness than as being able to (once again, alone) lead to victory.

35 This is true to the extent that the very idea of strategic surprise is traditionally associated with total strategies, understood as trying to defeat all a State's forces. Within a limited strategy, an electronic strategic surprise could, for instance, come as an attack trying to break down a country's banking network.

36 The example has been shown in fiction. In the "Debt of Honor" trilogy, Tom Clancy presents a scenario where an super-nationalist Japanese government engages computer operations on Wall Street, taking Washington and Tokyo into a virtual war. However, it is kept as a secret by both governments, both fearing for their respective governments. In practice, Tokyo used the economic crisis created to take a series of territorial guarantors, in fact leading to a military confrontation, obviously discreet but nonetheless real.

infrastructure, include unprecedented violence and last over time[37], which raises a few questions on the difficulties a party could encounter when launching these attacks;

– thirdly, the probability of an electronic strategic surprise occurring (getting the exact figures is a tricky exercise) also involves a reflection on the nature of its real effects on the attacked organizations. It seems obvious that the dependence of our States and institutions on computer systems has not stopped growing over the last 20 years, which once again raises the question of the function and vulnerabilities of the technically oriented system which was brilliantly analyzed by Jacques Ellul [ELL 77]. This is particularly the case when our institutions and kinds of political organization themselves have become metaphors for the network and that they are considered to be new fields of conflict [HEN 02]. This single conceptual change, which carries within itself the appropriation of the characterization of specific forms of a reticular act [FOR 97], tends to make others perceive of an increase in the risks induced by an electronic strategic surprise. In such a configuration type, society, institutions or even armies are naturally mobilized by computers and networks and appear especially vulnerable.

In such conditions, applying rationalities specific to networks also brings about several advantages in terms of defense. Reticulation induces redundancy, in such a way that attacks performed on one node in particular might not necessarily have repercussions on others. This type of phenomenon has been particularly well explored in publications on terrorist and guerilla groups, showing that bringing down the head of these organizations brought about their loss less often than hierarchical organizations.

For Arquilla and Ronfeldt, the consequences are as such: the networks have to fight with other networks. In their view, networks have their own resilience, which is considered as being superior to hierarchical organizations [ARQ 96]. At the same time, we cannot help but notice also that an electronic strategic surprise is enhanced by the fact that several vital and critical systems[38] (water and electricity supply, rail networks, air traffic, banking systems, etc.) are not entirely automated and that human and direct control is still possible. In other words, governing systems could be affected but total paralysis is difficult to imagine. However there is a lack of experience of serious attacks on these systems, which hardly allows us to draw lessons from it and understand the interactions which could probably take place with

---

37 In fact, disruptions to networks, computers or water conveyance, either accidental or deliberate, are relatively abundant. Regarding water supplies in industrialized countries, these disruptions have never led to panic and terror. There are many reasons which can explain this phenomenon, including that they have only ever been temporary [LEW 02].
38 We traditionally distinguish vital and critical systems according to the degree of dependence that our societies, and more particularly their cohesion, maintains.

the rest of society. Only alarming information on the quality of water will be available (its truthfulness is hardly important), and the reaction of the population will undoubtedly be impossible to predict [HEN 10].

At this stage in our discussion, the question of knowing to what extent a strategic surprise aimed at paralyzing armed force networks may occur. As François Géré points out, the best way of paralyzing these networks for a long time is, without a doubt, to physically destroy them rather than stopping them from working by the only arsenal of possible measures in information warfare [GER 97]. The conduct of military operations led over these last 20 years shows how, in the preparation for strike plans, the enemy's detection and command and communication systems have been targeted by a combination of computer and air strikes and jamming. Information warfare takes place as often in software spaces as "real" places, and just constitutes one aspect of what the most apt military organizations are in a position to do [HEN 05].

Military history, as with the sociology of innovation, shows that new weapons and new war methods must be combined with older methods and systems in order to produce maximum effects. This does not fail, however, to raise the question of information warfare as the military revolution as many analysts see it[39].

The sole use of electronic massive attacks on military systems in an attempt to paralyze them seems difficult indeed. The Pentagon recorded 43,785 attacks in the first semester in 2009, against 54,640 for the year 2008, and 1.415 in 2000 [MCM 09]. This sequence is absolutely astonishing and yet, at no point does the American force's capacity to lead its missions seem to have been put into question[40]. The attacked systems have been both the most exposed (email networks, websites accessible to the public such as the Naval War College's site) and yet the less criticized at the same time.

Similar examples have been seen in the private sector[41]. If the digitalization processes of military units themselves are making advances and networks are

---

39 In this sense, it would not change the deep nature of war, not sweeping away underlying laws.

40 The policy on the matter still remains that we must not communicate on penetrations which would have been successful and the extent of the damage they could have caused. Several computer systems belonging to US forces are still blocked off and are ultimately not linked to the Internet. Networking systems happens by links, such as data links which are still easy to control.

41 Thus in 2000, Ford suffered an attack of 140,000 infected emails in 3 hours, shutting down its network for just under a week. The company's 114 factories however pursued their operations and the affected networks ordering and sending spare parts were never infected. Communication with the sales centers were not affected either [LEW 02].

becoming vital factors there, then the adopted position is still, in France, the UK and the USA in particular, to keep training the staff for action in an environment described as being "damaged" [DEN 05].

A paralysis of computer systems, whatever the reason, would not lead to a physical paralysis of the units using them – at least if the adopted principles are applied[42]. They could, however, considerably slow down their actions on the other hand.

New computer attack systems that we could liken to electronic warfare systems, however seem to be reaching a level of "maturity", like *Suter* for instance. Supported by a combat device, it enables the user to enter enemy air defense networks to gauge what their operators are seeing, but also in order to delete the radar echoes of attacker devices from their screens[43].

In practice, these radar paralysis systems (if we were certain of their existence[44]) by no means prevent us from resorting to more classic detection methods (like visual observation), and it is not certain if they can be used on a large scale[45]. We must add here that the single paralysis/destruction of an air defense system (if it is a real military challenge) in itself is neither a sign nor the materialization of a strategic surprise, nor is its decision to strike which is capable of almost instantaneously submitting the enemy's will. The loss of control over the skies is not the guarantee of a near defeat. From a strategic point of view, any attack must be combined and involve hitting practically all the sectors allowing the enemy's forces to act. Moreover, infiltrating command and communication networks and controlling an army, on the operative and tactical front, far beyond the only servers connected to the Internet and from where emails are forwarded, seems necessary but eminently complex and requires, in exchange for and from strategic entities attempting to do it, strong abilities.

---

42 Most land force units do not require computers to fight. The digitialization process essentially involves sharing information via portable terminals, making it possible to locate friend or enemy forces. The limits specific to these systems (particularly problems of perfect information regarding th position of enemy forces) are considered in the doctrine corpuses of the armies implementing them. And so, the systems are considered more as tactical decision aids than systems describing the behaviour of other forces.

43 The system was used in the Israeli strike on a Syrian nuclear plant in September 2007.

44 This seems to be the case, a study from the US Congressional Research Office seems to warn of the existence of a program based on an article from the magazine *Aviation Week* which, in the past, has spread false information about US programs [CRS 07].

45 Already in 1991, rumors on the use of a virus able to paralyze Iraqi air defense systems had started to circulate. It was then confirmed to be a rumor.

If literature on the subject only mentions this possibility[46] (consequently, there is no truly available example), then historical examples on the use of electronic warfare on enemy radar and radio networks (intrusion, jamming or listening) show that, if the adversary were able to see a serious reduction in his capacities, then he could have continued to fight[47].

Despite its assets, electronic warfare has never been able to carry away the decision by itself and, by analogy, we are able to estimate that this could also be the case for information operations whether they use systems like *Suter* or more conventional information warfare capacities. Moreover the question of the possibility that States other than the USA and European countries can design them, and also the question of their potential spreading (even their proliferation) is also being raised. But in the end, for now the threat does not seem to be imminent. The capabilities of information warfare do not seem to be in a position to send armies into a state of failure.

If the hypothesis of a strategic surprise targeted at military networks cannot be completely isolated, then we cannot help but notice that it would require a concentration of the enemy's extremely high computerized capabilities, were it only in view of a saturation attack. The resultant hypothesis of an infiltration into to the most vital sectors of the software for a weapon system or a C4ISR network, if it cannot be isolated, however depends on the difficulty of accessing it – at the same and in a more general way, to fully produce a strategic surprise in due form. This is especially the case as a lot of military software is relatively simple in comparison to civilian software, and any potential error can be detected quicker[48]. We could add here that, if it was confirmed, using a system such as *Suter* would raise the question of the quantity and quality of the intelligence needed before its use. The types of command systems targeted, the radars through which the system penetrates have been involved a considerable intelligence infrastructure, as this type of action could

---

46 When it refers to it, at least in the public domain: the Israeli attack, relatively recent, only led to descriptive analyzes which appeared in magazines and whose prospective analytical value remains limited [FUL 07].

47 This is, notably, the case for the least technologically advanced adversaries. Egypt or Syria in the face of Israel during the war of Kippir (1973) pursued combat (but it is also true that the Israeli capacity for electronic warfare, although real, were still limited). In 1982 the Syrian capacity to use their networks was also reduced but organizational modalities (implemented by autonomous anti-tank units) partially made it possible to compensate for the Israeli actions which turned out to be more useful in the fight against air defenses in Damas.

48 We estimate that the software systems of F-22 count around 2 million lines of code, versus 8 million for F-35. Comparatively Windows XP counts around 35 million lines of code.

not be reproduced on a large scale, in a strategic surprise, for example[49]. The classic measures for operational safety, from this point of view, certainly constitute a factor which makes it possible to limit risks but it is also important to be aware of the risks run by new forms of information warfare, such as *Suter* or similar systems which might be developed.

In this regard, the intelligence services clearly have a part to play in defining information safety measures, but also in describing potentially critical network operators. Fundamentally, knowing the flaws in these networks or more generally their modes of function, creates a certain vulnerability, with their operators being able to forward sensitive information to an adversary, questioning again the networks' natural resilience. The threat is, then, *real*, with the majority of the malicious acts led by a company coming from their employees who are often misinformed of elementary safety measures [BAU 06]. This threat indeed raises the question concerning the evolution in recruiting armed forces[50].

The intelligence services also have an important part to play, perhaps a more classic one, in the implementation and maintenance of a device combining both monitoring and research on the arsenals of information warfare that a potential enemy could be capable of putting into place. At any rate, intelligence has always run into the above mentioned problems, as a matter of analyzing the adversary's intentions and apprehending the threat on the decision front – in the space where adversary actions have been, essentially, converted into strategic surprises. From this point of view, the problem does not concern the many methods used by an enemy to create a strategic surprise (conventional or electronic attack, diplomatic action) but rather the sociology of strategic organizations.

The only exception to this type of reasoning might stem from using strikes with directed enemy weapons (DEW) which are capable of creating an electric saturation phenomenon similar to that seen with nuclear weapons. This type of threat, if it is located around the concept of information warfare as we have been using it in this chapter, is nonetheless real: any non- "hardened" electric or electronic system will be "grilled" by such an attack, which amounts to a rationale of destroying the targeted systems [KOP 04]. In the meantime, several States are working on the concept, moreover with this type of weapon seeming relatively cheap. In view of the operations aiming at enemy information infrastructures, the penetration of networks in light of the difficulties that it brings could not be the option with the best return

---

49 This is particularly the case as national defense systems involve different types of sensors and management systems, potentially put onto a network. The hypothetic paralysis of a single type of sensor does not compromise the functioning of the other sensors.

50 Where the recruitment of civil workers according depending on their qualifications tends to increase, to the detriment of more traditional methods of military recruitment, based on loyalty to the institution and the country.

for a strategic surprise. Using weapons with DEW effects, comparatively, offers long-lasting physical paralysis of the system (the effects of such of an attack are irreversible) and engaging targets is made easier by the wide variety of vectors available[51]. In this regard, using this type of weapon seems more suitable for paralysis and surprise on a strategic level. Here too, however, the first strike might lead the enemy to exploitation, running the risk of seeing the attacked entity recover.

3.4. Concluding remarks: surprise in strategic studies

If it is obvious that the excellent technological and doctrinal evolution observed for the last 30 years in the armed forces does not, by any means, make strategic principles and laws outdated and obsolete [COU 99], then we cannot help but notice that the different ways of applying force (lethal or not) have become considerably more diversified. Information warfare has a major role in this evolution, and the thousands of publications produced over the last 20 years can bear witness to this idea. However, we cannot help but question the real strategic effects of the appearance of this new type of art of warfare, particularly with regard to the concept of surprise. The analyst's feelings are shared here.

Surprise implies an element of cognitive shock, which is both disorienting and paralyzing to the victim, at least in the short term.

Yet how, when computer attacks on large companies and state-governed infrastructures and armies are frequent, can we consider that one attack being more violent than another would count as a strategic surprise? Here we find ourselves, logically, in the permanent dialectic of opposed wills, in what we can call the "routine of conflict". Indeed, the attacks may be extremely violent (and historically tend to be increasingly more so, as much in quantity as in quality) but they hardly ever only occur in a dialectic continuum between defensive and offensive. This implies, in return for phenomena of adapting materials, software and organizations. All in all, these attacks will not be the first, and for those getting information on the subject, there is nothing surprising to be learned. But if this is not a question of surprise, then is a strategic surprise in its electronic form, for all this, impossible to conceptualize? Here the analyst is questioning the deep dynamics of the surprise. Historically, surprise (whether it is tactical, operative, strategic or technological) stems from the combination of many factors, as much in terms of doctrine and capacity as political, which do not all constitute as surprises.

---

51 According to some analysts, such weapons could be of a similar size to those of a classic aviation bomb weighing 227 kg. they could be dropped by combat devices but also by equipping with ballistic and cruise missiles. The possibility of such weapons being implemented on the enemy's side by putting them into sea containers also allows them to imagine using them without a classic military attack taking place beforehand.

The German invasion on the USSR in 1941 thus relied on a finely balanced combination of a doctrinal corpus and relatively well tested capacities from September 1939 (which the USSR also contributed to). It takes it roots from Hitler's desire to conquer and to make Europe submit to the Nazi order, whose content was known to intelligence services – including Soviet services. The space/time where the attack took place was preceded by a logic which was accessible to any person with some knowledge of military history: attacking in June, Hitler sought to benefit from the best season, avoiding the terrible *raspoutitsa* (quagmire season) and thus taking advantage of a better level of mobility, which would not have been limited by a low number of roads in a bad condition. The method used is also well known, so much so because the forces there were relatively used to the army officers wanting to avoid having to suffer the winter, and thus the offensive was led at a high *tempo*. From this point of view, military logic is irrefutable and, on the strategic front, everything proved to be predictable. But in fact, the surprising element of the offensive lies in the decision to conduct it. Already engaged on the West front, Hitler should not have attacked, according to what we might describe as "strategic wisdom" [SCN 06]. Added to this is Stalin's deliberate belief in the German promise to respect the Molotov-Ribbentrop pact. Consequently and in return, the Red Army was not prepared for what was going to happen. It was the Soviet military system, all the way to the tactical front, which was shocked by the intervening surprise on a political-strategic level[52].

Military logic, regardless of its relevance, has thus been subjected to political logic. In many respects, we can still learn lessons from the German invasion, including the hypothesis of a surprise attack via computer systems/electronic channels.

Firstly, being controlled by political views is still current. If it has been proven that a large number of the attacks on the Pentagon have come from China or North Korea, and that the attacks on Estonia had come from Russia, then these strikes have not met any real retaliation from the victims. Military logic has not managed to win out against political logic, with this reigning over the military domain.

Secondly, a surprise attack will probably intervene by a complex combination, if it *does* occur. Only using arsenals from cyberwar will, undoubtedly, be insufficient. This is especially so when faced with the degree of apprehension of the threat, which is currently the States which could be a victim of it – even if an awareness of the threat might legitimately be considered as being not enough. This is particularly the case with the exception of a terrorist attack with limited objectives; a computer

---

52 If it is true that some Soviet generals had pre-empted the possibility of this attack, then the politically incorrect nature of such a hypothesis was sufficient, where purges having brought down the forces still reigned supreme, to naturally block necessary preparations.

attack in the backdrop of a war between strategic organizations (state-governed or not) would need to be exploited. Just like the air forces, computer viruses do not conquer terrorists in the "real" world, even if they commonly show an undeniable strategic utility.

Thirdly, surprise cannot come so much from the *types* of capacities used, but from the attacker's intentions, and these capacities are all political and not technical.

On the other hand, the new types of strategic surprise that we could assist with might involve combinations of more complex means than in the past, or even build on technological surprises. Thus, as a result, these forms of strategic surprise must be not conceptualized or analyzed in a monocausal approach, but actually in a system analysis.

Considering a system analysis approach rather than one based on capacity in methodologies for conceptualizing future threats seems especially adapted, as we cannot fully understand the concept of surprise without considering the fact that it, in itself, is part of the art of warfare. It is both the component and, to a certain extent, one of the conditions of its materialization. However, considering that a strategic surprise could come via an electronic channel does not mean that we can take into account the very complexity of what a new form of strategic surprise (taking inspiration from past experiences) might represent. Until now, through a lack of tools or shrewd judgment, strategic surprises have not acted as a factor of victory for the party putting the surprise into action. Of course we can, in the absolute, conceive of an efficient strategic surprise and lead on to victory by operating it, or even taking it into account using information warfare[53]. But it would also involve considering other factors, whether they are technical, tactical, doctrinal, and above all, political. At this stage, we are only able to understand the role played by intelligence services in the totality of the analyzes they can provide. Whether intelligence services use information warfare methods or not, for these services it is a matter of considering the entire correlation of an enemy's forces, from his intentions to his capacities and operatory modes.

If these services' analytical methods are not fundamentally put into question by new technologies, then their work is made much more difficult, with the mass of information to be analyzed ever growing. However, the fact still remains that the real difficulty caused by using information warfare in a strategic attack could, and more than probably would, come from its combination with other more classic military approaches.

---

53 Were it not only from its mediatized aspect.

Historically, using new weapons has only proven to be greatly useful, revealing their potential to break, when combined with technological systems and older forces. It is without a doubt in this type of context that information warfare would prove to be the most efficient, shocking the enemy's devices and heightening the chaos following on from a combined attack.

It is, then, a completely plausible idea that new combinations of forces engaged in strategic surprise will come forward, and will, in fact, raise the question of knowing the exact place where information warfare will play out. However this is a question which falls beyond the boundaries of this chapter: such a use of information warfare would fall into the classic context of strategic surprise.

3.5. Bibliography

[AMB 89] AMBROSE S. E., "The Bulge", *MHQ: The Quarterly Journal of Military History*, no. 3, vol. 1, July-September 1989.

[ARQ 96] ARQUILLA J., RONFELDT D., "Information, power and grand strategy: in Athena's camp", in SCHWARZENSTEIN S.J.D, *The Information Revolution and National Security: Dimensions and Directions*, CSIS, Washington, USA, 1996.

[BAR 05] BARGER D. G., *Toward a Revolution in Intelligence Affairs*, Rand Corporation, Santa Monica, USA, 2005.

[BAU 06] BAUTZMANN A., "Quand l'employé devient cheval de Troie", *Défense & sécurité internationale*, no. 15, Paris, France, May 2006.

[BEA 85] BEAUFRE A., *Introduction à la stratégie*, IFRI/Economica, Paris, France, 1985.

[BRA 93] BRACKEN P., "The military after next", *The Washington Quarterly,* vol. 16, no. 4, Washington, USA, Autumn 1993.

[BRU 08] BRUSTLEIN C., "La surprise stratégique. De la notion aux implications", *Focus stratégique*, no. 10, IFRI, Paris, France, October 2008.

[CHA 04] CHALIAND G., BLIN A., *Histoire du terrorisme. De l'antiquité à Al-Qaïda*, Bayard, Paris, France, 2004.

[CHE 08] CHEM, "La surprise stratégique", *Défense Nationale et Sécurité Collective*, no. 3, Paris, France, March 2008.

[COU 99] COUTAU-BÉGARIE H., *Traité de stratégie*, col. Bibliothèque stratégique, Economica, Paris, France, 1999.

[CRO 97] CROPSEY C., "Omniscient, omnipresent, omnipotent: O3", *Défense Nationale,* Paris, France, April 1997.

[DEL 04] DELAFORCE P., *Battle of the Bulge. Hitler's Final Gamble*, Pearson, Edinburgh, UK, 2004.

[DEN 05] DE NEVE A., MATHIEU R., *Les armées d'Europe face aux défis capacitaires et technologiques*, col. Axes, Bruylant, Brussels, Belgium, 2005.

[DEN 06] DE NEVE A., HENROTIN J., "La network centric warfare", *Stratégique*, no. 86, April 2006.

[ELL 77] ELLUL J., *Le système technicien*, Liberté de l'esprit, Calmann-Lévy, Paris, France, 1977.

[EUR 09] EUROPOL, TE-SAT 2009. EU Terrorism Situation and Report, The Hague, The Netherlands, 2009.

[FOR 97] FORGET P., POLYCARPE G., *Le réseau et l'infini. Essai d'anthropologie philosophique et stratégique*, col. Bibliothèque stratégique, Institut de Stratégie Comparée, Economica, Paris, France, 1997.

[FUL 07] FULGHUM D., "Why Syria's air defense failed to detect Israelis", *Aviation Week and Space Technology, January* 14th 2007.

[GER 97] GÉRÉ F., *Demain la guerre*, Calmann-Lévy, Paris, France, 1997.

[GER 00] GÉRÉ, F., "RMA or new operational art? A view from France", in GONGORA, T., VON RIECKHOFF, H., *Toward a Revolution in Military Affairs?*, Greenwood Press, Westport/London, UK, 2000.

[GOO 05] GOODMAN M., "9/11: The failure of strategic intelligence", in WARK, W.K., *Twenty First Century Intelligence*, col. Studies in Intelligence, Frank Cass, London, UK, 2005.

[GRA 05] GRAY C. S., *Transformation and Strategic Surprise*, www.strategicstudiesinstitute. army.mil/Pubs/display.cfm?pubid=602, Strategic Studies Institute, Carlisle Barracks, USA, April 2005.

[GRA 97] GRAY C.H., *Postmodern War. The New Politics of Conflict*, London, 1997.

[GUO 09] GUO-QING Z., QING-FENG Y., SU-QI C., TAO T., "Evolution of the Internet and its Cores", *New Journal of Physics*, no. 10, 2008.

[HEC 09] HECKER M., RID, T., *War 2.0. Irregular Warfare in the Information Age*, Praeger Security International, Westport, 2009.

[HEI 04] HEISBOURG F. (ed.), 11 septembre. Rapport de la commission d'enquête. Rapport final de la commission nationale sur les attaques terroristes contre les Etats-Unis, Paris, Editions des Equateurs, 2004.

[HEN 02] HENROTIN J., "Vulnérabilités des sociétés techniciennes et contre-terrorisme", *Stratégique*, no. 85, 2002/1.

[HEN 05] HENROTIN J., *L'Airpower au XXIe siècle. Enjeux et perspectives de la stratégie aérienne*, Réseau multidisciplinaire d'études stratégiques, Bruylant, Brussels, Belgium, 2005.

[HEN 08] HENROTIN J., *La technologie militaire en question. Le cas américain*, Stratégies et doctrines, Economica, Paris, France, 2008.

[HEN 10] HENROTIN J., *La résilience dans l'antiterrorisme. Le dernier bouclier*, Défis du troisième millénaire, L'Esprit du Livre, Sceaux, 2010.

[HIN 93] HINSLEY F.H., "Introduction: The influence of ultra in the Second World War" in HINSLEY, F.H., STRIPP, A., *Codebreakers: The Inside Story of Bletchley Park*, Oxford University Press, Oxford, UK, 1993.

[JOH 96] JOHNSON S.E., LIBICKI M.C., *Dominant Battlespace Knowledge*, National Defense University Press, Washington, USA, 1996.

[KAH 97] KAHLE B., "Preserving the Internet", *Scientific American*, March 1997.

[KEE 03] KEEGAN J., *Intelligence in War. Knowledge of the Enemy from Napoleon to Al Qaeda*, Alfred Knopf, New York, USA, 2003.

[KOP 04] KOPP C., *The Electromagnetical Bomb – A Weapon of Electrical Mass Destruction*, Air & Space Power Chronicles, July 2004.

[LAW 99] LAWRENCE S., GILES C.L., "Accessibility of the information on the Web", *Nature*, July 8th 1999.

[LBD 08] GOUVERNEMENT FRANÇAIS, Le livre blanc sur la défense et la sécurité nationale, Odile Jacob, Paris, France, 2008.

[LEW 02] LEWIS J.A., *Assessing the Risks of Cyber Terrorism, Cyber War and Other Cyber Threats*, csis.org/files/media/csis/pubs/021101_risks_of_cyberterror.pdf, CSIS, Washington, USA, December 2002.

[LIB 95] LIBICKI M. C., *What is Information Warfare?*, National Defense University Press, Washington, USA, 1995.

[LIB 09] LIBICKI M. C., *Cyberdeterrence and Cyberwar*, Rand Corporation, Santa Monica, USA, 2009.

[LON 04] LONSDALE D.J., *The Nature of War in the Information Age. Clausewitzian Future*, col. Strategy and History, Frank Cass, New York, USA, 2004.

[MCM 09] MCMILLAN R., *Cyberattacks on the US Military Jump Sharply in 2009*, www.networkworld.com/news/2009/112009-cyberattacks-on-us-military-jump.html, Network World, November 20th 2009.

[MOL 96] MOLANDER R.C., RIDDILE A.S., WILSON P.A., *Strategic Information Warfare: A New Face of War*, Parameters, Fall 1996.

[MUR 05] MURPHY D.E., *What Stalin Knew: The Enigma of Barbarossa*, Yale University Press, New Haven, USA, 2005.

[NAT 02] NATO, *Open Source Intelligence Reader*, www.oss.net, 2002.

[OWE 00] OWENS W.A., OFFLEY E., *Lifting the Fog of War*, Ferrar, Strauss and Giroux, New York, USA, 2000.

[RAZ 99] RAZOUX P., *La guerre israélo-arabe d'octobre 1973: une nouvelle donne militaire au Proche-Orient*, Economica, Paris, France, 1999.

[SCH 96] SCHWARTAU W., *Information Warfare*, Thunder's Mouth Press, New York, USA, 1996 (2nd edition).

[SCH 00] SCHWARTAU W., *Asymmetrical Adversaries*, vol. 44, no. 2, Orbis, Spring 2000.

[SCN 06] SCHNETZLER B., *Les erreurs stratégiques du IIIème Reich durant la Seconde guerre mondiale*, col. Campagnes et Stratégies, Economica, Paris, France, 2006 (3rd edition).

[SHE 49] SHERMAN K., *Strategic Intelligence For American World Policy*, Princeton University Press, Princeton, USA, 1949.

[STE 07] STEELE R.D., "Open source intelligence" in JOHNSON L., *The Handbook of Intelligence Studies*, Routledge, London, UK, 2007.

[STE 09] STEED B., *Piercing the Fog of War. Recognizing change on the Battlefield*, Zenith Press, New York, USA, 2009.

[STU 93] STUDEMAN W. O., "Teaching the giant to dance: contradictions and opportunities in open source information within the intelligence community", *American Intelligence Journal*, USA, Spring/Summer 1993.

[SUS 05] SUSSAN R., *Les utopies posthumaines. Contre-culture, cyberculture, culture du chaos*, Omniscience, Paris, France, 2005.

[TER 08] TERTRAIS B., DEBOUZY O., "De la surprise stratégique", vol. 31, no. 124, *Commentaire*, Paris, France, 2008-2009.

[VAN 87] VAN CREVELD M., *Command in War*, Harvard University Press, Cambridge, USA, 1987.

[VAN 91] VAN CREVELD M., *Technology and War. From 2000 B.C. to the Present*, revised edition, Touchstone, New York, USA, 1991.

[VEN 08] VENTRE D., "Guerre de l'information: la prolifération des capacités?", *Défense & Sécurité Internationale*, no. 38, Paris, France, June 2008.

[WAL 95] WALLER D., "Onward cyber soldiers", *Time*, vol. 146, no. 8, USA, August 21th 1995.

[WAS 06] WASINSKI C., "Créer une révolution dans les affaires militaires: mode d'emploi", *Cultures & Conflits*, no. 64, Paris, France, Winter 2006.

[WHE 08] WHEATON K., *Revolution in Intelligence Affairs*, intellibriefs.blogspot.com/2008/10/revolution-in-intelligence-affairs.html, 6th October 2008.

[WHO 62] WOHLSTETTER R., *Pearl Harbor: Warning and Decision*, Stanford University Press, Stanford, USA, 1962.

[WIL 07] WILSON C., information operations, electronic warfare and cyberwar: capabilities and related policy issues, Congressional Research Service Report, Washington, USA, 2007.

Chapter 4

Cyberconflict: Stakes of Power

Strategies pursue objectives which cannot be fulfilled without a prior consideration of space, the actors, the interactions which might take place between them and the targets. The characteristics of the chosen space where the actors imagine their operations to be carried out condition the choice of these actors, the ways in which they carry out their actions and the feasibility of their projects. In cyberspace, it is indeed through cyberattacks and cyberdefense that such interactions will be implemented and the targets aimed. These are the two essential methods which will be used to reach the assigned objectives. Through battles led in cyberspace, States follow their quest for power or reconnaissance. But cyberspace cannot be controlled so easily: the rules are not entirely the same as those which reign in physical, conventional dimensions. When key concepts such as distance, time and proof tend to be eliminated, then the rules of the game can no longer be entirely identical. Cyberspace, then, slightly changes international relations, geopolitics and geostrategies, and the power struggles between different States on not just regional, but a global scale. In this chapter, we will be exploring the space of the conflict (cyberspace), the actors we can position there, the actions we might lead there, the targets we might aim there, and the approaches to power struggles between the actors.

4.1. Stakes of power

Defining cyberspace geopolitics is a matter of identifying strong and weak actors, analyzing the terms of their relationships, identifying regions, spaces and

Chapter written by Daniel VENTRE.

territories, which are more subjected than others to sensitive, strategic acts of violence, including the logic which aids the creation of power. Since its very origins, cyberspace has been dominated by the USA. Emerging powers are trying to develop their own solutions, in order to find relative autonomy in relation to that all powerful American giant. Thus, a Chinese space will see its day, with its own networks, its own physical infrastructures, and the development of a software industry and national content. The number of Internet users also goes against the USA. To what extent is the Anglophone world capable of dominating the duration of influence strategies in cyberspace? A State's power is also its military presence in cyberspace. Computing, computers, the Internet… these are all projects originating in the military world which were then transposed to the civilian world. States confront each other in unarmed conflict using the Internet. The never-ending espionage operations (system intrusions, the methods are not important here), reflect this. Each State observes the other, analyzes each other, pillages their respective secrets in the search for strategic information (sometimes, they do not even need to go looking in secure servers, as their projects[1] hand such information to the international community on a plate). Military cyber confrontations within a framework of armed conflicts (operational cyberwar) are, in the end, a marginal means of demonstrating these power relations. States are not the only ones seeking power through cyberspace. Hacktivist groups which make up a large proportion of the disturbances recorded on the net are not, however, looking for power so much as recognition: of their rights, their demands, their ideals, their religions, their cultures, their values, their singularities, their political convictions. All these together contribute to an antiglobalist[2] or alterglobalist[3] movement. But hacktivist groups do not demand these circles of influence most of the time.

Acquiring power and upholding it imposes both an offensive and defensive attitude on the States involved. Individual groups hardly really have to worry about anything, except for one thing: being on the offensive. Protection is given to them by small demanding, if not compliant, States. When new anonymous actors armed with the right skills to take the world's high powers as hostages through simple threats arrive on the international front, for them it is only a question of being on the offensive, as defense is given to them by the control over networks, codes and technologies. The stakes at play are therefore unbalanced. Only conventional actors are forced to think according to conventional plans (offensive and defensive). The model works well between similar actors (State against State, army against army). But this model is rendered useless when we put actors into the equation who can work on the offensive mode alone.

---

1 Wikileaks of course!
2 Antiglobalization is the line of thinking which wants to limit globalization.
3 Alterglobalization is the line of thinking which wants to change the content of globalization.

If today it is accepted that the USA is a global superpower and its domination does indeed extend to cyberspace, then this global balance is permanently being brought into question. With new powers emerging (China, mainly) and actors who are more modest but wishing to confirm their existence on the international front away from American influence, we will find a multitude of sometimes violent protests in cyberspace. The power of the US which is manifested via its control over cyberspace is a permanent target of attack. For some, this is a way of exploiting American wealth by creaming off as much of it as possible, where for others it is a way to make the giant falter on its own foundations. Due to the relative weakness of the necessary investments, there are more actors involved in this movement than could ever exist in the real world.

However, real domination in cyberspace is not within everybody's reach, because this assumes the imposition of norms, content, infrastructures, and ideas: in other words, upholding a leadership in each of the three layers making up cyberspace, namely the physical, logical/applicative, and cognitive layers. Non-state governed actors and small States may be involved in the last layer by making themselves heard, by seeking out reconnaissance there. The first and second layer are dominated by the USA and initiatives, projects, particular actions, and important developments regularly allow secondary actors to play a significant role in these two levels. It seems difficult for a State to dream of acceding to the rank of superpower or, simply, power through cyberspace alone. Being a great power or wanting to become one creates limitations, however: "as a quality of the most powerful State in the world, "defense" has a different meaning for the USA than it does for other nations"[4]. Power requires means. Cyberspace cannot be controlled without important resources. But these are turning out to be more important still. Cyberspace is growing, the number of actors within it does not stop growing, and the complexity also does not stop increasing. Vulnerabilities increase in proportion to the number of codelines deployed, Internet connections are open doors for humanity, the means needed for offensive operations do not stop decreasing when, at the same time, those means which are needed to guarantee security and defense are exploding out of control. In these conditions, it is difficult to maintain a balance, and the situation seems somewhat anarchic by the same single power in the long term.

If large land masses make great Empires, they do not always make great powers. In fact, it is preferable to be in possession of smaller territories but which are rich in resources, than larger without resources (better to have an oil field than an arid desert, even if they sometimes go together!). Cyberspace, at least theoretically infinite, gives power to those who set themselves up as masters, mainly due to its transversal nature to all conventional dimensions (air, land, sea, space). It is indeed this transversal nature which gives it its richness. The difficulty of the exercise

---

4 [AND 10], p. 33.

which consists of gaining power over cyberspace lies in its very nature: it is a *res communis*[5].

4.1.1. *Power relations*

The whole of international space is governed by power relations[6] which are not necessarily violent ones. Power relations exist between allies and friends. These relationships, for example, come in the form of diplomatic, economic, or even influential relations. Here, we are interested in violent relationships.

The most computer literate society, the most up-to-the-minute technologically, and the most dependent also, may have the highest offensive capabilities. At the same time, it will be the most vulnerable, and the most fragile. These societies are practically indefensible because their infrastructures are the most complex. Richard Clarke's thesis [CLA 10] makes even the least technically advanced States the least dependent, and the actors far more dangerous. In a certain way, this is the advantage for the poorest, the most powerless, the least connected, for all those who hardly depend on cyberspace, who have nothing to lose, and hardly anything to defend. An actor's vulnerability is, then, proportional to his level of technological development. The problem is therefore a question of decreasing vulnerability without decreasing power.

We could go back to the argument stating that the least equipped and dependent countries are also the easiest countries to destroy by cyberattacks, as the targets are both few in number and probably only have a low level of security. But with the level of dependence on cyberspace of these States being relatively low, carrying out violent cyberattacks on them would not be very fruitful. These States with their low level of technological advancement and dependent on cyberspace can, however, use capabilities allowing attacks on the more powerful. The entire matter concerns the level of capability needed for operations of significant violence and efficiency, to damage great powers with complex systems. This complexity is not only a negative point: from the defense point of view, it is more difficult to protect complex systems, but from the attack point of view, it is more hard work to find flaws in such a system and to really damage them.

We can define four different categories of actors[7], based on two essential criteria: "offensive capabilities" and "complexity/dependency". The first criterion

---

5 A wide common which belongs to all of us, and yet to no-one in particular.
6 [ENC 09], p. 143.
7 We presume this means States. The reflection could then be developed by integrating non-state governed actors, which would then require replacing the "complexity/dependency" criteria by other variables.

indicates the level reached by the actor in terms of attack. We assume that offensive capabilities integrate the motive. The second one indicates the level of complexity of its national infrastructure (interdependence on systems, levels of security, technological level reached, etc.) and society's dependence on cyberspace. Both aspects are combined here because we consider them to be tightly linked.

	Offensive capabilities	Complexity/dependency
A	High (+)	High (+)
B	High (+)	Low (-)
C	Low (-)	High (+)
D	Low (-)	Low (-)

Table 4.1. *Four categories of actors based on two criteria (offensive capabilities, complexity/dependency)*

We put the USA in category A, and States with very low or no connection in category D. In A we have actors which are strong globally. But the level of vulnerability is in proportion to the complexity/dependency variable, as well as another variable which has not been introduced into the first table: the defensive level. We could draw this to a close by adding this variable and generating the following table:

Offensive capabilities	Complexity/ dependency	Defensive capabilities
High (+)	High (+)	High (+)
High (+)	High (+)	Low(-)
High (+)	Low (-)	High (+)
High (+)	Low (-)	Low (-)
Low (-)	High (+)	High (+)
Low (-)	High (+)	Low (-)
Low (-)	Low (-)	High (+)
Low (-)	Low (-)	Low (-)

Table 4.2. *States characterized according to 3 criteria*

Based on the initial portrait (generated according to the two criteria, offensive capabilities, complexity/dependence) of the States, we will generate the first matrix of confrontation configurations:

	A (+; +)	B (+; -)	C (-; +)	D (-; -)
A (+; +)				
B (+; -)				
C (-; +)				
D (-; -)				

Table 4.3. *Based on the four defined State categories, we obtain ten possible confrontation combinations. The table must be made more complex because cyber confrontations may involve more than two States*

These elementary categories can be useful for generating scenarios of confrontation.

According to the current popular approach, which makes asymmetry the rule and symmetry the exception to the rule, the countries in category D are more advantaged or even stronger in cybernetic confrontations than the countries in A which, apparently, have all the assets needed to dominate or conquer. Nevertheless, we must examine all the different confrontation combinations and we cannot limit this debate to confirming that those who are less equipped are, in the end, better armed as they are also dependent on others. If they do not have the necessary resources, then they feel forced to call upon outside capabilities and thus create a dependent link, and therefore creating a relative weakness. The power relations between actors, as we have already discussed, come in different combinations. Here we present the most common, between which there will always be a range of subtle differences. In the strong to weak relationship, the strong will impose fire power. This demonstration of force has an impact on the target but also on its own side and other third parties who will be tempted to join the fight and will, perhaps, review their own positions. It often happens that the weak will fold in the face of the strong, but all too often we tend to imagine the opposite, as the theory of asymmetry and circumvention of superior forces is currently in vogue. Asymmetry is not always a weak to strong relationship, but a relationship between different forces. The weak do not always have the upper hand. When the strong is determined, supported by public opinion, well equipped with a strategy and good tactics, flexibility and adaptability, then the weak is in a bad position. The strong to weak relationship is bound to change, because the weak will not necessarily want to stay in this position. Weakness is, in fact, relative: it is appreciative of the state we find another actor in. Actors are neither weak nor strong in the absolute. For the strong, the aim is to stay that way, to conquer the weak and to preserve domination. For the weak, the aim is also not to be subjected to the pressure of the strong side and to become strong themselves. For the weak, there is a willingness to transform the relationship, and for the strong, there is a desire to maintain the power relationship.

Such a relationship can be illustrated by guerilla warfare, but this example is, of course, not restrictive. The weak can still be a strong State but one which confronts a superpower. In the guerilla-type strong/weak relationship, it will be a question of over throwing the adversary to avoid confronting it, playing on other aspects, morals, resistance, organization, surprise, etc. The mad to weak or mad to strong relationship is (for the mad) a question of acting irrationally, so that the adversary is taken completely by surprise. The process calls, with absolute certainty, for a retaliation which knows no limits[8].

We can propose rules to define or group together the actors. Various actors and actions, and their corresponding categories, generally fall into varied distinctions and criteria:

Distinction no. 1:

– political actions;

– non-political actions.

Distinction no. 2:

– actions led by state-governed actors;

– actions led by non-state-governed actors.

Distinction no. 3:

– actions led in times of peace;

– actions led in times of crises;

– actions led in times of conflict.

Distinction no. 4:

– actors whose actions are expensive;

– actors whose actions are inexpensive.

Distinction no. 5:

– potential threats;

– real and current threats.

---

8 [ENC 09], p. 166.

Distinction no. 6:

– attacks only led in cyberspace;

– attacked accompanied by physical operations.

Distinction no. 7:

– attacks on precise, individual targets;

– attacks not aiming for a precise target.

Distinction no. 8:

– attacks that we can trace back to the source;

– attacks that we cannot trace.

Distinction no. 9:

– individual actors;

– actors working in groups, networks, communities.

Distinction no. 10:

– when the impact is assessed in terms of "losses" (financial, power, credibility, guarantees, etc.);

– when the impact is assessed in other terms (change in behavior, feelings, resilience, etc.).

Distinction no. 11:

– visible attacks;

– invisible attacks.

Distinction no. 12:

– attacks requiring new defenses;

– attacks resorting to known defenses.

Distinction no. 13:

– actors capable of complex operations;

– actors only capable of simple operations.

This short list can of course be more thorough and complete. Let us now consider the criteria which are not, or only minorly, taken into account when defining the categories of actors of threats and conflict.

We must therefore include a new distinction, no. 14:

– the range of my threats;

– the range of others' threats.

The fact that international actors share cyberspace does not mean that an actor is separate from the others.

Distinction no. 15:

– the actors which affect me;

– the actors which do not affect me.

The following is the basic equation used here: each actor has his own opposing forces, each actor has his own range of threats. With each actor having his own environment and context, he has his own enemies and therefore potential attackers. Actors do not necessarily share their enemies with others. France's enemies are not the same as Japan's, even if they might share some of them. This is the case for the real world, as for cyberspace. The fact that cyberspace has no boundaries (a debatable point of view, we might add), does not entirely bring into question the existence of a range of threatening actors.

Distinction no. 16:

– media portrayed attacks;

– non-media portrayed attacks.

Distinction no. 17:

– attacks which can immediately be put into context;

– attacks whose context is not clear.

Distinction no. 18:

– attacks whose victims are aided by the international community;

– attacks whose victims are not aided by the international community.

Distinction no. 19:

– attacks which must be prevented;

– attacks where it may be preferable to let them happen, or that can be allowed to happen.

Distinction no. 20:

– attacks with negative consequences;

– attacks we can benefit from.

These are the possible threat classifications which enable us to develop the characteristic profiles of actors mediating threats and conflicts, through offering other perspectives.

The power relationships result in two essential means for cyberconflict and cyberwar: cyberattack and cyberdefense.

4.1.1.1. *Cyberattack*

Cyberattacks do not figure in the privileged domain of soldiers or authorities. The term is actually used indifferently to denote:

– criminal acts;

– military acts;

– attacks on information systems and information, whatever the motives (political, financial, etc);

– attacks on goods and people;

– attacks of vital, sensitive or not, private or public infrastructures, etc.

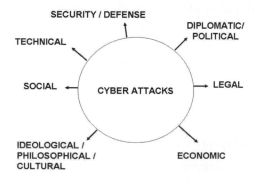

Figure 4.1. *Cyberattacks raise a multitude of questions*

Cyberattacks are characterized by several different criteria:

– useful weapons and targets are widely present across the world;

– if anyone can be a victim, then virtually anyone may claim for the attacks: anyone can lead attacks, a single individual can cause damage;

– there is a wide spectrum of targets and victims;

– the spectrum of cyberattacks is also quite wide, particularly in terms of power of destruction or disruption. The concept of major attack was introduced in the 1990s. This is the archetypal attack likely to put an end to the world as we know it today. This is the threat to social, cultural models: the model of a society wholly based on information and associated technologies. If cyberspace were destroyed, what would become of the societies which depend on it so much? This destruction may be the result of major attacks, but also from the particular uses of cyberspace or even its natural collapse;

– there is a wide spectrum of cyberattackers, as well as motives, means, and as many criteria allowing us to define the attacker[9];

– a single attack can hit millions of targets (but can we still speak of a "target", when the attacks have an impact on a target which was not specifically aimed at?);

– over the last few years, the number of victims in the world has not stopped increasing exponentially, and this is in spite of the efforts made in cybersecurity and investments. What would the situation be like if there were none of these security and defense strategies? There is no statistic in the criminal sector with such a comparison: complaints received by the IC3 (Internet Crime Complaint Center) in the USA were multiplied by 20 in the space of 10 years (going from 16,839 in 2000, to 336,655 in 2009)[10]. It has gone from 6 incidents relating to losses and thefts of nominative and sensitive data reported in 2002, to 780 in 2008 in the USA alone[11].

– a target can be struck millions of times over very short periods;

– statistics relating to cyberattacks are staggering. We are talking in millions of attacks, sometimes on the same target. What other kind of attack can tally up millions of victims in one single strike?[12];

---

9 See [VEN 11].

10 http://scamfraudalert.wordpress.com/2010/03/13/fbi-2009-cybercrime-statistics/.

11 According to data published by DataLossDB.org.

12 There are many examples of this. Let us remember the millions of machines compromised by botnets, launching spamming campaigns or DDoS attacks. Let us not forget the millions of nominative data which was lost or stolen in a single case, as was the case in 2003 – but there are hundreds examples of this kind – for the company America Online which had 92 million user names and email addresses stolen by one of its employees. The database was used to send 7 billion spam mails across the world.

– the most frequently struck targets are those with the highest symbolic meaning: the US DoD, US military targets, government bureaus, large companies: in other words, everything symbolizing power and representing American hegemony. The importance of the symbolic stature is high, as we were able to see in the Stuxnet affair, whose media success can be partly explained by the manipulation of symbols, myths, utopias, etc.;

– anybody may contribute to attacks without knowing it (zombie machines). 25% of machines in the world are zombies;

– cyberattacks can be invisible and leave many victims. This is what is also known as the perfect crime (leaving behind no traces)[13];

– the attack can be concealed behind a fake advertisement;

– speed is one of the essential elements of the attack, even if the preparation takes weeks;

– cyberattacks generate hypotheses: they threaten the stability of international relations. They can sometimes be considered as acts of war, with the difficulty being knowing when this is the case;

– cyberattacks are now part of military doctrine in their own right. But soldiers seems to have an object in their hands that they do not always know what to do with;

– cyberattacks can threaten national defense in times of peace. The virus Conficker led to French Rafale fighter planes being pinned to the ground in January 2009;

– cyber attackers could be considered as "heroes" fighting against the American enemy, against Big Brother, against the enemies of freedom, against the dominant American cultural oppression, against an adverse country, for political, religious, ideological causes;

– the effects of cyberattacks are sometimes hardly visible;

– a natural incident (climatic influences, maintenance errors, programming problems…) might seem like a cyberattack (and vice versa). After the death of Michael Jackson, Google saw a sudden spike in searches, wrongly mistaking the searches as a series of cyberattacks, whereas it was obviously only a natural movement of interest in the star's death[14]. Cyberattacks have conditioned actors in

---

13 The perfect crime is characterized by the difficulty of detecting it, of being designed so that nobody can point the finger at the potential guilty party, a crime which may affect a lot of people but on a low level.

14   http://www.computerweekly.com/Articles/2009/06/29/236681/google-mistakes-michael-jackson-searches-for-cyber-attack.htm 29th June 2009.

such a way that even the smallest abnormality in a system's operation is taken as an attack;

– cyberattacks may range from ordinary criminality or armed conflict;

– nothing resembles an attack more than another attack: criminal or war related, they may come in the same forms;

– attack strategies differ but are not immediately visible for the victims;

– cyberattacks may pursue many objectives: destruction, interference, chaos, and destabilization;

– more often than not, the creator of the attacks is an "invisible enemy", opening the door to all interpretations, fantasies, all discourses wishing to build up representations which fill a void. The invisible is not satisfying. To fight against what it represents, we must give it a body, we must be able to adapt this enemy, to describe it;

– the creators do not sign their work (or rarely);

– one target is no more important than another. Only the target allowing the fulfillment of the desired objectives is important;

– only a developed strategy can give a meaning to cyberattacks;

– cyberattacks raise the question of the use of technologies (new, or more conventional) as power tools. Now, the question is knowing how to use information and information systems to gain, but also to maintain and defend power, striking force, reconnaissance;

– cyberattacks represent questions of security for potential targets, sometimes presented as a matter of life or death (of the system, of a social model);

– before, cyberattacks were called "computer pirating". The name tends to be fading out, leaving space for a terminology which goes back to more violent, or war-like concepts. This linguistic derivative marks a progressive transition within our mindsets. Cyberattacks are no longer the only matter involved in cybercriminality and, therefore, civil justice. They call up political, diplomatic operation and they could call up military responses.

The palette of tools at the attacker's disposal is relatively well known: computer theft, destruction of hardware, data theft, intrusions, viruses and other malware, denial of service, identity theft, communication interception, glitches, etc. We all have access to this "palette" of tools, regardless of the actor. The hacktivist may use the same tools as the government bureau trying to spread propaganda. A mafia network might use botnets to launch spam or phishing operations, whereas an army might use botnets to launch attacks. Social engineering might also be used as much by an intelligence agency as by a business or a modern day Arsène Lupin acting alone. The means used are therefore not criteria for characterizing threatening actors, since they all share the same. More or less sophisticated, complex codes might be the signatures of specific individuals. But individuals or groups with large means are still potentially too large in number for us to be able to confirm, for example, that a complex program such as Stuxnet, was the doing of a State rather than a community of programmers or research bodies.

The tools at hand (or to be built) are used to lead actions fulfilling specific objectives[15]. The operatory modes and methods may be very different. We might be confronted with attacks that are:

– launched at random (launching a virus which spreads over the entire planet, without knowing who will be hit, when, what the impact will be, for how long);

– targeted (against a country, a business, an individual, an ideology, a political movement. The Stuxnet worm was, it has been said, intended to specifically strike SCADA systems, Siemens applications, and Iran);

– massive attacks (phishing, scam, spam, characteristics of cyberwar covering a wide range, but also propaganda operations which may want to be heard as much as possible);

– isolated (one against one, one against many or groups of many, but a potential attack);

– in waves (attacks on Estonia in 2007 happened in successive waves);

– direct or by rebound;

– left without a trace;

– looking to create more or less high secondary effects;

– led from the inside or outside;

– led from abroad;

– claimed, signed, anonymous;

– visible or invisible;

– highly portrayed in the media or, on the contrary, covered up;

– variable in power;

– of a variable level of complexity, as the complexity of the tools used is not a criterion of success, harm, capability to destroy, nor is it a signature (relatively

---

15 We therefore assume that there is no such thing as a free act.

simple tools are not reserved for small time actors; no more so than complex tools are only reserved for States). So that these tools are available on the shelves, and these shelves are available to the general public, it is becoming possible now to connect a certain behavior or type of tool to a certain type of actor;

– within a certain time frame;

– etc.

The advantage for security, if there is one, is that it does not really have to worry about the nature of the attacker, only the forms that the attacks might take. However, it must focus on the evolution of the different contexts (political, social, cultural, economic) which are likely to create new conditions which may favor attacks. The operatory modes and tools used by the actors of information warfare and cyberwar[16] are chosen according to their objectives, which are, remember, the following:

– destabilizing an adversary, temporarily or in the long term;

– weakening the adversary;

– paralyzing the adversary;

– observing our adversary;

– changing the adversary's behavior;

– altering the adversary's decision making process;

– isolating the enemy, cutting it off from the rest of the world;

– dominating information space;

– taking the lead in the OODA loop;

– seeing beyond the horizon;

– making the fog rise in the battlefield space;

– non-combat win;

– non-contact win.

Today we know that:

– attacks can be targeted;

– attacks can strike targets which are hardly connected to the Internet;

---

16 For definitions of these notions, see [VEN 07] and [VEN 11].

– large scale attacks (i.e. striking several types of actors at the same time, over one or several territories) can be envisaged using means such as botnets or long term operations;

– the means to react are rarely operational;

– in extreme situations (catastrophic situation) the authorities are rapidly overwhelmed;

– that means to react, if they even exist, probably fail through a lack of coordination;

– solidarity between States remains a pious wish and is limited for political reasons and sovereignty;

– the Internet can be cut off across a whole region or country by the authorities;

– physical attacks on infrastructures can cause as many interruptions as for software attacks;

– a number of actors do not have the means to protect themselves;

– the most dangerous attacks are not necessarily the most spectacular, visible, portrayed in the media, or the most violent;

– attacks on vital infrastructures are possible, if we are to believe the interpretations on the Stuxnet case and the tests carried out;

– cyberattacks must not only target computer systems, or just individuals, but most likely both;

– natural incidents may produce effects similar to human attacks;

– system malfunctions may look like attacks and vice versa;

– the effects of cyberattacks may be immediate or delayed;

– cyberattacks may have consequences (desired or not) on allies and more generally, third parties;

– the most efficient cyberattacks (efficiency being defined by reaching our objectives and not attracting media impact or striking thousands of targets, if this was not the aim), do not rely on the most modern, complex and powerful tools, but on those tools which are strictly necessary for fulfilling the objective.

Attack scenarios take all these factors into account.

Whatever the operations considered, one of the major factors is the consideration of the context in which they take place. In the Estonian case (2007), the context was ethnic tensions (Russians and Estonians living in the Estonian territory) and political tensions between Russia and its former satellite state. In the Ambalat crisis

(Indonesia), the context is still ethnic tensions, this time between the Malays and Indonesians. In the Xinjiang riots, the initial context was an ethnic crisis. When the Chinese were defacing American sites, the context was not the incident which triggered off the actions (spy plane shot down, bombed embassy), but the particular relationship which exists between the two giants, the USA and China (two cultural models, two different political systems: competition).

Within this context, an event occurred which threw oil onto the flames. In Estonia, this was a political decision (moving a statue of symbolic value). In Indonesia, this was the transfer of exploitation rights to a foreign oil company, on a territory of disputed sovereignty, claimed by both Malaysia and Indonesia. In China, this was provocations and attacks which lead to the Xinjiang riots, etc.

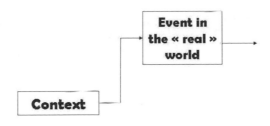

Figure 4.2. *"Context" as a model starting point*

This provocative event puts the actors in a position of confrontation: the crisis starts, develops, and may go as far as armed confrontation. In Estonia, the protests in the streets were violent. Between Indonesia and Malaysia, provocations and insults followed and military troops were sent in as intimidation. In Xinjiang, the riots left hundreds of deaths in their wake.

This tension, these confrontations in the "real" world may be accompanied and extended in cyberspace. Actions led by populations (protests, revolts) and by armed forces in a combat situation may also be extended in cyberspace. This use of cyberspace comes in the form of operational attacks and operational cyberwar.

The expression "confrontations in the real world" is developed concomitantly with "confrontations in cyberspace". In the real dimension, confrontations may take place on the diplomatic, political or military ground, with varying degrees of violence. The virtual world thus offers a new dimension to these confrontations, prolonging them, encouraging them, supporting them, fanning their flames. Cyberattacks are thus led in this virtual dimension (DDoS attacks, use of botnets, spreading viruses, attacks on adversary communication means, server and information system paralysis, misinformation campaigns, almost constant site defacements, and as many now well-known methods, grouped under the term of Computer Network Attacks (CNA), which have many different objectives. Let us recall her, in a non-exhaustive list: psychological operations, system destruction, influence, propaganda, weakening the adversary, winning international public opinion over to our own cause). The "confrontations in the virtual world" dimension may have its own identity. It may even end up making a move in the conventional political dimension. This was the case for Estonia, where cyberattacks practically made the political dimension and the street protests forgotten. Faced with the publicity on cyberattacks, there is no longer any talk of confrontations in the streets, or the fate of the communities who rose up.

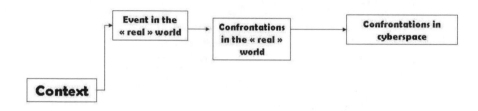

Figure 4.3. *Origins of the conflict*

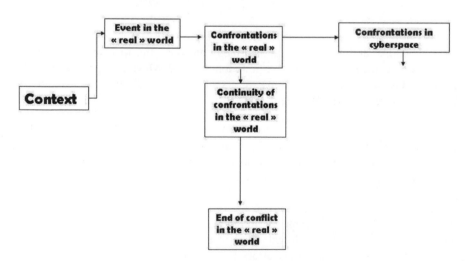

Figure 4.4. *Each dimension is developed*

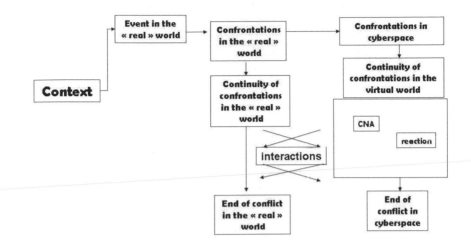

Figure 4.5. *Interaction between the two conflict dimensions*

Interactions are created between the two processes, "confrontations in the real world" and "confrontations in the virtual world". Cyberattacks may use military operations in the real world, and political decisions in the real work may trigger retaliation in the form of cyberattacks, for example.

Each of these processes may develop at their own pace: attacks in cyberspace might be led at a quicker pace than for confrontations in the real world, or on the contrary, extend after the crisis in the real world has apparently ended.

Conflicts reach their end, at least temporarily. Each process will reach its end: either because a solution was found, or because the limits of the process were reached. Two processes might end in sync with each other, but not necessarily. We may record, for instance, cyberattacks perpetrated as retaliations or because the feeling of injustice or vengeance lives on.

Each finished process will leave traces which will feed into the initial context and change it: leaving behind little pieces of history which stay in memories, changing power relations (in cases of victory/defeat, for example), heightening awareness of vulnerability, changing allies, etc.

Both expressions, "confrontations in the real world" and "confrontation in the virtual world" are two dimensions of a single conflict, which could have their own identity (specific actors, for example), their own way of proceeding, their own pace (not starting or finishing at the same time, not knowing the tensions at the same moment), their own consequences. One might have an end, the other might not, one might have a more or less high impact on the context or the conflict, on another dimension, and they might be different (imagine a conflict where asymmetry only exists in cyberspace and not in the real dimension).

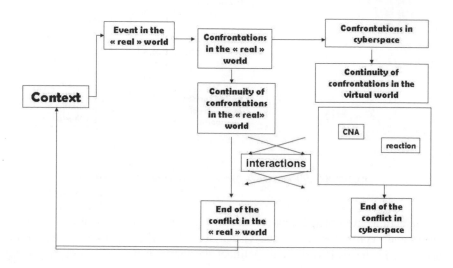

Figure 4.6. *Both dimensions feed the context*

The sequence of the two "real" and "virtual" components might be different when, for instance, virtual operations are carried out to prepare or even specifically to trigger a crisis or conflict. The "virtual" element will then come before the "real" one, in our diagram.

We could imagine cyberspace to be behind a conflict which is propagated or prolonged in the real world. Could a conflict in cyberspace only originate from this single space, independently of any consideration for the real world, and play out until its final end only in the virtual world?

This is the meaning given to the concept of cyberattack or strategic cyberwar. Thus, in our diagram, the cyberoperations on the right hand side are operational. Those on the left, remaining independent of the context of course, are strategic to the extent where they are not accompanied by actions in the real world.

For now, this last scenario is utopic. But whether a conflict starts or is prepared in cyberspace, or not, is indeed imaginable. We might consider a case where the event in cyberspace is used as the trigger, and thus results in virtual confrontations, able to open up or be accompanied by confrontation processes in the real world. Cyberattacks are still operational in the real world and are non-tactical. They aim to accompany, even if it is by coming before them, operations in the real world. This is not a cyberwar, but cyber confrontations which prepare an attack in the real world. For example, we refer to the attacks on Iraq led by the USA before launching their military operations on the ground.

Absolute cyberwar is when the context is entirely cybernetic, the cybernetic spark, the pursuit of uniquely cybernetic confrontations. This is cyberwar in isolation, away from the other dimensions, which is hardly imaginable, due to the cyberspace/real world interdependence.

Each input on the diagram must then be considered as an element of conflict or crisis, which we must be in a position to act on, to intervene, to influence the sequence of the loop and its exit. Decision makers, commands and C2s have a certain number of "cursors" which are the means enabling us to modify these components. These cursors, are, for example, military interventions, media interventions, and political decisions.

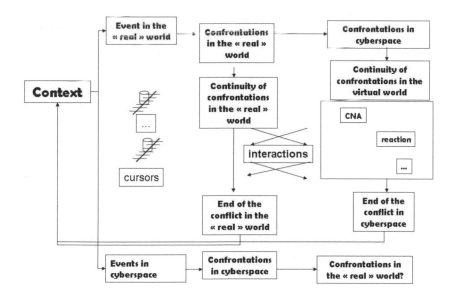

Figure 4.7. *Components and cursors*

We will use the Ambalat crisis as an example, although there are many others, where Indonesia and Malaysia were in opposition in 2005[17], a period when politicians played the role of the stop/go control button. The beginning and end of the tensions and hostile exchanges generally depend on the politician's statements, decisions, stances and attitudes.

When a political decision maker calls populations to be calm and reserved, it is to decreases the tension levels. When the politician decides to move a statue (Estonian case), fully aware of the risks that a symbolic gesture might have on social peace within a context of ethnic tension, then a choice has clearly been made, sounding out the beginning of the violence. The stop/go button was pressed. When politicians decide to deal with problems using treaties, it is in the hope of putting an end to these tensions, the sources of confrontations, crises and combats. The political decision is the essential cursor.

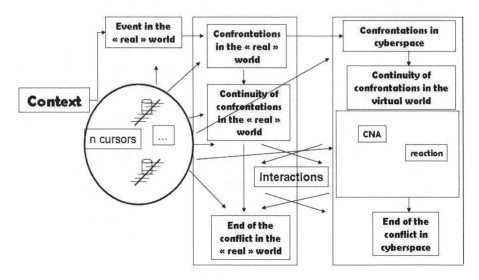

Figure 4.8. *Cursors acting on components*

As for the press, the media, and websites, they play their traditional role of voice box/spokes person. This is the "volume level/control" button. We are not saying that the media decide on the intensity of the battles, but that in a number of situations, particularly ethnic conflict battles, they play an important role.

---

17 Conflict of sovereignty on a maritime space.

Of course, the politician also holds the "volume" cursor because he can decide whether to turn the intensity up or not on these confrontations, and whether to deploy more troops on the ground.

Regarding C2 (command and control), we go back to the question of activating the cursors or not. But within this flow chart, things would be too simple if this were just the case as non-state governed, uncontrollable actors come to be involved in the crisis or conflict's sequence. These actors have their own logics, motives, interests, stakes, objectives and strategies. The hacktivist, whose intervention may be involved in the playing out of a crisis, does not fix the same objectives or stakes as the main actors in this crisis. When hackers become involved in international conflicts (hacking into enemy information systems as self-proclaimed warriors or soldiers), their actions might, however, be more detrimental than useful to the actors in the conflict, by creating a fog of information through their untimely intervention.

In this process, we can replace the OODA (observe, orient, decide, act) loop. Speed plays a determining role here. It is a question of leading, not only on the loop, but also in the materialization of each of its components, taken to be independent loops. Power, success, victory, will go to those who act before and quicker than the others, forcing the adversary to react. The model that we designed here is thus a sequence of OODA loops.

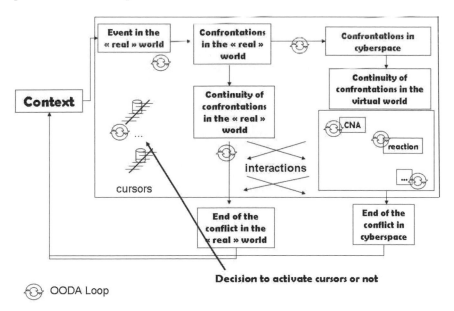

Figure 4.9. *Integrating the OODA loop*

A crisis or conflict will have its own processes. Two distinct conflicts will have two distinct processes. However one or many actors from process 1 may find themselves in process 2, related to another conflict. Interferences and interactions are, on the other hand, possible between the processes of different conflicts. Therefore, at a certain moment, we can imagine a crossing over between the processes of two previously distinct conflicts.

Reading and understanding a cyberattack type incident may prove difficult. Is the attack, that we think is related to the context and process 1, related more to another context and another process?

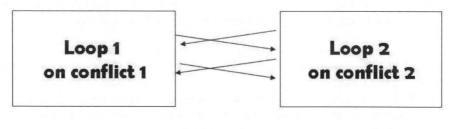

Figure 4.10. *Interaction between two a priori distinct processes. We call the described process the "loop", because it closes by feeding the initial context*

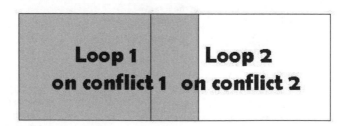

Figure 4.11. *Possible intersection between a priori distinct loops*

The utility of this formulation as a process or sequence of processes and loops, is in the ability to replace cyberattacks in a context or chain of actions, and not to consider them as isolated elements. It also means that the components of an entire situation can be arranged and we can understand that cyberattacks are not an unavoidable fact and that protection through reinforcing the security of information systems is not the only way to be secure. Without a doubt, there are cursors that can be activated in order to prevent cyberattacks from happening or striking us.

We look for the cause of a cyberattack and the immediate context seems to offer satisfying responses. In the Estonia case, the context might be constructed by the nature of relations with Russia. But it is, perhaps, more generated by the NATO-Russia relationship. Cyberattacks can be associated with two processes.

The model we propose raises many questions:

– How do we break the reiteration of the loop constituted by the entire process?

– How do we break the process, where, and by what means?

– How do we make cyberconflict stop?

– Will stopping or influencing the course of a confrontation in information space make it possible to stop/change/influence the confrontation in tangible space?

– Vice versa, will stopping/changing a confrontation in tangible space influence the confrontation in virtual space in the long term?

– What is the respective impact of changing the components of a confrontation in relation to each other? How are tangible/intangible confrontations linked? Which cursors are involved and influence each other?

– Is it possible to manage the various components of the model independently?

– To what extent does the sequence of events in the virtual world contribute to changing the original context?

– What are the major interactions/interferences within the loop?

– Which cursors modulate the intensity, other than the media?

   - the object of the confrontation: more or less "sensitive", subject to consequences, involving the sovereignty, values, etc.,

   - the actors: motives, organization, relations with the law, values, impact, status (military, non-military);

– What is the dimension of the process which must be stopped as a priority: the virtual or the real?

4.1.1.2. *Cyberdefense*

Since 2007, undoubtedly the consequences of the Estonian case, not only in Europe, we are assisting with the implementation of new policies and strategies for cybersecurity and defense which are accompanied by the creation of agencies or specialized units:

– the US Cyber Command was launched in May 2010, managed by General Keith Alexander;

- within the US Cyber Command was Army Cyber Command was created (ARCYBER) in October 2010, which centralizes the US Army's means in protecting its networks, involving some 21,000 soldiers and civilians[18];

– the 24th Air Force, on the Lackland base (Texas, USA) which is the Air Force's cyber unit, was created in August 2009. It has been fully operational since October 2010 and responsible for defending the Air Force's network from cyberattacks[19].

The USA is not the only country in the world with specialized units:

– Germany created a cyberwar unit, installed in the city of Rheinbach in 2009[20]. In February 2011, it set up a national cybersecurity council, responsible for coordination operations from the national defense center in Bonn. It made the police, intelligence services and the armies cooperate. The Stuxnet affair was proposed as an argument to justify a necessary improvement in the coordination, of the consideration of real risks, everything based on the knowledge that, with Stuxnet, security was not at its highest level. Above all, critics see an opportunity to bring police and intelligence services together, to the detriment of the principle of separating these powers.

– The Netherlands published a new cybersecurity strategy in February 2011, announcing the creation of a National Center for Cyber Security. The country also put the Stuxnet case forward, a recent incident, as an example of the threats which weigh down on information systems. Memories are short. Each incident has its own wave of strategies, politics, statements, and organizations being created. Estonia is already nearly forgotten in the discussion.

– In 2010, South Korea created a center of command for cyberwar, to counter possible attacks coming from North Korea and China[21]. The unit was composed of

18 http://www.defensesystems.com/Articles/2010/10/15/Cyber-Defense-Army-Cyber-command .aspx.
19   http://www.signonsandiego.com/news/2010/oct/01/air-force-declares-cyberwarfare-unit-operational/#.
20 http://benmazzotta.wordpress.com/2009/02/11/new-german-cyber-warfare-unit/.
21 http://www.theregister.co.uk/2010/01/12/korea_cyberwarfare_unit/.

200 engineers responsible for countering the some 95,000 daily attacks on the army's networks.

– North Korea, according to South Korean intelligence services, has units specialized in cyberattacks. The number of engineers is unknown.

– In 2010, Switzerland had plans to create two units dedicated solely to cyberwar within the Centre des Opérations Electroniques de l'Organisation de Soutien au Commandement des Forces Armées (electronic operations service for the organization of support in the armed forces command) [CAV 10][22].

– In January 2011, the Estonian Ministry of Defense proposed creating cyberdefense units based on the expertise in the country's computer technician communities. This unit operates within parliamentary forces, a voluntary organization co-financed by the Ministry of Defense, helping to guarantee the country's defense. The activities of this unit are led together with NATO's center of excellence in Tallinn[23].

– In March 2009, the UK announced the creation of a unit dedicated to cyberwar[24], the Cyber Security Operations Centre – CSOC, within the GCHC. The centre was staffed with just under 20 people. In January 2011, General Sir David Richards expressed the desire to create a cyber command, based on the American model, protecting the country from cyberattacks, and being capable of launching its own cyberattacks. This approach was written into the extended conclusions in the Strategic Defense and Security Review in the UK in October 2010[25].

– Israel created Unit 8200 based in the Negev desert.

– We are giving Iran the willpower to develop cyberwar capabilities. But this is only one State amongst 30, 40 or 120 other States (the figures change over time and according to the sources used) supposed to have or want to have cyberattack capabilities.

– France's "LIO/LID" policy assumes the implementation of specialized means lending themselves to cyberwar units. ANSSI (France's national agency of

---

22 Defensive units, the first one in the form of a military CERT which must be coordinated with the GovCERT. But the Center of Electronic Operations must also implement a CNO cell. From a legal point of view, CNDs are legal, but CNAs and CNEs are only legal in a state of attack. This means that Switzerland has made it forbidden to use CNAs other than in a situation of war, if its systems are attacked.

23 http://www.defensenews.com/story.php?i=5556484.

24 http://www.theregister.co.uk/2009/11/12/csoc_date/.

25 http://www.direct.gov.uk/prod_consum_dg/groups/dg_digitalassets/@dg/@en/documents/digitalasset/dg_191634.pdf?CID=PDF&PLA=furl&CRE=sdsr.

information systems security) was created by the decree of July 7th 2009, and its powers were increased by the decree of February 11th 2011[26].

– In March 2011, Australia announced the creation of a specialist unit within its intelligence system[27], whose mission is to lead enquiries on state-governed cyberattacks, and identifying cyber threats.

– China is reputed to have had specialized units for over 10 years now, if we believe in the American reports. Beijing also accused Taiwan of leading cyberattacks using specialist military units.

– NATO has 15 centers of excellence, one of which is dedicated to cyberdefense cooperative (CCDCOE), an attack prevention center.

The nature of these units and centers is very different from one example to the next. There are civilian units, military units, others which unmistakably have their motives in war (and therefore attacks), and others which are for defense. Whatever the case may be, there are more and more States displaying their strategies and implementing cyberdefense methods, which are underlying the possibility of leading confrontations. States are preparing for war. No one wants to be at a disadvantage. The fact of the matter is that this dynamic contributes the weaponization of cyberspace, even if – a little like for nuclear strategies – each side swears that they will never be the first to use their capabilities for an attack.

To prepare or refine security and defense, many actors regularly carry out tests, variable sized exercises which involve a sometimes high number of participants (civilians, soldiers, private and public actors, those from industry, defense and security, etc.). The objectives of the exercises consist of testing the reliability of existing systems and processes, identifying flaws, testing the feasibility of particular operations and improving the performance of the systems currently in place. These exercises also transpose into the real sphere everything which has just been put onto paper, theorized on or model up until now. Security exercises test resistance and the fortress's capabilities.

Such high magnitude security exercises do not come without their risks. Military maneuvers may sometimes end in disaster: the sinking of the Russian submarine Koursk in 2000, flight 655 from Iran Air, shot down by USS Vincennes in the Persian Gulf in 1998, the unexplained sinking of the ferry "Estonia" in the Baltic

26 ANSSI, the birth of the French Cyber Command. 15th February 2011. http://www.linformaticien.com/Actualit%C3%A9s/tabid/58/newsid496/10342/anssi-aissance-du-cybercommand-francais/Default.aspx.
27 Australian Security Intelligence Organisation (ASIO).

Sea *en route* from Tallinn to Stockholm at the end of September 1994[28]. We even sometimes read that the 9/11 attacks in the US and on the London Underground on July 7th 2005 occurred when, at the same time, security exercises based on scenarios very similar to those attacks were taking place. Some propose that the simulations are just decoys, masking the real act wanting to be committed[29]. Such exercises may mobilize resources at the same time as real incidents occur: the concomitance of both test and reality may disturb the vision of this reality.

Name of exercise	Organiza tion and country involved	Date	Content and conclusions
Eligible Receiver	USA	1997	Objective: measuring the vulnerability of the government's IT systems. This exercise involved the USA NSA and DoD. 35 agents from the NSA were sent across the globe with the mission of launching attacks on American information systems, only using tools bought legally via the Internet. In less than 2 weeks, all 35 agents had taken control of 911 systems, and had attacked 41,000 out of the Pentagon's 100,000 machines [ADA 01].The exercise demonstrated how easy it was to get into the Pentagon's networks, and to familiarize themselves with its emergency systems, for example.

---

28 http://www.alterinfo.net/Quand-des-exercices-d-antiterrorisme-tournent-au-vinaigre-11-9,-attentats-de-Londres-et-naufrage-de-l-Estonia_a18224.html. This unexplained sunk ship happened at the same time as the military exercises. The day before the accident, Estonia was also the area of an anti-terrorism exercise, whose scenario was a bomb attack.
29 http://www.alterinfo.net/Les-trois-villes-des-etats-Unis-les-plus-susceptibles-d-etre-la-cible-d-attaque-sous-fausse-banniere-en-2008_a17134.html In this article, it is mentioned that on September 11th 2001, an agency of the American Ministry of Defense and the CIA led a terrorist attack scenario, where an imaginary airplane coming from Dulles International Airport in Washing crashed on one of the four towers of the National Reconnaissance Office, in the suburb of Chantilly in Virginia, a few miles west of the Pentagon.

Blue Cascades	USA	2002	First exercise in North America (USA and Canada) involving the public sector and private businesses (the Navy, FEMA, the Canadian Office of Critical Infrastructure Protection, Verizon, Boeing, etc.). Conclusion: governments underestimate their dependency on information technologies.
Black Ice	USA	November 2002	Exercise led in preparation for the Olympic Games in Utah. The exercise was sponsored by the Department of Energy. It showed how a terrorist attack would be worsened by simulataneous cyberattacks.
Digital Pearl Harbor	USA	2002	Organized by the Naval War College. Conclusions: to launch a decisive and large scale attack, hackers should have $200m and at least 5 years to lead the offensive well. As many say that it is possible. Conclusions also say that such an attack would not lead to death or catastrophic losses[30].
Silent Horizon	USA (CIA, NSA)	May 2005	Assessing the way in which the government and businesses react to attacks led via the Internet: who assumes responsibility of defense? In theory, this is the State's role, but a large portion of the defense infrastructures are the property of private telecommunication companies, which makes the task more complex still.
Operation Liver-wire	USA	2005	Cyberterrorism exercise organized by the DHS. Questions the role of the government in a cyberattack situation.

---

30 Some might say the opposite. See the article "Cyberterror – potential for mass effect", in *IANewsletter*, vol. 4, no. 4, Winter 01/02. http://iac.dtic.mil/iatac "One incident can have a catastrophic ripple effect around the globe".

Cyber Storm I war game	USA	6th-10th February 2006	Coordinated by the DHS, involving 115 government agencies and businesses[31]. The exercise tests the away in which leaders respond and react to a cyberattack with high national implications. To make the exercise as realistic as possible, a number of people were unaware of the situation and thought they were being confronted with a real incident.
Han Kuang[32]	Taiwan	April 2007	5 day long exercise, simulating a Chinese attack. Exercise on a computerized simulation platform[33].
APCERT Drill 2007	Pacific Asia[34]	November 2007	Scenario of a cyberattack aiming to cause chaos at the Beijing Olympic Games
Cyber Storm II war game	USA	March 2008 (5 days)	CDX coordinated by the NSA.
8th Annual Cyber Defense Exercise (CDX)[35]	USA	April 2008	Organized by the NSA

31 This experiment was developed by the independent study group from the American Bipartisan Policy Center (BPC), with the help of the ex-director of the CIA, Michael Hayden. Its objective? Sensitizing the American government and opinion on the country's vulnerability in the face of cyberattacks. The trailer for the event was available on YouTube: http://www.youtube.com/watch?v=8xpV5JjnEdE. The exercise was organized in a hotel room, the Mandarin Oriental in Washington. Amongst the high ranking officials involved were: the ex-Director of National Intelligence (DNI), John Negroponte, ex-secretary to the Internal Security for ex-president George. W. Bush, Michael Chertoff, ex-director of the CIA, John McLaughlin or even the senator Bennett Johnson. To face the rise of cyberattacks head on, after the attack on Google, the White House decided to define new strategies, according to the *New York Times*. It also plans to put a new unit into action, the United States Cyber Command. If it is backed by Congress, then it will be managed by General Keith B. Alexander, head of the NSA.

32 http://www.taipeitimes.com/News/taiwan/archives/2007/04/22/2003357691.

33 This is not testing cyberattack scenarios, but using computerized platforms which simulate attack scenarios by the Chinese army along the Taiwan coasts, underwater confrontations, air attacks, missile shots, etc.

34 Participating countries: Australia, Brunei, China, Hong Kong, India, Japan, Malaysia, Singapore, South Korea, Taiwan, Thailand, Vietnam. The exercise was organized and coordinated by the Malaysian Computer Emergency Response Team (MyCERT), CyberSecurity Malaysia, in collaboration with the Australia Computer Emergency Response Team (AusCERT) and the Singapore Computer Emergency Response Team (SingCERT).

Cyber Coalition 2008[36]	NATO	November 2008	Exercise is limited to NATO. Scenario includes multiple cyberattacks launched simultaneously against NATO members.
Estonian-Swedish Cyber Defense exercise[37]	Estonia, Sweden	6th December 2008	The exercise is carried out by students at the Tallinn University of Technology
APCERT Drill 2008	Pacific Asia[38]	December 2008	Simulation of cyberattack destabilizing the regional economy
Cyber War Games	USA	2nd April 2009	Cyber war games, organized at the beginning of 2009 by the DHS control Systems Analysis Center, simulating attacks on critical infrastructures (chemical industry, in particular), and grouping together 40 participants from 12 countries (USA, Australia, Canada, Finland, France, Germany, Hungary, Italy, Japan, the Netherlands, New Zealand, Sweden)[39]. During these exercises, the teams were responsible for protecting the infrastructures against hacker attacks.
Cyber Defense Exercises – CDX[40]	USA	21st to 24th April 2009	Experts from the NSA, American military schools, and teams from the Air Force of Institute of Technology took part in the exercises[41].

35 CDX: Cyber Defense Exercise http://www.wired.com/politics/security/news/2008/05/nsa_cyberwargames.

36 http://www.ccdcoe.org/212.html.

37 http://www.ccdcoe.org/91.html.

38 Brunei joins the exercise. The APCERT Drill 2008 was organized by the Malaysian Computer Emergency Response Team (MyCERT), CyberSecurity Malaysia, in collaboration with the Australian Computer Emergency Response Team (AusCERT). The exercise involved 13 countries: Australia, Brunei, China, Hong Kong, India, Japan, Malaysia, Singapore, South Korea, Taiwan, Thailand, Sri Lanka and Vietnam.

39 https://inlportal.inl.gov/portal/server.pt?open=514&objID=1269&mode=2&featurestory=DA_327137.

40 Exercise won by the Air Force Academy in 2006, in 2007-2008-2009 by West Point, in 2010 by the U.S. Naval Academy.

41 http://www.afit.edu/en/ccr/news.cfm?na=detail&ncat=CCR&item=206. In 2009, for the first time, soldiers from an ally nation took part in the exercise (Royal Military College of Canada).

Cyber Coalition 2009	NATO	12th-13th November 2009	CDX sponsored by NATO
Cyber ShockWave	USA	February 16th 2010	Exercise led nationally. One of the striking conclusions is the the state of unpreparedness on behalf of the USA to confront large scale cyberattacks[42].
Initiative Three Exercise[43]	USA (DHS)	March 2010	Tests the deployment of new technological solutions which could be introduced into the security program, EINSTEIN.
10th Annual Cyber Defense Exercise (CDX)[44]	USA (NSA)	20th-23rd April 2010	Organized by the NSA[45]. The command center was installed at Greenbelt, at Lockhead Martin (one of the NSA's security solution providers). The exercise was awarded to the Navy. The competition for the exercise was out of the West Point Military Academy, the US Air Force, the United States Merchant Marine Academy and the Air Force Institute of Technlogy.
Baltic Cyber Shield (BCS) Cyber Defence Exercise 2010[46]	CCDCOE (Tallinn) and SNDC (Swedish National Defense College), NATO	May 2010	Cyberdefense exercise (CDX), setting 6 blue teams against a single red team each other. The aim was to improve understanding of the cyber environment and, in particular, the security of critical infrastructures and SCADA systems, and also to increase the capabilities of a necessary cooperation in terms of cyberdefense. The cooperation between agencies, and public and private sectors is not improvised: the way in which these cooperations are developed must be understood.

42 http://www.bipartisanpolicy.org/sites/default/files/Final%20Cyber%20Brochure.pdf.
43 http://www.dhs.gov/xlibrary/assets/privacy/privacy_pia_nppd_initiative3exercise.pdf.
44 http://uscybercom-watch.blogspot.com/2010/04/navy-wins-cyber-defense-exercise-trophy.html.
45 http://homelandsecuritynewswire.com/national-security-agency-holds-2010-cyber-defense-exercise.
46 http://www.ccdcoe.org/publications/BCS2010AAR.pdf.

Piranet 2010	France	23th-24th June 2010	The States is trained to meet a large scale computer system attack head on[47]. Organized by the SGDSN.
Cyber Storm III	USA (DHS)	September 2010	Tests the capability of facing a cyberattack. The following countries were part of the exercise: USA, Australia, New Zealand, Canada, and the UK. European countries and Japan were also invited to take part.
Operation Cyber Forward	USA	16th October 2010	Exercise carried out in Fairfax (Viginia, USA), within the network warfare branch of the Virginia National Guard Data Processing Unit[48]. The first cyberdefense exercise worked at Unit level, testing a unit's capabilities of anticipating, identifying and responding to unauthorized access to the US Army's networks.
Cyber Europe 2010	22 EU Member States	4th November 2010	Tests organized by l'ENISA and the CCR[49].
Cyber Coalition 2010[50]	NATO	16th – 18th November 2010	Exercise led from the NATO center in Mons. The objective is to test to decision making processes, the responsibility circuits in cyberdefense, and the methods for collaboration between NATO member countries. The official page on the NATO website confirms that the results are highly satisfying, with the systems in place making it possible to react when faced with incidents, and to demonstrate the capability of those involved to collaborate.

Table 4.4. *Cybersecurity, cyberdefense and cyberattack exercises[51]*

---

47 http://www.ssi.gouv.fr/site_article248.html.
48 http://www.ng.mil/news/archives/2010/11/110310-cyber.aspx.
49 http://www.generation-nt.com/cyber-europe-2010-exercice-cybersecurite-avec-320-news wire-1112181.html.
50 http://www.nato.int/cps/en/SID-1CC2A18E-31A193DB/natolive/news_69805.htm.

For us, one of the main flaws in real life exercises is the absence of surprise[52] and the relative confidence in everything taking place. In fact, the essential ingredients which characterize real attacks are missing here: surprise, shock, stress, fear, panic and chaos.

Faced with growing threats (or presented as such in media and official discussion) in the cybernetic domain, in businesses, States, and armies, we have been led to face large scale attacks head on for many years now. The tests are often led globally and aim to test the resistance of existing organizations to attacks.

4.1.1.3. *Cyberwar*

The neologism "cyberwar" has diverse meanings. The two terms which make up the word are equally as polysemous: "war" has many definitions, as indeed does its prefix, "cyber".

Sometimes not suitable for the objects it is supposed to describe, the concept is often subject to confusions. The hacking of servers, either State-governed or belonging to businesses, blamed on hackers – not always Chinese for that matter – is often classed as cyberwar. This is the same case for the wave of site defacements occurring during specific events such as a major crisis or an armed conflict. Defacements happen in ordinary times also, and during periods of politically intense activity. We only have to scour the sites of the international media to realize this.

Let us cite a definition of the Internet at random. The site Qfinance Dictionary for example, describes cyberwar as the use of information systems such as the Internet to exploit or attack the adversary's computer control processes[53]. From such a simple definition, we take from this that:

– the Internet is not the only vector of cyberwar;

– actors are adversaries;

– actions are limited to aiming at computerized systems;

---

51 There are cybersecurity exercises (national security) aiming to identify flaws and capabilities in security systems and national infrastructures (capability to detect an attack and to confront it), and war game type exercises (computerized warfare simulations), more specifically intended for army formation.
52 As an example, see the preparatory operations schedule such as was published in a report by the CIA and the NSA, more than 6 months before the exercise http://knight.segfaults.net/EE579/CDX2011Directive%20v1_0.pdf.
53 Qfinance Dictionary, 2010, http://www.qfinance.com/dictionary.

– there are at least 2 targets: the information system, and the adversary linked to this information system[54].

However, the approach is imprecise and raises many questions:

– What is an adversary?

– What is the origin of the attack?

– Is this really a definition of cyberwar? Does it not relate more to cyberattacks?

– Are the adversary's information systems really the target of cyberwar?

– Who is this adversary?

– When does cyberwar take place?

– What are the factors triggering a cyberwar?

Let us remember how J. Arquilla and D. Rondfelt defined cyberwar in 1993 in their famous article, "Cyberwar is Coming!": "Cyberwar refers to conducting, and preparing to conduct, military operations according to information-related principles. It means disrupting if not destroying the information and communications systems, broadly defined to include even military culture, on which an adversary relies in order to 'know' itself: who it is, where it is, what it can do when, why it is fighting, which threats to counter first, etc. It means trying to know all about an adversary while keeping it from knowing much about oneself".

For J. Arquilla and D. Rondfelt, cyberwar is a war of knowledge. "It means turning the 'balance of information and knowledge' in one's favor, especially if the balance of forces is not". This form of war is closer to the concept of information warfare, since it encompasses means of reconnaissance, communication interception and electronic fog. But what differentiates it from former concepts, is that it must not be considered as a simple set of technology based measures.

Cyberwar is a true transformation of the nature of war. It involves organizations as much as technology, and man is the permanent link with technology ("machine"). This first rough definition, which does not focus on the "cyberspace" dimension, confirms further that speed is not the essential or only characteristic of these new forms of war. "In some situations, combat may be waged fast and from afar, but in many other situations, it may slow and close-in; and new combinations of far and close and fast and slow may be the norm, not one extreme or the other".

---

54 We will come back to this notion of target later. Targeting and reaching target 1, a technical target, does not automatically mean that target 2, *a priori* a human target, will be disrupted, struck, destroyed. Everything depends on the degree of dependency on resistance, resilience between the two.

Currently, theoreticians and analysts of conflicts in or with cyberspace seem obsessed by the concepts of speed (everything should happen at the speed of light) and distancing (targets can hit from afar, across the planet). It is rare to speak of resorting to cyberconflict to attack nearby adversaries, or to include long term operations.

From their discussion on the subject, we also understand that cyberwar does not necessarily mean resorting to high-tech means, and the arms race is therefore frantic. Useful tools (weapons?) are simply necessary tools. There is no need for important, superior, costly means, just suitable, adapted, sufficient ones. "Cyberwar may actually be waged with low technology under some circumstances".

Other approaches, perhaps less expert ones[55], simply confirm that cyberwar is a "type of war" where computer systems are used to damage or destroy the enemy's systems. Cyberwar is sometimes considered as a synonym for information warfare [MEL 09][56] or a sub-set of information warfare. Cyberwar is a war of information led by regular military forces[57].

This approach was introduced by Martin Libicki, and widely adopted afterwards. This sub-set involves actions carried out in the cybernetic world [PAR 01]. Cyberspace is therefore a sub-set of information space, a place of information warfare. With cyberwar being limited to cyberspace, it is, then, a sub-set of information warfare. The place where this war plays out is the cyber world, defined as any virtual reality contained within a set of networks and computers.

This cyber world is characterized by the fact that it is composed of several sub-sets[58], with the most important one being the Internet and its related networks. Furthermore, cyberwar is defined as a combination of CNA + CND and information operations[59]. Thus, cyberwar is characterized, for a military oriented approach, by combinations whose rules must be defined.

Documents from military doctrine consider cyberwar as one of the forms or components of information warfare. Let us the example of the Indian Army's approach which, in its 2004 doctrine, defined cyberwar as the set of "techniques enabling destruction, damage, exploitation or compromise of the enemy's computer systems. Cyberwar includes attacks known as hacking, on enemy computer networks. Computer hacking has evolved in such a way that it is possible to

---

55 MacMillan Dictionary, 2010, http://www.macmillandictionary.com.
56 Also see http://www.psycom.net/iwar.2.html (2010) and http://www.thefreedictionary.com /cyberwar (2010).
57 *RAND Review*, vol. 22, no. 2, 1998-1999, USA.
58 [PAR 01] "There are many cyber worlds", p. 122.
59 [PAR 01], p. 122

interfere with information stored in or passing through computer networks, in order to damage the adversary's C2 structure" [IAD 04].

In the same military vein, the Tradoc document (US Army) dated February 22nd 2010 [TRA 10] also considers cyberwar as a constitutive building block, in fact here it is one of the four components of cyber operations (CyberOps), alongside cyber network operations (CyNetOps), cyber support (CyberSpt), and cyber situational awareness (CyberSA). Cyberwar is an operational component (and therefore non-strategic). The term "cyberwar" in this text is, in fact, a contraction of the term "cyberspace warfare".

A 2010 report by the CSS states that the concept of cyberwar only covers a small part of all cybernetic attacks. "Cyberwar" is therefore a sub-set of all the existing forms of cyberattack [CAV 10]. Cyberwar is also a sub-concept [CSS 10], a sub-set of cyberconflict.

Cyberwar and war are often tightly linked. There can be no cyberwar if there is not war to start with [SCH 08]. For a cyberattack to be classed as cyberwar or an act of cyberwar, then it must figure in the framework of military operations.

"Cyberwars are currently defined as computerized attacks which accompany physical military operations to destroy the enemy's military forces, or which originate from political conflicts between nations" [DAN 10]. The 2010 DoD lexicon proposes the following: cyberwar is an "armed conflict led entirely or partly by cybernetic means. Military operations led to deny an adverse force the efficient use of cyberspace systems and weapons during a conflict. Cyberwar includes cyberattack and cyberdefense" [JCS 10].

Cyberwar is a form of war which, through its singularities (its asymmetrical capabilities, mainly), seems closer to terrorism and guerilla warfare than conventional warfare [BAR 10]. Moreover, it can be considered as an art, in the same way as war. Cyberwar is considered as a force intensifier for some (a complement to conventional warfare, a support function), and a strategic tool for others (making it possible to be militarily engaged, to win the war through other means).

Cyberwar as a force intensifier, corresponds to the Russian approach. For Martin Libicki[60], operational cyberwar is a support function, such as air warfare was throughout the 20th Century. Cyberwar is a war within a war.

---

60 [LIB 09], p. xviii.

"A pure cyberwar – where cyber weapons are used – is unlikely. Future wars and previous skirmishes will be a mixture of conventional or kinetic weapons, and cyber weapons used as a subversive or force intensifier" [SOM 11].

Pure cyberwar, which only takes place in cyberspace and which is commonly considered as being utopic, is simply a natural complement to contemporary and future wars. These will be a mix of conventional, kinetic and cybernetic weapons. Cyberwar will play the role of a force intensifier. Cyberwar will not replace short wars [MUR 99]. "It completes it, supports it, re-organizes it. The cyber warrior does not replace the warrior." Traditional operations, contrary to common knowledge, could also be, in turn, force intensifiers of cyberwar [SHA 10].

Cyberwar, as a strategic tool, corresponds to the Chinese approach. It consists of controlling an adversary without needing to use physical engagement on the battle ground. Paraphrasing Chinese strategists, Richard Bejtlich[61] considers cyberwar as a means of making the enemy submit without using traditional combat. This reminds us of the Sun Tzu Treaty which sees the height of the art of warfare in making the enemy submit with using combat. This tells us that cyberwar could be entirely virtual, without using the real world, without resorting to lethal weapons. This is a way of winning the war using other means. It specifies, however, that "cyberwar is real". The virtual is real, it is not a myth, and what happens there has immediate implications for the real world.

Cyberwar is sometimes presented as a major risk, sometimes undervalued in its supposed effects. Cyberwar thus has little strategic value and a low capability to cause real damage.

In the military domain, cyberwar is a strategic war which can be used as a principal method for reaching strategic objectives. Strategic cyberwar is defined across the whole spectrum of cases, from the strategic level to the tactical level [SHA 10][62]. The concept of protecting the national infrastructure – particularly its critical components – against attacks is also called "cyberwar" and in a wider context, strategic information warfare [MOL 96].

In the current state of knowledge, it seems that highly aimed attacks are still too complex to be implemented. If we are able to aim an attack, then it is still dangerous to predict the consequences of it. The attack could become one of the attack's indirect victims. Due to this risk, the concept of strategic cyberwar is still in the

---

61 Tao Security Blog, http://taosecurity.blogspot.com/.
62 Amit Sharma, author of the article where this definition was taken from, is an Indian expert on security and defense. He carried out some of his studies at the UK Defense Academy. He is a researcher within the Indian Ministry of Defense.

theoretical domain. As an example of this risk, we inform readers of the misadventure which happened to the new American Cyber Command, in around 2010 [BEA 10].

Cyberwar remains tightly bound to reality, because it may have physical, material consequences, and may cost the lives of humans [SHI 01]. Peter Sommer considers that "true cyberwar is an event whose characteristics are those of conventional cyberwar, but which takes place exclusively in cyberspace [SOM 11]. But this type of war is highly unlikely.

We can comprehend cyberwar by considering what it is *not*:

– cyberwar cannot be simplified to cyberespionage, no more than war could be reduced to espionage;

– above all, cyberwar is not a fixed, defined object with precise and unchanging contours;

– cyberwar cannot be summarized as the simple defacement of websites belonging to rival nations, organizations or political movements [SHI 01];

– cyberwar must not be a matter for hackers and hacktivists. A letter dated on January 7th 1999 signed by German hacker groups, group 2600, the Chaos Computer Club, the Cult of the Dead Cow, recalled the declaration of cyberwar (referring to a process of the one by the group Legion of the Underground at the end of 1998 which had "declared war" on Chinese and Iraqi governments to punish their lack of respect for human rights), was a wholly irresponsible act by the hackers, recalling that cyberwar had nothing to do with ethnic hacking. The argument consists of stating that we cannot fight against repressive States regarding information by contributing to the destruction or disturbance of these information systems;

– cyberwar is not a cold war [STI 10].

There are those who consider that, simply, cyberwar does not exist. For these people, the computerization of the army and society does not open up a new battlefield. Cyberwar, for those people, is just a fantasy, a utopia, an object of science fiction. An article published on the BBC website was even entitled "Cyberwar or Science Fiction" in connection with the Stuxnet case [FEI 10]. Whereas we do not know if cyberwar even exists or is really possible, States invest massively in protection against cyber threats [FEI 10].

4.1.1.4. *Confrontations in the information dimension (CID)*

"Thinking (wrongly) that all conflicts are like wars, then we are giving social existence an entirely aggressive character" [ARO 76].

Not all conflicts are war, but we are indeed lacking in words when we must describe certain operations or events which use methods of the art of warfare, ranging from conflicts in cyberspace, confrontations between individuals or groups, on States or between States sometimes. These are not war but, in fact, cyberwar.

Lifting ambiguities involves proposing new more precise terminology, combined with specific configurations. Lifting ambiguities would result in more peaceful discourses. This is because we cannot speak about cyberwar without immediately thinking of war, and then imagining all sorts of fantastical situations and imperfect visions which may influence political decision makers on the highest levels.

We thus introduce the concept of "confrontations in the information dimension" (CID), which denotes conflicting acts led in cyberspace which are distinguished from cyberwar, without, however, completely raising issues of cybercriminality.

Thus let all sociopolitical, ethnic and religious movements come under the category of CID[63]:

– the use of social networks by citizens who reject them political regime. Here we could speak of cyberrevolts, cyberprotests, cyberrevolutions, or simply the cybernetic dimensions of opposition movements;

– site defacements or virus attack operations, for political ends, involving nationalist hackers or hacktivists;

– any form of militantism, whatever the reason, cause and targets attacked (companies, institutions).

Current discourse which protests high and mighty against the democratic power of social networks undoubtedly deserves us to dwell on it more than we actually do in this book. Web 2.0 is a weapon of democracy, of the oppressed, and of anyone who, from any point on earth, could easily contribute to the birth of social battles, defense of social justice, to the appearance of new political forces. Web 2.0 is the weapon of the weak against the strong, above all justice against injustice, of the people against oppressive powers in all their forms – not only political, but also economic and cultural. The usefulness of these tools and movements has yet to be shown. But as for this discourse, this is in line with fashion which makes each citizen the hero or star of a day, an event, in a mediatized context. "Become the hero of the revolutions that you can lead from your own living room!" the partisans of Web 2.0 tell us. Andy Warhol claimed that, in the future, everyone would be famous for 15 minutes. With Twitter, blogs, and web 2.0, everybody is on the web, dreaming of being heard, seen, recognized, to come out of the darkness of

---

63 Athina Karatzogianni [KAR 06] identifies two types of cyberconflicts: sociopolitical and ethno-religious.

anonymity, of being *someone*. We are being told that we can be militants, revolutionaries without risks, even warriors, and even heroes. Why not? This is not really a question of being famous, but of being part of history, which is a form of participating in major events. The individual is not trying to single himself out in these movements, since he is, in fact, the single drop of water which comes to broaden the river. But one day he could say, "I was there". The real power of social networks and tools like Twitter on the course of revolutions and other forms of opposition still has to be demonstrated. Revolutions need other conditions to succeed. On the other hand, the future of these forms of organization and communication is not guaranteed.

Intelligence operations led by States or private actors are also part of the CIDs. The multiple intrusions into information systems belonging to large industrial groups contribute, by the information they take, to the industrial and economic power of the actors involved (we are speaking of economic war). Intrusions into state-governed systems (The Ministry of Finance, in France, 2011, and the European Commission in March 2011, for example) for political, economic, and industrial means still come under the function of CID.

CID's are often similar to cybercriminality. Their actors may be pursued in States they act in, and fall under the arm of the law. Hacktivists, indeed activists in their soul, in their methods, may also come under cybercriminality. Computer hacking, were it is motivated by political or ideological, remains an act of delinquency. In the same way, citizen using social networks to spread hostile information to the authorities fall under the arm of the law (dissidence, terrorism), according to the contexts and law in force in each State.

CID's seem to be distinguished from cyberwar through the motivation which rallies its actors. But this is not a distinguishing feature, certainly no more so that the actor's identity is, which could be a citizen, an institution, a State. The target does not make it possible to differentiate CIDs from cyberwar or cybercriminality. Hacktivists or criminals can also target civil as well as state-governed, military or even critical infrastructure websites. Soldiers do not have control over sensitive target, or over the level of cybernetic violence which could be imposed. However, only soldiers have the capability to integrate attacks in information space on a more complex process, involving the deployment and use of armed force in all dimensions (air, ground, sea, space).

4.1.2. *Expression of sovereignty*

Sovereignty is a State's capability of being a sovereign (being independent and free in its future), and to exert its authority. If we consider that cyberspace – or parts of cyberspace – make up one or several territories, and that these spaces can be separated and become *spaces* of sovereignty, then it must be in a position to confirm and defend its sovereignty over this space. This involves great efforts, means, investments, and the use of space. The State's absence in this space, any loss of control over the territories would, then, be the mark of this sovereignty losing its power.

Sovereignty can be broken down into three criteria. First of all, we have the symbols, such as the flag: an object of collective identity which "has virtually infinite spaces to be displayed"[64]. The flag comes in different forms in cyberspace: the use of language, the imposition of norms, and the occupation of space by content.

The flag is one of the most commonly used images by hacktivists during the multiple site defacements: Turkish, Chinese and American flags, etc. The mark of sovereignty is, then, the existence of an armed force which will defend the territory's integrity. The United Nation's Charter gives this right to States. The only zone in the world which is deprived of any militarization is Antarctica. The army is present in cyberspace. States therefore have their sovereignty in this way. The third criterion is the law. Sovereignty is based on a legal system, and this is demonstrated through its legality. The imposition of norms applied to cyberspace (technical norms, for example) is a variation of this lawful presence of a State which is imposed on the presence of other actors.

Furthermore, sovereignty is manifested in a State's capability to exert its authority over its entire territory. Zones which inside this territory escape its authority are gray zones. They promote instability. In a certain way, cyberspace is the gray zone of the States: it is impossible to exert full authority over parts of cyberspace which depend on them. When a cyberattack is launched from a State, the State either confirms that the attackers on its territory are to be ignored and unable to be located, in which case there is a "gray zone"; or, the State acknowledges the act, the attackers, and can locate them, in which case we have sovereignty and compliance.

4.1.3. *Cyberpower*

Power is a relationship (A has the power in relation to a subordinate of power). It is a capability with its trusted agents (power materialized in the government and State). We distinguish power from coercion (use of force), the power of injunction (an order given by a judge), and the power of influence (soft power). Power is

---

64 [ENC 09], p. 93.

localized in States, capital cities, in the center of the capitals. Power is also a capability, it has its own actors (States, but also not state-governed actors can climb amongst the rank of power), and it involves a hierarchy. A multipolar world is organized around two dominant powers. A unipolar world only counts a dominant hyper power. On an international scale, power is expressed by force (hard power), by coercion, by brute force.

Exerting power in cyberspace not only assumes the State to manifest its presence, its authority, to have respect (make laws, bring order by fighting against crime in all its forms) and to limit the negative effects that using this space might have on power: controlling content, Chinese "harmonization" and censoring after often appropriate. To lead these objectives well, the States can still count on the support of the industrial sector: "The growing sophistication in Internet content filtering can be claimed by, partly, services provided by Western Internet services and software companies (most of them are based in the USA)"[65]. Market law takes on ideological and political considerations.

In each State, from the most democratic to the most authoritarian, the increased controls over content and internet user practice will always find their justifications: battles against pornography, content attacking cultural, religious and social values, intellectual and industrial property rights, attack the nation's image, politicians, security, etc. Political party or opposing sites (sometimes described as being terrorists), rebel sites, separatist movement sites, religious sites, human rights defense groups, social network platforms, sites spreading security tools and cryptography are all filtered, blocked and censored.

According to studies by ONI, States concentrate their control on content produced in the national language. This is why filtering results are more useful in China on the Chinese language than in English[66]. The States use many methods: either the Internet is left open but will be controlled during electoral periods for example, or it is filtered and what varies is the page shown to the internet user. Once the censoring and blocking tools are installed, their use has no other limits than those fixed by the authorities. They just have to legitimize it to justify their action. Government critics generally start by demanding the battle against pornography, protecting minors and citizen, protection against attacks on religious values and then forbidding political movements, independence, any form of claim, all in the name of national security.

---

65 [DEI 06] This article cites Microsoft, Cisco, Yahoo!, Skype, Google, all accused of colluding with the Chinese government. It also recalls that the business applications of Secure Computing, Fortinet, and Websense in particular, were reused by governments for means of control and censoring. http://www.feer.com/articles1/2006/0612/free/p022.html (site consulted on July 3rd 2010).
66 [DEI 06].

Information is considered as an interference in national affairs. In a number of countries, filtering is presented as a necessary means to combat American hegemony and Western propaganda. Power may be the search for control over massive elements, such as territory, men, primary resources, and of course ideas and information, Power consists of having a reserve of resources, as big as possible and the most strategic as possible. Building empires and continent States stems from this logic of power. If the construction of a dominion over cyberspace (which will be the territory this power will rely on) is based on information domination, the flaw in this power lies in the lack of solidarity in this resource, which is fragile and attackable in its elementary building blocks. Cyberpower is the capability to use cyberspace[67]. For Dan Kuehl, cyberpower is the capability to use cyberspace to create advantages and influence events in all the other operational environments[68]. The cyberpower in question is, then, a necessary element for guaranteeing national security:

– cyberpower is an element of national security;

– cyberpower and cyberspace are components of international security;

– cyberpower works for national interests.

Cyber power may be understood as the "capability to use cyberspace to create advantages and influence events in all operational environments and across instruments of power"[69]. Cyberpower is a measure of the capability to use this environment. This cyberpower is therefore determined by several different factors:

 technological knowledge;

– objectives, organizations, aims, the way in which we use this approach to power, this method of power, to influence other elements of power (power of information, economic power, military power, etc.).

In 2010, J. Nye published his "Cyber Power" [NYE 10], an extract from a title being published in 2011, "The Future of Power in the 21st Century".

Power is a function of context. The growth of cyberspace provides a new important context for State power. The key ideas in its development are the following:

– the concept of transferring power from a dominant State to another one is a familiar one. What is new, is the idea of spreading power. More and more things are happening today which are escaping the control of States and their power;

– for some, this spreading of power could mark the end of Westphalian order;

---

67 [KRA 09].

68 [KRA 09].

69 [KRA 09].

– the era of information globalization has started many new problems for the strong States, themselves the instigators of these problems;

– states will remain dominant actors on the international front, but this will be more and more difficult to control;

– power is a concept, an object which is difficult to measure: power is the capability to do something, to do something so that others act at our will;

– J. Nye distinguishes two forms of power: hard and soft. Hard power consists of restraining using force, and soft is by influence and attraction;

– cyberpower is a new concept. It depends on the resources which characterize cyberspace. It consists of benefiting from the use of information resources which are electronically interconnected. This is the capability to use cyberspace for creating advantages, influencing events in other operational environments and by using instruments of power. Cyberpower can therefore be used by considering cyberspace as an aim or an instrument;

– an analogy is made between power and the ocean: we can use the seas to win sea battles, or use the resources which we find in the oceans to create effects on land, and to influence battles on land;

– the cyber domain is unique because it is manmade and subject to technological changes which are quicker than in any other domain. The geography of cyberspace changes more than in any other space;

– the barriers at the entrance to cyberspace are so low that non-state governed actors and weak or small states can claim stakes there and play important roles, which is not the case on land or at sea, or in the air or space (a domain where a number of actors are considerably reduced);

– speaking of "dominance" in cyberspace makes no sense, even if States are reputed to have more capabilities than others (USA, Russia, UK, France, China);

– extreme conflict in cyberspace is cyberwar;

– in this context, the attacker may remain invisible, anonymous, be distinct, and one single attack might not cost anything financially[70];

– the attacker has the advantage, not the defense, because cyberspace was designed to be easy to use, not for security. This situation is not necessarily going to irremediable forever, but this is what we know at the current moment in time;

---

70 The idea that cyberattacks cost nothing or nearly nothing should be put into context. During the Stuxnet attacks, some people were talking of millions of dollars. Of course we can put forward the figures that we want. But the development of sophisticated tools, whatever the case, requires men, skills and this comes at a cost. When the USA created CyberCommand and financed cyber soldiers, all this has a cost. It is therefore wrong to speak of gratuity or quasi-gratuity. At this price, it is possible to get a popgun.

– dissuasion is possible, but consider the problem of blame;

– J. Nye considers extra-cyberspace power, and intra-cyberspace power, which relates to the distinction between naval force on the seas and naval protection force on land;

– intra-cyberspace: information can be used to produce soft power (attracting the open source community and making it adhere to a new standard, providing servers to human rights defending hacktivists). Hard power will come in the form of DDoS attacks);

– extra-cyberspace: attacks on SCADA systems or physical attacks on infrastructures for the hard power part, or campaigns to win over the public opinion of another State for the soft power part;

– the relative reduction of power due to its dispersion does not mean equalization or leveling. Large power States still have more resources than the small ones and non-state governed actors. Actors remain unequal due to the question of resources;

– a teenage hacker with basic knowledge or a state organization with lots of means can both cause heavy damage;

– the geographical location of the resources in cyberspace is an important concept, because we can confirm that the States will remain sovereigns there;

– attacks are not all equal. More skills are needed to attack the extremely secure information systems belonging to a State agency or critical infrastructure systems, than to strike low value targets. Resistance to the attacks can differ greatly;

– cyberspace is not an environment which favors self-organization due to the high number of users and the importance of the resource;

– more Internet is needed, out of necessity (development of our model of society), but less is needed, out of reasons of security.

4.1.4. *Measuring and locating power*

Measuring power is a real challenge, *a fortiori* that in cyberspace where it is difficult to count the active population, actors form groups with moving and sometimes intangible shapes, and their actions may have uncontrollable or even imperceptible implications. The power found in cyberspace must, however, be assessed. Let us propose some criteria in order to do so:

– the capability to harm: actors capable of rallying up the means, human resources namely, quickly, and to mobilize them in the long term, to identify targets, to communicate about their capabilities, to be fully aware, to have an exact vision of their own capabilities, have the basic requirements to allow good strikes;

– striking force: this is generated using the elements described above. This is also the capability to reach targets (capability to hack websites is not a reflection of *real* power);

– the capability to unite and arouse alliances: this informs us of the actor's caliber and acquired recognition. A will form an alliance with B, because B appears as an actor who can ensure protection, come to help during situations of crisis, to confront attacks, to give aid.

But power sometimes needs to be demonstrated. The recognition of this power cannot always be obtained on the basis of single political declarations, publicity documents ("State A wants to become the world's leading cybersecurity hub"), published figures, or lab tests. This could, then, involve leading aggressive operations. Attacks over the last few years can at least be interpreted as such: they used "demonstrations" of their force. This is undoubtedly the reason why they have not managed to destroy the targets. Being strong does not guarantee domination, but not being strong guarantees decline. The loss of naval power is largely responsible for the decline in high powers over History. One analogy is still possible: the States in cyberspace or who are dependent on it do not always guarantee their development and power, but those who cannot access it sufficiently and impose themselves there, guarantee their delay. The loss of power for certain States in the cyber sphere is indeed the gauge of a rapid decline. Power in cyberspace is becoming increasingly more localized, in the absence of being centralized. In each case, power is not as dispersed as common discourse would have us believe on sharing, spreading, globalization and the transnationality in influxes and exchanges. We worry about the fate of critical infrastructure which are fully localized, we worry about the risks run by a society, by actors, and we identify or try to identify the source of threats, to redesign the structure of these attacker networks (where botnet machines are located, where master servers are found, which are the silent partners, etc.).

Even when causes find support in various points around the world, and even when hacker communities might be made up of help from individuals spread all over the planet, we cannot speak about the spreading of power in the sense of the lack of localization. Even when distributed, force has a center. Power can be located, we just desire proof that it constitutes the favored attack targets. Power in cyberspace follows the forms of the real world:

– the power of strong States (economy, army, politics);

– the power in capital cities;

– the power in rich States, in places of wealth.

Statistics on server and zombie computers perpetrating the cyberattacks led using botnets offer a visualization of the location of a form of cybercriminal power, but which might also encompass resources and state governed actions. The geographical distribution [ZHU 07] of C2 botnet servers are the following: USA 38.8%; China 4.4%; Korea 3.2%; Germany 2.7%; the Netherlands 2.6%; Canada 1.7%; UK 1.3%.

The location of the bots (compromised machines) is concentrated in developing countries where security is at a weaker level still. Even if 15% of bots are in Brazil, with concentrations in China, Malaysia and other Asian countries, the distribution widely covers the entire planet, with 197 countries affects [ZHU 07]. However, the distribution of DDoS attack victims is concentrated in the USA (31.8%), Italy (11%) and another 76 countries. All studies must be taken as photographs at time T [ZHU 07]. Bots move, servers frequently change location, as well as the zombies and the victims.

Mapping power in cyberspace or linked to cyberspace can be drawn according to multiple criteria, such as:

– the penetration rate of the Internet in the population;

– the location of Internet root servers;

– the number of IP addresses in each country[71];

– well connected States, but which do not host, or hardly, botnet C2 servers. This reveals the State's capability to guarantee control over cyberspace, and to decide on its usage;

– the presence of cyberwar and cyberdefense units within the States;

– relationships between armed forces, governments and non-state governed actors (criminal networks, industry, relays in the civilian population), made it possible to reinforce State power, thanks to the added value of this relationship, particularly within a framework of aggressive and/or defensive operations;

– the existence of a strong national industry in the ICT domains which is able to impose its norms on an international scale, or simply to ensure the State has technological independence. This mapping is relatively simple. The USA dominates the world, projects are gradually coming to life (China and North Korea have developed their own application systems, Internet, search engines, etc.);

Power is also a question of perception. However, the more a target is attacked, the more it becomes an interesting object in the eyes of the attackers. Servers belonging to the DoD are taken as a favored target because they represent American

---

71 http://www.domaintools.com/internet-statistics/country-ip-counts.html.

power. Thus, we could say that power is proportional to the mass of attacks the target is a victim of: the more a target is attacked over the long term, the more power it symbolizes.

4.1.4.1. *Cyberspace, place of conflict*

We may represent cyberspace as a transversal space with conventional dimensions, putting aside the transversality and globality of "space" here, putting it in the same rank as the others, so we are only focused on the characteristic of cyberspace. The only space which is truly transversal to all the other spaces is information space, of which cyberspace is a component.

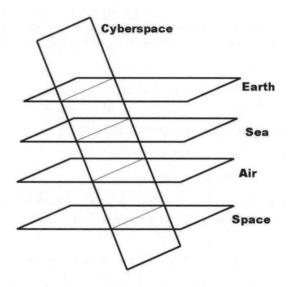

Figure 4.12. *Cyberspace, transversal space*

By flattening the four conventional dimensions, we obtain the "real" dimension (R) in relation to the "virtual" dimension (V) which is a synonym of cyberspace here (or even, information space).

Information warfare and cyberwar are a set of processes which thus make it possible, from the operations led in V or R, to obtain a certain effect in R or V. In R, the ultimate target is the individual. In V, the target is a component of cyberspace. Actions can be led uniquely in V so as to only strike V, and we are still in cyberwar in such a case. However, actions led uniquely in R with no impact of V are no longer a case of information warfare or cyberwar.

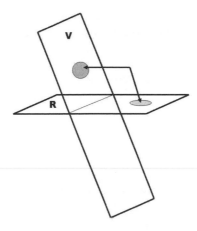

Figure 4.13. *Cyberwar defined as an interaction between V and R*

When analyzing phenomena of information warfare, or when leading information warfare type operations, we must ask the following questions:

– which action (attack, decision, operation) led in R produces a shock wave likely to have repercussions in V?

– which action in V produces a shock wave likely to have repercussions in R?

The means, methods, logic, strategies and tactics implemented will be different, depending on whether we go from R or V, and whether we are aiming at V or R. In information warfare, we aim to control R, V and R+V, but it must always have an impact in space V. This space will not stop growing, so as to cover more and more parts of the real dimension. Objects themselves will gradually have digital existence. Each object will have an RFID microchip (radio frequency identification) connected to it, enabling it to "enter" cyberspace. The object will have a digital identity, like the individual for example: a reference, a location, a digital, virtual existence. Furthermore, it will be easier to lead an operation in or on V.

4.1.4.2. *Measurement criteria*

The consideration of current, existing capabilities is a vital element for measuring power. The creation of cyber units discussed previously in this chapter help us to understand this idea. Considering politics, strategies and doctrines is another important element, because these may reflect the States' willingness to invest in the development of means to respond to these strategies. However, between the plans on paper to materialization, and the theory to real implementation, there is, sometimes, a potential gap. Once the means are developed, particularly in terms of structures (units, agencies, militia), it is not sufficient for them alone to make up the efficient capabilities. The men which make up these capabilities must be of good quality, and well controlled. The sociological dimension is just as important in this discussion of power, as the pure mathematical calculation of the resources involved: the number of individuals, the millions of Euros or Dollars invested in developing means for attacks and cybernetic defense, the number of exercises (CDX) performed every year, etc.

This appreciation of power must use several different approaches and multiply the perspectives.

The Internet penetration rate within populations can, then, be used as a force and vulnerability index of these States. In fact:

Internet using citizens are likely to constitute available resources for the attacks (in the theory of the people's war, for example[72]; or if we use the means of the Internet users themselves as resources, in the case of botnets which enable us to launch attacks, perhaps; as a means of spreading malware able to propagate to more critical systems);

– the number of Internet users will reveal the level of dependency of a society on cyberspace, and therefore its sensitivity/vulnerability to cyberattacks;

– the rate is a measurement of the level of a society's technological development, whilst a measurement of the wealth of a country and its level of development is undoubtedly also is part of its openness to the rest of the world, and therefore its permeability to the influence of different cultures;

– the penetration rate of the Internet in a society is an indication of the volume of potential targets or entry points for attack on the given territory;

– it also reveals the level of addiction of a society to technology, and the level of knowledge.

Based on statistics published by http://www.internetworldstats.com, we group States into different categories, according to penetration rate:

– G1: rate between 80 and 100%;

– G2: rate between 60 and 79%;

– G3: rate between 40 and 59%;

– G4: rate between 20 and 39%;

---

72 For example, it has been said that in China, its high number of Internet users is a natural reservoir for leading cyberattacks.

– G5: rate between 10 and 19%;

– G6: rate between 1 and 9%;

– G7: rate lower than 1%.

Unconnected countries are discounted from the statistics and do not have a specific group here.

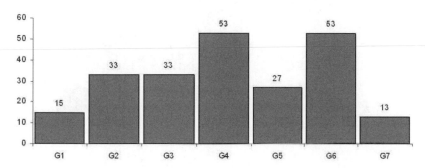

Figure 4.14. *Number of countries listed in each group*

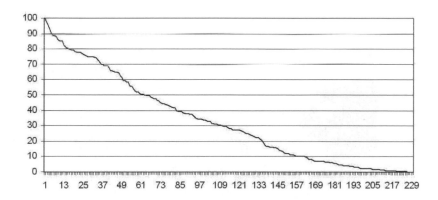

Figure 4.15. *Ratio of number of countries/Internet penetration rate. Out of 230 listed countries, nearly half have a penetration rate higher than 30%*

A high penetration rate does not particularly mean that the Internet is equally present over the considered territory. There are strong discrepancies between cities and the countryside, and large cities and less important cities. Inside these spaces, strong discrepancies may still appear, between cities and the suburbs, between high earning districts and poorer districts, etc.

G1

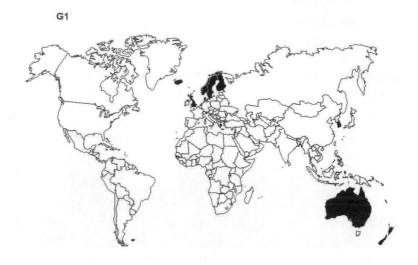

Figure 4.16. *Countries in group 1*

G2

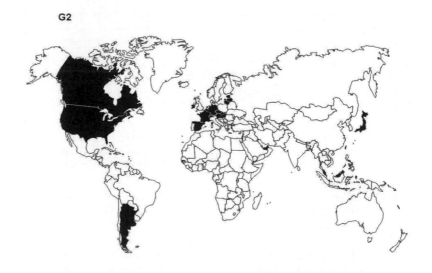

Figure 4.17. *Countries in group 2*

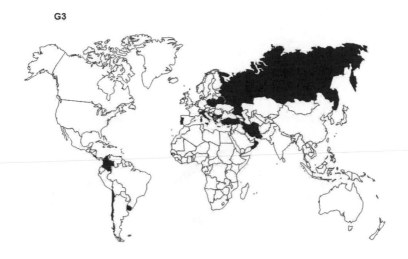

Figure 4.18. *Countries in group 3*

The previous comment regarding discrepancies between certain geographical areas especially applies to territories as large as Russia or China.

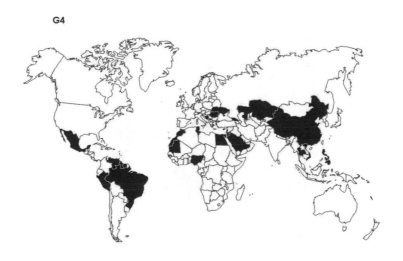

Figure 4.19. *Countries from group 4*

G5

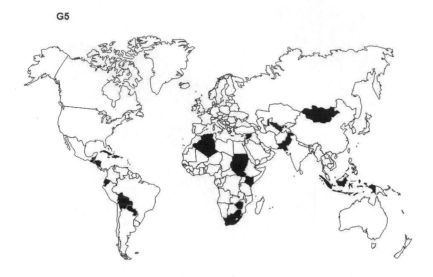

Figure 4.20. *Countries from group 5*

G6

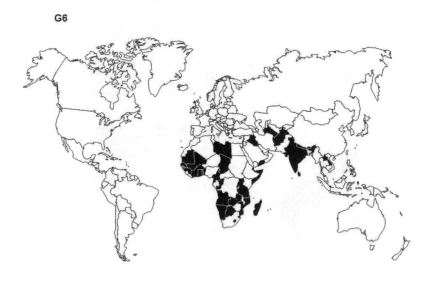

Figure 4.21. *Countries from group 6*

G7

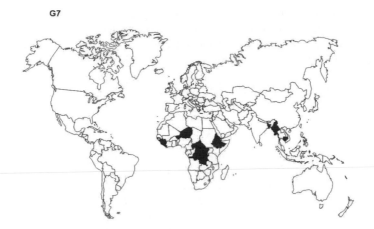

Figure 4.22. *Countries from group 7*

Forces can be analyzed in terms of other criteria, such as the presence (or non-presence) of cyberwar or cyberdefense units.

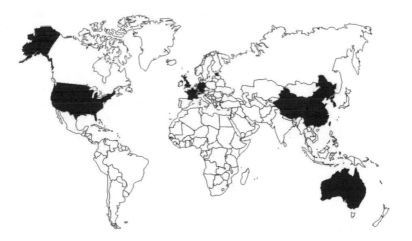

Figure 4.23. *Map displaying cyberdefense centers or cyberwar units*

This visual demonstration brings us to notice that the States which appear able to defend themselves and/or to act aggressively, are concentrated in groups 1 and 2. China is in group 4, but this separate case does not seem to have the same structures as the other nations. China will not remain in group 4 for long, with its staggeringly fast growing Internet. It is clear that the better connected States who seem to have a better awareness of the important nature of their cybersecurity and cyberdefense. If security must be developed in the most well connected countries, which seems logical, then the capabilities to defend and confront will also be concentrated in these same States. We have not included Russia in this map. There are no displayed cybersecurity and cyberdefense agencies. But the offensive operations there, apparently [CAR 10] are led in the tight partnerships between Moscow and criminal networks.

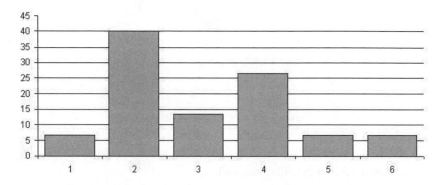

Figure 4.24. *Relative share in % of groups of countries (defined according to the Internet penetration rate). Countries mentioned in the results of the search for "cyberwar"*[73] *on Google (February 2011)*

The following table shows the known confrontations or those usually used as examples in discussions on cyberwar, and those centered on groups 2, 3 and 4, meaning countries whose Internet penetration rate is between 20% and 80% (119 countries out of 230, or 51%).

Country	Group
Israel – Iran (Stuxnet affair, for example)	2 against 3
USA – Iran (Stuxnet affair)	2 against 3
Estonia – Russia (2007)	2 against 3
USA – Russia	2 against 3
USA – China	2 against 4
USA – Iraq	2 against 6
Russia – Georgia	3 against 4

---

73 Average for the results offered on the two spelling variations of "cyberwar" and "cyber war".

4.1.4.3. *The concept of vital space*

Herbert Spencer believed that the object of the fight between States was survival on a vital space[74] (the Raum). This perception of international relations, linked to social Darwinism, confirms that the State is connected to the ground and cannot develop or live without it. The State, then, is considered as a living being, responding to natural laws in the same way as all organisms, animals and plants. The vital space (lebensraum), a concept which flows through these ideas, is the main source of conflicts between different States (Ratzel, Haushofer)[75].

When we describe the world as a system, as an organism, whose brain is the Internet; when we describe cyberspace as a system made up of millions of computer-brains, then we are validating this organicistic approach. The world is an organism responding to natural laws, and cyberspace is an organism. State power is linked to cyberspace, and therefore, in a certain way, to the survival of modern States which find themselves depending on their presence in this new dimension, on the possession of spaces within the total cybernetic space. This battle for vital space is confirmed in the confrontations between States or private actors within international authorities for the domination of the Internet.

If cyberspace resources were to dry up, if IP addresses were to be lacking in the long term, then undoubtedly cyberspace would become the place or object of confrontations between States. This is because these States have transformed their information systems into their central nervous system; for them, it really is vital. The dependency which links States to cyberspace can be very strong. Does this battle take the form of a conquest for free spaces or spaces belonging to others? The answer is yes, at least symbolically.

With cyberspace being a vital infrastructure, anything which could gravely attack it or question the balances which are defined because of it, will lead to reactions which go beyond the stakes in hand. States are agreed on the right to respond in the way which is the most relevant to them: "The nation reserves the right to respond to intrusions led by States, terrorist groups or other adversaries, in the way which seems most appropriate to it [...] The responses to an enemy attack will be determined by the context of each attack in particular. Intrusions into government systems, military systems and national infrastructures are threats to our national security" [KEY 08].

---

74 *Der Raum des Cyberspace*, Martin Warnke, 28 pages, http://www.njoerd-ffm.de/cyber/cyberspace.pdf.
75 Let us remember that for Ratzel, the bigger the State, the more resources it has. This explains the need to reduce the number of States, and to create a State-continent.

4.1.4.4. *The gravity model*

This theory produces the hypothesis that the interaction between two actors is proportional to the geopgraphical distance which separates them. The smaller the distance between them, the more interactions there will be (peaceful or aggressive). The gravity model was formulated by Ernst Georg Ravenstein[76] in 1885, Emile Lavasseur in 1889 or still William J. Reilly in 1931[77], transposing Newton's law (universal law of gravitation) to geography. Using Newton's theory in this way consists of saying that any geographical space exerts gravity on other spaces according to its mass, and the distances which separates them from this mass. This is indeed verified.

Countries which are geographically close to China but which remain distanced from it for political and historical reasons, find themselves, at the beginning of this 21st Century, sucked into the Chinese economy, entering again into the fold of their Empire. This is the case for South Korea, whose top business partner is no longer the USA, but China. This immense country has become attractive once again, its mass irremediably attracts its neighboring countries in the immediate vicinity, and also those who are greatly distanced.

This theory for cyberspace could be reformulated in the following way: the probability of there being a link between two actors decreases the more distance is increased (there is less chance of a French internet user being in contact with a Chilean internet user than with one from Switzerland, if only for linguistic reasons, because the distance is not only geographical but cultural and linguistic), and gets larger according to the mass (there is more chance of having relations with an American internet user than with a Luxembourg user, due to the high North America internet using population, and the force of American culture, etc.). But the volume of internet users in a country is not enough to turn it into a gravitational mass in cyberspace: the linguistic barrier may block these gravitational forces (French or Spanish internet users will hardly go towards the Chinese internet naturally, due to the difficult access through the language – automated translation tools are relatively useless still). We may, however, find reduced yet very attracting spaces.

The concept of "mass" or "distance" must be interpreted. The distance is not only geographical or physical. If an actor is politically "close" to another, then the distance is low between them, whether one is in France and the other in Australia. If a "small" actor has the capability to attract projectors towards him, then his symbolic "mass" will become high, meaning that he has a high gravitational pull (the "buzz" effect, for example, which is produced spontaneously around a video

76 Laws of Migration, 1885.
77 The Law of Retail Gravitation, 1931, New York.

uploaded by a previously unknown Internet user). Large spaces may have low gravitational power, if they only have small interests. An immense territory but without the least useable natural resources has no great interest. Thus, saying that cyberspace is "infinite" brings no specific value to this dimension. It is not the "infinite" character which brings its value and gravitational nature. This is the opposite of its position. Gravitational pull is not, on the other hand, a permanently fixed factor. It is more of a variable. That which has little attraction today might have a high gravitational power tomorrow. What is far today might be close tomorrow.

Cyberspace, in its totality, has a high attracting power: the exponential growth of the number of internet users and individuals linked by mobile telephones is the proof of this. The share of global growth which is attributed to the Internet is a factor with high gravitation, particularly for countries looking to grow. Within cyberspace, there are attracting zones which can be defined according to several criteria. The English language, and there the whole English-speaking Internet is a gravitational factor due to its over representation. Anglophone culture, and therefore all the content adding to it, can have this attractive character. The closer we are to this culture, the closer we feel to it. The more curious we are to get to know it, the more we move towards it. The more a culture is represented on the Internet, the more it must exert its power of attraction. Social networks and developing communities may have a power of attraction which exceeds national boundaries. But it is indeed probable that in cyberspace, the laws of gravity generally respect the laws which exist in the real world. There is more chance of an internet user or a blogger being interested in national information, in national sites, and possible sites for the part of the world they live in (Europe, Asia, the Americas).

4.1.4.5. *The Second World*

Parag Khanna divides the world into 3 sections [KHA 09]. He distinguishes:

– the rich world (which he calls the "first world"), composed of the large Empires, namely the USA, the European Union and China. It is the relations between these empires which shape the world, and not the inter-civilization relations;

– the third world;

– and in between, we have the "second world", where we find emerging countries such as Eastern Europe, Central Asia, South America, the Middle East, and South Asia.

The second world is a new set of central regions which the global economy revolves around. Rich countries will find markets in the second world, and the second world will find business opportunities in the first world, and use it as a platform for economic development in the third world. Parag Khanna believes that the best thing which could have happened to the third world is, in fact, the second world: it offers opportunities that it would not have with the rich, first world. If we were to adopt this approach, then cyberspace, or rather the population linked to cyberspace, would be cut into three sections:

– rich, well connected countries;

– third world countries, victims of digital divides, and who will perhaps never have access to the Internet;

– between the two, there are neither rich nor completely impoverished countries which have little connection, but which dream of being developed. These are territories, and not countries (because within a State's borders, there are high discrepancies according to the regions), which will go as far as using mobile Wi-Fi ports, carried on the backs of elephants, as is the case for certain regions in China.

Populations forever separated from cyberspace or destined to have little connection have only one way of moving forward to be present in cyberspace: access it by using their diasporas. Cyberconflicts are confrontations between the first and second world. The third world is still removed from this type of conflict.

4.1.4.6. *Speed as a determiner of power*

"The speed of light" is a frequently used expression in several documents on the subject of cyberspace. This is the fast moving world, with data processed there, transferred, exploited, with no latency time. But this time is necessarily the time of cyberspace. Indeed, data is processed at the speed of light, but we will always need a certain delay for the data to reach its destination. It may be delayed, stuck somewhere along the way. Calculations are still limited by physical capabilities. The race for calculating times is one of the major stakes in computer processing. But immediacy is an illusion. It only concerns data. However, any process or calculation needs a specific amount of time. Actions performed by users are part of human and not machine time. The decisions which call upon these actions respond to a longer time. But popular discourse seems to want to give only a partial image of cyberspace, one which is not entirely wrong, but which is not entirely exact either. According to the 2007-2008 report by the Canadian Security Intelligence Service, cyberspace is characterized by its continuous connectivity, which facilitates attacks in a few seconds, from inside or outside a country[78]. Space-time is shortened, our ports are being threatened, it is impossible to detect the attack and to prevent it from reaching its target, are just some of the recurring arguments. But the attacks are not led in just a few seconds. They need days, sometimes weeks or months, to program

78 Page 17 of the report. http://dsp-psd.tpsgc.gc.ca/collections/collection_2010/sp-ps/PS71-2008-fra.pdf.

a malware which is capable of attacking targets; they might need to think several years in advance about the possibility of planting hidden ports in applications which be sold abroad and used later on.

The notion of a boundless, fluid cyberspace could mean that the battlefield is likely to change its configuration somewhat instantaneously, that there is no fixed territory, that any potential target can be found at just a few milliseconds from the attacker. Time is a key factor in the control over cyberspace. The famous OODA loop is still a current affair: for the adversary to take the lead, he must decide and act quickly, and in terms of cyberattacks, we believe that the first to act will have a lead which is difficult to catch up with. But implementing the attack itself cannot forget the preparation time, the observation, analysis time, and the time take to make the decision. In the name of sacred "speed", law absolute in cyberspace, today everything could become invisible and intangible. As it is a question of always moving quicker so as not to be taken over, of staying at the top; as calculation speed has become an objective criterion of quality, efficiency and power, then this technological race imposes actors of security and defense to follow, to adapt: "unfortunately, we don't have the luxury of 20 years to develop strategies, techniques and doctrines to face this revolution and uphold American superiority in this fast changing environment" [ALE 07].

4.1.5. *Limits of exercising power*

Powerlessness can be manifested in many ways. First of all, there are recurrent reports and flaws which persist. There are also persistent discussions, which have been striking up the same arguments for the last 15 years on threat, fragility, and the imminence of major attacks. This is a sign of powerlessness because nothing has been able to put an end to these worries. Unless there is a useful discussion, on the contrary, working in favor of power.

Powerlessness also concerns individuals and official institutions and governments having to control their data (data leaks, theft, loss, daily intrusions into so called secure systems). Powerlessness is displayed through the difficulty of finding traces of our attackers in this universe which is made for them. This is, then, a large limitation on defense which sees itself placed in the realm of the impossibility of reacting within a reasonable time limit (limit on the exercise of legitimate defense). Powerlessness is partly created by the absence of a legal framework, or at least an international agreement, which makes it possible to harmonize essential concepts such as "cyberwar", "cyberspace", "cyberconflict", "cyberattack". This absence[79] of an international legal framework is the manifestation of the inertia displayed by States who cannot manage to agree on the subject. But, can power really find a way of exerting itself out of the legal framework?

On their own territories, the authorities are sometimes forced to accept a relative loss of power. This is a widespread idea, according to which the Beijing government controls all its Chinese citizens, knows everything, deals with everything, and nothing happens in the society without Beijing knowing about it or giving it the go ahead. But Beijing cannot control what happens from a computer in its territory, nor can it completely control the data which passes through its systems, nor can it control its citizens any more than Paris or Washington can. China is also prey to cybercriminality, a victim of intrusions in its systems, DDoS attacks, etc. The police acts, as in all the world's States, but the task is difficult. In January 2010, the Jingzhou police (in the Hubei province), closed the pornographic site "Dingxiang", based in Chongqing, which had pulled in 30 million members in 6 months. This site had been added to 9,000 other sites closed in 2009. 5,400 suspects were arrested, and 4,100 enquiries were in progress[80]. China certainly hosts servers used for massive attacks everywhere in the world. This does not mean that Beijing approves or disapproves, nor does it mean that there is a gray zone in China, confined in Chinese cyberspace. In cyberspace, what happens very often to express Chinese power (through the many attacks attributed to it), is sometimes the manifestation of the lack of control by authorities over whole sections of society and cyberspace.

International alliances are often said to be one of the best ways to fight against threats, of organizing legal and security[81] or defense systems for confront problems considered to be global and widespread. Alliances are also one of the ways of the ways that the attackers operate: criminals, States and independent actors are, at certain points in time, more or less linked, combined together, brought together to share their resources and know-how. Alliances, of course, do not only concern the international dimension. Agreements and partnerships are established on a national scale. Actors wishing to lead specific operations but who do not have the means necessary (or who do not want to use their own) will resort to outside means and skills. This principle is widely spread in the field of cyberattacks, with hackers very often acting for others:

– activists acting for their own ideals, and called upon to lead actions for various interests;

---

79 We say "absence" because even if the law of conflicts applies, then other variations may be considered. But a consensus has never been expressed officially on an international scale.
80 *South China Morning Post*, Hong Kong, January 4th 2010.
81 See a study on the partnership between India and the USA on cybersecurity [NAI 10].

– states call upon the skills of other States: North Korea uses China's means to launch cyberattacks; Burma also uses China for these ends;

– states call upon hacker groups, within their own borders, but also on an international scale;

– states rely on criminality: Russia sub-contracts aggressive operations on the country's mafia networks;

– cybersecurity and cyberdefense of certain States is sub-contracted to private, national or even foreign actors;

– an actor A wishing to attack B may use services that it will pay for: this is not an alliance, but a contract of provision of service or sub-contracting.

The phenomenon of subcontracting tends to make up for the lack of internal skills. The attackers adopt this model for reasons to do with cost: launching an operation at time T would assume that preparations would have been made well in advance (investing in training individuals, thinking about strategies, gathering intelligence, identifying targets, doing tests). When this is not the case, it is more economical to use outside skills. But this formula has its limitations. It is difficult to imagine a State accepting being subjected to groups, networks and actors with capabilities and being capable of imposing their laws on it or to threaten it with things that it would not be able to control.

Whatever the case, the subcontracting chain can be a long one: a State A may subcontract the use of its capabilities to State B, which will then use criminal networks to actually lead the operation. Thus, State A will depend on the criminal network belonging to State B. Using outside skills may also come in the force of rallying up feelings or values (nationalism, for instance). When States use crime networks for their operations, it is perhaps to hide their involvement, or maybe because these networks have superior means. This is, however, sometimes the same as admitting that neither the army nor the intelligence services have these capabilities internally. These are failing States with a weakened sovereignty.

The situation Estonia was a victim of in 2007 encouraged States to face up to their responsibilities. Should the international community help Estonia? And if yes, how? The limitations of this quickly come to the surface. There are many reasons for this. First of all, let us remember that the law, both international and (often) national, and the official documents of the EU, UN and NATO have not, or had not until recently, considered the specific nature of the computer attacks that certain States were victims of. This is a situation which, in fact, makes the States face up to their individual responsibilities: each victim must, then, first of all count on himself and then, possible, hope for outside help. Collective action is, however, held up by the specific approach that States may have of the various matters at stake. The range of definitions and stakes actors, and the importance given to these questions, vary from one State to the next. The definitions of the concepts of "cyberattack", "cyberdefense", "cyberwar", "information warfare" or "acts of cyberterrorism" constitute the many points where the different States diverge. The different ranges and the actors involved are therefore not the same, do not have the same skills, the perception of threats varies, as well as the measures of protection. A collective willingness can only be manifested when a consensus is possible.

The way in which UN members managed the Libya situation in March 2011, although this is an entirely different context, allows us to measure the complexity which sometimes comes before the international community consensus. The urgency of the situation was not felt in the same way by everybody, no more than the real stakes, the threats and the honor. Each State is, as a matter of urgency, inclined to defend its own interests and to convince others to follow its course. International solidarity is not always displayed spontaneously, and is sometimes the fruit of fierce negotiations which take place over time, to a pace which is not, in each case, the same for the belligerents, the victims and the attackers. It is, then, highly probably that a State which has been a victim of cyberattacks will find itself alone when it calls upon the international community to help it. Then again, what could the international community actually do, in terms of reaction, for example? The victim State will be confronted with solitude, expecting action from the international authorities. The restraints on any quick and consensual reaction are lawful, conceptual, political, and simply technical: when the guilty cannot be identified for certain, then the international community has no way of chasing him.

The question of cybersecurity will still find no useful answer in international cooperation. Let us simply cite the case of the Japan/USA cooperation. In 2005, both countries had decided to organize regular meetings on information security, but the project did not go on longer than 2008[82]. In 2010, new discussions were held between both States, always at an official, ministerial level, planning the exchange of information relating to cyberattacks and measures to be put into place. International cooperation cannot function based on agreements or draft projects between governments alone. Projects must be given the means to get processes under way, to create infrastructures if needs be. Cybersecurity is only, in the end, one question amongst so many others in the group of nations which may sometimes be ignored to favor more important or simply easier subjects to set in motion. In terms of security or defense, one of the main limitations is probably the reluctance to share information.

---

82 *Japan–US talks on cyber attacks set for early February in Tokyo*, 25th January 2010, http://www.istockanalyst.com/article/viewiStockNews/articleid/3805623.

4.1.6. *The Monroe doctrine*

During a speech to the National Congress, General Alexander was interrogated on the need for the USA to apply an equivalent to the Monroe doctrine[83] in cyberspace. This doctrine was stated on December 2nd 1823 by American president James Monroe during the 7th annual speech to the Congress[84], and stipulates that the efforts on behalf of European governments to interfere with American States must be considered as acts of aggression, an imposition of American intervention, as a suitable response. On the latter point, the doctrine left a large margin for maneuvering as it did not define the suitable responses and means. This doctrine has been referred to on several occasions by the USA. Recent reflections on the matter are trying to bring back the Monroe doctrine and, in particular, to see a solution in it to clarify the government's positions and choices in terms of cyberspace. This is notably the case for the current context of non-stop attacks, as much on the government's infrastructures and security agencies as on American businesses. This reflection is illustrated by the intervention of a Mrs. Mary Ann Davidson[85] before the sub-committee dealing with new threats, cybersecurity, and science and technology[86].

She proposed the following ideas in her presentation:

– the definition of cyberspace and its real nature, or the one we choose to give it, is important from the point of view of international relations, geopolitics and geostrategies. The fact that this space is called "virtual" does not remove it from being applied to principles in the real world. This is especially not only "virtual": it is based on a physical infrastructure. An IP address indicates a machine which can be found on the national territory. In this sense, cyberspace and dealing with its associated problems must be part of a global approach. We must, still according to Mrs. Davison, stop seeing cyberspace as an object operating with its own rules that the real world does not know. Cyberspace is not a parallel universe. The problems linked to cyberspace must be considered using the same approach as for the real

---

83 http://security.nationaljournal.com/2009/06/how-can-cyberspace-be-protecte.php Quotation in the article by Shane Harris, "How can Cyberspace be defended?", 8th June 2009 (site consulted July 2nd 2010).

84 Text from the message available on the following site: http://www.ushistory. org/documents/monroe.htm (site consulted June 20th 2010).

85 Notes on Mary Ann Davidson's intervention, March 10th 2009, before the Homeland Security Subcommittee on Emerging Threats, Cybersecurity and Science and Technology. Document entitled: "The Monroe Doctrine in Cyberspace". http://www.whitehouse.gov/files /documents/cyber/Davidson%20MaryAnn%20-%20The%20Monroe%20Doctrine%20in %20Cyberspace.pdf Site consulted June 21st 2010.

86 http://homeland.house.gov/about/subcommittees.asp?subcommittee=12 (site consulted June 21st 2010).

world. We must above all admit that there are solutions available, and we must demystify cyberspace;

– the Monroe doctrine recognizes an American sphere of influence (SOI), a space of American national interests and the right to defend these interests, with limits over the responses. The Monroe doctrine is the confirmation of the concept of "territory", of sphere of influence, of sovereignty. Referring to this would negate the idea of an absence of boundaries in cyberspace. These borders and boundaries must be defined, and they are extended with the notion of sphere of influence. The American SOI is limited by its physical, material dimensions;

– but we cannot summarize cyberspace a set of spheres of influence. It is built around infrastructures which are critical for all the actors involved, and for the international community. The USA must contribute to defending these common infrastructures;

– if the USA claims a cyberterritory, they must be in a position to defend it. One of the most realistic ways of managing this is to adopt the Monroe doctrine in cyberspace, which would be recognizing that cyberspace is no different from other spaces, and that what happens there can be dealt with using the same rules which apply and govern the real world (the "offline" world, as Davison says). Adopting a cyber Monroe doctrine would be a signal thrown at the rest of the world: play with fire, and you'll get burned. Any foray into this sphere is likely to create a response from the USA. It is, therefore, a position which claims to be dissuasive;

– applying a cyber Monroe doctrine would force the government to make a choice: define the threats which are bigger than all the others and which must be dealt with as a priority. This implies that this is not the case today, that the means might be distributed, that there might not be a summary of threats and their materialization;

– with the means of response not being defined before in the Monroe doctrine, then they will be adapted to these threats;

– adopting a cyber Monroe doctrine could lead the armies to evolve (new missions), and the creation of new troops, weapons and also technologies.

This whole argument is based on one main principle: repetitive incidents and attacks that the USA is a victim of in cyberspace have generated a new situation of conflict. Problems in cyberspace must be understood in the same was as we understood situations of crisis and war. This implies that the situation must have political, diplomatic and possibly military responses. Questions on the difference, or lack thereof, of the nature of cyberspace, which has its own rules or, on the contrary, which has common rules with other dimensions, does not seem like an absolute necessity. Nobody brings into question the differences which separate other dimensions in the real world (the sea has its own rules, even if only physical ones, which are difference from those in space, for example). If cyberspace has its own rules, then this difference must not be linked to the idea of incompatibility with other affairs in this world. If it does indeed have it own rules, then they must simply be integrated and manipulated in order to imagine new geopolitics. The whole difficulty lies in the clear marking of the assets of sovereignty in cyberspace. The limitations of a cyber Monroe doctrine concern the way in which the USA can confirm its power in cyberspace, make their laws apply, and ensure that their warnings are taken seriously.

4.1.7. *Globalization*

In "Le Grand Echiquier" (a French television show) Zbigniew Brzezinski, future counselor to President James Carter, proposes a geopolitical interpretation of the effects of the technetronic revolution on the evolution of East-West confrontations. The planet is becoming a global society; the USA is the only real global society; American society is a model; thanks to the control over information and communication networks, the USA has the capability and the power to influence the world, to impose its model in means other than force; network diplomacy will conquer the world. This theory established the Soft Power concept (Joseph Nye). Information technologies are the vector of American diplomacy, a real force intensifier. In the 1990s, globalization went hand in hand with the information age, and networks were the instrument of globalization, with the potentially best armed nation to rule this globalized world being the US. This globalization, dreamed of by Americans (whose notion of "the global village" is a famous allegory) is a process of growing interconnection between economies, societies and civilizations. This interconnection is facilitated largely by technological revolutions (transport, telecommunications). Globalization, a phenomenon of expansion and harmonization of interdependent links between States on a global scale, has found one of its principal supporting pillars in the Internet. Networks have made it possible to renew the genre. The term "globalize" first appeared in the beginning of the 20th Century, and was generalized in the thesis by McLuhan (the global village), but the idea was not as new as it may have seem. In the 15th and 16th Centuries, the world was already built around large cities (Genoa, Amsterdam, London, etc.) which were the capitals of financial or economic networks, which extended to a worldwide scale. The construction of the Internet as a star, with its concentration nodes of exchanges is sometimes rather similar to this world of global business exchange networks organized around large centers which are forces of attraction.

4.1.8. *Shock theories*

In "The Clash of Civilisations", political scientist Samuel Huntingdon in 1993 confirmed that the East-West conflict of ideologies gave way to a clash of civilizations [HUN 00]. He proposed a representation of the world where the end of bipolar equilibrium (characteristic of the Cold War) resulted in an increased division between men, stemming from the fact that they belonged to civilizations[87]. He distinguished 8 competing civilizations: Chinese (Confucianism), Japanese (Shintoism), the Muslims, Western Christians, Eastern Christians, South American, Hinduism, Sub-Saharan Africa. He confirmed that the relations between these civilizations were intrinsically conflicting. His approach was far from being unanimous, and sometimes faced fierce criticism: "Let us insist. The clash of civilizations as an explicative tool and globalizing conflicts in the 21st Century seems neither efficient nor relevant"[88]. His critics believe more in concepts such as the representation of identity of values as factors which explain conflicts between civilizations. There are, of course, confrontations between Chinese and Japanese hackers, based on cultural issues, and some religious ones (aggressive Chinese and Korean hacktivism when the Emperor of Japan visits an Shinto war memorial); there are certainly waves of strictly religious content, particularly visible in claims and slogans on site defacements everywhere across the world (pro-Islam); but we have not yet seen today conflicts claiming Western Christian, Eastern Christian, South-American or other statuses. Cyberspace is moving away from S. Huntingdon's vision.

The Shock Theory is also the title of a book by Naomi Klein published in 2008 [KLE 08]. The argument running through this work is simple: when a war or a natural disaster destroys a country, when whole populations are damaged by high scale phenomena, they go into a state of shock. Some (governments, leaders, but more generally, capitalism) use this temporary state of total chaos to their advantage to occupy the land, to take extreme measures to their benefit, before the capabilities to be resilient against it all can take the upper hand. They exploit human misery when the individual is at its weakest, wholly unable to go against the least amount of resistance; they apply shock therapy methods on their populations for economical reasons. This theory establishes a direct relationship between super disorders and mega profits. This doctrine explains how the politics of the free market were imposed on the world by exploiting situations of psychological shock that the populations and States found themselves in.

The process is relatively simple: a country finds itself in a state known as A; some actors might want to change this state, but certain resistance gets in their way. A disaster happens, either natural or deliberate; the country is now transformed and can go onto state B, under the blow of a radical transformation, quick, with no concessions. Naomi Klein develops her analysis with the support of several examples: before the floods, the New Orleans education system offered a standard

---

87 According to him, a civilization is above all, based on a religion.
88 [ENC 09], p. 199.

education, accessible to a high number, but public schools were in a bad condition, suffering from a lack of financial means. After the floods, everything had to be rebuilt; liberalists redesigned the city, private schools became the backbone of the education system, moving the poor even further away. They went from 123 public schools, to only 4. New Orleans became a sort of laboratory for a new form of education system. According to Klein, this is just one example of how capitalist nests in situations of extreme chaos, and also fear. They use tragedy as an opportunity for radical change.

The theories of Milton Friedman developed at the University of Chicago are behind this method which was applied to New Orleans. According to Friedman, says Klein, the State must only intervene in one domain: security and defense. Not, however, *education*. In the State's school cuts, he sees the stamp of socialism and interference in the free market[89]. The example of Iraq is used, a country which has undergone many shocks: the violence of war to control will and perceptions, plus economic shock therapy (massive privatizations, inflations, etc.). This author also discusses the Falklands War (Argentina), the riots in Tiananmen (China), NATO's attack on Belgrade, and of course, 9/11 (USA). The method does not necessarily force fate. The important element is opportunism, knowing how to use this time filled with vulnerability, and having the ability to do it, which also assumes a prior state of preparation, and a capability to possibly create a new shock to ensure the treatment we wish to implement.

For Friedman, only a real crisis produces real change. Shock and crisis make it possible to move from the politically impossible to the politically inevitable. The art of major reform comes from the way of making it accepted, making it inevitable, but further still, making it considered as a savior and something positive. Reformers must act quickly, because a certain time window will open up after a disaster, where anything is possible: an opportunity is created which just has to be taken, before society goes back to its initial, pre-crisis state. Can this model be transferred to cyberspace?

We could imagine that actors profit from situations of disorder and chaos that a major cyberattack might generate, for example. A major attack which strikes the system's "brain" could land the social body in danger. A brutal cut in access to cyberspace would probably create a void, felt by the social body, which would be the same as being deprived of our senses: no longer seeing, hearing, or feeling the world as we felt it before. Under the effect of the blow, would the social body become vulnerable, exploitable, useable, malleable? Thus, in the same way as there was a pre 9/11 and an after (the after being the liberticidal laws passed in the name of security), there will be a before and after to a "major cyberattack". The before

---

89 [KLE 08], p. 5.

and after of the Estonia affair differ as the policies put into place for security and defense know how to benefit from the example to justify new measures, creations, investments. A before and after was also discussed during the Stuxnet affair. But Stuxnet did not strike populations closely, and still remains an affair for specialists or those curious about the phenomenon.

The Friedman theory is behind the military "Shock and Wave" doctrine, written by Harlan K. Ullman and James P. Wade in 1996 [ULL 96]. The essential principles of this doctrine consist of acting quickly, shocking the adversary psychologically, imposing the vision of oversized forces on him and annihilating his resistance, his will to fight. The "shock and awe" theory has similarities with the Blitzkrieg approach (speed, precise strikes). This strategy is based on information technologies: spreading information, controlling information space (our own, that belonging to the allies, international public opinion, and of course, the adversary's, conveying messages, gaining control over information systems (requiring computerized attack-type operations), having this dominating vision of the battlefield which is necessary for victory (data collection, intelligence, monitoring, recognition). This theory cannot be applied to all contexts and is certainly not a recipe for victory [GIB 01]. Cyberspace is not only used to create shock. If we follow Friedman's argument, a major cyberattack would not be a disaster for everybody. The anticipation of major events must not be limited to imagining solutions for security and defense, but also solutions for recuperation and exploiting shock, which does not consist of rising up everybody, but strengthening the power and capabilities of a few. Friedman's strategy, however, cannot take advantage of a major destabilization in cyberspace. In fact, liberalism, capitalism and globalization have made cyberspace their vector of development. A major attack on cyberspace would be more of an attack on the economic and political models, which would be weakened by this attack.

4.1.9. *Naval and maritime power strategy*

The maritime strategy emphasizes the marine environment and the advantages offered by the ocean in times of peace and war. The naval strategy emphasizes the fleets, the conduct of war on the water. This is the violent sub-category of the maritime strategy[90]. In these strategies we find many analogies which can be applied to cyberspace. In terms of naval power, Navy development has always been associated with emerging economic and cultural flows. In the same way, we could link the need to develop cybernetic military capabilities with the need to protect commercial flows in the new dimension. The biggest developments are made in States with the highest economic growth (China, South Korea, etc.). The growth of

90 [MON 07].

cybernetic power follows the same dynamic. The growth of the navy in Asia reflects its good economic condition and, undoubtedly, also the strengthening of these States. This also happens in cyberspace. If there is a relation between the GDP and the level of development in the naval forces, then China, South Korea and India, for example, still have a margin for progress. The USA, harboring worries with regard to the development of Chinese military power, are not ready to relax just yet. The developments in capabilities relating to cyberspace go by the same logic.

Marine environment	Cyber environment
Isotropic environment	Isotropic environment
Total maneuvering freedom, because we can choose the route we wish	Here, we can choose the path that the data will take
Seas and oceans are interdependent Geographically, the navy of one region can access all maritime space in all other regions	Sub-spaces in cyberspace communicate
The sea is a restrictive environment: climate, hostile regions (the Arctic, for example)	Cyberspace has its own restrictions: limited data rates, for example

Table 4.5. *Comparison between the logic of the marine environment[91] and the cyber environment*

The functions given to cyberforces used by the USA and gradually other nations as well, will probably not be limited to accompanying operations in war time, or to protecting the national, working population in peace time and conflict against enemy attacks. Their role must be expanded. Let us imagine that cyber units are becoming forces of pressure in the collection of nations in their own right, and instruments of diplomacy. Cyberdiplomacy using cyberforces would remain as an OOTW[92], and could be exerted in times of peace and crisis, and not only in war, aiming to have an effect on operations or simply manifest its presence (demonstrative deployment of forces). A coercive diplomacy may be conceived of, a coercion aiming to fulfill political objectives (dissuading actors from engaging in war, for example). The States could use these bodies as the armed wing of the new politics of the gun-vessel (using or threatening to use force in international crises, for example), or as an instrument of diplomacy and influence. If confrontations in cyberspace are limited when face to face with state-governed enemies, then we could well imagine here that the enemies agree on rules and a standard precise framework, or are inspired by the principle of habits and customs which govern naval warfare. But, amongst these actors, we must count the others, the non-state

91 For more of the logic of the sea environment, see the Revue DSI special edition no. 14, p. 9, October 2010.
92 OOTW: operation other than war.

governed actors, and the irregular actors. For Vice-Admiral Arthur K. Cebrowski, cyberspace is a new strategic space, similar to the sea, as an international domain of business and communication [CEB 04][93]: "The synergy of these events has established cyberspace as a new strategic wide common, similar to Mahan's theories, according to which the sea is described as a "wide common", which is the international domain of business and communications" [CEB 04]. The same applies to power in cyberspace as for naval power[94]: not being powerful in this domain does not guarantee domination, but weakness does guarantee decline. The navy domain is not only intended for combat: humanitarian actions, global business security, a place to express one's power over other States to stop them attacking (weakness encourages aggression), gathering intelligence, contributing to national security, etc. The same characteristics can be applied to cyberspace.

In Table 4.6 we are looking for possible comparisons between the cybernetic world and the maritime and naval space.

Sea		Cyberspace
Use of the sea according to Ken Booth[95] – 1976	Diplomatic role: Negotiations in a position of force	Diplomacy based on cyberspace is indeed possible in the long term. When a State can prove its cybernetic fire power, its superior capabilities, it will be able, maybe, to use this argument in negotiations. This is perhaps what creators of cyberattacks are looking for when they launch them before or during international summits, which is increasingly more often now
Use of the sea according to Ken Booth – 1976	Diplomatic role: Manipulation	Cyberspace is clearly a place of manipulation: of data, information, images, ideas, individuals
Use of the sea according Ken Booth – 1976	Diplomatic role: Prestige	Controlling cyberspace, whether this is on the military, industrial or content front, is an instrument of prestige
Use of the sea according Ken Booth – 1976	Police role: Coastal responsibilities	If navy forces can play the role of the police, guaranteeing security over the land, then cyberspace can also be used as a source of information making it possible to contribute to securing the States

---

93 Quoted in [NEA 09] page 208 http://www.ndu.edu/CTNSP/docUploaded//International%20Transformation.pdf.

94 Navy War College Strategic Studies Group XXVI briefing, "Convergence of Sea Power and Cyber Power", 13th July 2007.

95 According to the diagram published in DSI, special edition, 14, October 2010, p. 94.

Use of the sea according Ken Booth – 1976	Military role: Projection of force	Cyberspace facilitates the deployment of forces into the various parts of the world. It also facilitates the projection of forces. Cyberspace itself, as the maritime space, is the place chosen to project forces: attacks can be led out of our own territory, whilst staying in the same cyberspace
	Maritime pirates[96]	Computerized pirating[97]
	Pirates	Cyberpirates; Michael Tanji[98] produced the hypothesis of resorting to web "pirates", in comparison with ocean pirates, to make up for the difference between the capabilities of the LEAs[99] and pirates. Is this model (using private resources to fight against piracy) transferrable to cyberspace?
Alfred Thayer Mahan[100]	Maritime power makes it possible to dominate the world. There is, then, an environment which is superior to all the others, in that it gives power to those to adapt to it[101]	Cyberspace in its entirety is necessary for gaining power, and for upholding it. If it not a matter of seizing it, then it is indeed a question of guaranteeing a dominant position there in spite of everything, or total freedom to act. This, really, boils down to the same thing, because this freedom is only possible through domination and the inabilities of others

---

96 The role of sea wars in the fight on piracy on the oceans in order to ensure the protection of global commerce, could provide a model for the fight on computer crimes which attacks global commerce in cyberspace.

97 The image of hackers is the skull and crossbones of piracy and looting. Besides this symbol, the space itself can be likened to the sea space in terms of how the pirates use it. Like in Indonesia, where 17,000 islands became a landmark of piracy, the Internet is a space for piracy. Some isolated States virtually entirely depend on sea channels for their commerce in the same way that high connected States virtually entirely depend on the Internet for their activities. This state of dependency makes them a target for the threat of sea piracy.

98 "INFOSEC Privateering as a Solution to Cyberspace Threats".

99 Law enforcement agencies.

100 His works deal with the influence of sea power on history.

101 The idea consists of confirming that there are territories which are more necessary than others for gaining power.

Halford Mackinder	The domination of Eastern Europe ensured domination of the Heartland[102]. Mackinder introduced the notion of the World Island[103]	Mahan's theories, like those by Mackinder, confirm that there are spaces, or parts of these spaces, which are more important than others and which guarantee world control. If we consider that cyberspace today is a substitute for the continents, then the whole challenge consists of defining the spaces within cyberspace, the sub-spaces, whose control must be guaranteed to maintain the rest. This might be all the Internet's root servers. But it could also be an infrastructure outside cyberspace, but which cyberspace depends on, such as the electrical distribution networks. Controlling the whole of cyberspace is probably a challenge with no solution, as it is growing every day. It is also a challenge that does not come under the jurisdiction of the States or non-state governed actors. Is cyberspace really the space which should be dominated, or is it only the vector making it possible to reach the essential space, the space of ideas?
Spykman	Rimland[104]	See the same comment as those relating to Mahan's and Mackinder's theories
Hugo Grotius – 1630	Concept of *mare liberum*[105] (open sea)[106]	Cyberspace is also an open space, but one which has closed ports, controlled access, denials, restricted domains. We can open or block access according to our own interests

102 A turning zone, a central part of the world, a continental zone, located in the middle of the earth, not accessible to sea powers, thus a natural advantage.

103 World Island: a notion which underlines the disadvantaged position of the USA, which is located in an inner crescent. This position puts the USA in a position of potential inferiority (Z. Brzezinski, 1997).

104 Rimland is a term coined by Spykman to denote the set of coastal and Southern regions of Eurasia (which is the equivalent of Mackinder's world island). Spykman turns Mackinder's argument around: he who controls the Rimland (and not the Heartland, as with Mackinder), controls the world.

105 Opposing principle to closed sea/*mare clausum*.

106 Principle stating that ships from all States can sails in the waters of a State, if it is for commerce and transport. For example, the principle is applied by the Dutch who prosper from their sea commerce.

John Selden – 1635	Concept of *mare clausum* (closed sea)[107]	In this approach to the Internet, we find the same dichotomy between open and closed, between free and ownership. Choices are only made according to the interests specific to each individual. But an internet ocean where all ports are denied would not make any sense
Cornelius von Bynkershoek – 1702	Bynkershoek principle (1702): the seas are a wide common[108]. A State's control over its neighboring sea must be limited to the cannon's range the littoral zone	Cyberspace is a wide common, but which has many owners. Actors try to section their own spaces according to criteria other than the gun or cannon range, since the notion of distance is completely wiped out in cyberspace. Rather they use renewed criteria: when soldiers are forced to put aside the spaces where they can act freely in cyberspace, then this is the same as leaving spaces from which any non-desired actor is removed

Table 4.6. *Research on comparisons between theories of sea/naval power and cyberpower*

Attacks led through networks, by their invisible, discreet and silent nature, and the surprise effect that they cause, remind us of submarine maneuvers; cyberspace in the oceans and sea-beds. Cyberattacks, like submarine attacks, can sink (we use terminology such as pirating, paralysis, destabilization, and sabotage for cyberattacks) the enemy ship (the target, the server, the information system, the network, the satellite), by taking advantage of the shelter offered by the environment they evolve in. Made invisible by their environment, the attackers may act and withdraw without being seen, attacking in an unpredictable way, acting where they want to with complete discretion, leading their actions in foreign or adversary spaces or territories, fighting from their environment to strike targets outside this environment (today, the submarine may be part of land operations; cyberspace makes it possible to strike targets beyond its dimensions by producing effects). There are many common points between them, due to the shadows that the cyberattacks and cyber defenders can operate under, the shadows which offer them significant power. But this analogy is ignored in geostrategic analyzes, and in the perception of cyber power as an instrument of power.

---

107 Only ships flying the flag of the neighboring State can sail in their waters.
108 See his book *De Domino Maris* published in 1702, the first modern conception of sea sovereignty.

The multitude of attacks in the cyberspace world today are the banderilla whose strikes are carried out against all sorts of targets, and particularly by small actors against much bigger ones; the submarine was also perceived as a "mosquito", able to attack much more imposing ships[109]. "The first submarines were only local defense weapons; they could not be distanced from their home port. We have managed to replace nearly all of them with high action range ships, used for offensive in high seas and on enemy coasts. But in both cases, their tactic is the same. Invisible or hardly visible, depending on whether they are completely submerged or only have their periscope out, they act by surprise", we read in 1915 [BLA 15][110]. The first submarines could not be considered as thorough attack tools, but through their silence, their invisibility, the discreet nature of their approach (stealth) and the surprise caused by their action, from the very beginning they had qualities which, today, can be found in cyberattacks.

Maneuvers in cyberspace share discretion with submarine maneuvers. The environment where these maneuvers operate, and their respective technologies, means that they can operate without being detected, to get closer to the object they want to observe or hit. It is possible to maneuver within cyberspace as a submarine does, which can travel along the coasts of an enemy country without the adversary being able to detect it. This is what has happened many times to South Korea, which seemed unable to detect the presence of North Korean submarines however close they could be to its coasts these last few years. But how many countries have been victims of intrusions into their sensitive information systems, intrusions for purposes of espionage, without any security service noticing it?

It is only often by chance that we can know about intrusions, submarine intrusions as much as cybernetic intrusions. It was through analyzing its log book that the South Korean services were able to know that North Korean submarines had entered the South Korean waters in the previous months[111]. It is sometimes in the few months or years after a cyber intrusion that the victims discover the facts of what they had been subjected to. This could be, for instance, divulging sensitive documents on the Internet which were claimed to have been saved and stored well away in secure machines. Attacks on the first submarines and cyberattacks have the common fault of lacking precision in their shots, and the need for the first attacks to be as close to their target as possible to get a chance of hitting them, and for the second attacks to have intimate knowledge of the target to have a hope of hitting it seriously and destabilizing it. The submarine gives an adversary the impression that threat is everywhere. It can appear and disappear, strike where it wants, and can go

---

109 *Défense & sécurité internationale*, special edition, no. 11, April 2010, p. 09.
110 Pages 12-13.
111 *Yet Another Gaping Hole in S. Korea's Defenses Revealed*, April 6th 2010, http://english.chosun.com/site/data/html_dir/2010/04/06/2010040601060.html.

into enemy waters. Cyberspace gives attackers the same advantages and incites the same feeling in their potential targets. The two approaches differ on a few points, however: the first sub-marines were vulnerable once spotted. Cyber attackers have always played on anonymity and the difficulty, if not the impossibility, of being able to blame them. In the absolute, cyber attackers are not restricted by distance, they can strike from afar and are hardly identifiable.

A number of cyberattacks share the idea of aiming at economic targets with German army submarines during WWI. The German army, in fact, used sub-marines to torpedo merchant navy ships in the North Sea and in the English Channel during WWI. Faced with the new strategy, the term *new war* was then used, of a war on economy, of threats against the progress of civilization: "If using a sub-marine would allow any nation, when it wanted, to completely stop and with impunity maritime traffic in part of its seas […], then civilization risks seeing itself threatened once more in one of the elements necessary for its development, namely the progress of intercontinental exchanges" [BLA 15][112].

Contemporary attacks share the same economic targets, and we are offering them the capability to put our civilization in danger. Today, 90% of goods are shipped via the sea, and therefore it must be protected. Cyberspace ensures the operation of our globalized world. So we must guarantee *its* protection, protect its service exchanges, and its financial transactions. Operations led in cyberspace have the following in common with submarine missions: an intelligence function over long periods, defense, protecting the country's interests, exercising a potential threat. As this is the case for all technology, introducing submarines into war has raised questions with regard to its impact on the art of warfare.

These questions have, of course, fueled debates on the RMA around the 1990s, amid the introduction of ICTs. In his book, *Chronique de la Grande Guerre*, Maurice Barrès wrote in 1918 on the submarine and its intensive use by the Germans: "This is not to say that our enemies have a fearsome weapon. But they now recognize, in the secret of their counsels, that this weapon cannot control the decision to start war. Persius, who we take to be the biggest naval critic of the time, always considered submarine warfare to be a bluff. The element of being submersible is an element which will be added to other elements used in naval art, but which does not transform maritime warfare. If the submersible changed the very nature of war, then it would change the very nature of peace. This is not true, however. It is an instrument which took its place amongst the battleships; but,

---

112 pp. 37-38.

politically, far from being a revolution which creates a decisive superiority, it is a great deception" [BAR 18][113].

Today, we more or less hear the same arguments regarding the advantages or limitations of cyberwar: the cybernetic weapon cannot decide on the outcome of war; it is neither superior nor inferior to other weapons, but will come to be added to the plethora of weapons we have and modes of confrontation. Cyberwar does not fundamentally transform the art of warfare (there is no RMA associated with the appearance of cyberspace); the cybernetic weapon takes its position alongside other weapons; cyberwar is more an instilled fear than a real threat; whatever the case, its psychological dimension is essential in cyberwar which remains as a component of information warfare. Submarines and cyber weapons equate to the same combat, dare we say.

Submarines are complex weapon systems, state of the art technology, but their usefulness largely relies on the control that men and crews have over them. The quality of the submarine forces depends on their training, their experience, their motivation, and their capability to transmit knowledge and know-how. This aspect, critical in the domain of submarines as it seems to have missed its vocation, is just as important in the cyberwar domain. Cyber units or cyberforces which are being created in the USA and practically everywhere across the world, must be made up of individuals, and the usefulness of implementing nice theories, doctrines and other strategies developed on paper over the last 20 years will depend on their capabilities. Man will make the difference, man will be able to define the cyberwar capabilities, and not just the number of individuals making up a unit, the available data rates, the number of servers, satellites, the capacity to store or process data. Modern submarines are also in cyberspace, because they must communicate between them. The US Navy is planning to give submariners data transmission systems and access to the Internet[114].

The counterpart to the power bestowed on submarines? Their vulnerability. These vessels are made vulnerable to detection systems due to their communication needs. The force/vulnerability pair is also a characteristic of cyberspace. From a geographical point of view, today we reveal a subtle increase in the number of submarines in the world, which seems to express an idea of going back to competing for control over maritime spaces. The confirmation of State's desire to implement cyber units, to define cyberspace as a place of combat, is part of the same logic: the logic of competing for control over cyberspace, this time, a virtual competition. Underwater warfare may also be involved in cyberwar, for example, by attacking the infrastructures which are essential for the Internet network to survive.

113 Page 23.
114 *Défense & sécurité internationale*, special edition, no. 11, April 2010, p. 33.

Communication cables which run through the oceans are regularly damaged (bad weather, broken cables). In peace time, repairing these damages is an easy task. However, submarine cables are easy targets. A physical target on these cables would undoubtedly have effects which are as useful and radical as the operations led by a software attack. Protection of these cables must be guaranteed. Threats on submarine Internet cables are very similar to those threats already felt in the 19th Century on communication cables.

The link between cyberwar and underwater warfare is so strong that the lexicon developed by the US DoD in 2010, commissioned by the Chief of the Defense Staff, combined the two definitions[115]. The definition of "undersea warfare", taken from JP 1-02 is formulated as thus: *operations conducted to establish and maintain control of the underwater environment by denying an opposing force the effective use of the underwater systems and weapons. It includes offensive and defensive submarine, anti-submarine and mine warfare operations.* The definition which is similar to cyberwar is formulated in these terms: *an armed conflict conducted in whole or part by cyber means. Military operations conducted to deny an opposing force the effective use of cyberspace systems and weapons in a conflict. It includes cyberattack, cyberdefense, and cyber enabling actions.* Novels using underwater warfare in their narratives will once more help us to illustrate the analogies which really exist, or which must be established between the cyberspace environment and other environments. Let us draw images and analogies found in "The Hunt for Red October" by Tom Clancy [CLA 09], published in the USA in 1984. We can explore these analogies from the following aspects:

– The importance of the human being, the individual, and the notion of trust. As soon as well confide the responsibility of handling particularly destructive, strategic weapons to men (as is the case in the novel's Soviet nuclear submarine, Red October), the authorities must be able to trust them entirely. "The crews of such vessels had to be trusted"[116]. What would happen if mankind decided to exert the fire power that they have within arm's reach? This applies to cyberdefense also. The individuals making up the cyber units must have confidence in their commanders and authorities. Hackers may come from a very special class of soldier, with an astute technological knowledge. The power of those who hold this knowledge in their hands can be huge. Imagine a State developing programs designed to launch cyberattacks on opposing forces. Then imagine that the developers activate programs on their own State or army or take the initiative against enemies.

---

115 USA. DoD. Joint Chiefs of Staff. Joint terminology for cyberspace operations. 2010. 16 pages. See definition 18, p. 8 on "cyberwar". http://www.nsci-va.org/CyberReferenceLib /2010-11-Joint%20Terminology%20for%20Cyberspace%20Operations.pdf.
116 [CLA 84].

– Computers bring errors into our appreciation and understanding of the environment. "As important as the computer was its programming software. Four years before, a PhD candidate in geophysics who was working at Cal Tech's geophysical laboratory had completed a program of six hundred thousand steps designed to predict earthquakes". This program was introduced into the army. But the program had "a nasty habit of analyzing the wrong signal – and you couldn't tell it was wrong from the results. Besides, since it had been originally designed to look for seismic events, Jones suspected it of a tendency to interpret anomalies as seismic events [...]. It was one thing to use computers as a tool, quite another to let them do your thinking for you. Besides, they were always discovering new sea sounds that nobody had ever heard before, much less classified"[117]. All the same, we notice that cyberspace can produce errors or interfere with our perception of reality in a damaging way (too much information making relevant information, or creating an image which does not relate to reality).

– Asking questions in light of large scale navy maneuvers, American soldiers are asking themselves questions. Are these exercises or real maneuvers? "Well, sir, it might not be an exercise at all. It could be the real thing. This could be the beginning of a conventional war against NATO, its first step being interdiction of the sea lines of communication"[118]. Aggressive actions concealed behind banal actions which seem like criminal acts, or even disguised as cyberdefense exercises as is happening more and more in the world, could perhaps also hide the preparation for a conventional war. Observers confronted with imminent threat, who detected signs of suspicious activities in cyberspace, are in the same position as the commanders and government in the novel, namely in terms of doubt and the questions asked: "this can't be [...], this might be [...]" a test, a real attack in preparation, the premises of a war, a provocation, a spreading out…Some activities and operations are, sometimes, not what they seem to be.

The novel talks of the advantage held by the Soviet submarine. Actors in cyberspace benefit from the same advantages. It is a limitless space which acts as their refuge, and offers the possibility to act and remain invisible at the same time (or almost), and finally, to escape all detection. Earth and air environments do not offer the same advantages.

4.1.10. *Air/space and cybernetic power: analogies*

The birth of aviation did not appear to soldiers as a time for revolution. This technological break took time to be imposed and accepted as a significant advancement, as being useful to the art of warfare. The first exploits by the Wright

---

117 [CLA 84].
118 [CLA 84].

brothers were little known and they were only considered as real, in France, with the possibility of using airplanes as war engines. It would be logical to explore whether the new apparatus, displaying special and hugely different operating conditions, could be used in future wars, either as fighters or as scouts [NAN 11][119]. These few lines from a study by Max de Nansouty published in 1911 in the use of airplanes in warfare, raise two questions. One concerns the conditions of accepting and introducing new technology, whatever that might be, into military affairs, and also its transformation into an instrument of war. The other question deals with the impact and place of this new technology amongst existing weapons. Skepticism, reluctance, hesitation, timid adoption, acceptance, discussions on the rupture, on the revolution in military matters: the process is sometimes long and complex, and goes from one extreme to the other.

Confronted with the beginnings of aviation, soldiers showed themselves to be more prudent, and more reserved. They were faced with a new piece of technology, that they clearly had no idea what to do with. The airplane was first of all seen as a sport, not a strategic military instrument. Using this technology as a tool for war did not happen on its own, and went against resistance, as if military machinery ran too much like clockwork, and that introducing a new cog into its intricacies could risk disturbing it, which might explain the reluctance surrounding the issue. The Italian Giulio Douhet was part of those who turned flight into a strategic war instrument. Around 1910, he confirmed the new battlefield which had been declared open: the sky[120]. This is not the discourse, it must not be forgotten, of our contemporary military experts in question, who are making cyberspace a new field for battle and confrontation today. At the beginning of the 20th Century, the technological breakthrough of flight seemed to open the doors to a revolution in the art of warfare. It is, now, possible to imagine striking the opposing force beyond the front line, in their own territory (striking where civil populations are to be found). This idea can be found in the new dimension today: by using cybernetic weapons, it is possible to strike a society at its heart (seeing and striking beyond the horizon). The capabilities offered by cyberspace authorize, for example, aiming critical infrastructures, and sensitive targets, such as banks, energy distribution services, vital industries. This strategy of striking the opposing force's capabilities at the source is part of the theories of information warfare and cyberwar[121].

If the theories formed by Giulio Douhet seem to guarantee an easy victory (these deep strikes are used to destroy the opposing force's capabilities to fight, and to hit

---

119 Chapter on "Utilisation des aéroplanes à la guerre" (Using airplanes in warfare) page 15.
120 Quoted in *Aux origines de la stratégie aérienne, Histoire et Stratégie, La puissance aérienne*, no. 2, Paris, France, September 2010.
121 International law is then damaged, attacks on critical infrastructures consequently directly attack the civil population.

the civilian populations in the heart, so the enemy admits defeat), then history has shown that even intensive bombings on populations are not always enough to secure victory. It seems that cyberattacks cannot win through an adversary either, and can only complement war, in its more classical forms and dimensions. Both dimensions, spatial and cybernetic, thus present us with a multitude of analogies. Flight as a new weapon raised questions regarding the hierarchy of dimensions in relation to each other: was space more superior than the sea, than the earth? Should weapons (land, marine army) be subordinate to flight, and should the contrary be imagined?

The debate is also continuing today concerning the cybernetic dimension. Should a new weapon be created (a cyber army), or should this function be subordinate to an already existing weapon, and in this case, which weapon should be stated as being the head of the natural hierarchy? The answer is, of course, not irrelevant, because the weapon which would control cyberspace would control the others also, in a way, due to the transversal nature of cyberspace to all the conventional dimensions. We can look for answers in the conventional distinction that has been made of the use of cyberspace, between tactical and strategic conception. Tactical conception consists of making cyberspace into an additional instrument used in other dimensions. Cyberforces, then, only are simply a "weapon" to be integrated within already existing forces. This is the approach which is applied globally to cyber units which are integrated and not independent. Cyberspace, cyberattacks and cyberwar are force intensifiers. In strategic conception, it is accepted that cyberforces make it possible, on the contrary, to reach strategic and political effects by striking the vital centers in society directly, along with the critical infrastructures and military information systems. This approach is similar to Giulio Douhet's theory (the utility of striking against demographic centers), or even Sherman's theory (recommending attacks on industrial sites).

The consequence of this specific power given to flight, according to Douhet is that: flight should be put on a higher level of hierarchy than the land and marine army. The Severksy model (1894-1984) may also be cited here. Seversky, researching a new geopolitical theory, and particularly the definition of space which must be controlled to guarantee world domination, confirmed that land and sea power were, from then on, subordinate to air power. He who controls space controls all other spaces at will, he told us. This was the modern counterpart to undersea power.

Today, strategic conception concerning cybernetic space is *not* imposed, yet many questions still remain. It seems possible to launch cyberattacks on critical infrastructures (Estonia or the Stuxnet affair, for example), but the decisive impact of these attacks has yet to be proven. Cyberattacks and cyberspace are perceived more as additional methods and dimensions, used for conflict and war, and not as substitutes, and not as absolute weapons capable of deciding on the war's fate (it does not seem likely for now to base a victory on action led in a single dimension). It seems clear today that air power is no longer able to decide on the outcome of wars. The successes had by American aviation in Iraq and Afghanistan are tactical successes, but were not transformed into strategic successes.

This is indeed an independent dimension. But in the US, the Air Force nonetheless tends to want to impose itself as a natural controller of cyberspace. At any rate, the Air Force has certainly invested in its domination. In 2005, General Michael Moseley and the US Air Force secretary Michael Wynne stated that the Air Force's mission was to fly and fight in the air, in space, and in cyberspace. The transverse nature of cyberspace makes this approach entirely necessary. The US Air Force wants to impose its influence in three dimensions, guaranteeing total freedom to act within these spaces.

In 2006, a task-force was created within the Air Force to think about how the army could be positioned and act in this new environment of combat. In September 2006, Moseley and Wynne signed a document proposing that an operation command by created for cyberspace. In November 2008, General Moseley created the Air Force Cyber Command (the AFCYBER was created from the 8th Air Force). It implemented the Air Force's organization, training and equipment to turn it into a operational cyberforce. In July 2010, the US Air Force published a document entitled "Cyberspace Operations, Air Force Doctrine Document 3-12", which, in its 55 pages, laid out the main principles of the Air Force's doctrine in terms of cyberspace operations.

By winning over and upholding superiority in cyberspace, the US Air Force aims to maintain its freedom to act in this domain as in the other dimensions (air, space). To guarantee this freedom of action in the air, space and in cyberspace, it must counter the capabilities of an opposing force which disturbs the American capabilities to project power and influence[122]. The Air Force will not strive to gain control and lead operations across the whole of cyberspace – which is *not* a monolithic domain, but one which is composed of sub-domains – but only across parts of this dimension which will be useful for carrying out its missions (for example, a set of IP addresses, only representing a small section of cyberspace). Superiority in cyberspace appears as a vital precondition, making it possible to

---

122 The report deals with the dual nature of cyberspace which is the source of force, power and vulnerability at the same time. But we must remember that this duality is not specific to cyberspace. The oceans also have this characteristic: attacks may come from the sea, but we can use them to project our forces. We can be powerful and vulnerable at the same time. Air space also has this dual nature: we can attack from the air, but can also be attacked via the air without being able to protect ourselves (a missile coming from the air, a plane which crashes into the Twin Towers, etc.).

express full power. It could not take the lead in the air without preliminary control over cyberspace. The most important stake is the fight against asymmetrical threats, which will be the rule from now on.

The introduction of cyberspace operations is part of a specific context; a major evolution in the operation environment and the nature of the conflicts, which make irregular wars the rule, and make regular actors the exception to the rule. But the battle against unconventional, non-state governed, irregular actors raises specific problems: there are multiple actors, unpredictable at that, who do not abide by the same rules. New orders in conflicts are imposing the implementation of an ever more important need for information, and information collection and processing. Networks now have an incredible importance. The document refers to the growing threats against American heritage: the USA is a target and the increasing amount of attacks against their networks is indeed the proof of this. There are many obstacles which need to be removed before they can achieve real superiority and freedom to act, especially as vulnerable points may originate within the very operations of the armed forces. An example of this is the vulnerability of using products (software and hardware), commercial products (off-the-shelf), and sometimes even foreign products[123]. This brings to mind the fact that the US Air Force uses commercial, even foreign, applications for its cyberspace operations.

Information space extends to space[124], particularly via communication and observation satellites[125]. Satellites are the keystone to the cyberspace and communication systems, but also the security system: monitoring (Echelon network is the symbol), observation, communication. These are at the heart of the C4ISR systems, without which a concept such as network-centric warfare could not exist. There would be no drones without satellites. It is even a question of extending the Internet to extra-atmospheric space. Projects in this vein (InterPlanetary Networks) were being formed in the 1990s, but ran into several technical difficulties (delays in important transmissions due to high distances and costs) [GEL 06]. NASA dedicates a few pages on its website to this project[126]. The development of communication

---

123 This vulnerability was again underlined during the Stuxnet affair, which made the headlines between August and October 2010 in a wide part of the world: Iran used foreign applications in its control systems and nuclear plants. But is the use of foreign application really a source of more vulnerabilities than using home-made solutions? Is using foreign or commercial products avoidable when there is a lack of companies and specific developments?
124 The quest for space started 50 years ago, initiated by the USA, for military requirements of reconnaissance. Since, space has become one of the main catalysts for means of security and defense. In this domain, as well as many others, the USA remains in an overwhelming, hegemonic position, with a share of 95% in the global total for space defense spending.
125 NASA's website gives a good representation of satellite position in real time, http://science.nasa.gov/realtime/jtrack/3d/JTrack3D.html.
126 http://tmo.jpl.nasa.gov/index.cfm.

systems based on the infrastructures in extra-atmospheric space will also raise questions for legal, geopolitical and geostrategic domains: questions of seizing this space, questions of regulation of human activity in this space, of sovereignty, new territoriality and independence.

The Treaty on the Principles governing State activities in the exploration and use of extra-atmospheric space, such as the Moon and other celestial bodies, came into force on October 10th 1967 and classified the use of this space by making it forbidden to send objects into orbit carrying nuclear weapons or any weapon of mass destruction. Moreover, extra-atmospheric space is militarized, but is not weaponized. It is exempt from confrontations, not so much due to international rules but because of the low number of actors which exist there, and the risks that these confrontations would have for the belligerents.

No one has any real advantage in fighting in space. Destroying satellites is potentially risky for any actor, because of the debris which floats around in space after some of them are destroyed. Over the last few years, the reappearance of Anti-Satellite Activities led by China and the USA put the theme of space war back on the agenda, and raised the question of the impact that such attacks would have on State security and communications. This threat is both a political and technological issue. Means for destruction or interference in satellite operation have been thought up by the Americans, as much as by the Soviets, Russians, or the Chinese from the beginning of the 1960s. Between 1968 and 1982, the Soviet Union led a good 20 ASAT type tests [BHU 07], and the USA led 35 tests between 1959 and 1986. On October 18th 1975, the Soviets blinded an American satellite using infrared rays. On October 17th 1997, the American blinded a satellite using a 30 watt laser (test on the Air Force satellite MSTI-3, orbiting 420 km from Earth). The Chinese were focusing on ASAT operations from the 1960s (the 640-3 program, then the 863 program). On January 11th 2007, China tested its capability to destroy satellites, carrying out the test on an old weather observation satellite, Fengyun 1C. The most vulnerable satellites are, of course, in low orbit.

The development of an interplanetary Internet could, then, be subject to these threats and become the pretext for a new source of confliction in extra-atmospheric space. Means for space warfare go alongside the objective for information warfare and cyberwar. Destroying or interfering with satellite operation would have immediate consequences for the operation of data transmission systems, for C4ISR type systems operation, for navigation systems, for accessing the Internet is certain areas of the world, and on telephone communication. "Objects which evolve in the space environment actually retain an intrinsically vulnerable character. Identifying the character of a collusion or maneuver or even the cause of malfunction to be intentional or not, or hostile or not, is today still far from being guaranteed on all fronts, even for military satellites"[127].

In the table below, we have categorized the many comparisons which can be drawn between discussions on space and cyberspace. There are many reasons for these comparisons:

– space is clearly natural, but we must have technologies to access it. In the same way, accessing cyberspace requires the use of technology, without which it would not exist anyway;

– space technologies, except for stations and rockets transporting men, consist of satellites, whose main function is to transmit data and information, whether these are telecommunication, observation or other satellites;

– satellites are the integral part of the infrastructure making up cyberspace;

– building and conquering cyberspace both have contemporary chronologies: everything really started after 1945;

– the analogy between infrastructures and technologies which access to both domains is strong. These are modern technologies, communication technologies which require hardware infrastructures, software layers (acquisition, processing, data transmission) and which use a part of the electromagnetic spectrum.

Space	Cyberspace
In August 1945, the USA planned to send satellites into space to increase their means of observation and intelligence	During WWII, the USA and Europe launched the development of computer processors enabling them to decipher enemy messages (intelligence)
Large initiatives started in the USA	Large initiatives started in the USA
Today, there are around 20 countries in space	Virtually the entire planet is being called to connect to the Internet
High costs to access it	Relatively low access cost for users, but we must not forget the very high costs of developing and deploying the necessary infrastructures
Will space be American?	Will cyberspace remain American? The base for it is American (Internet, protocols, control)

---

127 [PAS 10] p. 80

For a long time, a part of the world paid tribute to American capabilities (China, for example, asked Nixon to provide satellite images of the USSR. During the First Gulf War, the French only had satellite images provided by the USA). This situation is changing, with a number of States becoming autonomous and powers in space	Many countries have paid tribute to the USA by developing their own cyberspace (China developed its own Internet based on American equipment). The development of national industries, software and hardware is leading this country towards autonomy in this field
Since 1990, space has become strategic in warfare	Since 1990, information space and cyberspace have become strategic in warfare
Space is militarized	Cyberspace is militarized
Will space be weaponized?	Cyberspace is weaponized (made up of combats in space)
Space shortens the decision making loop	Cyberspace makes it possible to strike beyond the horizon, without seeing nor being seen, striking from further afield is possible
Space shortens the decision making loop	Processing data digitally enables capture, processing, and quicker data analyzes and decision making
Space enables better accuracy (strikes, images)	Cyberspace is more accurate through the advantage of the information which is available and can be processed
The power given by space is also a source of vulnerability (the satellites we depend on here on Earth are vulnerable)	Cyberspace brings power, force, and vulnerability all at once
The USA is at the mercy of a space Pearl Harbor (an idea formed in 1993)	Cyberspace is at the mercy of a cyber Pearl Harbor
Duality: soldiers can use civilian satellites, particularly during war time	Duality: soldiers can use civilian networks, commercial civil applications, and hardware designed for civilians
There are passive systems (listening, voice, interception) for military space	Cyberspace also has passive systems
There are active systems for military space (capable of bringing combat to space)	Soldiers have systems able to bring combat to cyberspace
Space is in danger due to the debris cluttering it up	Cyberspace is threatened with implosion, due to a too high number of users, of data, of fluxes, etc.
Civil satellites have equivalent, or sometimes better than, military satellites	The capabilities of solutions developed in the civil sector have no reason to envy military solutions. The capabilities used by soldiers come directly from the civil sector
Mankind has known how to bring war into all the elements it has conquered (fire, earth, sea, air). Will it bring war into extra-atmospheric space?	Mankind has known how to bring war into all the elements it has conquered. It *has* brought war into the element is conquered: cyberspace

Without ground bases, space is nothing (means to control satellites). Leading an attack on means in space may consist of destroying means on the ground	Without the physical infrastructure, cyberspace is nothing. Attacking cyberspace may consist of leading an attack on infrastructures there (cables, servers, etc.)
Space was alongside the Cold War and is accompanying modern wars more and more today	Cyberspace has been accompanying modern wars since 1990, particularly the war on terrorism
Observation satellites are becoming more and more accurate: this precision leads to misinformation (fake submarines made out of cardboard to lure in observers). Precision does not guarantee control, domination or success	Cyberspace gives access to masses of information and to an increasingly more accurate processing. Precision does not guarantee control, domination or success
The objective of using satellites: seeing everything	The objective of using cyberspace for intelligence means: seeing everything
In 1967, an international Treaty forbade the use of nuclear weapons in extra-atmospheric space, but combat is not forbidden	There is currently no international treaty forbidding combat in cyberspace
Everett Dolman distinguishes 4 distinct areas in space, which their own characteristics: terrestrial area, circumterrestrial space, lunar space, solar space	We can distinguish at least 3 areas in cyberspace. Which are its constitutive layers: the physical layer – the infrastructure – the software layer, and the cognitive dimension
Dolman [DOL 02] imagines astrostrategic points (the essential points which must be controlled): terrestrial space, transit or stopping bases for space operations on the moon, Lagrange's positions L1 to L5	Soldiers had considered creating Botnets for military means, relying on civilian networks: military operations can be led at a later date from these strategic points. Other strategic points are DNS servers, for example
In 1961, D. Cole put forward the idea of colonizing asteroids	We may consider necessary presence in cyberspace as a variant of "colonizing" a territory: establishing colonies means living in new territories
Dolman [DOL 02] confirms the necessary domination of space by the Americans, allowing them to become the shepherds of those who venture there. Domination means that they can impose the true vision of the American world, which must spread the liberal economic model across the world. Through this, they convey American values	We can see a similarity with the American desire to keep the monopoly over the Internet, and the American efforts for info-domination, as well as soft power which aims to extend its power in cyberspace and to use cyberspace to project its power. They want to impose their values as universal values
Domination in this domain, as with all other domains, results in much resistance	As in other domains, hegemonic desires result in resistance

Table 4.7. *Comparisons between space and cyberspace*

4.1.11. *Cyberconflict/cyber weapons, chemical/biological weapons: comparisons*

Cyberconflict, cyberwar and cyber weapons are often compared to nuclear conflict, to the Cold War, to nuclear weapons and to chemical and biological weapons. In Table 4.8 we have summarized the main points where they are similar or dissimilar.

Chemical weapons	Cybernetic weapons
Weapons of mass destruction	Weapons of mass disruption
Direct effect on humanity	Indirect effect on humanity
Capability to destroy	Can be transformed into capability to disrupt
High psychological effect	High psychological effect (PYSOPS are one of the consequences of cybernetic operations)
Sudden nature of attacks	Surprise effect
Efficiency depending on certain conditions (weather, environment)	Efficiency depending on conditions (environment, condition of the target, security systems, reaction measures, etc.)
Efficiency depending on the level of target protection. An actor with good chemical defense keeps its operational capabilities	Efficiency depending on the level of target protection. An actor with good cybernetic defenses, redundant systems, and procedures enabling them to return to the pre-attack date, partly retains its operation capabilities
Defense consists of detecting danger	Defense consists of sensing signals warning of danger
Defense consists of guaranteeing individual protection	Security and defense depend on measures taken individually
Defense consists of collective protection	Defense consists of collective protection
If the target is in possession of chemical weapons, there is a risk that they may use these weapons in reaction to an attack	Must a cyberattack respond to another cyberattack alone?

Table 4.8. *Comparisons between chemical and cybernetic weapons*

Biological weapons	Cybernetic weapons
They do not act immediately	Can act with a delay
Many different ways of spreading them (airplane, drone, bomb, insects, animals, etc.)	Many ways of spreading virus attacks (any format)
Undefined targets: either civilian or military	Both civilian and military targets possible
Major psychological effect	High psychological effect
Threat of terrorist use	Possible terrorist use
Difficult to implement, can limit its usage	Relative ease to implement thus facilitating usage
Uncontrollable attacks (may hit the attacker)	Partly uncontrollable effects (may hit the attacker)

Table 4.9. *Comparisons between biological weapons and cybernetic weapons*

4.1.12. *Cyberconflict/cyber weapons, Cold War, nuclear weapons: comparisons*

Nuclear weapons	Cyber weapons
Weapons used by the powerful, the rich, States	Everybody can use these weapons
Rare	Very wide spread
Difficult to access	Easy to access
High financial cost	Low financial cost
Massive destruction	Massive disruption
Lethal (a nuclear attack between great powers would result in hundreds of millions of attacks)	Not immediately lethal[128]. A large scale cyberattack on a State's financial systems is not lethal

---

128 Cybernetic weapons are part of the line of non-lethal weapons which have been developed since the 1960s: lasers, infrasound, paralysers, tear gases, psychotropic drugs...Non-lethal weapons do not wipe out violence. They are used as an addition to, in support of, lethal weapons. They put their users in a situation of risk and unacceptable asymmetry when faced with actors in possession of lethal weapons and who are likely to use them.

Suitable for the military	Not suitable for the military
Countries in possession of nuclear weapons are identified. Threats are localized and identified. The dissuasion strategy worked because the armed actors were known, though limited in number	Threat can *a priori* be localized[129]. All the "connected" actors are likely to pose a threat which is therefore more widespread. With the number of actors being higher (or indefinite) than for nuclear weapons, then the threat is difficult to trace. The attacks may come from anywhere, at any time, and strike anyone
Threat is omnipresent	Threat is omnipresent. But it is not *a priori* directed towards specific targets
Dissuasion and nuclear arms claim to be strictly defensive	As for nuclear arms, cybernetic arms are (officially) strictly for defensive use
Protects and defends a country's vital interests	Threatens a country's critical infrastructures
Contributes indirectly to partner security	As the threat of using cybernetic arms is not, or is very little, written in full in doctrines, it contributes little to security
Must prevent war	Cybernetic arms do not prevent war
Keeping attackers doubting the way in which the victim will retaliate	The use of cybernetic arms is always restricted by an unknown factor: the victim's reaction
National independence in terms of planning and deciding on the use of arms	Systems are interdependent. Nations can consider remaining independent regarding their choice to use cybernetic arms. With the use of these arms potentially having an impact on the allies, then being independent cannot ignore collateral risks

---

129 "Cyber attacks can be launched against any nation and on any continent. And from any continent", declared Toomas Hendrik Ilves, President of Estonia during an intervention before the UN General Assembly, September 24th 2008. http://www.un.org/en/ga/63/general debate/estonia.shtml.

An attack on vital interests could justify a nuclear retaliation. States in possession of a nuclear weapons confirm that they will never use their weapon first. However French dissuasion, theoretically at least, moves in all directions: its leaves the possibility open to exert a nuclear retaliation, whatever the nature of the threat and weapon used (conventional, chemical, bacteriological), and whatever the opposing force's identity [TER 00]	Using cybernetic arms can be considered for retaliating against conventional attacks, and using conventional weapons to retaliate against cybernetic attacks also. Doctrines are still not confirmed on these points: what level of reaction can be authorized when faced with cyberattacks?
The inalienable right to legitimate defense is applied (article 51 of the United Nations Charter)	Does the legitimate right to legitimate defense also assume that States offer the right to respond to cyberattacks by kinetic means and conventional weapons? If cyberspace is considered as a domain in its own right, without a specific hierarchy in relation to other dimensions, then it is unlikely that the reaction to cyberattacks will be cybernetic. Nothing can foresee that the reactions are led in the same dimensions as the attacks
The State which has nuclear weapons for retaliation confirms its willingness to expose all its opposing forces to unacceptable damage (does not forbid strikes on civil populations)	This is undoubtedly partly on this point (the concept of unacceptable damage) that the cybernetic weapon, if it can be used as such, cannot match the nuclear weapon just yet. The cybernetic arm is not yet, until proven otherwise, capable of causing unacceptable damage (notion that the French nuclear doctrine defines it as recourse to a high lethal power exerted on civil populations)
Heavy environmental impact	Clean war
The use of nuclear weapons sped up Japan's surrender: nuclear weapons thus guaranteed victory in this case. Thereafter, the nuclear arm became the guage of not just victory, but of mutual destruction	Having good offensive capabilities does not guarantee victory
The strategic dimension of using nuclear arms was not imposed straight away. The dissuasion strategy was created gradually.	We have a weapon, but we do not currently have a method for using it (we have innovative technology, but a lack of strategies)

Table 4.10. *Comparisons between nuclear weapons and cybernetic weapons*

Cold War	Cybernetic war
Bipolar system (two great blocks dominating the world)	Multipolar system
The balance of the Cold War rested on the Russia/USA relationship	Through the American discourse in particular, cyberwar focuses on the USA/China[130]
Known threat	Threat that everybody has heard about
In the case of an attack, we would immediately know who the attacker is	In the case of an attack, we cannot know immediately who the attacker is
We know when there is an attack	We do not always know when there is an attack
A threat that everybody understands, since the bombings on Japan	A threat that only a few people understand
A threat which is easy to define	A threat which is difficult to define
Priority threat	A threat which is still only slightly considered by States
Military balance based on the bipolar system	Risks changing the global military balance
The Cold War put strain on international and economic relations	Risk of fundamentally constraining international, political and economical relations[131]

130 Many American experts think that there is no other country in the world as vulnerable as the USA. The Quadriennal Defense Review in February 2010 identified the Chinese threat to the American capabilities to act freely on the oceans, in space, and in cyberspace. In the game of power struggles between two high powers, other countries may play an important role, like Japan for instance, which contributes to the regional reinforcement of the American position. But if we understand the function that Japan might have in the air domain (offering bases to the U.S. Air Force), the sea domain (controlling sea space, offering bases for American ships), even the space domain (observation and communication satellites, Echelon network), we can easily see the role that it could play in the American cyberpower strategy. Could Japan perform tasks that the USA is not in a position to carry out from its own territory? Is the geographical closeness of Japan to China an advantage for leading cyberoperations? The question of the advantage of a regional approach to dealing with strategic problems is thus raised here. Could the role played by Japan in the Cold War find an equivalent today in the Sino-American relations and in the context of cyberwar threats?

131 Cyberwar is an international challenge and the neorealist approach to international relations is brought into question: the world is a dangerous place, States are in constant competition for power, the international systems is unorganized, and neorealists are telling us that the system is dominated by a small number of powerful States which limit the risk of conflict. But does cyberwar authorize the dominance of a few rare States or, on the contrary, does it open up an unlimited field of actors on an equivalent level of capabilities for violent acts and destabilization?

Having offensive nuclear capabilities has guaranteed peace between blocks, but has not wiped out wars around them	Having good offensive capabilities does not guarantee security
Today, we are in a post-Cold War period	We try to think about cyberwar using comparisons with the Cold War, as though it were a substitute
Based on the dissuasion strategy	Dissuasion seems ineffectual in a cybernetic context
The Cold War was a tense period of peace, extended over a long period	Cyberwar would be a punctual, regular war, and a brief one if it exploited cybernetic resources in the way we imagine, meaning, finding their added value in these surprise actions. We may speak of a period of cyberwars or cyberconflicts in the plural, but not of one single cyberwar lasting for many decades
The Cold War is characterized by the absence of using dissuasive arms	We could characterize cyberwar by the intensive use of cybernetic arms
Strategists thought about the way to avoid nuclear war	Strategists are thinking of ways to avoid cyberwar (Richard Clarke, for example), but also (and above all) the ways to lead cyberwar
The Cold War had access to important resources: scientific, technical, political, economic, industrial, military, media resources	Stakes of security and defense linked to controlling cyberspace and confrontations which may be led there, involve all these actors. All instruments of national power are mobilized

Table 4.11. *Comparison of elements characterizing the Cold War and the cyberwar era*

2007 was marked by cyberattacks launched on Estonia. The international community was vulnerable to these events which, with hindsight, proved to have gained an important symbolic dimension. Strictly technical reports seem to have been forgotten (the real content of the attack was, which targets were hit, what the consequences were, who the creators were, which methods they used), to the benefit of a single discourse on threats, on the necessary nature of security measures which are imposed, and reflections on the role of the international community in such situations.

The attacks on Estonia, in a certain way, became the symbol of what a major attack *could* be, or what a cyberwar could be. After the Estonia case, many countries in 2007 did not hesitate to declare out loud they were had also been victims of attacks, of intrusions in their most sensitive information systems (ministries, government agencies, large businesses): the USA (in June), Germany (in August), France (in September), the USA again in October, and the UK in November. The following focused on India, Belgium (May 2008), Russia and Georgia (in July and August) and the USA (in November). There is a long list of States which publically displayed themselves as victims of attacks coming mainly from two countries: Russia and, above all, China. It hardly seems to matter in these accusations whether we are speaking of Chinese authorities, of Chinese intelligence, of Chinese industrialists, hackers, or criminals[132]. The nature of the attacks is different according to each case.

In Estonia, the attacks struck the systems which were essential to the country's operation. In the USA, France and the UK, the attacks were intrusions which aimed to steal information (intelligence). In George and Russia, they were operations led in a war setting. Whatever the real nature of the operations, the States have not stopped revealing incidents that they have been victims of ever since, and above all, pointing the finger at the guilty parties. When we observe the geographical distribution of the victims/accusers on the one hand, and the guilty parties on the other hand, then the world appears to be organized into two blocks, as if there were a confrontation between Russia/China and the rest of the world. Are we to see in this setting the heritage of the logic of the Cold War blocks?

The discourse prior to 2000, of the emerging Internet, referred to developments caused by the arrivals of new technologies in the world. Thus, we are speaking of growth, of digital divide (by pointing out social classes which, within modern societies, cannot easily access the Internet and which are separated from the modernization race impelled by ICTs). This divide is, however, caused by two worlds, two blocks, but which do not cross over. The threat cannot come from there. The pre-2000 period was when the discourse on cybercriminal threats was to evolve. Let us remember the developments (which make us smile today) on violations of private lives linked to the misuse of cookies. From a military point of view, the pre-2000 era is the period of gradual computerization (sometimes very slow) in the armies. Should we speak of evolution or revolution?

In the backdrop of the Gulf War, we speak of the power of controlling information and information warfare, which was conceptualized during the 1990-2000 years. This was the period of utopia (or lies): it was possible to win only using the force of information; information warfare is a guarantee for quick victory; information warfare is a guarantee for war proper; information warfare tolls the bell for war) and the creation of threats (risks of major attacks, digital Pearl Harbor). The

---

132 When accusations are pointed towards China, then all interpretations are allowed. When they are pointed towards "Beijing", then the spectrum is more precise and of course, means the authorities.

post-2000 period did not break with this utopic, lie-filled phase, but marked a turning point. Of course, there was 9/11, and a little while after the war on terrorism. The question of security and of defending society against terrorism offers a major role to information technologies. The USA is still chasing domination over information space. Major threats are carried against critical infrastructures and the country's working population, and large scale tests and exercises prove this. From 2007 onwards, with the attacks on Estonia, there was a change in this discourse: the threat was not just cybercrime, apparently it came from a collusion between States with terrorist networks and criminal organizations.

We are moving on from the concept of "computer hacking" to cybernetic "attacks" (the term is much more aggressive). We are moving away from risk management to the battle against major threats, from questions on crime to questions on the act of war, from the difficulty of protecting ourselves from cybercriminality to the somewhat impossibility of protecting ourselves against major threats. We are no longer dealing with looking for information domination on the battlefield, with an extreme weakness in the whole system (an American discourse, see Richard Clark's thesis). We are finally departing from a discourse on threats, towards one dealing with a global or invisible threat. Foreign intrusions into systems had, of course, been denounced in the past (the terrorist threat was already present before 2000), but statistics show a high rise in cybernetic attack during the last years of 2000, occasionally lightly mixing statistics on cybercrimes with intelligence operations. After Estonia, the discourse focused rather on the fear of Chinese or Russian attacks on the West, and more and more accusations were being made. Above all, soldiers are not the only actors of confrontation in cyberspace. This was also being said and repeated half way through the 1990s. But, the Web 2.0 era seemed to bring the phenomena back to life, because in order to be an actor in cyberspace, it is no longer necessary to be a hacker: the relay of information on a large scale can rally up opinions. In this new generation of communication tools, authoritarian regimes see means for more control, but also a bigger threat. China opened its society to the Internet and to mobile telecommunications, but on the other hand, enforces control and censoring.

The USA follows the same principle, but dressed up as other concepts: America is the society of the freedom of communication and expression, but everything which goes around on the Internet is a pretext for making a census, analyses, tests – the whole legitimacy of the fight on terrorism which is threatening to put an end to the model of civilization and a political regime. At the dawn of 2010, cyberspace was imposed as a place for manifesting methods for information warfare. The hardening up of the discourse (States accused) is a dichotomous vision of the world. Two spaces, two blocks confront each other on the basis of espionage, but also influence.

A 1997 American report to the President's Commission on Critical Infrastructure Protection questioned dissuasion in Cyberspace[133]. The report recalled the conditions which gave way to the dissuasion strategy. The means deployed by the USA aimed to prevent any nuclear attack. The dissuasion strategy operated in a unique situation of threats of mass destruction, of surprise, which would make any reaction useless. Cyberspace imposes its own limitations to any simple transposition of the nuclear dissuasion strategy towards the cybernetic domain. Dissuading enemies in peace time assumes the possession of capabilities to demonstrate these forces. However, we must admit that in cyberspace, the American position (as well as the position of a good number of other nations) is far from fulfilling this need: States are still shouting loud and clear that they have been the victims of attacks (that they sometimes discover a bit late), that their security levels are insufficient, and that their fortresses are fallible. The discourse is against what it should be if it had to prove itself to be convincing and confirm its force. The impression of panic and disorder which sometimes reigns supreme in cybersecurity and cyberdefense is not likely to reinforce any dissuasion policy. In the same way that the nuclear dissuasion system is built on systems of detection and alarm in the case of an attack, then cyber dissuasion should develop warning systems preventing attacks.

The debate on dissuasion, with references to the nuclear debate, could therefore be removed with a simple argument: dissuasion does not work if we do not know who to answer to or lance preemptive attacks on. However, with blame being the main problem in cyberattacks, then any quick reaction is excluded. In fact, dissuasion is partly based on reaction speed or anticipation. Either, we must act first to stop the enemy's action, or we must be in a position to react before being struck by the enemy's shot, thus condemning both sides to mutual destruction. If weeks or months are needed to be sure of the blame of a cyberoperation, then dissuasion no longer works. We will now explain the logic of nuclear dissuasion: it is not a matter of ensuring that we can survive an attack, but that the attacker cannot survive a counter attack. Dissuasion is a theory based on assumptions (assumption that the attacker is acting according to rational behavior). Cybernetic defense and security and offensive use of the cybernetic domain guarantees (as a priority) that we can survive cyberattacks. The obsession with security pays all its attention on protecting vital infrastructures: it is a case of guaranteeing the survival of the system, of a society when faced with an attack, even before claiming to guarantee destroying the opposing force through counter attack.

If there can be cyber dissuasion, it must differ in the approaches, form, and in logic. Can there be any dissuasion other than the threat of mutual destruction? In cyber attacks, it is generally confirmed that the cost for the attacker is in fact low.

---

133 Toward Deterrence in the Cyber Dimension. Report to the President's Commission on Critical Infrastructure Protection, 1997, 9 pages.

The cost is low because accessing the targets is sometimes not very complex, because accessing "weapons" is easy, and because the targets often hardly resist. Through the years, the costs regularly get lower (there are more and more online data, targets and potential attackers), whereas in the mean time, the costs linked to security and defense do not stop growing (systems becoming more complex, becoming less and less easy to control, and sensitive to both surprise attacks and invisible and discreet ones). However, the cost of the attack, if it is low, is not always zero. The better the security and defense are, the more the cost of the attack will grow. Ideally, the cost of the attacks should increase so as to reduce their frequency. But right now, this is the exact opposite of what seems to be happening. Dissuasion through costs is not currently a topical affair.

Strategy of nuclear dissuasion	Is a strategy of cybernetic dissuasion possible?
Dissuasion denotes non-use, which is credible insofar as the opposing force perceives actual use as being possible	Use is not only possible, but is implemented. Damage is not likely to dissuade potential targets. Cybernetic dissuasion could therefore only be based on the threat of executing a process of a superior level of violence. The cybernetic weapon itself could only be used as a weapon of dissuasion if it had been proven or could be proved to be efficient
The strategy of dissuasion has a defensive nature	Cybernetic dissuasion also has a defensive nature
The actual position of the States in terms of politics on nuclear dissuasion sometimes goes against international dialogue and shared prerogatives. States are not prepared to give up a part of their sovereignty in this matter. Without referring to shared dissuasion, it is difficult to agree on collective dissuasion	With regard to threats and cybernetic wars, States go back to their responsibilities, their initiatives, despite the few international initiatives (CDX, treaty projects, etc.)

Table 4.12. *Is a strategy of cyber dissuasion possible?*

The only way to dissuade potential attackers today is to increase global interconnections and interdependencies. This is so that if *one* were to collapse, then the whole system would fall. Only the strategy of the mad against the weak or the strong, or the mad against the mad would not be affected by this dissuasion. It is not sufficient to say that we all breathe the same air to dissuade the sorcerer's apprentice from throwing chemical products into the atmosphere.

4.1.13. *Cyberconflict and new wars*

An economic war (with a widespread, international, constant threat), a cybernetic war, "attacks" or threats of attack from all parts of the world and different in nature (small delinquencies, criminality, aggressive competition), photos of wars portrayed in the media, our environment is, or could be, hostile and violent. Such is the discourse and such are the images which come to us every day and condition the perception of the world in which we are evolving. War is part of our landscape. This is not necessarily a military, murderous war, but a war of confrontations, conflicts, and competitions which seem to be at the root of societal life and which we do not hesitate to call a "war" (gang wars, the war on crime, the war against unemployment, the economic war to win market shares, etc.).

The economy and technology are "weapons", in the same way that knowledge or talent are, used in the conquest for power. The rhetoric used here permanently refers back to violent relationships, between individuals and groups of individuals, and between the strong and the weak. The Internet planet is the territory for the battle of the oppressed fighting against their oppressors, which is an asymmetrical fight as it is unbalanced. But the fantastic universe of the Internet can make it possible to rebalance this relationship, for the benefit of the weak. Thus, the anarchists, partisans of the free world, of open sources, are actors in the fight on monopole oppression, and great financial powers.

Everything should be shared freely, just like in an ideal world where there is only one source of competition: talent and creativity. We can also include rebels, those bringing about revolution whilst hiding their identities behind usernames, to deface institution websites which are effectively guilty of everything so as to hack government or institution servers, to call up the revolution on blogs. All of these actors are at war (at least ideologically), against systems, models, principles, values, cultures, religions, etc. The list goes on. The media continues to swamp us with the idea of utopia where the Internet (web 1.0, then 2.0, 3.0…) is the path to victory for the weak versus the strong. Overwhelming us with this idea means that States are convinced that their own over-equipped armies are now at the mercy of armed fighters using their cell phones alone. In the mean time, paradoxically, modern societies' relationship to war has never been, apparently, so removed: populations refuse war, and are gradually becoming lesser and lesser accepting of the image of their dead in combat. It is much more pleasant to make war virtual.

4.1.13.1. *Is cyberwar actually war?*

This is a relatively complex question, because it means defining war. It is a "concept of misleading obviousness" [MON 07]. But the very concept is brought back into question today. War no longer seems as simple as it was before. It has moved on, due to the multiple effects of the end of the Cold War, to globalization, modernization, technological progress, to the advent of the information society. Conventional benchmarks have disappeared: war no longer begins with a declaration and ends with a peace treaty. For a long time now, the battles organized on a battlefield where the armies name a place and time are over. The front lines have disappeared. Finished are the wars where it was relatively easy to distinguish enemies and allies. The blues on one side and the reds on the other – this works well in video games. Cyberspace did not come along to simplify matters. War, we see it every day on the television at least. We understand that it has retained its own characteristics: violence, fire, destruction, massacres, death.

When politicians hesitate to speak about war (the UN was not involved in the war on Libya!), the man in the street does not notice anything different, and considers the images he sees as coming from the war. Whatever the case, theorists have great difficulties in defining war today, which does not make it any easier to define cyberwar. We could even use the neologism, "cyberwar" to signify acts which resemble war, but which are not war itself [COR 10]. In war, there is radical nature that the operations we are faced with in cyberspace today do not have: the rejection of recognized values in peace time; the aim to systematically destroy the opposing force's societal structures; death of mankind; destruction of the enemy's heritage; domination of the adversary's willingness. Destruction is substituted for production. However, such acts are not enough to fulfill all these criteria to count as war. Certain degrees and levels of escalation in violence must be reached, and in the long term, which includes involving particular actors. Rivalries between crime rival gangs may meet these criteria, without there being a war. Then, there are wars, like the Cold War, which do not materialize this destruction.

The French joint lexicon of operation terminology (PIA 0.5.5.2) defines war as an "armed fight on social groups and especially between States, and is considered as a social phenomenon", specifying that "it results in a state of war or situation of war in the zone of confrontation". The state of war is defined precisely as a legal state "which stems from the declaration of war or an ultimatum with a conditional declaration of war". Cyberwar cannot, therefore, be a war in light of this conventional approach. For there to be war, we sometimes consider that there has to be a certain number of victims in the conflict. Such losses could be caused by cyberattacks, according to strategic attack scenarios. But this is undoubtedly not enough to define cyberwar as war itself. What can we identify with in war? What can we identify with in cyberwar? Are the criteria applicable to war also applicable to cyberwar?

Characteristics of war	Characteristics of cyberwar
Conventional wars: declarations of war	No declaration
Conventional wars: peace treaty	No peace treaty
Violence (war is a form of violence)	Violence (a cyberattack is an act of violence, but not necessarily war: a criminal act is an act of violence)[134]
What level of collective violence deserves the title of war? A minimum number of soldiers involved? A minimum number of victims? 300? 1,000? More? Only the deaths of soldiers? Deaths of soldiers *and* civilians? What about injured?[135] How many victims over how long?	We are forced to measure the level of collective violence (counting deaths, financial losses, etc.). Cyberattacks are subjected to these measurements: financial losses, number of machines used…Can measuring the level of violence become a criterion for discriminating cyberwar? Or must we also consider the political and social effects, phenomena which does not lend itself well to statistical measuring?
The duration of the conflict	Cybernetic operations may widely go over the strictly limited conflict duration: time to prepare, time for the effects of cyberattacks to fade away
A large scale confrontation, organized and bloody, involving political groups (G. Bouthoul)[136]. War is, therefore, a collective act	A large scale confrontation (possible), organized (possible), bloody (*a priori*, no), political groups (possible). Cyberwar can be a collective act
For G. Bouthoul, political groups confronting each other are acting in the name of sovereignty (inter-State wars) and internal actors (civil wars)	Political groups confronting each other are sovereign and internal actors
Inter-State military confrontation (sovereign States)	Cyberwar must be part of the conventional war framework in order to be a war itself

---

134 We can distinguish war from ordinary crime and violence: war is violence following collective and political objectives, whereas the latter are only used for personal interests [BOU 06].

135 There are many methods for accounting for victims, and they vary in criteria: military victims, military and civil victims, etc. The creators of such methods are: Quincy Wright, Jean-Pierre Derriennic, Pitirin Sorokin, Lewis Fry Richardson, D. Singer, M. Small, Ruth Leger Sivard [MON 07].

136 [BOU 06], p. 56.

Manifestation of extreme collective violence	Cyberwar can be an act of violence between two communities. Its extreme (lethal) nature is less relevant
Rules, the laws of conflict which are imposed on belligerents	Unclear laws: must the laws of conflict apply? If cyberwar operations enter into conventional war, then it is naturally subject to the same rules
Premediation	It is premeditated as it has to be prepared, planned, organized and then deployed. The "weapons" used for cyberattacks must be developed. The targets must be defined in advance. Often the weapons will be adapted to the targets. A weapon cannot always be used to hit non-specific targets
Aim: make the opposing force submit by using force	The aim may be identical. Any form of confrontation aims to impose its ideas, models, points of view, its willingness
Political objective	There is a political objective if it enters into conventional warfare
Limited war or low intensity war: has objectives which are more limited that total war, aims to weaken an opponent, at least temporarily, to achieve a major objective[137]. In limited wars, military confrontation may be absolute	Cyberattacks, which do not constitute as cyberwar on their own, make it possible to weaken an opponent temporarily, and to use this position to lead operations in other dimensions, in the aim to achieve a major objective. Cyberwars will probably be limited wars
Total war: mobilization of all the State's lifeblood, the war economy, control over all the intellectual activities within a country	Cyberwar and cyberattacks are tools available for accomplishing total war, but are total war themselves
Wars for reconnaissance: new theory explaining causes of war, trying to break away from utilitarian interpretations of causes for war. War for reconnaissance is a fight for image, for a place within nations. The more reconnaissance is refused, the more likely war will be. Putting a nation aside in this manner will radicalize its national or religious identity	Information warfare and cyberwar are usually more linked to the expression "war of knowledge". But cyberconflicts may also be wars for reconnaissance, or at least contribute to it

Table 4.13. *Comparison of the characteristics of war and cyberwar*

---

137 [MON 07], p. 299.

We could strive to make the characteristics of a "real" cyberwar adhere to the criteria making it possible to recognize war. But as we show here, war itself responds to relatively varying characteristics, which is a function of the observers' choices, and the eras as well. The object of "war" is not a fixed one. As for the object of "cyberwar", it is not only in the same condition, but in full creation.

Today we have seen very few events in cyberspace which could really trigger a war. No large outbursts of violence, no victims in the hundreds or thousands, no international headlines: nothing which in its form or consequences which reminds us of the outbursts of passion and worry that wars give rise to. We are tempted to overturn this obstacle by saying there is still no definition of cyberwar, and that this depends on us.

However, if the definition must retain a connotation of "war", then the "non-war" must be separated from the semantic field that is wrongly associated with it: terrorism, social claims, political movements, revolutions, activism, and criminality, for example. "War is a vitally important matter for the State", writes Sun Tzu in his famous treaty on the art of warfare. Yet, war has often been led to satisfy personal ambitions, clans, and families in order to satisfy a mentality of conquest or wealth, without it necessarily being at stake in the State's survival.

This notion of vital importance is omnipresent today in the discourse on global security: vitally important infrastructures, vitally important sectors of activity (SAIV)[138]. The dangerousness of cyberattacks likely to attack the critical infrastructures belonging to States raises this problem of security. Large cyberattacks on such infrastructures could be described as acts of war. To paraphrase Sun Tzu, we could say that cyberattacks have a vital importance for the State, insofar as they can destabilize it.

4.1.13.2. Cyberwar, new war?

The concept of "new wars" is often linked to the name Mary Kaldor [KAL 99], but the subject has also been dealt by other authors, such as Herfried Münkler [MUN 04] in Germany, Pascal Vennesson [VEN 08] in France, Jean-Marc Flükiger in Switzerland [FLU 11].

---

138 The Interministerial Decree no. 2006-212 from February 23rd 2006, in France in compliance to articles L 1332-1 and following the Code of Defense. The decree aims to define a list of particularly sensitive sectors and businesses, which are vital for the Nation's defense (those which must be protected, whose operation must be guaranteed as a matter of urgency, in order to maintain the economic activity and protection of the population). It is part of a global security process.

The innovation is not only associated with war. We are, of course, referring to new information technologies, new strategies, and new threats for example[139]. The trend is innovation, and warfare has not been able to escape this.

New wars differ entirely from those in the past. Thus, many questions are raised:

– What distinguishes past wars from new ones?

– When is this break established? When did we move from conventional wars to new wars? Strategic changes alter the conditions for using the forces. Must we, then, put this transition at the end of the Cold War, or the fall of the Berlin wall?

– Are new wars simply the wars of today and tomorrow?

– Are the wars of today all new wars, or are there wars amongst them which are conventional?

– To what extent do new information technologies contribute to the innovation of war? Are ICT's present in new wars?

– Is cyberwar a new war?

The basic postulate of partisans of the new war theory is simple: the risk of classic military confrontation has been wiped[140], due to major strategic changes. "If the nature of war has not changed, it has taken on different forms since the end of the Cold War" [DES 07][141]. Since the end of the Cold War, the war between States has become unlikely in Western space, and civil and inter-state governed wars reign over the world. "The end of the Cold War is more than a strategic revolution; it is an intellectual revolution"[142]. It concerns the end of a model primarily based on certainties, stereotypes, employment patterns, and the predominance of classic means of power. Operation superiority is now achieved by dominating the cognitive field.

---

139 Through a reference to the "Great Game", the expression the "New Great Game" has also recently appeared to describe the geopolitics of Central Asia. It explains their geopolitics as a fight between two nations for power, influence, and hegemony over Central Asia and the Transcausian Transition Zone. On one side, we have the USA, the UK and the NATO countries, and on the other we have Russia, China, and countries from the Shanghai Cooperation Organization (SCO). The fight is not centered on dominating territories, but on resources (oil, energy resources, distribution infrastructures, businesses, etc.). The concept is therefore also applied to cyberspace if information is considered as one of the essential resources.
140 Tactique générale, Edit. Economica.
141 p. VII.
142 [DES 07], p. VII.

New kinds of threats have appeared which overturn the pathways of classic confrontation, and which increase the uncertainty of war. Changes in the global strategic environment can be characterized by:

– the globalization effect;

– the major role of the media (conditioning behavior) and above all, its instantaneity;

– the spreading of theaters of operation in the world (coordination troops and sending in forces relies on cyberspace resources);

– irregular wars (which have become the rule);

– tensions regarding the costs of the operations: the margins are limited, and so is the budget and the materials;

– reduced time for decision making;

– "the immaterial, psychological element is once again become a dominant feature, at the same time the illusion of resolving conflict using an all-technological approach is being spread"[143].

Introducing the concept of new warfare requires that we identify discriminating criteria which can differentiate it from conventional warfare. These differences can be assessed in terms of:

– the frequency: are new wars more frequent, shorter, longer, than conventional wars?

– the identity of the actors: uniquely States, non-state governed confrontation, or even a war involving the whole range of actors in society, or the citizens army?

– the volume of the forces present (number of soldiers, number of pieces on the chess board);

– the way the army is composed (military reserve through conscription, professional armies[144]);

– the conduct;

– the respective role of different weapons (flights, navy, land, cybernetic). For example, is the predominance of the air force a characteristic of new wars? Can cybernetic force be prevalent? The transversal characteristic of cyberspace can be one of the characteristics of new wars;

---

143 [ADT 08], p.10.
144 In this regard, it is interesting to oppose the model for making up American or German cyber units for example, which are founded on the professionalization of actors, and units in Estonia who call up volunteers, or China and its militia for example, and the use of the concept of the people's war. The notion of soldier-citizen is not an outdated concept.

– the number of victims (the lethality of the conflicts, the violence of the confrontations)[145];

– the atrocity of the wars;

– the population's relationship with wars (mobilization, nationalism, etc.).

– the media's involvement in the wars;

– the capability of the confrontation to spread like wildfire, or to stay localized. If armed confrontations are not extended to bordering areas, then the Internet indeed makes it possible to involve actors way beyond they physical territory of the confrontations;

– the global, globalized dimension of wars[146]. With the help of cyberspace, wars may involve more actors who are physically removed from the confrontation terrain, but who play an important role (diasporas relaying information, supporting an effort for war, mobilizing foreign opinion);

– fixed objectives;

– the question of cost[147];

– the causes, the triggers;

---

145 Estimating the number of war victims is an exercise with many controversies around it. On the other hand, our developed societies agree on the importance given to the loss of human lives in the conflicts of yesterday. Populations struggle to understand or accept the loss of their citizens, in conflicts which seemed far away to them. This attitude has favored the utopic concept of a no death war, which seemed possible thanks to technology, including computers and modern means of communication. These technologies have a role to play on the speed, precision and perception of the environment ("situation awareness"), criteria which, once controlled, will make it possible to reach a lower level of deaths than for our own side. This step towards a lower level of fatality seems an important turning point and contributes to the nature of new wars. Wars have not always been as murderous as those in the 20th Century, or the Napoleon wars for example. It is also important to distinguish "war" and "combat" (or "battle").

146 In the 20th Century there have been world wars, and today we know the wars in the age of globalization. The latter, although geographically limited, have an impact on the economy and global society in its entirety: the security measures deployed by all States are an illustration of this. As for nuclear war, unlikely but still possible, it is global in nature and by the consequences it has on the planet. As for cyberwar, it is not necessarily worldwide, but if we tend to define its character by stating that all the world's networks are interconnected, that cyberspace is only one entity, and that attacks have impacts on the whole planet. Targeted attacks are now possible, and confrontations between States in cyberspace, or between state and non-state actors, inside or externally to a given territory, do not involve all of cyberspace. The "global" character of cyberwar is not naturally imposed.

147 Shrinking Costs of War, Human Security Report Project, 2nd section of report for 2009, Vancouver, HSRP, 2010.

– the consequences;

– the importance of technology, the relation between the military domain and technology;

– the nature of the weapons and the necessary role of technology: dual technologies, weapons available to everybody, proliferation of weapons. When fighters can make use of cyberspace, this has an impact of the war of conducting war: speed, access to information, manipulation;

– the relationship between the political leader and the soldier;

– the war's relationship with civilization and its evolution. Do wars evolve with civilizations, or do they make the civilizations evolve?

– the way in which we come out of war and rebuild ourselves;

– the necessary relationship with peace (we cannot think "war" without referring to peace);

– the definition of victory;

– and of course, today, in terms of the level of involvement of cyberspace in conflict.

War: what it was	War: what it no longer is, what it has become	Relationship between cyberspace and new wars
Mass war, nuclear threat, iron curtain	The battles of yesterday, far from the national territory[148]	Cyberwar authorizes actions far from its national territory
Irregular wars are the exception	Irregular wars are the rule	Cyberconflicts are characterized by the actor's involvement on all levels. But if the actors are different in nature (regular army, irregular actors, hackers, hacktivists, etc.), then we cannot really speak of asymmetry in cyberspace as all the actors have access to the same weapons, the same resources, and have equivalent capabilities. It is no longer truly a question of strong and weak

---

148 The French Army takes part in operations to destabilize regions, in the fight on terrorism, on international trafficking, and the national territory may find itself involved in disaster management operations, and more generally in protecting citizens.

Important role of the media, manipulation of public opinion, but the media is controlled by a few well identified sources	Major role of the media, real time information	The Internet is the favored place of media instantaneity. Citizens are being transformed into reporter/ witnesses and broadcast images, videos and comments on the net, sometimes quicker than the media itself, sending back even more images from the war (journalists cannot be present everywhere)
Decision making time has seen an acceleration with the introduction of communication technology in the 19th Century	Decision time shortened	The computerization of the battle field as well as global society has contributed to the shorted decision making time. ICTs have improved knowledge of the situation (knowing the opposing force better means shortening the decision making loop and reducing uncertainties)
Importance of technology (breakthroughs which guaranteed an advantage but not always definite)	Illusion of resolving conflicts by technological contribution, but a return to the importance given to the psychological element. Operation superiority is now achieved by dominating the cognitive field[149]	Cyberspace is the archetypal field of ideas, representations, manipulation, and the cognitive dimension
Shot imprecision	Shot precision	Computerization weapon systems has made shots more accurate
Uncertainty	Uncertainty	More information, means for collecting and processing, but uncertainty remains as a major factor in warfare
War and peace	Situation of unrealized crisis, able to degenerate into armed conflicts. There can sometimes be armed confrontations and peace actions on the same theater of operations	Confrontations cyberspace add to the confusion, because there are no real acts of war which are distinct from actions in times of peace: attacks can be led identically in both contexts

---

149 [DES 07], p. VIII.

War with declaration, peace with treaty	No more declarations, no more treaties	Attacks occur by playing the surprise effect card. The biggest fear for strategists is a surprise attack on vital infrastructures. It is no longer a question of declaring war
Example: the Cold War: certainties (we know the enemy), stereotypes, use patterns (strategy of dissuasion)	Example: post-Cold War. No more certainties (we do not know the enemy, the attack can come by surprise, strong return to uncertainty, asymmetrical strategies...)	The anonymity offered to the attacks increases uncertainty, the surprise effect, and makes any strategy of dissuasion impossible
Motives: ideologies	Motives: identity, political void. New wars no longer have geopolitical aims. These wars always have a political nature, but identity politics, contrary to conventional wars which involve politics of ideas. New wars are led in the name of particularism, exclusivism, and no longer cosmopolitanism. This is the universalism/fundamentalism opposition. The end of Western universalist and humanist political ideologies was approached by Daniel Bell[150] in 1960 in "The End of Ideologies" a concept appearing in a special context of the advent of the post-industrial society, "Towards the Post-Industrial Society" (1973). Raymond Aron, in "The Opium of the Intellectuals" (1955) dealt with the end of the ideological age	Cyberspace is the favored place for ideas to flow
Actors: state governed	Actors: infra-state governed	Cyberspace expands the field for actors of conflict

---

150 Daniel Bell, American sociologist, died in 2011.

Wars with and for the populations (strong people support)	Violence against the population: guerilla techniques, mass crimes, people forced to move	Cyberattacks can be led indiscriminately on populations or armies, by populations or armies
War economy: production mobilized, autarkic, centralized model	War economy: illegalities, pillaging, decentralized, global, scattered, transnational model, internationalized predation	Decentralized model, in a network, scattered, transnational, illegalities
	Dynamic: globalized wars (financed by diasporas, global economic aims, battles for accessing natural resources…). Conflicts extended due to trans-border economic interests	Role of diasporas and any supporting or opposed group
Decisive battles	There are hardly any more decisive battles	No decisive battles
Dominant actors: regular armies	Dominant actors: terrorists, warlords, soldiers to their own devices	For the time being we do not really know who is dominating: the army, intelligence services, hacker groups or any other group of actors?
State monopoly on war	States lose monopoly on war	States have no taken back the monopoly of violence with cyberspace
	Civilians taken as targets: hostage, extermination, ethnic cleansing, rapes…	Civilians taken as targets

Table 4.14. *Comparison between conventional and new wars*

But "if the environment changes, then the truth of war does not change"[151]. "Ultimately, wars will always be the confrontation of two wills, but force is not enough"[152], "if technology is a means which changes the conditions of combat, then it does not change the nature of war which remains as a profoundly human

---

151 [ADT 08], p.9.
152 [ADT 08], p.13.

phenomenon"[153], "the permanent principles of war… new processes"[154]. Since the end of the Cold War, wars have not disappeared, but they have undoubtedly changed. "They are no longer what they were" [VEN 10], as they are subjected to changes in the world (this is a reciprocal relationship: society changes the nature of war, and wars or the lack thereof influences the way a society evolves). The *Strategic Defense and Security Review* published in the UK in October 2010 describes what the new forms of conflict can be[155]:

– conflicts of globalization;

– inter-State conflicts are not disappearing;

– use of asymmetrical tactics: economic and cybernetic actions rather than direct military confrontations. As many state-governed actors as non-state actors seek the means to avoid confrontations with actors who conquer them in conventional conflicts;

– it will be more and more difficult to distinguish enemies from civilians, the media, non-state governed organizations, allies present on the confrontation ground;

– operations will be observed more, always more accurately, by the public opinion (transparent society?) which has high-tech and global communication means. The major role of information is a characteristic of new wars. Of course, information has always played a major role in the art of warfare as in political affair. But it is the digital aspect of this information which will make it all the more important, and the expansion of its field of processing, production, and dissemination;

– enemies will still attack physical and electronic lines of communication;

– communication technologies increase the enemies' capabilities to influence actors on the battlefield, but also society at the same time.

Cyberwar, a conflict in cyberspace, introduces the following new criteria into modern conflicts:

– disappearance of the notion of space;

– abolition of the notion of time;

– impossibilty to find a blame for the attacks.

---

153 [ADT 08], p.26.
154 [ADT 08], p. 33.
155 http://www.direct.gov.uk/prod_consum_dg/groups/dg_digitalassets/@dg/@en/documents /digitalasset/dg_191634.pdf?CID=PDF&PLA=furl&CRE=sdsr. Page 16 of report.

Only they are able to give a new face to conflicts, even if they do not entirely transform it, as has already been discussed previously on the very nature of war (the uncertainty remains, war is always a dual, etc.). There is a double dimension in the cybernetic conflict. The introduction of ICT's had an impact on the way in which wars led. On the one hand a battle is engaged to control cyberspace [SHA 10]. On the other hand, if cyberwar is new in its form, then in the strategies and tactics that it involves, it still remains a war with conventional objectives. Cyberwar is a kind of war which uses force intensifiers for conventional war. But the latter can also be considered as a force intensifier for cyberwar [SHA 10]. If cyberconflict can be described again, or if it contributes to the concept of new wars, then this is undoubtedly because it wipes out the notion of asymmetry. Indeed, the actors leading operations on each other are different: armies, intelligence, hacktivists, hackers, terrorists, etc. They are engaged in irregular and asymmetrical fights because some are legitimate, some are not, there are many of them, and there are fewer of them, some are made up of armies, some of them are spread out, some adopt frontal attack strategies, and others strategies of circumvention. But in cyberspace, these qualities are erased. Everybody has the same space, the same domain of action, the same techniques, the same tools, the same methods, the same means and capabilities. The targets that some might see are visible for everyone; it is no longer a question of identity, there are only capabilities and acts. Cyberspace allows confrontations between States; it enables confrontations between States and non-state governed actors, and between non-state governed actors. But this makes no difference at all to the struck target: whether the creator of the attack is small or big, weak or powerful, a State or other, it is still struck in the same way. This is not a question of asymmetry.

4.1.13.3. *Wars and technologies*

One of the main characteristics of new so-called technological war is not the disappearance of violence, but the considerable decrease number of deaths. If we may note a reduced level of lethality in conflicts, then this could partly be blamed on other factors than purely technological. Whatever the case may be, the introduction of new technologies into the field of war has always generated new hope: this could be guaranteed victory, quicker victory, or maybe destruction of the guaranteed opponent. Have new technology is having a lead over the opponent, so long as this adversary has not caught up by getting the same innovative technologies. So long as there is a technological divide, then the side who has the advantage can hope to take the lead (battle of the Earthern pot and against the Iron pot). The difficulty, then, is upholding the technological advantage (always having a head start), and having a better control over what the enemy does not know how to do: manipulating these weapons.

Today, information technologies offer us all identical, basic means and here, it is intelligence which makes all the difference. Knowing how to put together the applications we have to make new ones, knowing how to exploit the glitches in the systems before the others do, having a better understanding and knowing how to program better, before the others. The hope that is born from the technological advantage is between the hope of having less destructive confrontations for our own side, but not necessarily for the other side. With technology, strategists also dream of shorter confrontations in the long term, particularly enabling reduced costs (in human lives, salaries, hardware, logistics, etc.)[156], to benefit from the often decisive advantage offered by the surprise effect (surprise and speed are tightly bound, even if surprise is only the result of an operation which was prepared over the long term).

Technology should, and this has not always been the case, respond to the less inhumane wait for confrontation. ICTs leave in their wake the illusion of a totally virtual world, of dematerialized combats and thus a war proper, with no real victims, where the outcome is displayed on a computer screen, a bit like video game scores. Virtualization is made, ideally at least, of enemies that we can hit, although they are far away. We can therefore send war towards faraway lands, which shelters us from the violence of the barbaric people we are fighting: enemies who are held well away from us, but who we can fight in real time. for this, we have to manipulate the weapons that we can command using remote control via our computers. The war is more humane, then, because the enemy has no face; just an image on the screen. This all seems so similar, it could be mistaken for a video game, a movie. It has all become surreal. When to soldier still has to fight on the terrain, then technology puts a screen between him and the enemy[157].

Courage, fear and fatigue are still topical today [BAU 81]. The hopes vested in technology have not, yet, been fulfilled. We know for example that technical/technological superiority does not always guarantee victories[158]. There are multiple criteria which can be taken into account: the quality of the strategy, tactics, the operations, the decision makers, the men on the ground, their mental and physical resistance, their motivation and their resources. A new weapon calls for a new doctrine, and within a suitable doctrine, it is likely that the weapon will not have the anticipated efficiency. Methods of circumventing enemies who are both digitally and technically superior (better armed) also make it possible to put *a priori* superior actors at a disadvantage, at least on paper. We also know (and the atomic bomb is a major example of this), that using a high-tech weapon may have effects

---

156 High necessary investments in the design of weapons and high-tech equipment do not reduce the cost of war. Computerized weapons put a high strain on the States' budgets.
157 See the high-tech computerized equipment of soldiers in the modern age.
158 Weaponry alone does not make the army superior, does not decide the victory or the efficiency. The consequences of introducing technologies an army's capabilities appreciates with regarding technical performances of the army itself, of the technical control over their engagement, and finally the capability to integrate them in a concept of global use [MON 07], p. 33.

which are as harmful to ourselves as they are for the enemy (ecological pollution for nuclear weapons; risk of unpredictable damage during cyberattacks due to system interdependency). "Technology cannot change or transform war. New war domains do not change it either. We will soon be waging war in space, but this will not be 'space war'", confirms General Vincent Desportes [DES 08][159]. Techno-skepticism (or salutary prudence) is the current trend in several environments, with the soldier unable to escape this phenomenon. This position is an obstacle to the whole technological domain, for those see a future in technology, and those who see perfection and an answer to all their problems. These partisans are often considered with great irony, particularly in literature.

D. Buzzati, in his novel entitled "The Secret Weapon" [BUZ 66] speaks of a new technology, a secret weapon, which would allow the great powers of the Cold War to conquer the enemy. This new weapon is a persuasive gas that the great powers launch onto populations and the decision making centers, and which has the power to win the war in less than an hour by radically changing the ideology and thoughts of the individuals. After breathing in the gas, the communists become capitalists and vice versa. This does not change the balance within the powers, as the roles are simply reversed and the Cold War continues. Buzzati raises the idea of the myth of power awarded by modern technologies, and the belief that men hold in the power of these new technological weapons. He also conveys the utopias that we are finding over and over today in the capabilities of information warfare: rapid war [TES 10], easy victory, war proper, winning hearts and souls over to its cause. Technology offers more and more staggering capabilities every day for communications and data processing and exchanges, for instance. Speed and storage capabilities are the key words (ever quicker data processing and transfers, larger storage capacities). We can offer the reader a few figures to give an idea of such evolutions:

– in 1976, an iPod would have cost a billion US dollars, and would have been the size of an entire building;

– transferring 1 petaoctet of data between CERN in Geneva and the CC-IN2P3 in Lyon would have taken 3,900 years in 1990; it took 10 days in 2010 and just one day in 2011[160].

The cybernetic dimension of combat will inevitably be party to these evolutions. We cannot forget that technology never stops moving forward, and that the constant and variable factors that we use to develop scenarios, theories, strategies and doctrines of cyber confrontations must still undergo significant evolutions during the years to come. Technology was, and will probably remain for a long time still, an instrument of power. "Its circulation, adaptation and shared use are, then,

---

159 no. 37, p. 39.
160 *CNRS Journal*, no. 255, April 2011, Paris, France, p.36.

permanent strategic stakes for economic agents" [WAR 03]. Although the power of these States is based on mastering technology, we must however note that a number of attacks which could bring this power into question are today in the shape of a-technical attacks[161].

The introduction of ICT's into warfare is not without reminding us of the use of telecommunications in the same field in the 19th Century. Contemporary cyberspace comes under the branch of telecommunications. If warfare has been changed by the introduction of telecommunications, then maybe we will find similar processes likely to illustrate potential changes made to warfare by the appearance of cyberspace. Telegraphy quickly turned out to be useful for military operations. With the new means that we have today the concept of distance is revolutionized. But it also underlines the fragile nature of infrastructures, and the need to advance technology to reach more stable and reliable systems. The interest in these technologies is spreading across the whole planet.

For instance, the Japanese undertook research to develop wireless telegraphy at the end of the 19th Century. In Japan, in civil society, telegraphy was an instant success and one of the first infrastructures was developed on a very small time scale, similar to what would happen a century later with the arrival of the Internet. Electric telegraphy was invented in the USA in 1837, the first test was carried out in Japan in 1865, and the first Tokyo-Hokkaido line was installed in 1874. In 1871, it was possible to communicate with those abroad [IWA 02]. Speedy development and reduced distance equals success. These communication technologies were useful to Japan in the war between Russia and Japan in 1904-1905. During WWI, belligerents were able to make of communication technologies much more than they had been able to in previous conflicts. Germany turned communication into a weapon in its own right, whereas France left them as a part of engineering. Whatever the status that communication technologies take on within the army, they are imposed as a new decisive element in the art of warfare. "War is born, and with it comes the need to promptly transmit commands and important news from afar" [BEL 94]. A number of essential principles today which apply to the use of cyberspace in warfare are already applied to telegraphy and telephony in warfare: speed of the communications, reduced distances, network vulnerability, possible attacks on these networks, the necessary defense of these networks, and communication interceptions.

---

161 "A-technical" here means that the tools/weapons are pratically within reach of everybody, not requiring a high degree of technical knowledge on behalf of those who are using them. There is no need to really master the weapons used, especially when others can do it for us.

4.1.13.4. *Hybrid wars*

Are new wars simply "hybrid", a term used to denote armed conflicts which are neither totally conventional nor totally unconventional[162], but which are rather a combination of the two? The consequences for conventional forces is the obligation to prove themselves as being more flexible, and proving their adaptability in the face of actors able to use a wide range of tactics and weapons, and who will not hesitate to involve the population directly by fitting in with them, for instance. The concept of a hybrid war also goes back to the idea of complexity. The term has not yet been introduced into the official vocabulary of the U.S. DoD, although it has used it on several occasions in various reports, as the 2010 Government Accountability Office points out[163]. The American DoD uses "Full Spectrum Operations" as an equivalent.

The notion of a hybrid war does not have unanimous backing. The few definitions that we have of hybrid war show that this concept denotes conflicts which involve all kinds of actors using multiple combinations of violent means (mixing conventional and unconventional, regular and irregular, civil and military, state and non-state governed, legitimate and illegitimate actors, criminals, populations, etc.). The use of information and information technologies is therefore a necessary part of this widespread range of resources. Hybrid war may, then, appeal to cyberwar. In this case, operational cyberattacks would be used, and not strategic attacks. Cyberwar could also be called a hybrid war due to the nature of the space where it takes place: cyberspace is both physical and virtual. But even if we can just about perceive what "hybrid" means (everything is becoming hybrid, in fact: systems, networks, threats, wars), for now the term seems to be in the pursuit for recognition. It is often placed alongside "complex", "adaptive", and "global"[164]. It is also used to denote the process of computerizing armies which must seek to modernize their weaponry by incorporating the information systems needed for networking.

4.2. The Stuxnet affair

To conclude this chapter, let us take a look at the Stuxnet affair which was widely talked about across the world in the summer of 2010. It offers an interesting example of what threats can be today and the way in which they materialize. Equally so, it gives an insight into the way States find themselves involved (or not) in these incidents where actors are intervening in debates and holding the message

---

162 [GAO 10].
163 [GAO 10], p.2.
164 For example, see the rhetoric in texts such as the 2010 Tradoc Report [TRA 10], p.5, 13, 21, 24.

in their hands. We can also see in this case the interactions between these actors, and the way in power relationships emerge[165]. The media wave which broke out temporarily put the problems of cyberwar, its dangers and its realities back into the world's spotlight. It came across as an international invisible threat, with potential and indeed real consequences. But for the general public, Stuxnet was only an epiphenomenon. The media only used the subject in their headlines for a short while before moving onto something else, as is their wont. Behind the scenes, on the security and defense front, the case continued to feed discussions and research. The unique aspect of the Stuxnet case was that its Stuxnet Study raised more questions than answers. Where virtually an entire year has passed since the discovery of the famous worm by a Belarusian society[166], observers are still finding themselves deep in the fog of all the confused information and still have no tangible proof (and they probably never will, either). There is still a multitude of unknown factors which have opened up new footholds where all those who wanted to make their contribution to the phenomenon or get spoken about dove in head first. The question here is, "who"? Who could have launched Stuxnet?

Many hypotheses have been drawn up to answer this question. If Iran was the target, then Israel and the USA are the appointed creators of the worm (who benefits from the crime?). Other Western countries could also be nominated. It was said that China was guilty of wanting to attack India and more precisely, of wanting to destroy the INSAT 4B satellite in the fight for space that the two countries are currently engaged in[167]. Will there be a pre and post-Stuxnet, as the media are saying? It seems that this case presents at least as many conventional aspects as innovative ones. Amongst the conventional aspects, we will cite "uncertainty". The situation that observers are finding themselves in, undoubtedly including the creators of the worm and the direct and indirect victims, is clearly uncertainty. This goes back to Clausewitz, in terms of the fog and friction of war. We are faced with no information and too much information all at once. We do not know how to identify the right information. We are confronted with incomplete, partly true and partly false information. We have to put the puzzle together, but it seems like the prized piece is missing. It would be useful here to recall the discussion held by Donald Rumsfeld in 2002, who declared: "as we know, there are known knowns; there are things we know we know. We also know there are known unknowns; that is to say we know there are some things we do not know. But there are also unknown unknowns – the ones we do not know that we do not know. If we looks throughout the history of our country and other free countries, it is the latter

---

165 [VEN 10b].

166 On June 17th 2010, the Belarusian company VirusBlokAda published a report entitled: Trojan-Spy.0485 And Malware-Cryptor.Win32.Inject.gen.2 Review [KUP 10].

167 [HIG 10].

category that tend to be the difficult ones"[168]. We do not know who has acted. Is it an individual, many individuals, a network, or a team? Who is, or who are, the commanders? States or private actors? Soldiers? Today, there are many interpretations and a lot of explanations, but there is no definitive answer. Perhaps the right answer has been found, but nobody knows how to spot it.

There are still unknown factors regarding events. What we are still being told in 2011 is what we were being told in July 2010 about the Stuxnet worm which was discovered in June 2010. But we know that a version of it already existed in June 2009, perhaps even before. But we know nothing about the "life" of this worm between June 2009 and the moment it was discovered. We do not know what it would have become if nobody had found it. Could it have caused more damage? Was it slowed down or stopped by its disclosure? What is Stuxnet doing now? What are its designers and commanders doing: are they still hard at work or have they stopped all activity? It would have been interesting to see how the creators were active, when in July 2010 the worm was brought to the public's attention. The experts who analyzed the code discovered that the worm was exploiting a stolen license in Taiwan. In the week after the news was published, the worm was altered and another license, again stolen in Taiwan, replaced the first one. This means that the creators were watching, reacting, motivated by the will to resist, and to lead their operation well. But worse still, we do not know what the real target was. Let us not forget that the idea of the centrifugal machines in Iranian nuclear plants as the target is only a hypothesis, after all. Even if this were plausible, there are maybe others. Was Stuxnet really designed to only attack Iranian nuclear plants?

The statistics published mainly by two anti-virus software creators (Symantec and Kaspersky)[169] confirmed that the worm had been released in several countries. There were traces of it in India, Indonesia, China, Cuba, the USA, in Europe, etc. This is a matter which is still troubling analysts. If the worm was hell bent on targeting Iranian plants, then how and above all, *why*, was it found in so many different places throughout the world? Was the target itself even hit? Did the attackers know themselves? And as for the target, was it aware of the attack? If the target was Iran, then the answer is yes. The media responded to the arrests, and the authorities recognized that their nuclear schedule had been disrupted (but should we believe them?). Uncertainty also comes from the fact that we are lacking in sources to confront with our questions. The worm itself, although supposedly widely spread across the planet, was difficult to get hold of in order to analyze the code. We have far too sources to get statistics relating to the spread infection. The methods used to produce the statistics are unknown. But we do know that the results from the

---

168 Transcription of a meeting in the USA DoD, February 12th 2002, http://www.defenselink. mil/transcripts/transcript.aspx?transcriptid=2636.
169 [SYM 11].

statistics are highly dependent on the methods used to achieve them. All the communications around Stuxnet (statistics, reports, revelations, discoveries, etc.) are held by a relatively limited number of "experts" working in security and software industries. One of the characteristics of the case is the lack of discussions from official, state actors. A lack of proof and certainty left the door open to the imagination, and the experts had no trouble of walking into the world of fiction. Some saw references to the Bible, others saw mysterious codes supposedly encrypted with birthdays and signatures. We were in full Da Vinci Code swing. Some saw the stamp of Israel, others saw the USA, soldiers, or amateurs. But if the case had so much success, it is perhaps *not* due to its geopolitical dimension. It is perhaps, above all, because it manipulated values and symbols. In the eyes of the West, Iran is the devil. Nuclear power plants are the very image of apocalypse. The Japan earthquake in March 2011 quickly reminded us all of the dangers of nuclear power for mankind. The Internet, cyberspace...these are the new world. Stuxnet was stirring up threats, fears and the unknown, and this is why the phenomenon was interesting and intrigued the world.

We needed some answers. The idea of the attack being led against the Iranian nuclear system is indeed an attractive one. There are actors, somewhere in the shadows, fighting against the evil villain. Maybe these are soldiers, or intelligence agencies, or very talented hacker networks. Perhaps they are new righter of wrongs, speaking to us with masked faces through cameras, known as the anonymous. The most supported idea the intervention of a State against Iran, meaning a confrontation on the highest of levels. But let us not forget that, very often, mountains can easily produce molehills. The USA has accused Russia and China many times of certain attacks. Estonia accused Moscow of their attacks in 2007. But the only guilty parties arrested were simple hackers without the least political ambition.

In this case, how can Stuxnet be a divide, a decisive turning point? Some have confirmed that the worm was the first cybernetic weapons worthy of carrying the name, because it was complex. Faced with the same product, opinions differ greatly. On the contrary, others confirm that the worm was an amateur matter, and that the complexity is only superficial. They call it an amateur affair because the whole procedure lacked strategy and they did not reach their target. It is indeed remarkable to note at what point an object, a phenomenon, or an event seen from many points of view, can generate interpretations and standing points which are so different, and so radically opposed to each other. How can some see the work of amateurs, and others see the work of military engineers, wisely organized and innovative to the point of creating the global security event? How can some claim that a team of greatly talented engineers over several months was needed to create Stuxnet, when others say that it is not as difficult as all that to operate over four or five days, and that the process remains within reach of a single individual? Everybody sees what they wants to see, and find what they are looking for in their interpretations. Faced with the same observed object (but is it really the same?), then points of view differ again and lead to radically diverging conclusions. The phenomenon unmasks the fragile nature of the fundamental bases that security and defense policies are based on, as well as all theories on threats, violence, the level of disruption or destruction, the eminent nature of chaos, and of course, cyberconflicts.

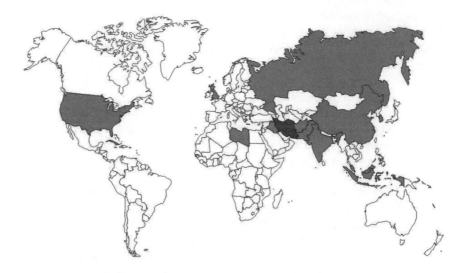

Figure 4.25. *Iran is only a hypothesis[170]. Several other countries were struck by Stuxnet according to statistics and anti-virus creators*

Whatever the case may be, the transfer to a higher level of complexity is not enough to mark a break in history. This break could be decided on by using a basic method encountering tough setbacks for the security of our most fundamental infrastructures. Or, even by striking apparently insignificant targets, which nobody is usually interested in, and which could turn out to be critical by the set of unsuspected effects happening in quick succession. This break, this *rupture* with history could therefore come from a strategy or a new tactic, and above all, from a technological leap.

If there is a break with history in Stuxnet, then only time will tell. The cyberattacks on Estonia are engrained in memories and people are still referring to

---

170 Stuxnet could also have targeted Siemens and not Iran directly, because the company has financial interests in this country, its helps financially in the construction of nuclear power plants. Siemens have been criticized for giving Iran dual technologies, and software to intercept text messages. It has international competition, and this could all be a simple matter of economic warfare.

them today. This case clearly marked a rupture, a symbolic one at least. It represents a benchmark in the history of security. Stuxnet will maybe play the same role again, but only the future will tell. We must not doubt this. The advocators and outcomes of the affair are not, and will never be, known. Iran, if it was the target, will not exploit the attack as Estonia did, continuing to portray the event in the media well beyond 2007.

We will formulate a hypothesis here, which would position Stuxnet is a more general position. We observe an extension of the field of targets and conventional actors of cyberconflict (USA, Asia, Russia, and few European countries) towards a new zone which we will call the "arc of crisis"[171].

Besides a few sporadic incidents here and there in the world, we have a set of actors historically involved in information warfare, all accusing each other of aggressive operations led in cyberspace. Over these last few years, cyberattacks have struck Europe, the USA, Asia, and all the connected countries to various degrees. Important incidents have been revealed: attacks on South Korea or the USA, blamed on North Korea; attacks on government sites virtually everywhere in Europe, but also in India, Japan and Australia; attacks on large American businesses, on the same rank as Google, which found a reason for its partial withdrawal from China in summer 2010.

Over these last few years, particularly since 2007 to be more precise, cyberspace has been the vector of confrontations in a set of countries which, as we can see on the map below, take up a particular region in the world:

– the USA have stated they led attacks on Iran in 2007;

– in 2008, confrontations between Russia and Georgia extended into cyberspace;

– in 2009, the Xinjiang riots in China involved cyberspace directly;

– Turkey, and particularly Turkish hacktivists, is very present in this domain. They took part in the Xinjiang riots. But they are also extremely virulent as the creators of millions of hacktivist type attacks;

– in 2010, Stuxnet may have been targeted towards Iran;

– in 2011, revolutions in North African countries would have been facilitated by Web 2.0.

---

171 The theory of the arc of crisis was formulated by the Islam specialist Bernard Lewis and updated by Zbygniew Brzezinski. The arc of crisis initially denoted a set of countries separating the Eastern block from Islam counties, and zone which extended from Egypt to Pakistan. The arc of crisis is a concept which was taken up again by the White Paper on Defense in 2008 (France).

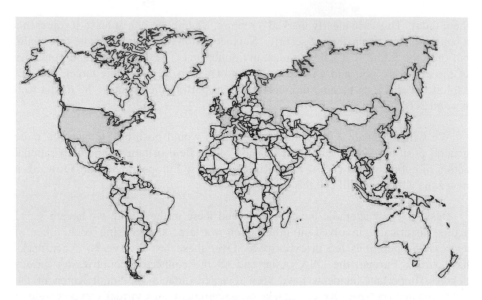

Figure 4.26. *The most notorious conventional actors in information warfare and cyberwar*

The countries which keep our attention make up a band where the people's riots are concentrated, along with wars accompanied by cyberattacks. In these countries, cyberspace is an accepted tool of confrontation. These countries were not traditionally taken for targets or actors of confrontation in cyberspace up until now.

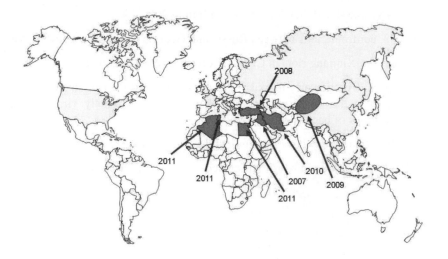

Figure 4.27. *A sequence of events with cybernetic dimensions*

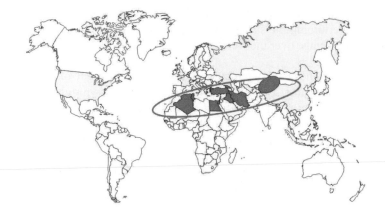

Figure 4.28. *Arc of crisis?*

Chronologically and geographically, Stuxnet is part of this succession of events, without there necessarily being a direct relation between them.

Besides Israel, the set of countries in this zone mainly come under groups 3 and 4.

Other threads have been relatively little explored regarding the possible source of the Stuxnet worm: terrorism, or the "anonymous". However, both are likely to bring real threats on States, and their infrastructures. If we can argue by using a comparison with conventional terrorism, then we can fully put cyberattacks amongst its ranks because it is lacking an essential element: the claim. But could terrorism not use the characteristics which shape cyberspace (transparency, anonymity) for its own interests? Terrorism aims to imprint people's memories by evolving and no longer just delivering the barbaric images it is accustomed to. We can envisage high-tech terrorism.

Can Stuxnet represent a break in the way of thinking about cyberwar? The answer to this is clearly, no. Stuxnet only confirms what we already knew: false flag attacks are possible, as well as totally anonymous ones invisible attacks. It is still difficult to attack critical infrastructures today, as the capabilities to accomplish objectives are still not well sized and mastered. Soldiers are not alone in the field, and it is difficult to know whether an attack has really hit its target when the victim does not react. In spite of everything, Stuxnet raises the question of the role of the military, of cyberoperations, of the choice of target, of the authorized limits in all the action. If Stuxnet did not hit its target, then it must use more means to reach it in future. The arms race is, then, on. It is unlikely that the small and weak actors, those with insufficient means, will make to follow suit, and we imagine that the asymmetry principle which currently prevails and confirms that the weak have the advantage in overturning the strong, gives up its place to return to logic, where the strong has an advantage over the weak.

Stuxnet also reminds us in international relations, in the game of power struggles between international actors, that lies are a weapon in their own right. Stuxnet is real game for liars. The victims lie about real attacks, about the level of vulnerability to viral attack, for instance. First of all Iran denied the impact of the worm by recognizing the infection, then recognized the negative impact on the nuclear program. The creators of the attacks also lie: many actors were accused, but none of them confirmed or rejected the accusations. Who should we believe? In this light, Stuxnet was above all an act of information warfare.

Whatever the questions we were raising at the time, the only that matters today is "who"? Who is guilty, who acted? When there is no answer to this, even all the best developed theories remain theoretical, and analyzes remain as pure hypotheses. It is impossible to do geopolitics and geostrategies, and even less so to venture into proposing a sociological analysis of these actors, as long as we do not know who did what. Then it will be the time to ask questions on the motives and methods of the attack, then thinking of a security or defense strategy based on this knowledge. For now, the challenge is finding the guilty party. However, we must ask questions regarding the impact that a certain blame could have. It is no longer enough to say "X led the attack". So we must assume the accusation with supporting proof, and give ourselves the means to react. But *how*?

Imagining economic, political measures, boycotting the international community, before considering using force? Besides the problem of blame, the problem of representation and interpretation is widely felt. The strategies that we define, the policies or the tactics that we decide on give a framework to the action (attacks, defense) that we can then lead and which are carried out by actors (cyber: warriors, fighters, criminals, activists) who evolve in a certain space (the cyberspace and the real realm). Actors think according to the realm they evolve in. Space, in fact cyberspace, is central. It conditions, influences, restricts, makes the action (its methods, scenarios, pace, power) and the choice of actors (who get involved according to their skills, capabilities, profiles, identify, objectives, motives, resources), and of course conditions strategies.

In fact, not everything is possible in every dimension. Cyberspace is not an exception to this rule, even if it offers a lot of new possibilities. Strategies are defined according to particular spaces. Therefore, the representation and definition of space are considered as being essential. But cyberspace is not yet well known enough. Thus, to represent it, the method consists of using metaphors or comparisons [VEN 11]. We start with a blank page, *cyberspace*, an undefined, non-specific concept in construction, then we lay a sheet of tracing paper over this page: references to known dimensions (earth, air, sea, space). Cyberspace is thus an ocean, an unknown land, a system, a jungle, a new territory. This imagery represents cyberspace as global systems, clouds, continents with their oceans, urban spaces (cities, data walls, tunnels, ports), transport systems (roads, highways), living systems (plants, insects, viruses, mankind). Cyberconflict is then thought about in the same way, meaning using continual references to conventional dimensions. Using imagery, cyberwar refers to air space, continents, the army (the computerized soldier), and to nuclear war. In the army, the computerization of the battlefield and the C4ISR systems are simplified as a networking of all the dimensions. Thus, theoretical approaches will inevitably be used as these references.

The beginnings of geopolitical reflections of cyberspace imagine cyberspace in comparison to maritime and naval power (Mahan, Corbett, etc.), air power (Douhet, Mitchell, etc.), space power (Star Wars), or the theories of Mackinder, Spykman, etc. The choices for these comparisons and metaphors are not without their consequences on the theoretical construction which results from it. Thinking of cyberwar in terms of nuclear weapons or the Cold War boils down to introducing specific notions such as dissuasion and weapons of mass destruction. Air and extra-atmospheric space deals with the freedom of movement, superiority, speed, modernity, technology and star wars.

Continents and oceans are geopolitical matters, of power, and of areas in the world which are bigger than others. The city signifies a particularly special concept today, namely the indefensible or impenetrable zone, the civilian/military mix, and the risks of collateral damage. Referring to the world of transport calls up notions of logistics, economy and distance, and the systemic approach refers to life, death, and the weakness of the body that is society. The cyberspace-brain of society, the nervous system, is threatened by the cyberattacks which try to crush it. Security is becoming a matter of life or death. Thinking about security in terms of the fortress principle, is a question of going back to principles from the Middle Ages, or the Vauban age. Perhaps this is not the most suitable model for security in the 21st Century.

The comparison has won over the legal domain. The question of a law being applicable to cyberwar and cyberattacks and has been widely dealt with in this vein: *jus in bello, jus ad bellum* (justice in war, the right to war), the international law of armed conflicts and the treaty on the non-proliferation of weapons of mass destruction are branches of law where we can apply copies of the still blank model of the law of cyberconflicts. What is an act of war? What is an armed attack? Perhaps the answers already exist in the current law. The problem does not so much come from the choice of comparisons and metaphors, as the difficulty to move away from them. Reality is not a metaphor and comparisons are never perfect.

4.3. Bibliography

[ADT 08] ARMÉE DE TERRE, *Tactique générale*, Editions Economica, Paris, France, 2008.

[ALE 07] ALEXANDER K.B., "Warfighting in Cyberspace", *Military.com*, http://www.military. com/forums/0,15240,143898,00.html, 31st July 2007.

[AND 10] ANDRES R.B., "Up in the air", *The American Interest*, vol. VI, no. 1, September/October 2010.

[ARO 76] ARON R., *Penser la guerre*, Clausewitz, Gallimard, Paris, France, 1976.

[BAR 18] BARRÈS M., *Chronique de la Grande Guerre*, no. 12, Plon, Paris, France, 24th April – 7th August 1918.

[BAR 10] BARLOW J., "Cyber war and U.S. policy: Part I, neorealism", *The Journal of Education, Community and Values*, vol. 10, no. 5, Pacific University of Oregon, USA, June 2010.

[BAU 81] BAUCOM D.R., "Technological war, reality and the American myth", *Air University Review*, http://www.airpower.maxwell.af.mil/airchronicles/aureview/1981/sep-oct/baucom.htm, September-October 1981.

[BEA 10] BEAUMONT P., "US appoints first cyber warfare general", *The Observer*, http://www.guardian.co.uk/world/2010/may/23/us-appoints-cyber-warfare-general, 23rd May, 2010.

[BEL 94] BELLOC A., *La télégraphie historique*, Librairie de Firmin-Didot Paris, France, http://gallica.bnf.fr/ark:/12148/bpt6k621150/f3.image.pagination.r=guerre+t%C3%A9l% C3%A9phonie.langFR, 1894.

[BEL 97] BELL D., *La fin de l'idéologie*, PUF, Paris, France, 1997.

[BHU 07] BHUPENDRA J., *High Altitude Limited ASAT Treaty*, Department of War Studies, King's College, London, UK, http://www.spacesecurityprogramme.org/uploads/ssp/space _sec_session%206_Prof.%20Bhupendra%20Jasani.pdf, 2007.

[BLA 15] BLANCHON G., *Les sous-marins et la guerre actuelle*, Bloud et Gay Editeurs, Paris, France, 1915.

[BOU 06] BOUTHOUL G., *Le phénomène guerre*, Petite Bibliothèque, Payot, Paris, France, 2006.

[BUZ 66] BUZZATI D., *Le K*, Editions Pocket, Laffont, Paris, France, 1966.

[CAR 10] CARR J., *Inside Cyber Warfare*, O'Reilly, USA, 2010.

[CEB 04] CEBROWSKI A.K., "Transformation and the changing character of war?", *Transformation Trends*, 2004.

[CLA 84] CLANCY T., *The Hunt for Red October*, Naval Institute Press, Annapolis, USA, 1984.

[CLA 10] CLARKE R., KNAKE R., *Cyber War: The Next Threat to National Security and What to do About It*, Ecco, USA, 2010.

[COR 10] CORNISH P., LIVINGSTONE D., CLEMENTE D., On Cyber Warfare, A Chatham House Report, November 2010.

[CSS 10] Center for Security Studies, "Cyberguerre: concept, état d'avancement et limites", *CSS*, no. 71, Zurich, Switzerland, April 2010.

[DAN 10] DANG S.T., *The Prevention of Cyberterrorism and Cyberwar. Issue one for the GA First Committee: Disarmament and International Security (DISEC)*, Old Dominion University, Vietnam, 2011.

[DEI 06] DEIBERT R., *The Geopolitics of Asian Cyberspace*, http://www.feer.com/articles1/2006/0612/free/p022.html, December 2006.

[DES 07] DESPORTES V., *Décider dans l'incertitude*, Editions Economica, Paris, France, 2007.

[DES 08] DESPORTES V., "Oui, il faut lire Clausewitz", *Revue Défense & Sécurité Internationale*, no. 37, p. 39, Paris, France, May 2008.

[DOL 02] DOLMAN E., *Astropolitik, Classical Geopolitics in the Space Age*, Frank Cass, London, UK, October, 2002.

[ENC 09] ENCEL F., *Horizons géopolitiques*, Editions du Seuil, Paris, France, 2009.

[FEI 10] FEILDEN T., "Cyber War or Science Fiction?", *BBC Today*, http://www.bbc.co.uk/blogs/today/tomfeilden/2010/10/cyber_war_or_science_fiction.html, 5th October 2010.

[FLU 11] FLÜKIGER J.M., *Guerres nouvelles et théorie de la guerre*, Infolio Coll. Illico, Switzerland, April 2011

[GAO 10] Hybrid Warfare, GAO-10-1036R report, Washington D.C., USA, http://www.gao.gov/new.items/d101036r.pdf, 10th September 2010.

[GEL 06] GELAS J.P., Réseaux Interplanétaires (IPN) et Réseaux tolérants aux délais (DTN), Laboratoire de l'Informatique du Parallélisme, France, http://symoon.free.fr/scs/dtn/biblio/IPN-DTN.pdf, 2006.

[GIB 01] GIBSON D.J., *Shock and Awe: a Sufficient Condition for Victory?*, Newport United States Naval War College, Newport, USA, http://www.dtic.mil/cgi-bin/GetTRDoc?Location=U2&doc=GetTRDoc.pdf&AD=ADA389508, 2001.

[HIG 10] HIGGINS K.J., "China likely behind Stuxnet attack, cyber war expert says", http://www.darkreading.com/vulnerability-management/167901026/security/attacks-breaches/228800582/china-likely-behind-stuxnet-attack-cyberwar-expert-says.html, 14th December 2010.

[HUN 00] HUNTINGTON S., *Le choc des civilisations*, Odile Jacob, Paris, France, 2000.

[IAD 04] INDIAN ARMY DOCTRINE, p. 21, October 2004.

[IWA 02] IWAO S., IYANAGA T., *Dictionnaire historique du Japon*, vol. 1, Maisonneuve Larose, Paris, France, 2002.

[DOD 10] DOD, Joint terminology for cyberspace operations, Joint Chiefs of Staff, Department
of Defense, USA, http://www.nsci-va.org/CyberReferenceLib/2010-11-Joint%20 Terminology%20for%20Cyberspace%20Operations.pdf, 2010.

[KAR 06] KARATZOGIANNI A., *The Politics of Cyberconflict*, Routledge, UK, 2006.

[KEY 08] KENYON H.S., *Collaboration Key to Network Warfare*, http://www.afcea.org/signal /articles/templates/SIGNAL_Article_Template.asp?articleid=1641&zoneid=5, July 2008.

[KHA 09] KHANNA P., *The Second World*, Random House, New York, USA, 2009.

[KLE 08] KLEIN N., *The Shock Doctrine*, Penguin Books, New York, USA, 2008.

[KRA 09] KRAMER F.D., STARR S.H., WENTZ L.K., *Cyberpower and National Security*, Center for Technology and National Security Policy, National Defense University, Washington, USA, 2009.

[KUP 10] KUPREEV O., ULASEN S., "Trojan-Spy.0485 and Malware-Cryptor.Win32.Inject.gen.2" Review, Belarus, http://www.f-secure.com/weblog/archives /new_rootkit_en.pdf, 2010.

[LIB 09] LIBICKI M., *Cyberdeterrence and Cyberwar*, RAND Corporation, USA, http://www.rand.org/pubs/monographs/2009/RAND_MG877.pdf, 2009.

[MEL 09] MELANI report, Guerre de l'information: mise en place d'unités spéciales dans divers pays, in Sûreté de l'information, situation en Suisse et sur le plan international, p. 16, Switzerland, January-June 2009.

[MEN 97] MENDRAS H., "La fin de l'idéologie, Lectures critiques", *Revue française de science politique*, vol. 47, edition 3-4, pp. 497-499, http://www.persee.fr/web/revues /home/prescript/article/rfsp_0035-2950_1997_num_47_3_395194, 1997.

[MOL 96] MOLANDER R., RIDDILE A.S., WILSON A., *Strategic Information Warfare: A New Face of War*, RAND Corporation, USA, 1996.

[MON 07] Montbrial T., KLEIN J., *Dictionnaire de stratégie*, Quadrige Presses Universitaires de France, Paris, France, 2007.

[MUN 04] MÜNKLER H., *The New Wars*, Polity, Oxford, UK, 2004.

[MUR 99] MURAWIEC L., "La cyberguerre", *Revue Agir*, no. 2, Paris, France, December 1999.

[NAI 10] NAIR S.K., *The Case for an India-US Partnership in Cybersecurity*, Takshashila Institution, India, http://takshashila.org.in/wp-content/uploads/2010/03/TDD-Cyber Collab-SKN-1.pdf, 14th July 2010.

[NEA 09] NEAL D., *Crosscutting Issues in International Transformation, The Center for National Security Policy*, National Defense University, Washington, USA, http://www.ndu.edu/CTNSP/docUploaded//International%20Transformation.pdf, December 2009.

[NYE 10] NYE J., *Cyber Power, Harvard Kennedy School, Belfer Center for Science and International Affairs*, Cambridge, USA, http://enews.belfercenter.org/ct.html?rtr=on&s= lj1i,lvy0,7oo,5oyu,uzw,f78b,40qe, May 2010.

[PAR 01] PARKS R.C., DUGGAN D.P., "Principles of cyber-warfare", *Proceedings of workshop IEEE 2001 Information Assurance and Security*, United States Military Academy, West Point, New York, USA, 5th-6th June 2001.

[PAS 10] PASCO X., "Arsenalisation de l'espace: un débat en trompe-l'œil?, Bilan géostratégie", *Le Monde*, Paris, France, 2010

[PIX 08] *La guerre*, Editions Pix'n Love, Les cahiers du jeu vidéo, France, 2008.

[SCH 08] SCHNEIER B., "For it to be cyberwar, it must first be war", quoted in "Marching off to Cyberwar", *The Economist*, http://www.economist.com/node/12673385, 4th December 2008.

[SHA 10] SHARMA A., "Cyber wars: a paradigm shift from means to ends", *Strategic Analysis*, vol. 24, no. 1, Routeldge, USA, January 2010.

[SHI 01] SHIMEALL T., WILLIAMS P., DUNLEVY C., *Countering Cyber War, NATO Review*, CERT Analysis Center of Carnegie Mellon University & OTAN, 2001.

[SOM 11] SOMMER P., BROWN I., Reducing systemic cybersecurity risk, Report for OCDE, Information Systems and Innovation Group, London School of Economics, London, UK, 14th January 2011.

[STI 10] STIENNON R., *Cyber war is not the Cold War*, https://www.infosecisland.com /blogview/6044--Cyber-War-is-not-the-Cold-War-.html, August 2nd 2010.

[SYM 11] Symantec, W32.Stuxnet Dossier, http://www.symantec.com/content/en/us/ enterprise/media/security_response/whitepapers/w32_stuxnet_dossier.pdf, February 2011.

[TES 10] TESQUET O., *La cyberguerre en 24 heures chrono*, www.slate.fr/print/209699, 6th May 2010.

[TRA 10] Cyberspace Operations. Concept Capability Plan 2016-2028. The United States Army. TRADOC Pamphlet 525-7-8, 22 February 2010.

[ULL 96] ULLMAN H.K., WADE J.P., *Shock and Awe: Achieving Rapid Dominance*, National Defense University, Washington D.C., USA, http://www.dodccrp.org/files/Ullman_ Shock.pdf, 1996.

[VEN 08] VENNESSON P., "Penser les guerres nouvelles: la doctrine militaire en questions", *Pouvoirs*, no. 125, p.81-92, L'armée française, April 2008.

[VEN 10a] VENNESON P., *The Transformation of War*, seminar, European University Institute, Department of Political and Social Sciences, October-December 2010.

[VEN 07] VENTRE D., *La guerre de l'information*, Hermès, Paris, France, 2007.

[VEN 10b] VENTRE D., "Stuxnet", *Revue Misc*, Paris, France, 2010.

[VEN 11] VENTRE D., *Cyberespace et acteurs du cyberconflit*, Hermès, Paris, France, 2011.

[WAR 03] WARUSFEL B., "Nouvelles technologies et relations internationals", AFRI, vol. IV, p. 892, Paris, France, 2003.

[ZHU 07] ZHUGE J., HOLZ TH. *et al.*, "Characterizing the IRC-based botnet phenomenon", http://honeyblog.org/junkyard/reports/botnet-china-TR.pdf, 3rd December 2007.

Chapter 5

Operational Aspects of a Cyberattack: Intelligence, Planning and Conduct

5.1. Introduction

Since the beginning of 2000, the increased amount of computerized attacks has triggered an increasing number of investigations. In particular, the generalized computer attack on Estonia in 2007 gave way to a wide field of reflection on what we call cyberwar and cyberattacks, without the difference between the two being clearly defined.

These reflections have gotten straight down to the State prerogative, and that States themselves have quickly come to understand, in an inevitable context of national security, the urgent need to rigorously define the concept. In addition, they have also seen the need for legislation, on the international front as much as the national, and to organize themselves in an aim for defense (defensive cyberwar). But more recently, as an unavoidable consequence from any field related to the State context, this may be in an aim to attack (offensive cyberwar). The publication of the French White Paper on Defense and National Security [LBD 08] has initiated this last aspect, as also other countries have.

If there is a relatively successful reflection on the human aspects (legal, societal, historical, etc.) of what a cyberwar might be, then on the other hand there is no open study on the technical and especially operational aspects regarding the materialization of a cyberattack. Yet, from a purely military point of view, this

Chapter written by Eric FILIOL.

"practical" question is very important. Any reflection on the matter, then, will inevitably lead to a certain number of questions:

– How do we conduct a cyberwar?

– Is there a cybernetic reality which is independent of the real world where cyberwars will exclusively take place? In other words, are our computerized systems and networks an independent territory, disconnected from the real world?

– Is computerized war fundamentally different (both technically and operationally) from a conventional war?

– Must we create weapons and (military) units in their own right with digital engineering, a digital infantry, etc?

– What are the targets (tactically and strategically), and what is a critical infrastructure in this context? The concept of a bunker itself, does it still have meaning?

– Are the concepts of law in cyberwar and the ethics of the cyberwarrior still valid on technical and operational fronts?

It is fundamental to answer these questions if we want to define a rigorous and applicable operational approach.

This double operational (military, police) and scientific/technical culture is vital. Simply understanding how a weapon works is not enough. It is incredibly important to know how to use it in the chosen context, and to know its boundaries and possibilities. The best hacker in the world will be useless if he cannot organize his tools and skills for a more general maneuver. The culture of intelligence is indeed essential. This concerns the technical aspect, but also and above all, the other forms of intelligence (human, electromagnetic, communications, etc.).

It is also fundamental to know our target perfectly, including its characteristics and its ability to act and react, its potential, etc. The target is often said to be a "critical" structure, so complex that it is vital to discover all its features beforehand.

Not only are these answers important, but they must lead on to an operational approach and a methodology which must confirm and convince others of the reality of cyberattacks, or at least of their technical feasibility. Too many authors (whose technical legitimacy is somewhat doubtful) are confirming that these threats are only a myth [GRE 02] in order to legitimize the existence of specialized agencies, whereas even since 2000 we have been made aware of the real, studied and valid attacks.

In this chapter, we will explain what attackers can do, and *how*. From this point of view, it is a fundamental point to cast out any ethical notion, and to think how the enemy would think. We will also endeavor to generalize the concept of a cyberattack. For our decision-makers, such an attack boils down to a distributed denial of service (DDoS) or defacing websites. This would also allow us to widen the concept of a critical infrastructure and to show that the line of defense, which consists of building bunkers, is deceptive.

We will use the different feedback we have acquired to construct this operational approach:

– the technical analysis of real attacks;

– the analysis of military doctrines in particular, and the author's 20 year experience in infantry weapons;

– legal expertises in attacks or computer crimes;

– NATO's InfoOps (*information operations*) followed by the author who has provided a very rich source of information and reflection [OTA 08];

– scientific and technical research in the computer security domain, favoring the hacker and attacker's vision, and going from theory to (and for) practice and the operational.

5.2. Towards a broader concept of cyberwar

5.2.1. *War and cyberwar: common ground*

The concept of cyberwar has not really been defined, or at least, nobody has managed to set a single definition which is universally accepted and recognized. In this chapter we will not consider the definitions and conceptions which already exist, as they will be presented in detail in other chapters, and because we wish to offer an alternative vision, one which is principally based on an operational vision.

The only founding text which relates to our approach (and which inspired our train of thought and approach) is that written by the Chinese colonels Qiao and Wang in their book *Unrestricted Warfare* [LAN 02]. In this major publication, there are two sentences which illustrate particularly well the real context where we wish to be: "The first rule of unrestricted warfare is that there are no rules, nothing is forbidden [...]. There is nothing in the world today that cannot become a weapon".

First of all, the concept of cyberwar uses a concept of war that we may define as an extreme form of communication[1] between two or several groups trying to protect or increase their wealth, interests or their influence, via actions on:

– resources (mining, oil, etc.);

– populations (human element);

– mindsets (intellectual or spiritual element);

– territory (geographic element);

– information (immaterial element), etc.

In other words, the final aim of war is for action on the physical and real world. The cybernetic dimension of it only constitutes an additional tool through new systems and tools in order to act on the physical world.

The computerized dimension (systems and networks) only adds a dimension which is comparable to the 3rd dimension, which was exploited by the use of flight at the beginning of the 20th Century. This is precisely the vision that Colonels Liang Qiao and Xiangsui Wang developed [LAN 02]: no dimension should be overlooked, and no dimension should be favored exclusively. The following passage from their work clearly shows that the digital field is just one dimension amongst others. It is namely the coordination of several dimensions, targeting the physical and real sphere, which is indeed the ultimate objective: "if the attacking side secretly musters large amounts of capital without the enemy nation being aware of this at all and launches a sneak attack against its financial markets, then after causing a financial crisis, buries a computer virus and hacker detachment in the opponent's computer system in advance, while at the same time carrying out a network attack against the enemy so that the civilian electricity network, traffic dispatching network, financial transaction network, telephone communications network, and mass media network are completely paralyzed, this will cause the enemy nation to fall into social panic, street riots, and a political crisis." [LAN 02].

The vision of a war which only aims at a purely digital realm, a sort of *Second Life* type, seems to be extremely limited. It would be possible (author's thesis) to compare it with one which consists of replacing conflicts and other armed confrontations with football tournaments. This leads us to define the concepts of cyberattacks and cyberwar in the following way:

– cyberwar is a classic war where at least one of its elements, in its materialization, namely the motivations and tools (weapons in the broadest sense) relies on the computerized or digital field. These elements are called cyberattacks;

---

1 Expression adapted from Wikipedia (fr.wikipedia.org/wiki/Guerre), the rest is the author's own.

– a cyberattack is an attack on the real realm:

- either *directly*, by going through an information and communication system (ICS). In this case, the computerized field is only a tool or a means (attack on people, for instance);

- or *indirectly*, by attacking an ICS where one or several components from the real realm depend on it (for instance, an attack on an electronic voting machine network).

From this point of view, we will take the legal definition of cybercrime[2].

5.2.2. *New orders in cyberwar*

If cyberwar (or cyberattacks which make it a war) is only one new dimension in the domain of armed conflict, then on the other hand it has intrinsic features which radically change the order, and above all power relationships between belligerents. There are essentially three of these features: obliterating the concept of time, the concept of space and above all, the concept of proof. These three characteristics are interdependent of each other, even if for the purpose of simplicity we will set them out separately. They help to make the relations between attacker and target very *asymmetric*, and this is for the benefit of these relationships.

5.2.2.1. *Obliterating space*

Whereas in the case of conventional warfare, the spatial dimension is a critical strategic and tactical set of data – an air attack happens after the planes have had to travel a long distance with the possibility of being detected by satellites and radars. In the case of a cyberattack, it is possible to strike any point in space instantly from any other space.

Figure 5.1 which describes the action of a *botnet* (malicious network made of thousands of infected machines and controlled by a pirate) shows this obliteration of space.

This disappearance of the concept of space consequently removes the target's capacity to react, who then cannot easily link the attack to a specific origin. With no geographic reference, the target is then no longer able to identify with certainty the nature of the enemy. Without an enemy, war is impossible.

---

2 We will use the definition Computer Crime Research Center, http://www.crime-research.org/articles/joseph06/.

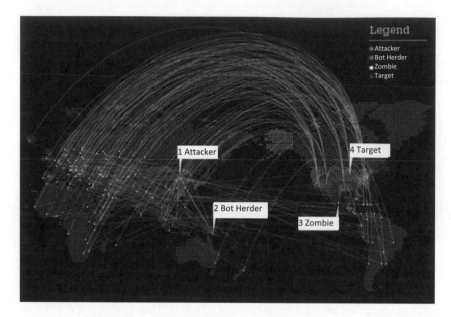

Figure 5.1. *General principle of a botnet operation*

5.2.2.2. *Obliterating time*

This primarily concerns the victim who perceives the attack as being sudden and immediate. On the other hand, if the attacker must make his move that very instant, then his preparations and planning may be spread over time, up to months beforehand. With the attack perceived of as sudden, then this will consequently deny the target of:

– the possibilities of obtaining intelligence, due to the loss of time references (real sequence of events and their chronology). Its analysis capacities are more than limited;

– reacting and leading its own maneuver. With no temporal reference, the target can no longer organize its retaliation in a way which is adapted to the attacker.

If the attack is powerful and well led, then its sudden nature and its consequence (surprise) remove all abilities to react. Or rather the target, in the worst case, never manages to take the initiative. Figure 5.2 shows such an attack by the *Slammer* worm.

Current research shows that such an attack could be led in 2009 and would have had a global effect in a matter of minutes.

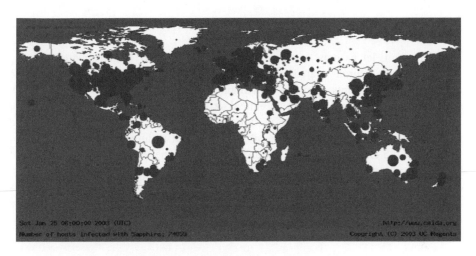

Figure 5.2. *Slammer worm attack in January 2003*
(15 minutes after the attack started)

5.2.2.3. *Obliterating proof*

This is probably the most important characteristic, to the extent that not only does it remove any exact image from the "battlefield" and from the tactical situation, but it also allows the attacker to send a potentially falsified image, and one which is distorted from reality.

In the digital world, everything can be falsified (MAC address, IP address, documents, etc.) and the notion of proof (in the legal sense) no longer means anything. Due to the single fact that the concept of copying is dying out – we cannot copy an electric phenomenon – the very idea of proof is no longer valid. A worm such as *Blaster* could not be traced because it was connected to target machines through the theft of IP addresses [FIL 06]. Moreover, it was not possible to trace the attacker either. An attacker might also use the certainty of tools such as cryptography against the person trying to analyze the available data [FIL 10] and wrongly incriminate an innocent third party. Furthermore, with the disappearance of the concept of proof (and therefore intelligence, in a military context), the idea of repercussion and legitimate defense is no longer valid either [BEN 05]. The target's operational capacity is obliterated.

In this context, it is getting easier to understand that, devoid of truth, any idea of legislation is getting trickier, and the application of some unspecific law (in an international court) is more fanciful still.

5.2.3. *Who are cyberwarriors?*

First of all, let us draw out the main consequences of what happens initially. Total dematerialization related to the computerized and digital realm, with the removal of all concepts of proof as a main primary effect (digital in particular), means that any attempt to obtain an ethical or lawful notion of cyberwar is in vain. Moreover, a cyber attacker who no longer fears being identified, revealed and incriminated, will exploit all the possibilities offered to him entirely. This is total warfare, in the Qia and Wang definition [LAN 02]. The very notion of control (of weapons) no longer means anything: if we can count warheads, tanks and planes, essentially all material, if we can trace the critical know-how for weapons of mass destruction, then this becomes completely deceptive in the case of weapons of mass infection (viruses, for instance). It is hard to imagine NATO inspectors trying to control cross-border digital influxes and streams.

In such a context, it is easy to understand how the computerized domain, more than any form of terrorism, gives an excellent dimension to the relationship from the weak to strong. Any individual with a sound knowledge of ICS's (or ICT's) is a potential cyber attacker. This makes any grad student studying computer science a potential hacker. Knowledge in computer science is freely available, universally spread (free software has greatly contributed to this irrefutable fact, opening up a real Pandora's box) and therefore accessible to a large number of people: we just need a laptop, or even the latest cell phone, and an Internet connection to get up and running and have access to the most sophisticated techniques and tools.

On a more serious note, the responsibility of Western countries may also be incriminated via the real transfer of critical knowledge in our grad school classes (computer sciences, security, etc.) which welcome many foreign students whose experience shows, for some of them, that they had been connected with radical environments or movements.

Yet, if technical knowledge is indeed necessary, then it is far from being enough to lead large scale cyberattacks. It is essential to have a logistic ability offering coordination, planning and conduct. In this context, cyberattackers are just a link, obviously an important once, in the general chain. The main terrorist movements[3] (al-Qaeda, Hezbollah), mafias and above all certain States offer this logistic support [ALM 08], [MES 99], [BAN 06], [PAR 10].

------

3 However, let us note that it is difficult to assess the real capacity of these groups. On the other hand, it has been perfectly established that these groups have understood all the potential of the computer domain for terrorist means. The operational capacity will come with time, and our own inconsistencies regarding security management.

Since 2009, new actors have appeared on the scene as a structured movement: the *hacker movement*. Groups such as Antisec or more recently, The Anonymous have launched high-level structured operations on States (Iran, Zimbabwe, France, the European Union member states, etc.), entities (churches of scientology) and large companies (Mastercard, RSA Laboratories, HBGary, Maersk, etc.) These groups, structured into many sub-groups and layers have a high technical expertise at their disposal, and have access to the most vital technical resources. This is because a vast number of them work for the benefit of large software or security companies. Through what is called the "digital alter-globalist" [MAN 11], this international hacker is beginning to get a real political awareness and has technical means to make himself known and impose himself on others.

5.2.4. *Is formalization possible?*

After having put forward a definition of the concept of a cyberattack, the temptation might be to try to define it more formally. Probability theory or fuzzy logic are the two domains which come to mind naturally. Logically, operational thinking imagines the attacker's movement or its very own, in terms of events, hypothesis or options which we could attach probabilities to initially, or even afterwards within a Bayesian approach. But, if this means something in the safety/reliability domain[4], then on the other hand in the security domain, this approach cannot be applied. Security deals with managing intentional threats, which can be summarized by the famous duo of "sword versus shield". These threats are unpredictable by nature, cannot be modeled and are adaptive. A good attacker will make sure to permanently innovate and above all, as a feature of the computerized field, to delete all traces of proof but, especially, to make up false proof.

In this context, assigning probabilities or using a more descriptive model, such as fuzzy logic for instance, to manage events which cannot be defined by nature, are no longer scientifically valid[5].

5.3. Concept of critical infrastructure

This is the key concept in the warfare domain: the target must be known, evaluated, and its weakest elements identified. This is the role of the intelligence

---

4 Discipline mainly dealing with unintentional threats and therefore which are predictable because they can be modeled; the code theory and reliability theory are very powerful tools in this context.

5 Let us remember that the concept of probability relates to predicting the occurrence of events. It is not possible to attach such a probability to an event which is still unidentified and undefined.

stage. Moreover, we must have an acceptable definition of the notion of the criticality of infrastructures. It is also necessary to have useful methodology so as to accurately determine the target's weak point.

5.3.1. *Generalized definition of the notion of critical infrastructure*

In the computer security domain, the concept of critical infrastructures came about at the beginning of 2000. However the definitions proposed and then adopted are a far cry from being satisfactory, particularly if we are not coming from the defender's point of view, but the attacker's.

Let us take the example from the European Council in 2006: "Critical infrastructures are those physical and information technology facilities, networks, services and assets which, if disrupted or destroyed, would have a serious impact on the health, safety, security or economic well-being of citizens or the effective functioning of governments in European Union (EU) countries. Critical infrastructure includes: energy installations and networks, communications and information technology; finance, health care, food, water, transport, production, storage and transport of dangerous goods and government" [EUR 10].

This definition is too restrictive because it only takes into account the infrastructure itself, without considering its environment and some of its elements. It is important to greatly expand what we understand by critical infrastructure, and to add a certain number of additional elements.

5.3.1.1. *The human element*

Considering the human element, which is nearly always forgotten, is fundamental. No system or infrastructure can function without humans.

It starts by the decision maker. An attacker will always aim for the top[6]. Experience (and particularly the author's, in the military field) shows that not only does a decision maker (often of a more humanist culture than scientific) not know about computer science, but above all, his role as decision maker and his importance in the hierarchy lets him think that the rules which apply to others do not apply to him. He is above rules. In the security domain (low material contingency), this is an everyday reality: the heart of the job, whatever it may be, is the priority and would not be vassalized by technical considerations, were they to determine the security of the job. This guilty and dangerous self-interest, and this narrow-minded view will be exploited with the attacker benefiting the most.

---

6 A Chinese proverb which says "a fish always rots from the head down!"

But often an infrastructure (or an organization) depends on a human. Let us imagine a serious crisis in a city known as "X" (riots, for example): the critical infrastructure is the head of the police force and, moreover, the head of the police and his high assistants. A preliminary computer attack (via the personal computers belonging to these forces, which are never secure) which attacks people (see section 5.5) will put these people out of action and will harm the operational capacity of the police's infrastructure.

In the same line of ideas, a leader with contempt for the most basic rules of security, who connects a PDA (personal digital assistant) to an internal network, slipping past all the security devices of the DMZ could put this network in danger[7].

But this also affects other types of staff:

– technical staff (not only computing staff);

– the staff or people with high media potential (Union representatives, journalists, etc.);

– any staff or person that the infrastructure depends on to function correctly, or any person able to impact this infrastructure through links or dependences.

These human elements, within system interdependence (section 5.3.2.) will be top targets.

5.3.1.2. *External elements*

Never taken into account, the target infrastructure will depend on these elements. They generally seem to be non-critical and are only somewhat protected. They are (non-exhaustive list):

– subcontractors;

– providers (of resources, services, basic products, etc.);

– *data-centers* (hosting company data);

– supervising services (e.g. telephone operators have relocated these services into countries where the culture of security is very far removed from our own);

– foreign or relocated sub-contractors;

– the target's environment, political and cultural in particular.

---

7 DMZ (demilitarized zone). This is the zone with all the network's security and protection functions. A real case occured in 2004 in many large companies whose activity was blocked.

It is important to take into account the political and public dimension (particularly the media). There is a high level of asymmetry between what public power could be in practice, and what an attacker might authorize.

Triggering a hard strike in a factory via a computerized attack, or causing a riot in sensitive areas will count as a series of diverted attacks which cannot simply be managed by sending in the police force. In the face of a sudden attack, the public power will be condemned to a long and perilous management strategy.

To reiterate our discussion, let us take the example of the possible introduction of one of the first flaws in the Windows XP core in 2001. The Microsoft editor sub-contracts the largest aspect of its operating system (OS) developments in India.

In 2001, a one Abdul Afroze Razzak was arrested in Bombay. As a proven member of al-Qaeda, he was an IT technician recruited into the Indian development teams for Microsoft. It was highly suspected that he had willingly introduced a critical vulnerability into Windows XP [GAR 01]. If Microsoft and the US service immediately denied it (nobody wanted to see such a terrible fact being confirmed), then this situation shows us just how dangerous sub-contracting abroad can be. On this point, let us note that introducing such a flaw is very easy and can easily be taken for a programming error.

As an example (taken from a real case of an attempt to introduce a serious security glitch in the Linux core), let us consider the following (healthy) code:

```
If (CriticalVar == function (arguments))

    {.... }
```

And let us change it as follows (just by deleting the single sign =):

```
If (CriticalVar = function(arguments))

    { .... }
```

A critical vulnerability has been introduced. In fact, the correct version of the tested code (operator ==), the value of the variable "CriticalVar" in relation to the value returned by the function. Changing the == symbol to = gets rid of the value of this variable for this value, thus creating a security glitch. Amongst the hundreds of thousands of lines of code, we can bet that this one will go unnoticed.

5.3.2. *System interdependence*

In the previous section, we saw how an infrastructure is built up of several interdependent components, which have a more or less critical role, and which are not all protected in the same way.

Today, analyses and experience show that trying to determine how many of them there are, and the dependent links between them, is an extremely complex task, if not impossible, in practice. It is necessary to construct a cartographic design, the most accurate as possible, of the interdependence of these different elements.

Let us now define more accurately the concept of system interdependence in our context. It describes all the direct and indirect dependencies between a target (final aim) and one or several components (primary aim) that this target depends on. The main tool is the dependence matrix[8].

This matrix is established during the intelligence stage (see section 5.4). Processing it makes it possible to identify and to chart all the dependencies and interdependencies within a complex infrastructure, particularly those which are invisible or difficult to see.

From the attacker's point of view, this makes it possible to identify a chain of dependence between the target and a sub-set of components. It will then be enough to attack the most external component, which is generally the least secure, and to play on the domino effect.

How can we define this matrix?

Let C_0 be the aimed target and a sub-set of components $C_1, C_2, C_3..., C_i...$ These are physical and human elements, and services gravitating around the target.

Each entry $M_{i,j}$ of the matrix M is defined by the matrix $M_{i,j}$ which is worth 1 if the component j depends on the component i, and is worth 0 otherwise.

If the binary factors are more intuitive, it is nevertheless possible to consider whole factors, or even real factors (weighting of the dependences), but this goes beyond the limits of this chapter (for more detail, see [PRI 94]).

In order to identify a chain of dependence between the target C_0 and any other dependence of length k, then it is enough to calculate the k-th power of the matrix.

---

8 This mathematical formalization was developed at ESAT– $(C + V)^O$, in the Gorgias project and the eponymous software aiming to gain techniques and a platform for analyzing the security of complex systems.

Let us take the first simple and didactic example for low dependence: the matrix is said to be hollow (Figure 5.3, left). Let us find a dependence with a rating of 5. It is sufficient to take the 5th power of this matrix (Figure 5.3, right).

$$
\begin{bmatrix}
0 & 1 & 0 & 0 & 0 & 0 & 0 \\
0 & 0 & 1 & 0 & 0 & 0 & 0 \\
0 & 0 & 0 & 1 & 0 & 0 & 0 \\
0 & 0 & 0 & 0 & 1 & 0 & 0 \\
0 & 0 & 0 & 0 & 0 & 1 & 0 \\
0 & 0 & 1 & 0 & 0 & 0 & 0 \\
0 & 0 & 0 & 0 & 1 & 0 & 0
\end{bmatrix}
\qquad
\begin{bmatrix}
0 & 0 & 0 & 0 & 0 & \boxed{1} & 0 \\
0 & 0 & 1 & 0 & 0 & 0 & 0 \\
0 & 0 & 0 & 1 & 0 & 0 & 0 \\
0 & 0 & 0 & 0 & 1 & 0 & 0 \\
0 & 0 & 0 & 0 & 0 & 1 & 0 \\
0 & 0 & 1 & 0 & 0 & 0 & 0 \\
0 & 0 & 0 & 0 & 1 & 0 & 0
\end{bmatrix}
$$

Figure 5.3. *Dependence matrices (left) and chain of dependence matrix to the power of 5 (right) in the simplest (sparse) case*

We can see here that such a chain exists between component 5 and the target. Therefore, it would be enough to strike component 5 in order to trigger a domino effect and to reach the final target.

If we consider a real case where the dependences are richer (heavy matrix, Figure 5.4), then we also see that there are 93 chains of dependence between component 5 and the target.

$$
C_0 \rightarrow
\begin{bmatrix}
0 & 1 & 0 & 0 & 1 & 1 & 0 \\
0 & 0 & 1 & 0 & 0 & 0 & 0 \\
0 & 1 & 0 & 1 & 0 & 0 & 1 \\
1 & 1 & 0 & 0 & 1 & 1 & 0 \\
0 & 0 & 0 & 0 & 0 & 1 & 0 \\
0 & 0 & 1 & 1 & 1 & 0 & 0 \\
0 & 1 & 1 & 1 & 1 & 0 & 0
\end{bmatrix}
\qquad
\begin{bmatrix}
37 & 104 & 88 & 87 & 99 & \boxed{93} & 39 \\
20 & 58 & 57 & 51 & 61 & 51 & 19 \\
51 & 147 & 128 & 127 & 141 & 132 & 57 \\
51 & 144 & 127 & 124 & 141 & 127 & 53 \\
20 & 57 & 46 & 47 & 52 & 53 & 23 \\
47 & 136 & 133 & 122 & 143 & 119 & 46 \\
56 & 161 & 152 & 142 & 165 & 141 & 56
\end{bmatrix}
$$

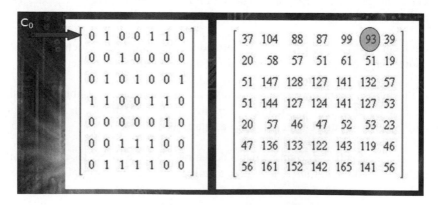

Figure 5.4. *Dependence matrix and chain of dependence matrix to the 5th order (right) in a real example*

This case is interesting because, on the one hand, there is a high number of "maneuver option switching" for the attacker, which is an advantage during the stages of planning and conduct (richness of the maneuver means more possibilities to adapt the attack to the actions/reactions of the target).

On the other hand, this means (from the point of view of the target defender) that the complexity of the dependence cartography is such that it cannot envisage and manage all of them.

A recent example[9] of this domino effect was given at the beginning of 2009 during global infection by the Win32.Conficker worm. This attack struck the French Defense and the British Marines hard. On January 15th and 16th 2009 [BSD 09], Rafale fighter planes from the French air force were "nailed to the ground". The attack had not aimed for the on-board computer system (it is hyper protected), but the air system control which, using Windows, was attacked and put out of service. It never released the flight settings, however[10]. The dependence on the systems did the rest. But this is an exceptional case and remains limited, because it was a direct dependence and therefore easily identifiable – at least we might think it is, above all it is limited to a purely technical frame.

It is precisely here that computer security still maintains a too restricted vision of the reality of the systems it is supposed to protect. Only considering the technical aspect, when identifying a system's dependences, can be deceptive. We often notice such a phenomenon when using FEROS[11] methods or implementing others such as Ebios[12]. Moreover, only the immediate vicinity is generally taken into account.

Matrix formalization – which only processes a graph structure on an algebraic level via its incidence matrix – allows for very in depth analysis of the interdependences.

Looking for a chain with a given length k (by taking the k-th power of the matrix) allows us to identify a chain dependence between k components which are more or less linked directly to the target infrastructure. It is possible to understand matters in a more qualitative way by searching, for example, specific combinations of structures. Thus, searching for a vertex cover – minimum set of point on the graph, or the components to strike, making it possible to hit all the other point/components – can be extremely interesting for a sudden, devastating attack [FIL 08].

---

9 This type of attack had struck the US Air Force in a similar way a few months beforehand.
10 This type of problem recently occured in a brigade of Chinese tanks.
11 Feros is a document expressing security objectives.
12 Ebios is the main method for identifying and managing risks, created by the DCSSI, www.ysosecure.com/methode-securite/methode-ebios.asp.

5.4. Different phases of a cyberattack

As with any coordinated military operation, there are three phases which must be considered:

– the intelligence phase;

– the planning phase and generating forces;

– the conduct phase.

It is important to note here that in no case can these phases be exclusive or independent. It is precisely for this reason that this type of operation can be reduced to a single digital aspect and requires a relatively high level of coordination. This is a complex task which is dealt with on an army rank structure, organized into offices or cells, each one responsible for a part of the operation.

5.4.1. *Intelligence phase*

This is the essential phase, without which any attack would be destined for failure, especially in a complex domain such as the computerized realm.

It is vital because it allows us to:

– identify the potential critical and non-critical components;

– establish the dependence matrix and to mathematically process them, then to draw an accurate precision of the target and its environment;

– provide elements for planning and conduct (using definite "maneuver option switchings" for heavy dependences).

This corresponds to the famous motto of infantry and cavalry soldiers: "nature, volume, behavior" of the enemy. Prior to this, during the initial phase, this intelligence is more strategic than during the course of action, it is more tactical, and it mainly functions as a way of supporting the maneuver and conduct. The intelligence phase is, by nature, the phase which contributes the most to the asymmetry between the target and the attacker:

– the attacker will plan his attack with a reverse temporal vision, starting with the desired effect and going towards the initial conditions and information which will allow him to carry out his plan. In other words, it is a question of organizing time to achieve a given effect. In this way, the approach is likened to that of a chess player;

– on the other hand, for the victim, the attack must seem sudden, inexplicable and without explanation. The intelligence phase – with all its deception techniques – has to think ahead of this phase, according to the general principle.

In the digital domain, contrary to generally accepted ideas, getting this intelligence is particularly easy, for two reasons which we will discuss now.

First of all, technically all the systems we use (systems of exploitation, materials, networks, etc.) leave behind a number of relatively exploitable tracks and hidden information, and which practically nobody – except for a few specialists in the forensics field – is truly aware of.

Secondly, on the human and sociological front, the digital field (because it is perceived of as a world apart, with no perceptible connection to the physical world) does not evoke a feeling of mistrust on behalf of those who use it. It is only a technique, and speaking about it openly will not cause serious consequences.

This is forgetting that intelligence is essentially very meticulous work, consisting of collating many pieces of meaningless information and to fusing them together with the aim of discovering closed information, or even information revealing the secrets of defense.

Consequently, this gives the attacker many different types of intelligence and, thus, sources. In each case, it is a matter of acquiring a precise image and all aspects of the target which is both static ("nature, volume") and dynamic ("attitude").

5.4.1.1. *Technical intelligence*

This is very easy to acquire, for the little that we know about where and how to look for it. The possibilities are virtually endless. Between used hard disks taken from the target's vicinity[13], laptops or other mass storage hardware left unwatched in a hotel room (notably abroad), mobile computing devices detained by customs over several hours (systematic in Israel, frequent in USA, to just name two countries), the attacker is spoilt for choice.

But the simplest is to exploit metadata which literally infests most document formats: PDF files, MS Word documents, images, audio files, etc., the range is huge.

---

13 On many occasions, the author has personally had the chance to check the second-hand market, the sales in certain domains, garbage analysis, etc., which has given some unbelievable findings and the ability to collect some, sometimes, very sensitive information (see [DUN 06]).

This metadata is information on the system, the user, his environment, etc., which is concealed in these files, with the user being completely unaware of it. This metadata, which is essentially passive, may be active in some cases [CHA 03] and transform into real data vacuums.

To illustrate this fact, let us consider two examples taken from real causes, out of many others studied by the author.

The first involves the fake report[14] drawn up by the British and presented by General Colin Powell before the United Nations, in order to try to legitimize the 3rd Gulf War, christened *Iraqi Freedom*.

This report, initially published in Word format, allowed the discovery, other than the clear manipulation of the British, of a certain amount of critical data, not only in the context of the time but in the absolute.

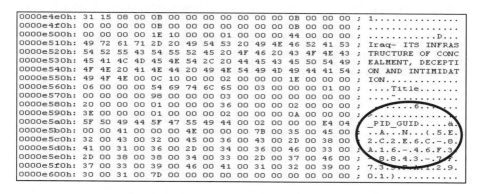

Figure 5.5. *Analysis of the British "report" on weapons of mass destruction. The circled section indicates the MAC address of a computer in Tony Blair's entourage*

This document made it possible to locate:

– the MAC address of a computer in 10 Downing Street (ex-Prime Minister Tony Blair's headquarters). The MAC address is unique data meaning that the computer's network card can be specifically identified;

– the complete history of the document with names, affiliations with the "real" different writers of this document. In particular, the first author of this document was simply identified as being Peter Hamill from CICR 22, Tony Blair's internal communication service.

---

14 "Iraq – Its infrastructure of concealment, deception and intimidation".

Another more ordinary example, it seems, deals with image formats containing metadata in EXIF format. They contain a large amount of information which, this time, concerns the user and his private life, rather than his computerized, technical environment (Figure 5.6).

Tag ID	Tag Name	Writable	Values / Notes
0x0000	GPSVersionID	int8u[4]	
0x0001	GPSLatitudeRef	string[2]	'N' = North 'S' = South
0x0002	GPSLatitude	rational64u[3]	
0x0003	GPSLongitudeRef	string[2]	'E' = East 'W' = West
0x0004	GPSLongitude	rational64u[3]	
0x0005	GPSAltitudeRef	int8u	0 = Above Sea Level 1 = Below Sea Level
0x0006	GPSAltitude	rational64u	
0x0007	GPSTimeStamp	rational64u[3]	(when writing, date is stripped off if present, and time is adjusted to UTC if it includes a timezone)
0x0008	GPSSatellites	string	
0x0009	GPSStatus	string[2]	'A' = Measurement Active 'V' = Measurement Void
0x000a	GPSMeasureMode	string[2]	2 = 2-Dimensional Measurement 3 = 3-Dimensional Measurement
0x000b	GPSDOP	rational64u	
0x000c	GPSSpeedRef	string[2]	'K' = km/h 'M' = mph 'N' = knots
0x000d	GPSSpeed	rational64u	
0x000e	GPSTrackRef	string[2]	'M' = Magnetic North 'T' = True North
0x000f	GPSTrack	rational64u	
0x0010	GPSImgDirectionRef	string[2]	'M' = Magnetic North 'T' = True North
0x0011	GPSImgDirection	rational64u	
0x0012	GPSMapDatum	string	
0x0013	GPSDestLatitudeRef	string[2]	'N' = North 'S' = South
0x0014	GPSDestLatitude	rational64u[3]	
0x0015	GPSDestLongitudeRef	string[2]	'E' = East 'W' = West
0x0016	GPSDestLongitude	rational64u[3]	
0x0017	GPSDestBearingRef	string[2]	'M' = Magnetic North 'T' = True North
0x0018	GPSDestBearing	rational64u	
0x0019	GPSDestDistanceRef	string[2]	'K' = Kilometers

Figure 5.6. *GPS coordinates in the EXIF metadata from an image*

Amongst this data, we find the following to be critical:

– the data and time of the photo;

– the GPS coordinates of the photo location (since 2008, several cameras have been integrated with this data).

Let us imagine now the photo of a person symbolizing an interesting target (system administrator, decision-maker, union leader, etc.) which he/she has posted on a site (Facebook, for instance). Analyzing this photo will enable us to locate, for example, the place where this person lives, if the photo is taken in their immediate environment.

Finally, and still to illustrate above all the ease of collecting technical information, let us finish by analyzing public market offers, in an example where the State is the target.

In 2005 a shrewd journalist showed [MAN 05] how such an analysis had made it possible to determine what the latest equipment/exploitation systems were, from one of the most sensitive units of the French army, the 785th electronic warfare company. The French article is shown in Figure 5.7.

Mais pourquoi la 785e compagnie de guerre électronique utilise-t'elle Microsoft/Office ?
09/06/2005, par jmm
[Impression | 1 réaction]

Le portail des achats du ministère de la défense fait partie de mes lectures épisodiques, parce que parfois cela s'avère intéressant.

On y apprend ainsi que la 785e compagnie de guerre electronique utilise Microsoft Windows, & Office.

En soi, rien que de très habituel. A ceci près que la 785e CGE « *représente la composante expérimentale de la Guerre Electronique* », qu' »*elle se doit d'assurer une veille technologique dans le domaine des télécommunications* » et que « *pour se faire, elle dispose aujourd'hui d'une palette de techniciens spécialistes de très bon niveau ayant fait leurs armes dan (sic) nos régiments de Guerre Electronique*« .

Et qu'on a donc du mal à comprendre pourquoi, dans son récent avis de marché portant sur l'acquisition de 18 micro-ordinateurs fixes, 24 micro-ordinateurs portables, soit 42 ordinateurs, le marché porte également sur une licence OPEN 42 postes Microsoft office édition professionnelle.

Figure 5.7. *"Why is the 785th electronic warfare company using Microsoft/Office?"*
Public market offer analysis (785th electronic warfare company)

Through concerns of transparency, the French State is making a high number of technical or peri-technical information available. Once it has been written, compared and cross-checked, it is completed with a relatively accurate image of the target.

With regard to organizations and companies, checking information is just as easy (professional open sources, chambers of commerce, account publications, etc.).

5.4.1.2. *Human intelligence*

This type of intelligence is even easier to obtain, as our organizations have forgotten the basic rules of professional discretion and have lost the culture of security. The other reason stems from the fact that we are living in an culture which does not consider the opening and sharing of information.

In a professional context, this is controlled by the desire to convince a client, to give him/her an image and, finally, to go away with a contract or the markets. Finally, the evolution of different mentalities means that modern organization probably no longer want to complicate their lives and have stopped asking questions. The attacker will exploit all of this. A simple piece of "soft" intelligence is often sufficient to collect a lot of information.

It would be laborious to list all cases (it is never possible to be exhaustive). Let us be limited to just a few cases, all taken from real situations:

– The analysis of blogs and other social networks (*Facebook*, *Twitter*, *Flickr*, *LinkedIn*, etc.) can reveal a terrifying situation. Between the senior officer explaining all our past, present and future activities through the menu (external operations, for instance); the engineer working for the defense industry talking about the project he is working on; the union leader exposing the internal problems within that business; the smallest executive exposing everything happening in his job and this, with plenty of details which make him the guilty party, the minimum of reaching a professional secret; etc. The examples are legion, and with an exasperating ease enable us to draw up a faithful image, both technical as much as human, of the next target very quickly (or of a component that the target depends on).

– The people who are guilty of deliberately leaking information act as much out of permissiveness as through a lack of knowledge of intelligence methods. From this point of view, the explosion of social networks is a golden opportunity for the attackers, but a source of calamity for the targets. Several tools make the search automatic, along with the extraction and multi-criteria processing of these forums and other networks. A tool such as Maltego[15] may act as a true cartography of relations and links between people, according to one or several criteria.

– The use of public places (function rooms, transport, restaurants, etc.) is also just as profitable. A simple discussion between different members of staff in a target-company is enough to give a clear image of it. As an example, let us consider the following real case, which is no less different, which our author was a direct witness to. During the journey from Rennes to Paris in a TVG (French high speed train), three engineers from a sensitive administration were discussing trivial matters which very quickly took a turn towards the professional domain. In a two hour journey, it was possible to:

 - determine which organization they were dependent on (seats for a soccer game at Rennes stadium had been sold by their company committee);

---

15 www.paterva.com/web4/index.php/maltego.

- learn what projects they were currently working on (including technical details such as the identification of those in charge, the clients, short and mid-term evolutions, the next meetings);

- obtain details on the personalities of some of their co-workers and people in the hierarchy, making it possible to get an exact idea of the nature of the relationships between them;

- get information on the computer environment through an observation of the Windows program on one of the engineer's laptops (what version of the system was being used, what security software was being used, and what applications were being used, etc.).

In sum, the mass of information collected had made it possible, probably, to at least perform a computer intrusion using telephone theft identify techniques (social engineering [COS 09])[16].

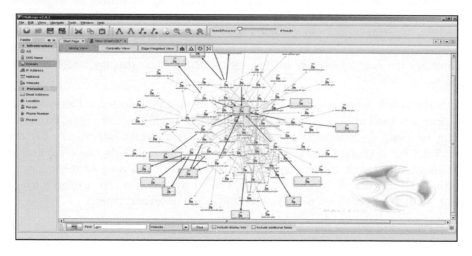

Figure 5.8. *Analysis of social networks with Maltego and information retrieval*

5.4.2. *Planning phase*

The objective consists of:

– predicting the general maneuver;

---

16 In 2003, such an attack was carried out on an organization, using elements collected in a public environment. The attacker with a very high knowledge of the internal life, structure and operation of this company, was able to get an account opened on the server by pretending to be a business engineer.

– generating the necessary forces (which includes those responsible for leading computer attacks);

– coordinating the different attacks on the "terrain" (conventional or computerized);

– incorporating the intelligence (afterwards) and conduct phases of the maneuver (before phase) in order to anticipate and to manage best as possible the unpredicted (target reactions, changes in the environment, etc.) and to allow the choice for the best "maneuver option switching" and the best available options.

From this point of view, this planning work corresponds, in a complex military operation, to the B5 army staff office[17]. The strictly cyberattack part, in this context, is built-in to the general maneuver within the framework of the desired global effect.

In other words, we could foresee this planning phase by using the *Black Info Ops* version [OTA 08].

5.4.3. *Conduct phase*

This is indeed the operational part. Each element of the attack (conventional, human, computerized) is not part of an isolated framework but is, in fact, in support of or in the preparation of another action, conforming to what has been planned. It is not only important to respect a strict timing, but also to cast out any form of improvisation on the terrain.

This conduct phase itself generates intelligence (intelligence in action) either willingly (first step of reconnaissance function, observation probes), or indirectly by using the outcomes of one or many specific actions (target's reaction, gained effects, etc.). Whether this is for the planning phase or the conduct phase, the reader will notice that there is no specific mention of the strictly computerized part. This underlines the fact that this is only one element in the general maneuver. As for any conventional force, a cyberattack will rely on:

– support forces. A DDoS will be similar to artillery bombing when a Denial of Service aimed at a server can be compared to the work of a combatant soldier. We could easily identify many other examples in order to establish correspondences with the transportation corps or transmissions;

– mixed forces (digital infantry, digital cavalry).

---

17 In NATO's nomenclature, the name is J5.

However, the cyberattack aspect is distinguished from others because it can and must apply methods which are inherent to it, and first of all, the partition principle which aims to:

– ensure that the attacker remains anonymous, either directly by deleting all traces leading back to him, or indirectly by laying false tracks so as to incriminate a third party as being the author of the attack;

– more generally, deleting any coherent vision and the entire target in order to annihilate any capacity for reaction and counter-offensive.

The wrongful incrimination of innocent third parties is a particularly interesting approach which must be favored so as to distort the victim's vision and for the attacker to lead in a "non-dangerous direction".

This is quite easy to carry out, and the basic principle is to create false tracks which must – as in the classic principles of intelligence and misinformation – be coherent with reality and the operational context (see the fictional scenario presented in section 5.6).

5.5. A few "elementary building blocks"

We will now endeavor to show the "building blocks" of existing computer attacks. We just need to have a coordinated vision in order to combine them in a wide scale attack by exploiting the methodology described previously.

Reading the publication by Qiao and Wang [LAN 02] from this point of view is fundamental. Studying it shows this exact coordinated line of thinking and the strategic and tactical framework of what constitutes a high amplitude computer attack, particularly as a precursor to more conventional operations/conflicts.

These foundation blocks are essentially used to demonstrate the technical feasibility of computer attacks: the problem is no longer a matter of knowing whether it is possible, but rather knowing *when it will happen*.

5.5.1. *General tactical framework*

A high magnitude systematic cyberattack on national or regional infrastructures can be set out into three main phases. The references for the principles used here are available in [BRU 09]:

– the first phase aims to disorganize, or even stop transport networks: rail networks, air controls, signaling, roads, communication channels, etc. In a more localized way, this includes area controls (starting a riot, for instance). There are three desired effects: trigger a social panic which cannot be managed by the authorities, limit its capacity to react and its mobility, and support other actions (computerized and/or conventional). The attacks on these types of infrastructures or services are in abundance: interference in the Los Angeles signaling network in January 2007, blocking rail traffic in 23 states in the south of the USA in August 2003 (via a virus striking the signaling system), paralysis of the Boston air control in March 1998 (via a computer virus which can be compared with the grounding of two French fighter planes in February 2009 [BSD 09]);

– the second phase is aimed at financial structures and those linked to the telecommunication network: stocks (Russian Stock Exchange in February 2006, all quotations frozen for an hour, alert systems on for the London stock exchange in June 2007 for 48 hours, European CO_2 emission recordings in February 2010 with markets frozen for a few hours, etc.), and messaging or telephone networks (diversion of transport messaging network in Canada in May 2006). Other than cutting off the target's capacities to react and reorganize, it strikes vital resources that the State's internal stability and functioning relies on;

– the third phase finishes by totally disorganizing the target by cutting off or seriously disorganizing the distribution of basic human services and resources for the State's inhabitants: the electric network (SCADA attacks in the USA revealed by the SANS Institute, January 2008), the network for distributing drinking water (attack in October 2008 in Harrisburg, USA), the nuclear industry (*Slammer* worm in the nuclear plant computer network in Besse-Davies, Ohio, USA), hospital structures (attack on a hospital[18] in 2006 in Seattle, USA).

The resultant social panic[19] and disorder monopolizes and puts a strain on the target's capacities to act, and in the mean time it removes all the resources necessary for its own action and survival.

In the end, everything which is managed and/or depends on information and communication systems falls. In fact (even if this is still a fictional scenario) this affects virtually all sectors, giving a maximum effect on a State's governmental functions, except if it has been able to anticipate such a situation by keeping independent resources which are exclusively intended to be used for these functions, and by ensuring the integrity of the operational availability (and its capacity) of the

---

18 In February 2009, the attack by the Conficker worm caused similar damage on computer networks which the intensive care units depend on in the South of France. These cases were never made public.

19 We can get a fairly accurate idea of the kind of panic that a situation of high disorganization in the main vital services of a country could generate. It is enough to observe the irrational reactions (mass buying and storing food, looting, etc.) during less severe situations (cyclone, for example).

decision-making chain. The domino effect must be exploited by the attacker to the maximum. It would be sufficient (see section 5.3.2 with the vertex-cover problem [FIL 08]) to strike a restricted number of secondary targets, which would make it possible to hit a maximum number of final targets. The question that immediately comes to mind concerns the apparent ease which seems to stem from what has just been presented here – even if it is still, once again, a prospective vision. Why have these cyberattacks not already happened? Is this really the case?

Faced with the complexity of an attack such as the *Conficker* worm and its impact, it is very difficult to imagine, as had already been the case with *Blaster* in 2003, that this does not involve the minimum amount of repetitions or making marks for a more systematic attack. Secondly, when such an attack really takes place and the effect of the surprise has passed (as was the case for the Estonia crisis), then intelligence will be drawn from it and an understanding will dawn on the victims. A cyberattack is, then, a single-strike weapon.

Finally this mainly stems from the fact (from the author's point of view) that a single cyberattack, outside a wider operational framework (military and tactical, political and strategic) is precisely something which cannot be considered. Therefore cyberwar does not fully exist on its own, but constitutes an additional dimension in conflict (particular before phases). These isolated attacks can be put into a system and coordinated to have a real devastating effect. A general scenario would consist of accumulating the effects by coordinating different blocks during the planning phase. The imagination and tactical creativeness do the rest. Once again, it is important to remember that the single technical vision (hackers, pirates) is insufficient if it does not take place within a true strategic and tactical mindset.

5.5.2. *Attacks on people*

Attacks on people aim to put any person with a vital role in management (particularly crisis management) out of operation for a somewhat long period of time in a critical infrastructure.

This aspect is systematically ignored in security policies. Moreover, these attacks are extremely simple to carry out. All we need is either the home computer system (which is never protected to the same level as the target where the future victim is working) or by mobile computer systems (cell phones, smart phone, pocket PC, etc.).

We can easily understand that, in these conditions, the notion of a bunker still remains fanciful, and that the boundary of the security target is at the very least fuzzy and unstable.

Let us use two examples, taken from real facts:

– The first example deals with *an attack on the domestic computer belonging to the union leader of a large company* (for example, by dropping compromising data). The choice of such a person is a well-thought out decision. This is due to the fact that the sensitivity of opinions with regard to the union, essentially, and the capacity to react and manage through employer or public power are limited. This is followed by anonymous denunciations, and the press is warned; this can lead to a climate where company strikes can be triggered. A second offensive consists of having new data which incriminates the company's management system, thus aggravating the strike even further and grinding the factory to an entire halt. If this (see section 5.6) is an element that the final target depends on, then the domino effect – due to the operational dependencies between them – will do the rest.

– The second example concerns a *coordinated attack on a small innovative company to liquidize it or re-buy it.* This company will play a key role in a vaster, delicate program, part of a bigger plan in which is it only a component, an essential one of course, but not exactly a critical one. The attacker is, for instance, an international consortium abroad. In this type of approach, the attack is far ahead of the desired effect. First of all, the decision-maker's computers and engineers are attacked. Data accrediting the use of industrial counterfeiting, and pirating are concealed in these computers[20]. A civil complaint is made against this start-up for counterfeiting. Searches and preliminary instructions, based on false proof, conclude by accepting the complaint. Investigating the main people in charge, and then a loss of trust in financial backers will follow on from this. In the end, a long legal procedure (that the consortium can allow, financially) will lead to the *startup* assessment.

5.5.3. *Opinion manipulation and area control*

Another type of approach may aim at opinions, through a few clicks of the mouse (and by combining the approaches presented in section 5.5.2) in order to achieve diverse effects. Moreover, the weighting of the opinion is a vital aspect, even explosive, which may, in itself, complicate police force tasks. Here we will use the example of an area control (physical effect) which may be used as a support for a future conventional attack. We are inspired by real events occurring at the end of 2008 in suburbs which are usually very susceptible areas.

In this case, let us imagine that the attacker wants to paralyze a given zone, by starting up riots or confrontations (blocking communication channels or areas).

---

20 This attack, to be coherent and credible, needs to have made this "proof" pre-conditionally after an analysis of the products developed by this company.

Firstly, videos of a highly racist, community-based and violent nature are posted on very popular sites (such as France's *dailymotion*, similar to YouTube), whose character is particularly insulting and offensive for a section of the population living in this sensitive area (see Figure 5.9). These videos received other videos as a response, heightening the tension during aggravation via interfering videograms (some coming from the real attacker to make the tension rise). Using classic intrusion techniques on computers belonging to the gang members (see previous section), and spreading rumors or facts on blogs etc., all contributed to the hornet's nest[21], kicking off riots and confrontations.

Public power, taken as a hostage, only has a limited means of reaction. The concomitant exploitation of international, critical news also helped to facilitate this scenario (see Figure 5.10).

Figure 5.9. *Videos posted in 2008 on France's site "dailymotion" to exacerbate hatred between rival gangs, one of which was said to be Muslim (Vince versus Morsay). The video titles include offensive and vulgar language of a sexual nature*

---

21 A similar case occurred in Italy in 2009: following comments on blogs and rumors spread on the Internet, ethnic and urban guerilla riots took place in Rosarno (Calabre). The Italian population blamed the demonstrators and the African rioters.

Figure 5.10. *Exploiting the news to provoke riots: "child decapitated by Israel" (top), "Gaza, Arab leaders are Zionists" (bottom)*

5.5.4. *Military computer attack in a conventional operation*

To show how a computer attack may also be led alongside a bigger conventional attack, we will consider the air raid from Israeli planes in October 2007 on Syrian plants suspected of harboring a nuclear plant for military means.

To monitor their air space, the Syrians had bought a system to digitalize this space from the Russians. This system has a certain number of ground receivers, linked to a computer center. In order to protect their planes from the Syrian anti-aircraft defense, Israeli soldiers infiltrated this computer network, directed some of the receivers so as to create a blind corridor that their planes could go through for their mission, without fear of danger [FIL 09a].

In this example: on the one hand, using a foreign critical military system was a major weak point. On the other hand, for the Israelis, without a preconditioned support by a purely computerized attack, then this conventional operation would have been impossible.

5.6. Example scenario

In this chapter we will firmly illustrate the subject and methodology by a fictional scenario. We will show how a military operation can be countered by cyberattacks.

We want to show that, in the end, a cyberattack is especially the best combination of InfoOps (*Information operations*) such as those formalized by NATO [OTA 08], and classic computer attacks…and a total lack of ethics.

To illustrate this vision, we will give a detailed tactical scenario[22] where all the elements, all the data, all the events, etc., are mostly inspired by recent events and solid cases, which are clearly limited. For clear ethical reasons, we will not discuss the real operational mode of the techniques and means used by the attackers who will be put on our stage in the following section. This will not hinder the general understanding. We will firstly present the tactics, then the apparent succession of the operations. Next, we will explain what actually happened and why. The reader will be able to find a similar scenario of a political attack in [FIL 09b].

5.6.1. *Tactical scenario*

5.6.1.1. *General situation*

September 20th, 2009. A conflict has broken out between two Mediterranean countries: on the one hand, we have the GREEN country, dominated by a fundamentalist faction which is widely supported by the population, and partly by national forces. On the other, the national forces of a bordering RED country which started the conflict as a result of repeated raids by fundamental GREEN militia. The population of the GREEN country is made up of a high fraction of foreign nationals from a BLUE country, also located in the Mediterranean.

Officially, the BLUE country is an ally with the GREEN and RED countries, but does not want to be politically involved for the moment, when its foreign nationals are at risk. There is a great fear that each belligerent section will use, for political or military means (hostage taking, civilians being killed, etc.), the existence of these nationals as a way of pressuring their country.

Faced with the worrying situation in terms of safety on the land (several bombings), an operation to remove the nationals was decided on by the political power in a state of emergency (less than 12 hours after the events started). The official statement from the BLUE government's spokes person is published on September 22nd 2009. After 9 hours, the BLUE country sends in a vessel from its

---

22 This scenario was initially published in [FIL 09]. Here we give an alternative of it based on more recent techniques. All the places here are imaginary, and any likeness is purely coincidental.

fleet, a VPC/LCT[23] type, with a few members from its special forces on board, an infantry unit (220 men) and 5 transport troop helicopters.

The BLUE National Marines has 48 hours to be put into place (latest departure, September 24th at 09:00). The vessel must go to the GREEN country's main port. The UN's Security Council, NATO's Commander and the European Council have authorized the BLUE country's intervention, and condemn any use of force on the BLUE country's military detachment, exposing countries guilty of economic and diplomatic sanctions. Officially, the two belligerents accept this mission to remove nationals on the basis of the proposed schedule.

In truth, analyzes show that the GREEN country's objective was to prevent the nationals being sent home, who could be used either as an implicit human shield (dissuade or at least delay this process), or on the other hand, for the BLUE country to lead a military intervention (nationals become victims of the RED forces). The aim of the RED country is also to delay the BLUE country's intervention, which is suspected of also covering an intelligence operation, partly to the benefit of the GREEN country. The BLUE country is an old colonial power in the region, and moreover, has kept its capacities to influence and its interests in this region of the world.

In summary, for both countries, a delay of 96 hours for the BLUE vessel is considered as a success. Each party must make others believe in the other's action, and not be incriminated. The ideal situation would be to ensure that the BLUE country is incapable of launching such an operation, which would demonstrate the vanity of its claims to intervene in the region.

5.6.1.2. *Environment and INT situation*[24]

The BLUE country has a very high diaspora from the two belligerent parties. The BLUE country is a democratic state where individual, union, and religious freedom is a sensitive societal aspect. The country is in its electoral period (renewing the Lower House).

The GREEN and RED countries officially (on the diplomatic front) approve of the operation to remove nationals. The GREEN country condemns it internally and informs its allies.

The GREEN's propaganda extends to the communities present in the BLUE country. The GREEN and RED countries have a high capacity in the CNO (*computer network operation*) domain:

---

23 Vessel Projection and Command and Landing-Craft Transport.
24 INT, military abbreviation for the "intelligence" in an operation.

– in the GREEN country or its allies, several organized pirate groups (malevolent hackers), and e-terrorist groups connected with world-known terrorist groups actively work to benefit the GREEN fundamentalist faction;

– in the RED country, state-governed structures, controlling hacker groups from time to time, are known to have a high activity involved in computer attacks; moreover, intelligence reports have established that the RED country manipulates certain hacker groups from the GREEN country.

The two belligerents have strong INT capacities.

Furthermore, intelligence reports from the BLUE country show that certain member states from the UN's Security Council secretly support one or the other of the two sides to counter the influence of the BLUE country in the area.

These countries have a high activity in the intelligence domain and in CNO type operations. The BLUE telephone operator, historical and the majority operator, has relocated its main call center into the GREEN country, along with a large portion of its telephonically supervised network, in particular managing the telegraphic network of the BLUE capital.

Several years ago, the BLUE country relocated its software production and data processing into the RED country (countable data, directories, data centers, etc.).

5.6.1.3. *Geographical situation*

The BLUE country has two military ports. Only the port in the SOUTH of Riencourt[25] may be used as a departure port, with the port in the NORTH of Chouest being too far away. Only a single road gives access to the Riencourt port, where the city is in between the sea and a mountain range. At 3 km from the port, the road passes through an important industrial zone.

In the GREEN country, the BLUE nationals (2,000) are mostly gathered in the city housing the main port. Around 150 BLUE nationals and their families are in the main city in the SOUTH, 250 km from the port.

The distance between the port/SOUTH city can be made by using a single road in the partially mountainous area, and is controlled by the RED forces. The RED country has control over the skies, outside a half of the country's South-West region, where forces can move freely. Using transport helicopters was judged by the BLUE country as being the only possible solution.

---

25 The choice of the name Riencourt bears no relation to the two French towns with the same name (one in the Somme, one in the Northern region).

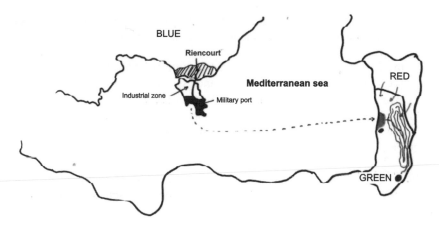

Figure 5.11. *Geographical situation of the RED, GREEN and BLUE countries*

5.6.2. *The order of events*

5.6.2.1. *Phase 1: before September 22nd*

September 21st, a serious strike has begun in the Oils SOUTH company, located in the industrial zone of the Riencourt port. The company's official documents were sent on the 18th to a daily newspaper, which triggered a massive plan for dismissal, motivated by heavy losses in the organization caused by, according to these documents, embezzlement on behalf of the factory manager. On the 21st, an investigation by the financial authorities into the company's computers confirms the truth inside these documents. The factory comes to a halt.

On September 22nd, confrontations between gangs get worse in the North region of Riencourt. This is a relatively frequent occurrence in these districts. Cars go up in flames, several people have knife wounds and an explosive situation monopolizes the police force's attention. The origin of these confrontations seems to stem from the threats and insults of a community and racial nature, in particular posted on sites such as YouTube and Dailymotion[26]. Tensions gradually rise but the powers that be, in this electoral period, want to manage the crisis carefully.

5.6.2.2. *Phase 2: from September 22nd to the 24th*

Following the new videos on the 23rd, new confrontations arise in the Northern districts of Riencourt, leaving two deaths in their wake by firearms. The situation is getting worse, and the police force intervenes. The situation is blocked:

---

26 This is inspired by a similar, real event in France, luckily in a very localized way, in November 2008.

demonstrations are taking place in the city of Riencourt in memory of the victims. The authorities are beginning to fear that the violence could increase.

On the 23rd at 06:00, a new investigation into the Oils SOUTH organization takes place, upon request by the court's finance sector and the Vice Quad, as well as at the main Union leader's home, who was taken into police custody and his computer seized. Indiscretions in the press show an aggravated matter for the Vice Quad. The trade-union denounces an attempt to break the strike and decides to strengthen it.

The 24th, at 06:00, in the city of Choucoulis, a 28 year-old soldier is arrested and investigated for serious matters. He is caught out through an analysis of his computer and his cell phone.

5.6.2.3. Phase 3: from September 24th to the 28th

On the 25th, following new revelations published in the press which gives a report on the prolonged custody of the union leader, the strike movement becomes even more serious. The trade-union, the majority in the region, manages to convince other factories in the industrial zone to join their movement. On the 26th, picket lines are drawn up, blocking off the single road giving access the military port.

Between the 24th and the 27th, frequent breakdowns in the telephone network affect certain regions, including the capital and large cities. These disturbances intermittently involve the mobile telephone network and Internet communications. Several journalists speak of a computer worm attack. The operator speaks of a breakdown in some of the network's hardware, which is being replaced.

On the 27th at midday, several BLUE nationals, many of whom are women and children, are victims of RED bombings. The BLUE beliefs are unsettled. On the 28th September, the BLUE National Marine vessel comes in with a 99 hour delay. The government's spokes person attempts to talk down this delay by speaking about logistic problems. The opposition bears witness to this opinion. The government accuses the unions of anti-patriotic behavior.

5.6.3. Analysis

Before presenting what actually happened, it is important to remember that in any conflict, the side(s) which start it have a depth in time that the other players do not have. Any operational planning foresees all the possible options for the opposite forces, by weighing them up against the time factor.

In the case of our tactical scenario, the operation to remove nationals by the BLUE country was easy to predict, and the INT analysts from the GREEN and RED country were able to anticipate this decision beforehand, and to include it in the tactical and strategic preparation, and then in their conduct and respective maneuver. Thus, such an analysis led these experts to reassure their operational leaders by saying that the BLUE vessel could only go from the port at Riencourt, as the VPC/LCT vessels were only available in this port. It is easy to study and identify the zones with local weaknesses from this, in order to act on an operational front.

This explains how the operations on the BLUE country had really started several days before the official date of the conflict and the country's political decision. It does not matter who started the conflict, the GREEN or the RED country. What matters is the nature and the conduct of the operations: uniquely through computer attacks, leaving no traces, leaving the analysts all the time in the world to endlessly go over and over the real responsibilities.

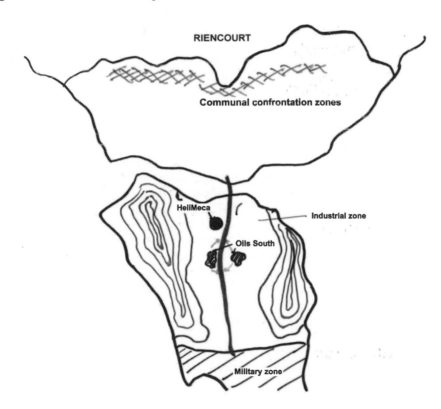

Figure 5.12. *Situation on the terrain at the port of Riencourt*

An initial computer attack strikes against the Oils SOUTH company on September 18th: fake documents, imitated from information processed offshore, were planted into the general director's computer. Then, later, they were put in the main union delegate's computer. Next, these documents just needed to reach the press, with a good timing which was compatible with the conduct of other operations. The Oils SOUTH organization provides the BLUE marines with specific vessel oil (public market study). Extra information (indiscretions on engineer's and marine officer's blogs, etc.) made it possible to assume that the BLUE Marines oil stocks were lower, and that the delivery was meant to come in as soon as the extra budget for the BLUE country's defense had been agreed at the beginning of October. Other indiscretions led us to determine that the BLUE country's Marines were short of parts for helicopters and that the delivery was meant to arrive at the end of September.

The parts in question are made by the HeliMeca group, located at the entrance of the Riencourt industrial zone. By starting this strike, the aim was to:

– block the emergency oil supplies (Oils SOUTH factory coming to a halt);

– block the access road to the military port (no access for HeliMeca trucks, for the sailors and the supplies on board and equipment);

– block the HeliMeca group's activity by extension in the long term, and reinforce the strike.

The second "attack" concerns the posting of provocative videos on two sites regularly visited by young people to exacerbate their rival groups and start riots. The idea, according to the classic covering principle, is to trigger a second zone for the police forces to attend to, and to deflect attention from social problems from the Riencourt industrial port zone.

Faced with these problems, the BLUE country's power tries to organize itself. This involves an increase in the communication needs between the different decision-making centers. The third attack aims to considerably obstruct these communications and to extend the times for decision making. Knowing the architecture of the national telephone network has made it possible to see that the R&D network is connected to the computer network exploitation.

A virus attack aimed at personal computers belonging to the many engineers and researchers of this operator (intelligence collection through blogs, social networks, etc.), enabled them to attack the network owing to the direct connection of their laptop on their internal network.

Finally, the soldier arrested on the 24th was no other than the Commander of the unit who was supposed to embark on the VPC/LCT with his brigade. A blog written by one of his warrant officers[27] revealed that on the 23rd, his brigade was on the vessel in question.

The attack was achieved in two phases: planting compromising data on the personal computer belonging to this officer and manipulating his cell phone (a model with a vital vulnerability) to further incriminate him with regard to the accusations. Arresting this officer involved, for internal reasons, having to find another brigade, starting off new delays.

In the end, the vessel, adding up more delays, could only come in 99 hours later.

5.7. Conclusion

The different aspects with regard to planning and conduct of cyberattacks allow us to draw out three main lessons:

– the technical vision alone is not enough, if it is not expressed in a coordinated and operational vision. This implies that behind the hacker or pirate, we must always look for the purpose and the mind behind it all, which reflects the classic and timeless principles of warfare;

– the final target must only be considered in a complex, fuzzy and moving environment. Considering this target as an unassailable bunker is simply fanciful. Knowing this environment perfectly guarantees the attacker the best action possible. The defender's lack of knowledge makes him extremely weak. Experience shows that, except in cases of very sophisticated, targeted attacks, it is more the victim's weakness rather than the attacker's real force which is decisive;

– the total and unrestricted exploitation of the human element is the key for any successful attack. Exploiting and revisiting the InfoOps potential and classic human intelligence techniques is therefore essential, as much for the attacker as for he who wants to be protected himself.

In this context, how can we consider a policy for defense and security? Is it possible to protect ourselves easily? The answer is clearly no, particularly with regard to the facility of doing so, so long as we admit and accept our dependence on information and communication systems to be inescapable and impossible to overcome. This is precisely the difference between the Estonian scenario and the case in Georgia. Where Estonia is weak, Georgia, whose computer infrastructure is somewhat non-existent, really had nothing to fear from these so-called Russian attacks, contrary to what might have been suggested in an objectively anti-Russian

---

27 These cases are not hypothetical. With the lack of professional discretion, all the professional sectors together become a major worry for police and security forces.

climate [VEN 07], [VEN 09]. In a broader sense, it is reasonable to hope to have the capacity to resist when we use uncontrolled means: exploitation systems, security software, cryptological concepts, etc. From this point of view, any solution must go through a necessary economical revolution which must:

– relocate important companies, particularly in all industries connected to governmental functions;

– relocate critical sources (data centers, supervision services, critical resource manufacturers, etc.).

In no way is it a question of creating a new Maginot line but of having a reasoned vision of our own desire for security. Since 1994, the USA (champions of free competition when it concerns countries other than itself) relocated and renationalized everything which affects the defense heritage and governmental functions (President Ronald Reegan's Union discourse). An interesting parallel to make is with the fall of the Roman Empire: it coincided with the instant when the Roman armies were recruiting mainly from the Empire's population, and no longer from Rome's strong forces. Sub-contracting security needs is the worst solution. Security must go through digital sovereignty!

A cultural revolution must also be led. This is probably the hardest thing to do. It is necessary to create a true security culture and professional discretion, which is a priority for decision-makers. This is another important point concerning a form of technological hegemony. There is too small a number of people who have understood that the problem begins much earlier: it is not so much the products but the concepts and norms which are important. As Bernard Carayon[28] quite right recalls: "the power of a country lies in its ability to impose standards and norms". Managing to impose a unique and controlled vision is a fearsome way of influencing and having power over mindsets.

5.8. Bibliography

[ALM 08] AL-MADHOUN O., *Islamic Jihad's Cyber War Brigades*, www.menassat.com/ ?q=en/news-articles/3966-islamic-jihad-s-cyber-war-brigades, July 17th 2008.

[BAN 06] BANGARÉ H., *Maroc-Israël: la Webtifada est lancée*. www.afrik.com/article 10160. html, July 27th 2006.

[BEN 05] BENICHOU D., LEFRANC S., "Introduction to network self-defense: technical and judicial issues", *Journal in Computer Virology*, vol. 1, no. 1-2, Springer Verlag, New York, USA, 2005.

---

28 French Member of Parliament, specialist reporter for questions of Defense at the National Assembly, during the opening conference at the SSTIC 2004, www.sstic.org.

[BSD 09] BLOG SECRET DEFENSE, *Les armées attaquées par un virus informatique*, secretdefense.blogs.liberation.fr/defense/2009/02/les-armes-attaq.html, February 5th 2009.

[CHA 03] CHAMBET P., DETOISIEN E., FILIOL E., "La fuite d'informations dans les documents propriétaires", *MISC - Le Journal de la sécurité informatique*, no. 7, May 2003.

[CON 09] CONHEADY S, *Social Engineering for Penetration Testers*, Brucon conference www.brucon.org/articles/p/r/e/Presentations.html#Social_engineering_for_penetration_testers, Brussels, October 2009.

[DUN 06] DUNN J., DETOISIEN E., *US Military Struggles with Data Loss*, Techworld, features.techworld.com/security/2436/us-military-struggles-with-data-loss, April 2006.

[EUR 06] EUROPEAN PARLIAMENT, Fight against terrorism: identification, designation and protection of European critical infrastructures ECI, Procedure File CNS/2006/0276, www.europarl.europa.eu/oeil/file.jsp?id=5425462, 2006.

[EUR 10] EUROPEAN UNION LEGISLATION SUMMARIES, Critical infrastructure protection, European Union, available at: http://europa.eu/legislation_summaries/justice_freedom_security/fight_against_terrorism/l33259_en.htm, 2010.

[FIL 06] FILIOL E., "Le ver Blaster/LovSan", *MISC, Le Journal de la sécurité informatique*, no. 11, July 2004.

[FIL 08] FILIOL E., FRANC E., GUBBIOLI A., MOQUET B., ROBLOT G., "Combinatorial optimisation of worm propagation on an unknown network", *International Journal in Computer Science*, vol. 2, no. 2, p. 124–131, 2008.

[FIL 09a] FILIOL E., RAYNAL F., "Cyberguerre: de l'attaque du bunker à l'attaque dans la profondeur", *Revue de défense nationale et sécurité collective*, vol. 2009-3, p. 74–86, March 2009.

[FIL 09b] FILIOL E., "Operational Aspects of cyberwarfare of cyber-terrorist attacks: what a truly devastating attack could do", *8th European Conference on Information Warfare and Security 2009*, p. 71–79, Lisbon, Portugal, 6-7th July 2009.

[FIL 09c] FILIOL E., *How to Prepare, Coordinate and Conduct a Cyber Attack*, Brucon conference 2009, www. brucon.org, Brussels, Belgium, October 2009.

[FIL 10] FILIOL E., "Anti-forensic techniques based on malicious cryptography", *9th European Conference in Information Warfare 2010*, Salonika, Greece, July 2010.

[FOL 09] FOLLATH E, STARK H., *The Story of Operation Orchard: How Israel Destroyed Syria's Al Kibar Nuclear Reactor*, www.spiegel.de/ international/world/0,1518,658663-2,00.html, February 11th 2009.

[GAR 01] GARDINER J., *Has Osama bin Laden bin Codin' XP?*, www.silicon.com/ technology/hardware/2001/12/19/has-osama-bin-laden-bin-codin-xp-11030037/, December 19th 2001.

[GRE 02] GREEN J., *The Myth of Cyberterrorism*, www.washingtonmonthly.com/ features/2001/0211.green.html, *Washington Monthly*, November 2002.

[LAN 02] LANG Q., XIANQSUI W., *Unrestricted Warfare: China's Master Plan to Destroy America*, Pan American Publishing Company, USA, 2002.

[LBD 08] GOUVERNEMENT FRANÇAIS, Le livre blanc sur la défense et la sécurité nationale, Odile Jacob, Paris, France, 2008.

[MAN 05] MANACH J.-M., *Mais pourquoi la 785e compagnie de guerre électronique utilise-t'elle Microsoft/Office?*, rewriting.net/2005/06/09/mais-pourquoi-la-785e-compagnie-de-guerre-electronique-utilise-microsoft-office/, June 9th 2005.

[MAN 11] MANACH J.-M., "Bercy: la piste de l'altermondialisme numérique", http://owni.fr/2011/03/07/bercy-la-piste-de-laltermondialisme-numerique/, *Owni*, March 7th 2011.

[MES 99] MESSNER E., *Kosovo Cyber-war Intensifies: Chinese Hackers Targeting US Sites, Government Says*, www.cnn.com/TECH/computing/9905/12/cyberwar.idg/, May 12th 1999.

[OTA 08] OTAN, Information Operations – Analysis Support and Capability Requirements, Research and Technology Organization, TR-SAS-057, ftp.rta.nato.int/public//PubFull Text/RTO/TR/RTO-TR-SAS-057/$$TR-SAS-057-ALL.pdf.

[PAR 10] PARR B., *Did Chinese Hackers Exploit Internet Explorer to Attack Google?* mashable.com/2010/01/14/google-china-attack-anatomy/, January 14th 2010.

[PRI 94] PRINS C.H., *Algorithmes de graphes avec programmes en Pascal*, Eyrolles, Paris, France, 1994.

[VEN 07] VENTRE D., "La guerre de l'information en Russie", no. 30, *MISC*, March 2007.

[VEN 09] VENTRE D., *Information Warfare*, ISTE Ltd, London and John Wiley & Sons, New York, 2009.

Chapter 6

Riots in Xinjiang and Chinese Information Warfare

Several times over the last few years, China has been accused of being at the origin of (meaning, *guilty* of) an incredible number of incidents regarding security reported over the world: intrusions into company and the State's most sensitive information systems, intrusion attempts into SCADA systems, data theft, espionage, etc.

Are these actions the implementation of the Chinese information warfare doctrine [VEN 07][1] (whose preliminary foundations were presented nearly 20 years ago by Wang Baocun, Wang Pufeng, Shen Weiguang, Qiao Liang, Wang Xiangsui, and closer to us, Dai Qingmin, or even Wang Houqing and Zhang Xingye in *The Science of Campaigns* [HOU 00], Peng Guangqiang and Yao Youzhi in *The Science of Military Strategy* [GUA 05])?

This chapter will keep in line with a context of ever-worsening cyberattacks (or simply an increased awareness of a phenomenon which has existed for many years already) or several studies, mainly American ones, which focus specifically on the strategy, doctrine and capabilities of information warfare, information operations and Chinese cyberwar.

In these publications we find, for instance, the report on the *Capability of the People's Republic of China to Conduct Cyber Warfare and Computer Network*

Chapter written by Daniel VENTRE.
1 A chapter in this publication is entirely dedicated to presenting the Chinese doctrine on information warfare and its main authors.

Exploitation [KRE 09], or Timothy L. Thomas' contribution in the excellent work *Cyberpower and National Security*, published by the *National Defense University* [KRA 09].

Some important questions still remain, however:

– What is the position of the Chinese doctrine today regarding information warfare?

– What are its real capabilities?

– What is the actual risk run by the various States in the world?

– What is the advance or delay in this global race to master information and cyberspace?

These questions interest the world's most important leaders on the highest level, for many reasons:

– the development of China's capabilities for information warfare is in line with the process of developing China's military capabilities: for the Chinese, the capabilities of information warfare have become a qualitative measure with regard to army development;

– a better understanding of the Chinese doctrine will mean being able to give a meaning to the cyberattacks that this State is responsible for, and to measure our own vulnerabilities;

– China is the only global bloc which can, in this matter, go against the USA, both being firmly engaged in the race to control information space;

– even if China cannot hope to meet the USA in the near future in terms of military capacity, it can fix itself an objective, from an asymmetry perspective, to compete with them, to be their equal, or even to take over on the information ground.

Let us note here that the USA is not China's only potential competitor in the dimension of cyberspace.

Although the Chinese doctrine on information warfare is essentially devoted to managing power relations with the outside (against the USA, ensuring China's position on the international stage), of course it strives to be applied within its own borders: controlling information and information space is a matter of power, within China.

Therefore, by analyzing the Xinjiang riots which took place over the summer of 2009, and particularly using the crisis management methods adopted by the authorities, then this chapter will discuss two aspects under the theme of information warfare:

– the first will deal with the level of sensitivity of Chinese cyberspace in the face of the political events affecting the country: is Chinese cyberspace vulnerable? How does it react to the shock wave caused by a major internal crisis with repercussions on an international scale?

– the second will involve the crisis management methods adopted by the authorities, and the position given to information space.

Taking inspiration from the conclusions given on these two matters, the last section will question Chinese information warfare philosophy: has the Xinjiang crisis illustrated the modern Chinese approach to information warfare, confirmed what we already know, or brought in new characteristics?

6.1. Xinjiang region: an explosive context

6.1.1. *Ethnic tensions, extremism, separatism, terrorism, and violence in Xinjiang*

The autonomous region of the Uyghur people in Xinjiang[2], in the North-West of China, is spread over a surface area of 1,660,001 km^2, which is relative to a sixth of the Chinese territory (the surface area of France is 632,834 km^2)[3], but it only has 20 million inhabitants.

If this region is characterized by a strong ethnic diversity (around twenty different groups), the November 2000 census showed that the Uyghur[4] population is the majority (45%), followed by the Han (41%)[5]. The regional capital Urumqi is populated with 75% Han people. The political system, which consisted of populating the region with Han people from the beginning of the 1950s, has reversed the ethnic proportions. On the other hand, an emigration movement was organized: the Uyghurs were sent to various regions in China to work in factories. These movements did not significantly reduce the presence of Islam[6], with nearly 62% of the Xinjiang population remaining as Muslims.

---

2 Xinjiang is one of the 5 autonomous regions in China (as well as Tibet, Guangxi, Inner Monogolia and Ningxia).
3 Figure taken from INSEE (2008), www.insee.fr/fr/themes/tableau.asp?reg_id=0&id=204.
4 In Chinese: 新疆, in Uyghur: شىنجاڭ.
5 *Chine, le Xinjiang et les Ouïgours* by Thierry Kellner, January 1st 2002. Article consulted December 28th 2009 on www.diploweb.com/Chine-le-Xinjiang-et-les-Ouigours.html.
6 Islam was introduced in the region during the 10th and 11th Centuries under pressure from Turkish ethnic groups.

The tensions seen in the region today, and the relations that it maintains with neighboring countries, are deeply rooted in history. Named Turkestan (land of the Turks) in the 12th Century, it was christened again as "Xinjiang"[7] (new territories) following the integration of East Turkestan into the Manchu Empire in the second half of the 19th Century. The presence of the Chinese was virtually always perceived as a foreign occupation, from which the Uyghurs[8] tried to free themselves. The Manchu period which reigned from 1759 to 1892 saw 42 Uyghur revolts. The First Eastern Turkestan Republic[9] was created, (short-lived, lasting from November 1933 to February 1934) and was succeeded from 1944 to 1949 before the region was finally reintegrated into Communist China in 1949. But it is indeed from 1884 onwards that Xinjiang stopped being a buffer zone in the eyes of the central power, becoming an "inalienable part of China" before "being part of a process of integration and assimilation intended to reinforce Chinese sovereignty"[10].

Ever since, the Chinese government has consisted of sinicizing the population[11], and maintaining the dynamics of constructing the Chinese Stat-Nation in the region. The Chinese regime defends the integrity and the unity of the Chinese territory which is "indivisible, inalienable and eternal"[12], which does not suffer any divisions: the designated enemies of these politics are those seeking independence, separatists and terrorists, particularly Uyghurs or Tibetans[13].

The shock between the Chinese dynamic and Uyghur claims largely explains the ethnic tensions which have given way to several violent incidents over the last decades. The Han people are targeted by these violent episodes, perceived as colonizers by the partisans of East Turkestan independence, the name used for Xinjiang "to show its allegiance to the Turk world and not the Chinese world" [CAS 04]. Out of these revolts, demonstrations, and uprisings, let us cite:

– the Uyghur uprising in Hotan, 1954;

---

7 In Chinese: 新疆, in Uyghur: شىنجاڭ.
8 Different spelling variations in English include: *Uighur, Uygur* and *Uigur*.
9 The Uyghurs belong to a Turkish ethno-linguistic group.
10 [CAS 04], p. 10.
11 For more on colonization in the 1950s, read the article on the conditions of those women sent to the region to be married, often forced, with occupying soldiers in order to populate the Han region: www.uyghurnews.com/ReadNews.asp?UighurNews=hidden-misery-of-maos-slave-teenage-brides&ItemID=MH882009790782557959107 (article consulted on January 7th 2010).
12 [CAS 04], p. 6.
13 In China, attacking national unity is liable for the death penality. As a single example, let us remember Ismail Semed who was executed on February 8th 2008 in Urumqi, in the autonomous Uyghur region of Xinjiang, after having been condemned to death on October 31st by the Urumqi People's Courth for having "tried to divide the motherland" after his exile from Pakistan in 2003, www.amnistie.ca/content/view/12246/462/.

– the huge Xinjiang revolts from 1956-1959 following the Central Committee of the Communist Party of China's refusal to rename the Xinjiang region as the Uyghur Republic;

– the armed demonstrations in many districts in Xinjiang in February 1978;

– the riots in Kashgar (1980, 1981), Aksu (1980), and Yesheng (1982);

– the 200 bombed attacks between 1987 and 1990 [KUM 98];

– the 200 murders during 1990[14] (exact figures are extremely difficult to get, there is no precise census available);

– the 1989 student demonstrations in Urumqi;

– the rising up of 2000 farmers in the village of Barin (20 dead), in April 1990, followed by an appeal to the Jihad launched by the Islamist Yusef Zeidin. The incidents in Yinin (*Guldja* or *Kulja* in Uyghurs) at the beginning of February 1997, also known as the "February 5th affair" (data from the height of the riots) during which Uyghur rioters attacked the Chinese Han people (official figures: 7 dead and 200 injured[15]; the Uyghurs and dissenters have much higher figures: 100 dead, 8,000 missing). The rumors of arrest, executions, repression of religious and cultural activities are behind these revolts.

Let us refer to the three bomb explosions on a bus in Urumchi, February 25th 1997 (9 dead, 74 injured). These attacks were connected to al-Qaeda. On February 12th 1999, the confrontations between young Uyghurs and police forces took on extreme measures, resulting in 5 injured. On September 8th 2000 in Urumchi [SEY 00], an army truck exploded in the middle of the city at rush hour killing 60 people. Nobody knows whether this explosion was an accident or an act of terrorism [SEY 00]. In the post 9/11 world, the authorities interpreted this act as a reinforced fight against terrorism[16].

Beijing considers the region to be the cradle for terrorists linked with al-Qaeda. "After September 11th 2001, the Chinese regime made an effort to integrate the repression of the Uyghur opposition into the international dynamic of the fight against Islam terrorist networks" [CAS 03]. The Uyghur extremists were the founders of the Islamic Part of Turkestan and the East Turkestan Islamic Movement[17]. In 2002, the latter, considered by the Chinese authorities as an Islamist

---

14 *True Nature of East Turkestan forces*, China Daily, January 22nd 2002. From a report issued by the State Council Information Office of the People's Republic of China.
15 Figures taken from fr.wikipedia.org/wiki/Incident_de_Yining.
16 According to the Uyghurs, when China accused them of having links to Islamist terrorism, the accusation is a standard strategy for incriminating Uyghurs in the eyes of the public opinion [USL 09].
17 ETIM.

separatist organization with links to al-Qaeda, was registered by UN's Security Council on the list of terrorist organizations linked to al-Qaeda [RIC 07]. 22 Uyghur fighters were, on the other hand, arrested during the Operation Enduring Freedom (OEF) and imprisoned in Guantanamo[18].

According to its detractors, Beijing used the context of the war on terrorism to lead a stronger repression against the Uyghurs in Xinjiang.

The revitalization of Islam in the region, which was very distinct from the 1980s onwards, may be considered as both a return towards tradition or the willingness to point out differences (claims for identity) in relation to the atheist Han ethnic group. In the post-9/11 context, the Uyghur case was presented by Beijing as a religious and terrorist matter, not only undermining China's national unity but also contributing to international terrorism. In 2004, the police carried out several arrests for "illegal religious activities", as well as executions[19].

More recently, violence and terrorist threats do not seem to have decreased: during the Akto raid on January 5th 2007, the Chinese police forces took down an Islamic terrorist camp[20].

On March 10th 2008 the police revealed that they had killed, two months beforehand, Islamist terrorists in Urumqi who were preparing an attack on the Olympic Games. On March 18th 2008, a Uyghur woman set off a bomb in a bus in the city of Urumqi. On March 23rd in the same year, following the death of a young Uyghur boy during his police custody, protests were organized in the city of Hotan which took place at the same time as the riots in the neighboring province of Tibet, without the two being so much as linked to each other.

On March 24th, thousands of demonstrators took to the street, this time to protest against a new law to stop women wearing headscarves. On April 9th 2008, the site of the Islamic Party of Turkestan broadcasted the video of three Chinese hostages being executed. On this party's site, hosted in Singapore, videos referring to the Uyghurs of Xinjiang as the *Jihad*[21] were found.

---

18 Their freedom and being sent back to China raises other problems. Read the report by the CCJR (Center for Constitutional Rights) regarding Abdul Nassar www.ccrjustice.org /files/AbdulNassar.pdf (site consulted on January 10th 2010).
19 fr.wikipedia.org/wiki/Xinjiang (site consulted on January 16th 2010).
20 www.chine-informations.com/actualite/chine-pekin-annonce-le-demantelement-un camp - terroriste-dans-le-xinjiang_5791.html, Bejing announces the deconstruction of a terrorist camp in Xinjiang, on January 17th 2007 (site consulted on January 10th 2010).
21 fr.wikipedia.org/wiki/Parti_d%27Allah_du_Turkestan_oriental_islamique, (site consulted on January 4th 2010).

On August 4th 2008, 4 days after the Beijing Olympic Games opened, 16 Chinese police offers were killed and 16 others were injured in the city of Kashgar during an attack led by two Uyghur separatists. On August 10th 2008, in the city of Kuqa, several explosions went off, leaving 12 dead in their wake. On August 12th 2008, attacks were launched on civil guards in the city of Yamanya (3 dead). On April 2nd 2009, a suicide attack in a building in the regional capital left 2 injured and 1 dead[22].

6.1.2. *Xinjiang: a strategic region*

This region is important for China as a whole because it is rich in natural resources: the Xinjiang underground contains petrol, natural gas, uranium, gold. It is also important from a military point of view: on the Lop Nor site, the biggest nuclear testing site in the world, there were 45 explosions between 1964 and 1996[23].

Although far from the capital (2,192 km), and although suffering permanent ethnic tensions, the region must remain under Beijing control, in order to preserve national unity. The challenges are high, internally as well as externally. We only have to look at the geographical position of this region on a map in order to understand the strategic position that it takes up, not only for China, but for regional and international balance.

For many centuries, the region was to be found on the silken road which linked the valley of the yellow river to the Mediterranean. Today it shares 5,300 km of borders with 8 different countries: Afghanistan, Pakistan, Kashmir under India's control (China manages the Aksai Chin region claimed by India as being part of Jammu and Kashmir), Russia, Kazakhstan, Kirghizstan, Tajikistan and Mongolia [ALL 06]. Internally, Xinjiang is in the immediate vicinity of Tibet. The attempts to destabilize the region and therefore China may help to find their sources in some neighboring States.

6.2. Riots, July 2009

6.2.1. *Chronology of facts*

In China, the year 2009 was marked by the 60th anniversary of the creation of the People's Republic of China, celebrated by shows and extravagant parades, a true demonstration of power and dynamism, at the height of ambitions and the role that China counts on playing on the stage held by large international powers. But 2009 also marked the 20th anniversary of the Tiananmen massacre (June 4th 1989), or even

---

22 fr.wikipedia.org/wiki/Xinjiang (site consulted on January 16th 2010).
23 www.nti.org/db/China/testpos.htm (site consulted on Decmber 28th 2009).

the 50th anniversary of the Dali Lama's escape in India[24]. This was, therefore, an important year, which was full of symbolic meaning. The authorities were vigilant on many fronts. But this vigilance seems to have been a mistake.

On July 5th 2009, extremely violent riots broke out in Urumqi, which between the Uyghur and Han people, during which 197 people perished and 1,721 were injured, according to official sources. Everything seems to have started up in another region in China. Zhu, an old employee licensed to make Xuri[25] toys in Shaoguan (Canton province) spread false information on the web saying that 6 Uyghur workers had raped two Han[26] workers in the company. The Han workers attacked the Uyghurs in retaliation. During the night of June 25th to 26th 2009, the quarrels resulted in the death of two Uyghur workers[27], and 120 people were injured in spite of the 400 officers in action.

Videos of the incidents were rapidly spread across the Internet, particularly on the site sohu.com, then on YouTube[28]. Following the incidents, all the Uyghur workers from the company were moved to another work place and did not return until a week later.

On July 5th, the Uyghur community organized a protest which was described in the media as being "pacifist", to express its discontent against the Chinese authorities, criticizing the way in which the incidents were managed in Shaoguan (the police had not protected the Uyghur workers). The thousands of Uyghur protesters confronted the police forces[29].

According to Rebiya Kadeer[30], president of the WUC, the Chinese police had provoked the demonstrators, and *agent provocateurs* were introduced into the peaceful demonstration (without it actually being a matter for Chinese police or soldiers). The confrontations with the police quickly turned into attacks on the Han people. Extreme acts of violence followed on from each other, and the authorities quickly communicated reports amongst the Han population.

---

24 In March 1959, following the Tibetan up-rising and confrontations with the Chinese army. In March 2008, Tibet saw violent problems.
25 Company as part of the *Early Light International* group based in Hong Kong.
26 The Uyghurs flowed in their thousands to the South of China to work in the region's many companies. There were frequent clashes between ethnic groups.
27 club.pchome.net/topic_1_15_3804013.html.
28 www.youtube.com/watch?v=6_PJTO2k0PM.
29 Some sources suggest figures of 3,000 protestors rallying against 1,000 police officers, see: www.google.com/hostednews/afp/article/ALeqM5hIFqKqC0nexK2ksxtwJC9bcn8r-g, AFP (French News Agency) from July 5th 2009.
30 Nominated for the Nobel Peace Prize in 2006

On July 6th, Beijing accused Rebiya Kadeer of having encouraged and organized this revolt. On July 7th the Chinese Han attacked the Uyghurs, as retaliation. The next day, Hu Jintao who should have attended the 35th G8 summit in Italy, cut his stay short and returned to China due to the situation in Xinjiang. Li Zhi, head of the Chinese Communist Party in Urumqi, promised a death sentence to all those who were found to be guilty of crimes committed during the riots. On July 9th, the authorities confirmed that they had intercepted R. Kadeer's communications, proving her implication in organizing the riots [WIN 09].

Thousands of Urumqi inhabitants tried to leave the city[31]. On Thursday July 10th, a decision was made by the authorities to close the main mosques to avoid crowds and the risk of new extreme behavior. The mosques reopened later in the day. According to a report (whose sources are debatable) from the London intelligence network *Stirling Assynt*, *Al-Qaeda in the Islamic Maghreb*, they called for retaliation on Chinese interests in Algeria in mid July[32]. The Chinese Embassy in Algeria, via its website, demanded its nationals to be vigilant[33].

In the weeks following the riots, the police carried out several arrests with the authorities promising death sentences for all those found to be guilty of crimes during the riots.

Ever since, the situation in the province has remained very tense.

In mid August, rumors were circulating about syringe attacks on the streets of Urumqi: individuals were attacking passers-by in the street and injecting them with poisoned needles. On September 3rd, Urumqi became the new theater of protests, this time against the authorities' behavior regarding the needle attacks. 5 people were killed during these protests.

---

31 *Chine: les gares prises d'assaut à Ürümqi (China: assaults on stations in Urumqi)* July 14th 2009, www.rtbf.be/info/chine-les-gares-prises-dassaut-a-urumqi-124553] (site consulted on January 15th 2010).

32 Other threats for violence action on China from Islamists were signaled by the following: Abu Yahya al-Libi, one of the leaders of al-Qaeda called upon the Jihad in Xinjiang in a video posted on the Internet in October 2009. In mid-July 2009, Seyfullah, leader of the Turkistan Islamic Party (TIP) called for violent actions on China on October 8th 2009, on the eve of the Olympic Games. Read *Al-Qaeda threatens to attack China*, October 8th 2009, www.chinadaily.com.cn/china/2009-10/08/content_8767743.html (site consulted on January 15th 2010).

33 *China warns citizens in Algeria of Al Qaeda Threat,* July 15th 2009, www.reuters.com/article/idUSTRE56E0KW20090715 (site consulted on January 15th 2010).

At the end of December 2009, 41 people were judged and condemned – 21 were sentenced to death for taking part in the Xinjiang riots[34].

Date	Facts	Symbol used on graphs/histograms
June 25th- 26th	Rumors lead to confrontations between Uyghurs and Han in the toy factory *Early Light International* in Shaoguan, in the Canton province	A
5th July	Protests in the streets of Urumqi turn into confrontations between Uyghurs and Hans	B
July 6th	The Chinese authorities accuse Rebiya Kadeer and the WUC of being behind the violence. In the 24 hours following the riots, telephone communications and part of the Internet was cut off	C
July 7th	Han retaliate against Uyghurs	D
July 8th	Hu Jintao who was meant to take part in the 35th G8 summit in Italy, cuts his stay short and returns to China because of the situation in Xiajiang. Li Zhi, head of the Chinese Communist Party in Urumqi promises the death penalty for all those found guilty of crimes committed during the riots	E
July 9th	Chinese authorities confirm the possession of proof regarding the WUC's implications in organizing the riots through intercepting Internet content, and telephone messages	F
July 10th	Mosques close in Urumqi	G
July 13th	The website of the Turkish Embassy in Beijing defaced	
July 28th	Rebiya Kadeer arrives in Japan. Chinese authorities react	H
August 1st	Melbourne Film Festival site is attacked. Anti-Kadeer slogans appear and Chinese flag is displayed	I
August 7th	Melbourne Film Festival site is hacked	
August 11th	Beginning of the most important military operation ever taken place in China, involving 50,000 men. The operations partly take place in Xinjiang (and in other various regions in China)	

---

34 *Uyghur American Association Strongly Condemns the Sentencing of 22 Uyghurs in East Turkestan*, December 23rd 2009, www.uyghurcongress.org/en/?p=1499, (site consulted on December 30th 2009).

August 17th	People start talking about needle attacks in the streets of Urumqi	J
August 27th	President Hu Jintao visits Xinjiang	K
September 3rd	Demonstrations in the streets of Urumqi against the behavior of the authorities regarding the needle attacks. 5 people are killed during the protests	
September 8th	One of the Taiwan Film Festival's organizers has their blog hacked	
September 27th	The Chinese government publishes a White Paper on ethnic policy which confirms that all ethnic groups are to be treated equally in China: same freedoms, same rights	
September 27th	The Xinjiang authorities vote on a law (Information Promotion Bill) which criminalizes any separatist discussions on the Internet. Access providers are asked to control their users and to inform authorities immediately of any violation of this law	
End of December	Announcement of the progressive reopening of the Internet in Xinjiang, with restrictions	
End of December	Since July 5th, 41 people were taken to trial and condemned. 21of them were given the death sentence	

Table 6.1. *Calendar of facts relating to the riots and situation in Xinjiang. Reference period: June 1st/December 31st 2009. The facts marked with a letter are the markers which will be used in the graphs later in this chapter*

6.2.2. Reasons for the riots

The Xinjiang riots in the summer of 2009, as exceptional as they may seem due to the number of victims and the extent of the damage, are not isolated acts of violence. The long list of violence acts in the region since the 1950s provides proof of this.

These are not the only acts of violence that China has had to lament over in the last few years. How can we forget the Tiananmen protests in 1989? More recently, in March 2008, we can add the Tibet riots, killing several people and making the international opinion focus on the Olympic Games for a few months.

296 Cyberwar and Information Warfare

More or less violent protests were shaking up the rest of the country, and were transforming the population's reactions into various situations: poverty, inequality, corruption, injustice. To a lesser extent, the Weng'an[35] (Guizhou) protests on June 28th 2008 witnessed thousands of students and citizens confronting the police (150 injured), and setting fire to hundreds of vehicles and buildings in 7 hours. The population was protesting against the police's behavior, which had tried to cover up the murder of a 16 year old girl as a suicide. The victim's family said the assassin was the son of one of the city's dignitaries. The rumor of the death of the young girl's uncle sparked off the riots.

The July 2009 events are part of a context filled with inter-ethnic tensions which have lasted for centuries. Two versions have been put forward, in order to try to explain the origin and cause for the riots; versions which, perhaps, complement each other rather go against each other: for the Uyghurs, they were simply reacting to the behavior of the Chinese authorities during the Shaoguan incidents. For the Chinese authorities, however, these riots were organized by the *World Uyghur Congress* (WUC)[36].

Whatever the spark, the tension may find its roots in the social inequalities which separate the Uyghurs who are kept away from the economic evolution and the region's growing wealth, and from the Han people who greatly benefit from the growth: the gross domestic product (GDP) doubled between 2000 and 2006, but only the Han people benefited from this, where 80% of the Uyghurs were still living below the poverty threshold [UNP 09].

Without a doubt, the tension is also partially rooted in the phenomenon of acculturation (at least felt to be as such) which the Uyghur victims are talking about: the Uyghur language is no longer taught in schools, practicing their religion is restricted, employment discriminations still exist, access to health care is not equal, the traditional Uyghur buildings are demolished, the historical truth regarding the Chinese presence in the region is twisted, etc. These are all the grievances against Beijing [UHR 09].

Each side has its own arguments: for the Uyghurs, the riots can be explained by the injustice, the social and economic inequality, the dominating role of the Han people in administration, the religious restrictions and repression, the oppression of Chinese power, the rejection of their legitimate claims for identity, colonization, acculturation. For Beijing, the riots are explained by separatism (the Chinese

35 en.wikipedia.org/wiki/2008_Wengan_riot.
36 www.uyghurcongress.org/en/?cat=149 (site consutled on December 30th 2009).The WUC was created on April 16th 2004 in Munich (Germany). Rebiya Kadeer was reinstated as president of the WUC during the 3rd general assembly which was held in Washington DC (May 21-25th 2009).

majorities feel that the claims of the minorities are separatist claims), extremism, Islamism, terrorism, and in the attempts at destabilization organized by foreign entities (starting with the pressure exerted by the Uyghur diaspora supported by countries such as the USA, where Rebiya Kadeer has been living since 2005, or Germany which hosts the WUC)[37].

The diaspora activities were organized at the beginning of the 1970s with action taken by Erkin Alptekin[38], founder of the East Turkestan Union in 1991, succeeded by the WUC created in 2004. Alptekin's action was delayed by Rebiya Kadeer, who, like the Dali Lama, crossed the planet to defend her cause.

However, let us underline that the US authorities did not deal with the Uyghur and Tibet matter equally, the latter receiving official support, which cannot be said for the Uyghurs [BOR 09].

Since 1949, the Beijing authorities have not stopped considering Uyghur separatism as an internal matter [SHI 09], whilst denouncing external influence and support that the movement benefits from, whether this concerns the interventions of diasporas or international terrorism (al-Qaeda in particular). This crisis in Xinjiang is sometimes presented as the direct consequence from outside disruptions: China suffered from the turbulences created by the situation in the neighboring Afghanistan, and the Xinjiang riots were the direct consequence of the recent American offensive launched in Afghanistan [CHA 09].

6.2.3. *The riots faced with international public opinion*

However, the Xinjiang riots, as important as they were, seem to have maintained less interest from the international public opinion than the Tibet riots in March 2008. A few statistics taken from Google Trends and the site Alexa.com can attest to this statement[39].

---

37 www.german-foreign-policy.com/en/fulltext/56104.10) *Strategies of Attrition*, October 22nd 2007 (site consulted on January 10th 2009).

38 Father was the government general secretary of the short-lived East Turkestan Republic in 1933-1934.

39 The graphs generated using Alexa.com offer information on site consultation. The *Daily Reach* indicator shows the percentage of all the Internet users who visited the site. The *Daily Traffic Rank* is the classification out of all the sites. These two indicators inform us of a site's popularity. The first indicator is based on internet users, the second is based on site classification. The graphs generated using Google Trends give an idea of the popularity of particular terms (put into Google by Internet users). These two approaches reflect the interest

The term "riots" shows a graph curve which is very clearly affected by the French riots in 2005, and is very little affected by riots which have taken place elsewhere in the world:

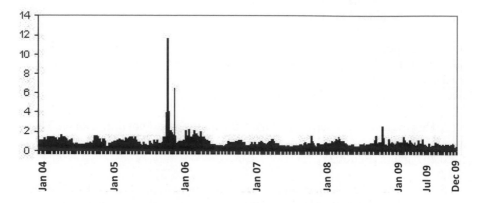

Figure 6.1. *Histogram generated using Google Trends data for the term "riots".*
Period covered: January 1ˢᵗ 2004-December 31ˢᵗ 2009. The scale is based
on the mean global activity over all the years collectively

French internet users are hardly interested in the Chinese phenomenon, which can also be said of the rest of the international community.

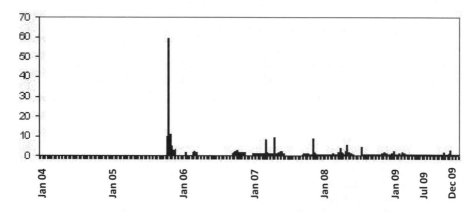

Figure 6.2. *Histogram generated using Google Trend data for the term* "émeute"
(French for riot). Period covered: January 1ˢᵗ 2004-December 31ˢᵗ 2009

---

of Internet users across the world on sites and topics and may also be used, with reserve, as indicators of the public opinions' interest in events.

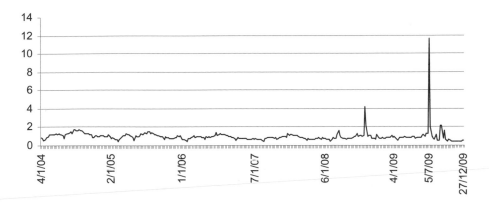

Figure 6.3. *Graph generated using Google Trends data for the term 新疆 (Xinjiang). Period covered: January 1ˢᵗ 2004-December 31ˢᵗ 2009*

Searches for the Chinese term 新疆 (Xinjiang) show a peak which coincides with the week of the riots. The outline on the last six years (2004-2009) shows no other peak as high as this, in spite of many other incidents (attacks in particular).

The intensity drops very quickly after the week of riots.

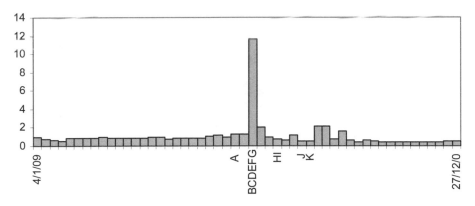

Figure 6.4. *Histogram generated using Google Trends data for the Chinese term 新疆 (Xinjiang). Period covered: January 1ˢᵗ 2004-December 31ˢᵗ 2009*

The internet users' interest in Tibet was particularly affected in the March 2008 period, which was the riot period in that region. Here, we still see the absence of the intensity lasting over the long term.

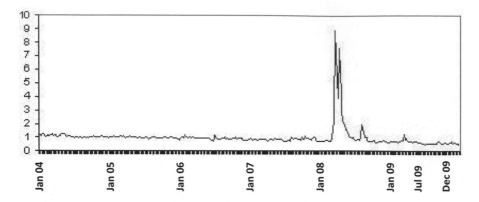

Figure 6.5. *Histogram generated using Google Trends data for the term Tibet. Period covered: January 1ˢᵗ 2004-December 31ˢᵗ 2009*

Public opinion was quickly turning away from the events. Interest was elsewhere. On the database provided by Alexa.com, the investigation on the popularity of websites shows the same phenomenon.

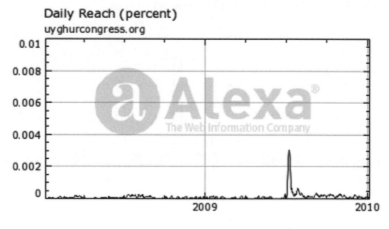

Figure 6.6. *Daily reach on the WUC site (2008-2009), recording on Alexa.com, January 7ᵗʰ 2010[40]*

The *World Uyghur Congress* (WUC) site recorded a frequentation peak trend during July 2009.

---

40 www.alexa.com/siteinfo/uyghurcongress.org.

But the period after the peak is clearly no more intense than the period before. There is no change in terms of frequentation, popularity, visibility and echo.

The visibility of the Uyghur American Association (UAA) is affected in the same way. Only major events seem to be able to produce new peaks.

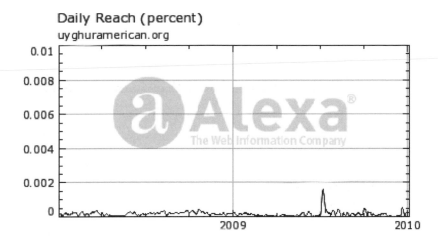

Figure 6.7. *Daily reach on the UAA site (2008-2009), recording on Alexa.com on January 7th 2010*[41]

The graphs for the most representative sites of the Tibet cause show no particular disturbances during the riot period in Xinjiang. The causes and dates are distinct, but the public's attention is specific and differentiated.

For example, the daily reach on the site tibet.net is concentrated for the month of March (2008, during the riots, and 2009, anniversary of the 1959 Tiananmen massacres).

The *Tibetan Centre for Human Rights and Democracy* (TCHRD) site, a Tibetan NGO for the defense of human rights in Tibet, recorded its high peak in March 2008, at the time of the disorder in this region, and has shown a flat line ever since.

---

41 www.alexa.com/siteinfo/uyghuramerican.org.

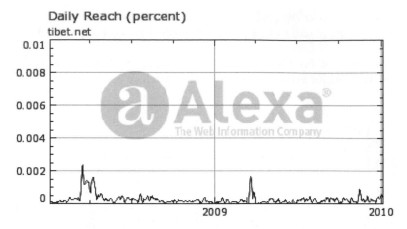

Figure 6.8. *Daily reach on the site www/tibet.net (2008-2009), recording on Alexa.com, on January 7th 2010[42]*

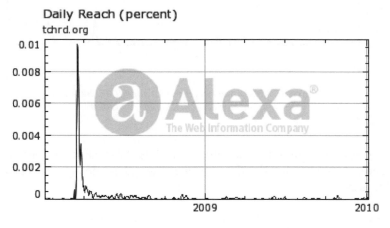

Figure 6.9. *Daily reach on www.tchrd.org (2008-2009) recording on Alexa.com, on January 7th 2010[43]*

The lack of high trends out of the period of important events also shows that these sites are not victims of DDoS-type attacks, which could in fact appear on these statistics as the same peaks.

42 www.alexa.com/siteinfo/tibet.net.

43 www.alexa.com/siteinfo/tchrd.org.

6.3. Impacts on Chinese cyberspace: hacktivism and site defacing

6.3.1. *The Internet in Xinjiang: a region dependent on information systems?*

No study or investigation into the question of information warfare and cyberwar could skip this initial question: is the region, the country, and the actor concerned connected to cyberspace in a strong or weak way?

Of course the impact that we may hope to have from an operation in cyberspace on the target depends on the answer to this question. A country with a low connection will be less vulnerable to CNO's than a wholly dependent state, as developed countries have become. If, in China, the Internet is developing at a staggering speed, then this is probably not the case for all its regions.

The Internet user population in China[44] in 2009 was estimated at 360 million people, meaning 48.8% of Asia's Internet users collectively, and a penetration rate of 26.9%[45]. The curve showing the evolution of Chinese internet users is constantly growing, and does not seem to suffer under the effects of the current global economic crisis.

For all this, at the current time the penetration rate of the Internet in China is still lower than in Russia or Brazil, and far behind the world-wide leaders in the field, such as Japan (73.8%), the USA (74.7%) and South Korea (76.1%). It is short of reaching the global average which is 23.8%. The 10-30 age group represents nearly 63% of Chinese Internet users, and students make up the majority social category amongst Internet users (31.7%).

According to the *China Internet Network Information Center* (CNNIC), the number of mobile Internet users has risen to 155 million, which is close to half of all Chinese Internet users. This figure will be particularly important in Chinese considerations for security, and therefore we will consider mobile communication tools as possible facilitators of protests, and mass movement organizations.

In Hong Kong, there are 4,878,713 internet users for a penetration rate of 69.2%. In Macao, the penetration rate is 46.3%. In Taiwan, it is 65.9% (15,143,000 internet users for a population of 22,974,347).

---

44 www.internetworldstats.com/stats.htm. The data may vary depending on the source. The report from July 2009 from the *China Internet Network Information Center* (CNNIC) lists 338 million, for a penetration rate of 25.5%.

45 360 million internet users for a Chinese population of 1,338,612,968 people. To enhance the comparison, let us add that the penetration rate in France in 69.3%, 68.3% in Estonia, and 7% in India.

The growth rate of the Internet user population is considerable. From 2000 to 2009, it reached 1,500% for mainland China, 113.7% for Hong Kong, 331.7% for Macao and 141.9% for Taiwan. Turkey, as we will see further on has played a particular role in the economic crisis, has 26.5 million Internet users, a penetration rate of 34.5% and a growth rate in the internet user population of 1,225% for the 2000-2009 period.

	Quantities		
	End of 2007	**End of 2008**	**July 2009**
IPv4 Addresses	135,274,752	181,273,344	205,031,168
Domain names	11,931,277	16,826,198	16, 259,562
.cn domains	9,001,993	13,572,326	12,963,685
Websites	1,503,800	2,878 000	3,061,109
Sites en in .cn	1,006,000	2,216,400	2,410,546
Number of web pages		16,086,370,233	

Table 6.2. *Statistics for the Internet in China*

In Xinjiang, the Internet penetration rate was 17.7% in December 2007 (3.63 million) and 27.1% in December 20008 (6.25 million), showing an increase of 72.1% in just one year[46].

If we believe in these figures, then the Internet penetration rate in Xinjiang is therefore higher, even if just by a small amount, than the national Chinese average. The comparative table below shows the values for the relative share of the three regions in China's internet: Beijing, Tibet and Xinjiang.

Beijing concentrates resources in a clear way.

Above all, it must be noted that Xinjiang has three times as many domain names as Tibet, twice as many Internet sites, and nearly thirty-five times as many Internet pages. Xinjiang is much more present on the Internet than Tibet, which is likely to have direct consequences on the way of approaching crisis management, and therefore it takes the cyberspace dimension into account.

---

46 Data taken from the annual report published by the CNNIC (*China Internet Network Information Center*), www.cnnic.cn/uploadfiles/pdf/2009/10/13/94556.pdf, July 2009.

	Beijing	Tibet	Xinjiang
IPv4 addresses (in national %)	24.3%	0.4%	0.2%
Domain names	3,839,778	12,479	40,958
Ending in .cn	3,446,010	10,908	34,545
Internet sites	340,439	3,651	8,317
Web pages (December 2008)	4,021,927,610	898,267	31,240,081

Table 6.3. *Internet statistics: Beijing, Tibet, Xinjiang (July 2009)*

With regard to security, Chinese cyberspace does not seem to be doing any better than the rest of the world. Still according to the CNNIC July 2009 report, 82% of Chinese internet users have anti-virus software, but 195 million of them have been victims of virus attacks during the first six months of 2009, and 110 million user accounts and passwords were hacked and stolen.

6.3.2. Website defacement in a crisis context

The relationship being established between political events and cyberspace attacks has been described for many years already. There are several examples of this. Let us remember the bombing on the Chinese Embassy in Belgrade by NATO in May 1999, which led a wave of attacks on Internet servers on both sides of the Atlantic. Let us remember the birth of the hacker group, the *Honker Union of China*, in 2001, following the collision between an American spy plane and a Chinese fighter plane. In 2005, when Malaysia and Indonesia were fighting over questions of exploiting areas of the ocean containing oil, hackers from each State who up confronted it, drawing out the diplomatic and political tension in cyberspace: the objective was to hit the maximum amount of targets (sites), but above all, sites with high symbolic values for the opponent side.

These confrontations have nothing to do with war, and are more like a game. But, however, literature (particularly from large public media) were speaking of "hacker wars" early on, making us believe in the existence of real combats led by real fighters, who were capable of influencing the course of events, politics, and the choices of decision-makers.

Up until now, the activities of "hacktivists" (activist hackers or nationalist hackers) have had no proven impact, other than disturbing systems for variable lengths of time, but not in a way so as to result in crises and conflicts. This *politics-hacking* relationship never stops being reinstated.

In November 2009, Switzerland voted by referendum for (or against) the building of mosques. This vote summoned up national opinion, the opinion of neighboring countries, and also the opinion of Muslim countries. In the days following the referendum, more than 4,000 sites were defaced in Switzerland, attacked by hackers demanding their Turkish identity, defending Islam, etc.

Figure 6.10 shows us the peak of the defaced sites recorded on the .ch domains during December 2009.

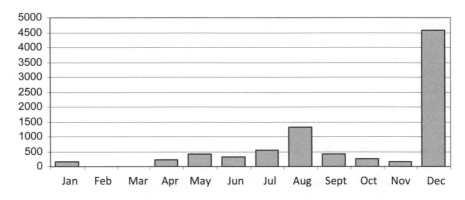

Figure 6.10. *Defaced sites on the .ch domain for 2009. Graph generated from reports published daily on zone-h.org*

The international press reported several cases of site defacing:

– According to a post[47] on July 9th 2009 by an Internet user known as *Sinbo*, more than 2000 pages of Chinese sites were hacked by the Turkish *Ayyildiz Hack Tea*[48]. This group had already hit the headlines in July 2008 when the magazine *German Focus* revealed in an article entitled *Turkish networks attack the European*

---

47   www.topix.com/forum/world/turkey/TBV96T5QTHCBPMGDB, (site consulted on January 11th 2010).
48 This figure cannot, however, be checked in light of the data that we have on the zone-h.org database. On the other hand, the actions taken by this group are not focused on China, and regularly target sites close to the terrorist organization PKK. After the appartment building fires in Germany where Turkish residents were living, this group of hackers went on to attack German bank and business sites.

Union that Ayyildiz had hacked into the European Union systems and tried to steal sensitive information[49].

– On July 11th 2009, the site for the Chinese Weather Center had been defaced by the Linuxploit_crew.

– The Turkish Embassy in Beijing (turkey.org.cn) was attacked on July 13th 2009 by a Chinese[50] (or pro-Chinese?) hacker, after the Turkish Prime Minster Recep Tayyip Erdogan had described incidents of genocide. The message posted by the hacker signing off as *Mafia Baron* demanded that the Turkish government stop interfering in the Xinjiang matter because it would reveal China's internal affairs.

– On August 7th 2009, the website for the Melbourne International Arts Festival (MIAF) was the victim of attacks from one signed *oldjun*, a Chinese (or pro-Chinese) hacker displaying an anti-Uyghur message. The motive for the attack resided in the festival program to show a film telling the story of the life of Rebiya Kadeer. According to the festival's organizers, the pressure was exerted in three stages: the first came from the Chinese Embassy who wanted the film removed from the program, the second stage was the withdrawal of 5 Chinese films from the festival (Chinese directors were removed upon the Government's demand, it seems)[51], and the third stage was the festival site's hacking, with the hackers demanding that, on behalf of the Chinese population, the projection of the film be removed from the program. The organizers were also bombarded with threatening emails[52]. In this context which favors anti-Chinese sentiment, fears seemed to be awakened, with Australian diplomacy revealing attempts of espionage operations from China, of which it was a victim[53].

---

49 *Turkish hacker group "AyYildiz Team" threatens Europe*, July 14th 2008, en.apa.az/news.php?id=52032 (article consulted on January 11th 2010). The article specified that the Turkish hackers had gotten into the private section (containing secret documents) of the European Commissioner's site, Xavier Solanas.
50 *Chinese Hackers attack Turkish Embassy Web site*, July 15th 2009, www.secuobs.com/revue/news/120697.shtml (article consulted on March 18th 2010).
51 *Australian Film Festival Site Defaced by Chinese Hackers*, July 26th 2009, www.france24.com/en/20090726-uighur-film-festival-australia-site-defaced-chinese-hacker cinema-internet (consulted on March 18th 2010).
52 *Hackers target Australian festival showing Uyghur film*, July 27th 2009, edition.cnn.com/2009/WORLD/asiapcf/07/26/china.australia.uyghur/index.html (consulted on January 15th 2010).
53 Autralian diplomats were warned in August 2009 of the distribution of fake emails (probably) coming from China, possibly attempts of cyberespionnage: www.thedarkvisitor.com/category/other-attacks/. Australia publised several reports listing the cyberattacks: www.smh.com.au/technology/security/fake-email-could-be-cyber-espionage-20090817-enp0.html.

– On September 8th 2009, the organizers of the Kaohsiung International Film Festival (the second biggest city in Taiwan) announced that one of their blogs had been hacked with a message posted accusing Rebiya Kadeer of being behind the Xinjiang riots[54]. The festival had not planned to invite the head of the WUC, but had scheduled the projection of the film telling her life story, the same film which was supposed to be shown in Melbourne, *Ten Conditions of Love.*

But these few site attacks, highly portrayed in the media, could not alone summarize the disturbances that cyberspace could have been a victim of during the crisis.

Any major political event is likely to attract the attention of hacktivists, who find causes to defend, targets to hit, a worthy context, a strengthened motivation for their actions, and also a voice box for their own actions because at that very moment, interests are particularly focused more on possible exploits which will take place and be connected to the event.

The hacktivist may thus be an opportunist, who will take advantage of a specific context and use it as a play ground, a place to express his own claims.

By its multi-ethnic (Han, Uyghurs, Turkish speakers, etc.), religious (Islam), international (around Afghanistan, implication of the diasporas, opinions formed by governments, etc.) dimension, because it involves China (which is a target of choice in its own right, whatever the time, like the USA, the NSA, or other actors on the global stage), because it held a relationship from the strong to the weak (Han people and Uyghur playing this role in turn depending on the partisans adopted point of view), the Xinjiang crisis grouped together the conditions favoring the implication of hacktivists. Site defacing, the hacktivist's main method of expression, does not only aim to cause immediate damage, to disrupt a site, a server, a company, or an institution. It also aims to convey a certain message. However, the higher the number of servers and sites hacked, then the higher the vulnerability in the information systems will be. Beyond the odd anecdote, there are frequent operations aimed at a country's infrastructure security.

Have the Xinjiang events had an active effect on the international hacker community, a community which could be considered as a particular sub-set of what we would normally call *public opinion*? Or, on the other hand, have hackers forsaken the event to get together elsewhere in the world? At least the hacktivist phenomenon is not following other methods of action, tending to spread messages more, or is no longer the favored mode of confrontation and expression, at a time when Web 2.0 is opening up new simpler, more legal, possibilities.

---

54 *East Turkestan: Taiwan Festival Hacked over Uyghur film*, September 9th 2009, www.unpo.org/ content/view/10033/236/ (consulted on 15th January 2010).

For the anecdote, let us remember that in the meantime, the riots (week of the 5th to 10th July) and important cyberattacks launched using botnets (DDoS attacks), were hitting servers in South Korea and the USA in three successive waves: the 4th, the 7th and finally the 9th July 2009.

6.3.3. *Defining the dynamics of the relationship between "political events" and "site defacement"*

Chinese cyberspace is indeed vast. It is not due to part of the Internet being cut off during this period which significantly reduced the possibility of attacks on information systems towards, or from, this country.

If we are used to considering China as an aggressive actor in the field of cyberspace, then let us consider it here also as a potential target, like an actor in a defensive, reactive position. Was Chinese cyberspace a victim of major disturbances coming directly from the Xinjiang crisis? Did the Chinese hackers act against activists for the Uyghur cause in the world? What intensity could these "confrontations" take by intervening information systems? Did a "hacker war" really take place?

Perhaps we can find a few answers to these questions in the defacement of sites that we will analyze thanks to the information available from the Zone-h project.

For this study, defacements have been identified which have affected the ccTLD's of countries which are directly involved, and other less directly affected countries, namely:

– .cn (China), .hk (Hong Kong), .tw (Taiwan), .mo (Macao);

– .tr (Turkey);

– .jp (Japan);

– .au (Australia)[55].

The statistical data was established using information available online on the zone-h.org website. The reports were made daily, whilst isolating defacements relating to aforementioned extensions.

---

55 The first 4 represent Chinese space. The .tr domain is from Turkey, likely to take the side of the Uyghurs. The .jp domain is Japanese, and we will analyze it here for measure the effect of the choice of welcoming in Rebiya Kadeer a short while after the riots. As for the .au domain, it has been chosen to try to identify the effects other than the single defacement of the Melbourne Film Festival's site.

The period used is from June 1st 2009 to August 31st 2009, surrounding the July when the riots took place, two periods of equal length in order to show a potential change in the intensity of the attacks during the crisis. June was also an important time which was likely to change the intensity of the attacks: the anniversary of the Tiananmen massacre.

The analyses that we can carry out using this data must try to show a lot of information. The "confrontation" dimension between hackers may be observed through the speed of the Chinese, Uyghur, pro-Chinese, pro-Uyghur website defacements (actions, reactions, responses, repercussions). This dimension may be visible through the content of the claims (insults, warnings, racist talk, etc.).

Confrontation may still be perceived through the nature of the targets hit. Do targeted defacements (meaning those defacements which not only affect specific targets, but whose claims are directly linked, by their content, to the Xinjiang crisis itself), in all their intensity, thus enable us to speak of confrontation or are they only specific actions?

The level of hacktivist implication in this crisis must call for many comments on the nature of the events which are likely to lead to reactions and, therefore, significant disturbances in cyberspace, as well as certain types of incidents, crises or conflicts on a level of sensitivity and fragility.

What shock wave in the real realm can have an impact in cyberspace, and how is it propagated? Analyzing this relationship between two spaces (real and virtual) relies on ccTLD's which facilitate the geographical reading of the phenomenon. Identifying targeted defacements, meaning those which are directly motivated by the crisis, had relied on analyzing the claim content[56].

The following terms (and the translations into Chinese, Turkish and Uyghur) were isolated in the analyzed content: Xinjiang, Urumqi, East Turkestan, Uyghur and Rebiya Kadeer.

A search for the terms China and Turkey (as well as their derivatives and translations in Chinese, Turkish and Uyghur) made it possible to isolate defacements showing an anti-Chinese, pro-Chinese, anti-Turk or pro-Turk sentiment, without these defacements able to be linked to the Xinjiang crisis directly, as such feelings were expressed in all the periods. In this case, only one potential demonstration of exacerbated sentiments was meant to be researched.

---

56 The content could be a word or an image, for example a photograph of the WUC President, Rebiya Kadeer.

6.3.3.1. Defacements on the .cn domain

The annual graph for the defacements shows a slight increase in the number of attacks during July (+77.4% against the previous month). The monthly average for the number of recorded defacements is 1,198 sites[57].

In July, some 2,095 defacements were recorded, meaning nearly 75% more than the average. However, the week of the riots was not characterized by a spectacular growth in the attacks against the rest of the trimester, even if a slight high trend can be identified on July 6th, the second day of the riots.

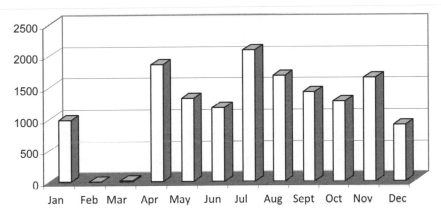

Figure 6.11. *Defacements of .cn domain sites (from 1st January to 31st December 2009)*

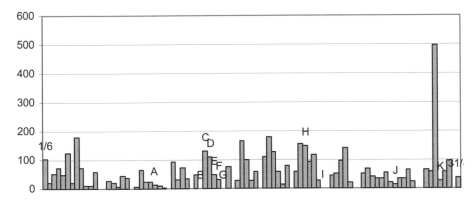

Figure 6.12. *Defacements of .cn domain sites (from June 1st to December 31st 2009)[58]*

---

57 14,387 defacements recorded in the zone-h.org base for 2009 on .cn alone.

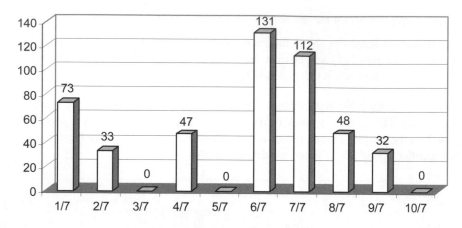

Figure 6.13. *Defacements of .cn domain sites*
(from July 1ˢᵗ to August 31ˢᵗ 2009)

The graphs for single defacement and mass defacements do not highlight a remarkable increase in the attacks, which gives us nothing to conclude in the demonstration of a wave of attacks, linked (or not) to the crisis.

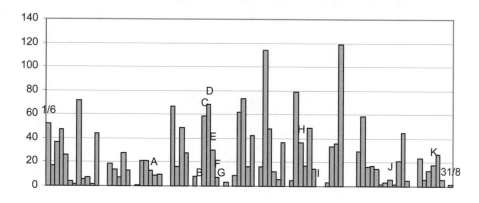

Figure 6.14. *Defacements of .cn domain sites (single attack)*
(from June 1st to 31st August 2009)

---

58 As with all the histograms, which will be presented further on, the important moments in the crisis will be identified by letters (A, B, C, D, etc.), whose meaning is shown in Table 5.1.

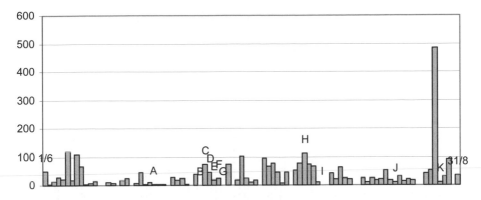

Figure 6.15. *Defacements of .cn domain sites (mass attack)*
(from June 1ˢᵗ to August 31ˢᵗ 2009)

Sites considered as important, meaning those ending in .gov, were not subjected to a series of targeted attacks during the Xinjiang crisis period, contrary to the period connected to the Tiananmen massacre anniversary (but this simple observation does not mean that we can say whether the attacks at the beginning of June were linked to Tiananmen or not, in the absence of a precise content analysis).

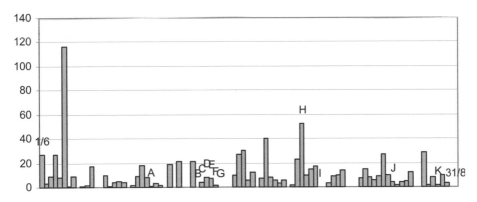

Figure 6.16. *Defacements of sites from the .gov.cn sub-set domain*
(from June 1ˢᵗ to August 31ˢᵗ 2009)

The number of signatures involved in the attacks on the .cn domain reveals the rallying up of hackers on the international stage on a given subject, on a given event.

The amount subtly increased on the second day of the riots, but globally, there is no peak/high trend allowing us to observe a particular act of mobilization, certainly no more than during the Tiananmen massacre anniversary.

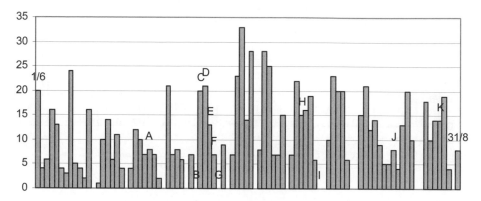

Figure 6.17. *Number of "signatures" having defaced the .cn domain sites (from June 1st to August 31st 2009)*

It seems that the hackers were no more in number, and no more effective either, during the crisis period since the average number of sites defaced by each signature had stagnated.

Amongst the mass of defacements, it was imperative to identify those which could be linked directly to the cause, meaning, to identify the "crisis effect" on the common phenomenon of defacement.

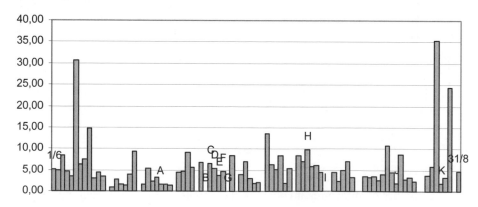

Figure 6.18. *Average number of sites defaced by signatures on .cn domain sites (from June 1st to August 31st 2009)*

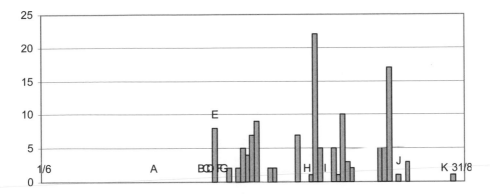

Figure 6.19. *Number of defacements with direct content from .cn domain sites (from June 1ˢᵗ to August 31ˢᵗ 2009)*

Here still, the conclusions drawn from the analysis show the appearance of defacements which were directly motivated by the crisis, but without the phenomenon seeming to have taken on any remarkable proportions. The phenomenon seems very limited to the crisis management period.

In minimal proportions, the attacks motivated by the crisis affected a few sites considered as important, because they ended in .gov. The authorities had no serious attacks.

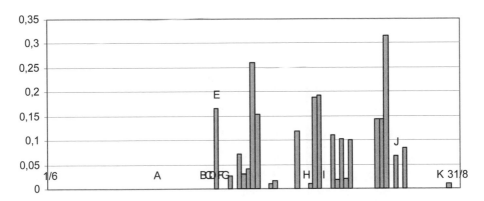

Figure 6.20. *Daily proportion of targeted attacks/total number of attacked sites for the .cn (from June 1ˢᵗ to August 31ˢᵗ 2009)*

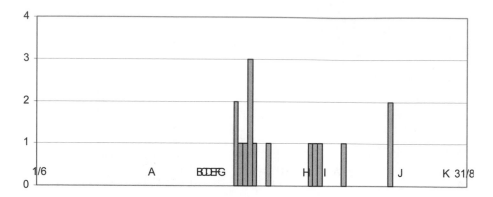

Figure 6.21. *Defacements with both direct content (targeted) and on an important site (.gov.cn) (from June 1st to August 31st 2009)*

6.3.3.2. *Defacements on .hk domains*

The same type of analysis was carried out on.hk domain sites. We may draw similar conclusions. The general curve for the defacements over 2009 shows a remarkable increase for July. The close-up on the June-August 2009 period confirms the acceleration of the activity around the riot period, and July 6th also recorded a specific peak in the studied week.

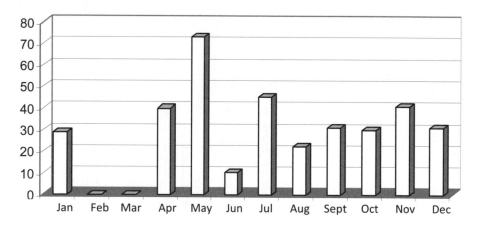

Figure 6.22. *Monthly number of defacements on .hk domain sites (2009)*

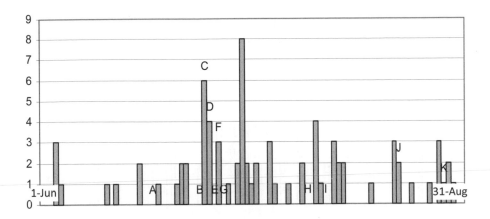

Figure 6.23. *Number of defacements on .hk domain sites*
(from June 1ˢᵗ to August 31ˢᵗ 2009)

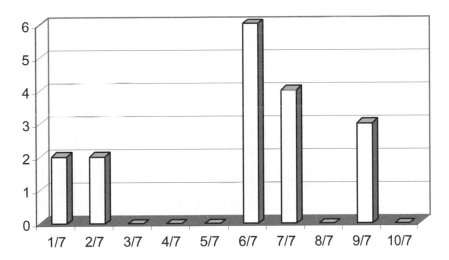

Figure 6.24. *Number of defacements on .hk domain sites*
(first ten days of July 2009)

The mobilization of the hackers is not noticeable on this domain, no more than their effectiveness which is interpreted by the average number of sites they defaced.

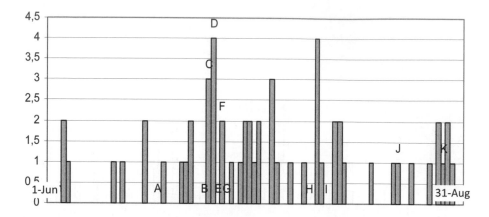

Figure 6.25. *Number of signatures which hacked .hk domain sites*
(from June 1ˢᵗ to August 31ˢᵗ 2009)

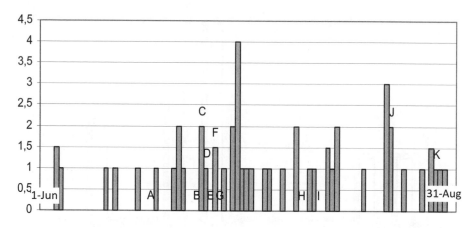

Figure 6.26. *Average number of sites defaced by signature on .hk domain sites*
(from June 1ˢᵗ to August 31st 2009)

The number of defacements which are likely to be motivated specifically by the crisis is low: there are only 2, which is distanced from the week characterized by violent incidents.

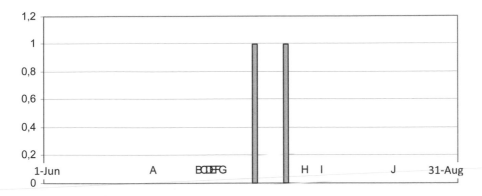

Figure 6.27. *Defacements with direct content from .hk domain sites (from June 1st to August 31st 2009)*

The defacements showing content which is indirectly linked to the crisis (meaning slogans carrying pro or anti-Chinese/Turkish messages) are also low in number, even less than those with content directly linked to the crisis.

The hacktivists did not focus their activity on the .hk domain during the crisis.

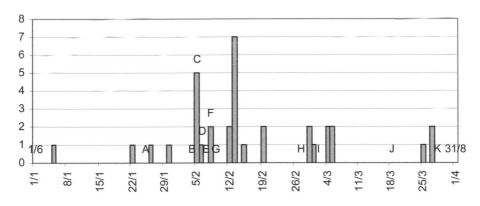

Figure 6.28. *Indirect content in defacements on .hk domain sites (from June 1st to August 31st 2009)*

6.3.3.3. Defacements on the .tw domain

We analyzed the .tw domain, not for political reasons (is Taiwan part of China?) but because it is included in what we call the Chinese world. For this reason, its servers are vulnerable to attacks in a context where the anti-Chinese sentiment can be exacerbated.

We observe a rising trend in July but particularly in August.

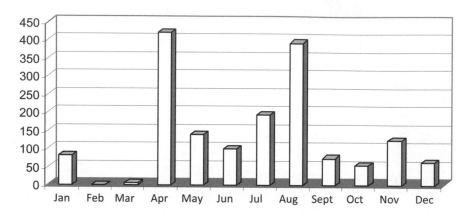

Figure 6.29. *Number of defacements on .tw domain sites (2009)*

During the riot week, the pace of the defacements only saw a slight low period if we compare it to the pace of the trimester studied. However a close-up on the riot week shows a very clear rise the day after the riots (July 6th and 7th).

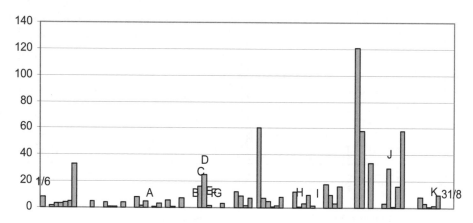

Figure 6.30. *Number of defacements on .tw domain sites*
(from June 1ˢᵗ to August 31ˢᵗ 2009)

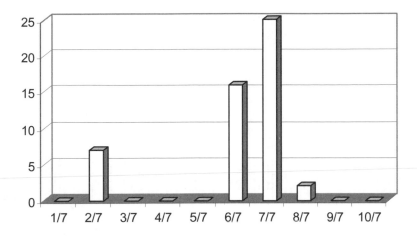

Figure 6.31. *Number of defacements on .tw domain sites*
(first ten days of July 2009)

The sites considered to be important are not targeted in particular.

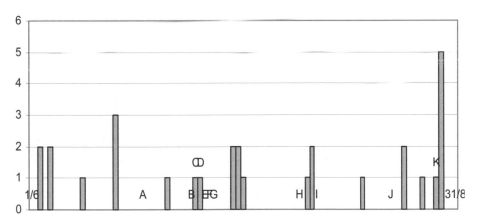

Figure 6.32. *Number of defacements on .gov.tw domain sites*
(from June 1ˢᵗ to August 31ˢᵗ 2009)

The number of signatures does not show more of a concentration of the interests in the .tw domain during this period, or an increased effectiveness at this time.

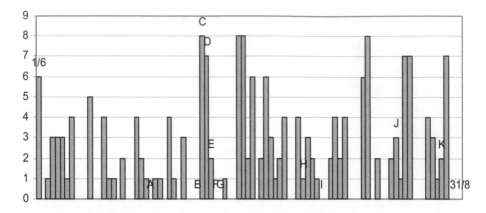

Figure 6.33. *Number of signatures which hacked .tw domain sites (from June 1ˢᵗ to August 31ˢᵗ 2009)*

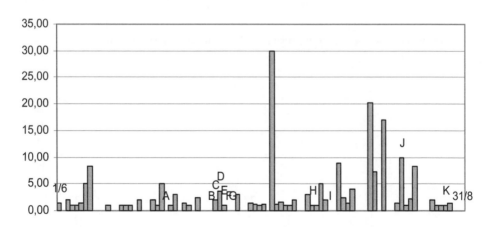

Figure 6.34. *Average number of sites hacked by signature on .tw domain sites, daily average (from June 1ˢᵗ to August 31ˢᵗ 2009)*

There are very few defacements which can be directly linked to this context, namely 12 over the period in question and far from the riot week, which does not result in any "retaliation" type behavior.

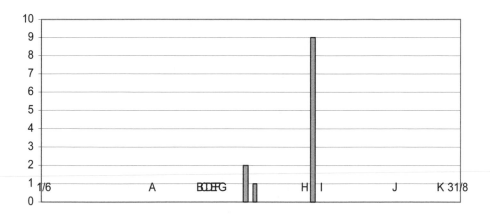

Figure 6.35. *Defacements with direct content on .tw sites (from June 1ˢᵗ to August 31ˢᵗ 2009)*

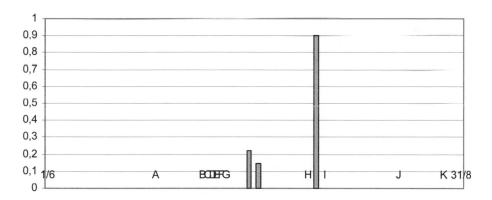

Figure 6.36. *Proportion of targeted attacks/total number of sites attacked daily (from June 1ˢᵗ to August 31ˢᵗ 2009)*

6.3.3.4. *Defacements on the .mo domain*

Investigating defacements on Macao sites did not reveal any specific trend, and this is probably due to the extremely low number of defacements generally recorded on this ccTLD.

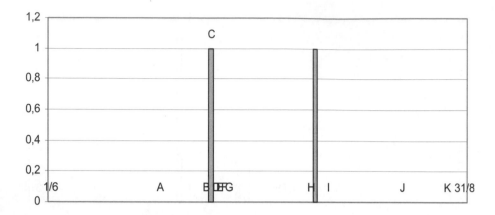

Figure 6.37. *Number of defacements on .mo domain sites*
(from June 1ˢᵗ to August 31ˢᵗ 2009)

The number of reported defacements hitting the .mo domain is still insignificant. We will simply note the defacement content:

– the first, taking place on July 6th, was signed by *1923 Turk*. The site was the victim of a massive attack. The message is pro-Turk and the signatory was identified as a cyberspace solider;

– the second, taking place on July 29ᵗʰ was signed *sexy kuala*, and the signatory was identified as a Turkish hacker: *Hack Turkyie*.

6.3.3.5. *Defacements on the .tr domain*

Turkey was directly linked to the context due to: ethnic bonds between its population and the Uyghur population in Xinjiang, authority stances, the religious community (Islam) with the Uyghurs, and the presence of Uyghur diasporas in this country. Anti-Turk hackers were able to find a ground for exercising their skills in this context, i.e. a ground which is highly portrayed in the media.

Therefore these are hackers motivated by anti-Turk, anti-Islam, anti-Uyghur or still pro-Chinese sentiments, who were likely to make their presence known in the Turkish cyberspace at this time. But these could also be pro-Turk, pro-Islam hackers. The changes in the defacements over 2009 show no specific activity for the June-August period, with no peak for the month of July. Were the .tr domain sites spared from the Xinjiang crisis?

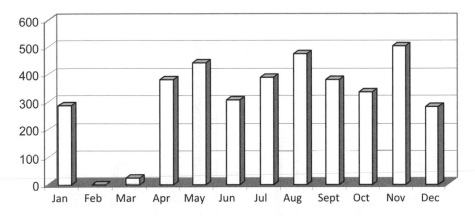

Figure 6.38. *Number of defacements on.tr*
domain sites (2009)

However, a high trend was recorded on the second day of the riots on July 6th.

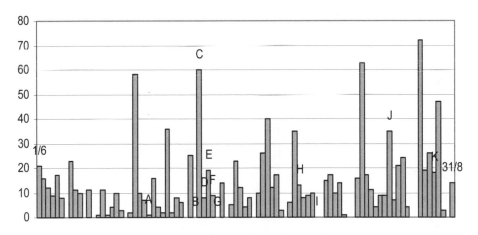

Figure 6.39. *Number of defacements of .tr domain sites*
(from June 1ˢᵗ to August 31ˢᵗ 2009)

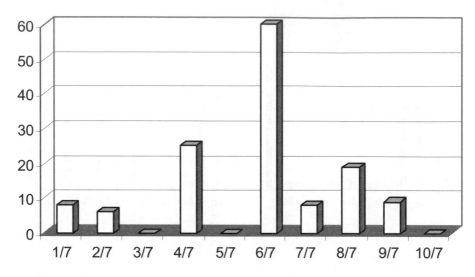

Figure 6.40. *Number of defacements of .tr domain sites (first ten days of July 2009)*

The important sites (.gov) were specifically taken as a target.

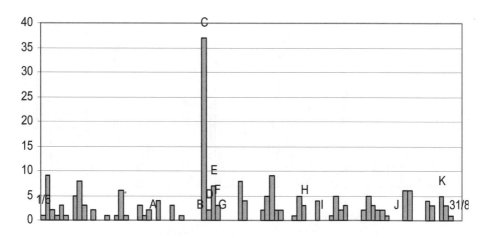

Figure 6.41. *Number of defacements of gov.tr domain sites*
(from June 1st to August 31st 2009)

However the number of signatures involved is not noticeable between July 1st to 10th, no more so than the hacker's effectiveness (ratio of the number of sites defaced by signature). It is impossible to conclude on the existence of a "confrontation", "retaliation" or "mass reaction" type movement against Turkey.

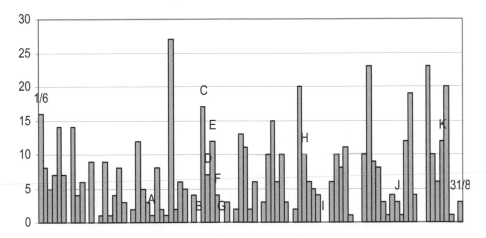

Figure 6.42. *Number of signatures which hacked .tr domain sites (from June 1ˢᵗ to August 31ˢᵗ 2009)*

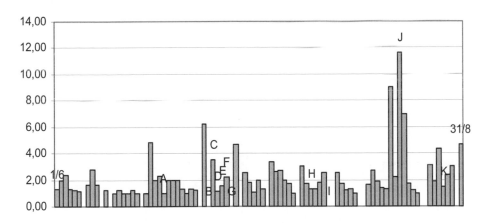

Figure 6.43. *Number of sites (daily average) defaced by hackers on .tr domain sites (from June 1ˢᵗ to August 31ˢᵗ 2009)*

As for the defacements which are directly motivated by the crisis (or taking a message linked to the crisis as a slogan, perhaps not the simple opportunism as we mentioned previously in the chapter), they are still in small quantities.

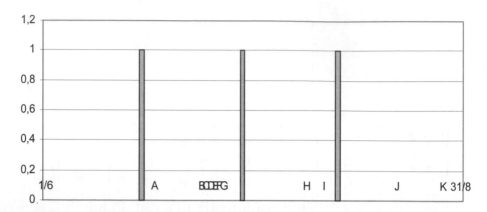

Figure 6.44. *Defacements with direct content on .tr domain sites (from June 1ˢᵗ to August 31ˢᵗ 2009)*

The defacement on July 14ᵗʰ is the only one which hit an important site with content directly linked to the crisis. The site is the following: www.milliparklar.gov.tr (site for the general management of nature and national park conservation) and was hit by the signature *Starturk*.

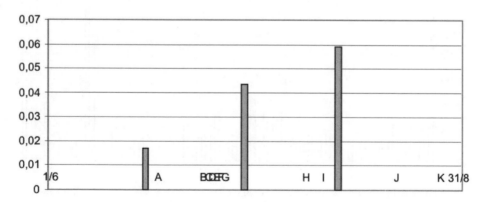

Figure 6.45. *Proportion of targeted attacks each day/total number of sites attacked each day for .tr domain sites (from June 1ˢᵗ to August 31ˢᵗ 2009)*

6.3.3.6. *Defacements on the .jp domain*

The study can be carried over to.jp (Japan) sites due to its role in the order of events: Japan welcomed Rebiya Kadeer and this was enough to receive criticism from Beijing.

The day after the Shaoguan riots, we recorded a high peak (more than 70 defacements) with no equivalent peak for the rest of the period studied (June-August 2009). A pure coincidence of dates? Due to the fact that Japan was not involved in the Shaoguan affair, there was therefore no reason for the attacks to be led as a reaction to an intervention from Japan.

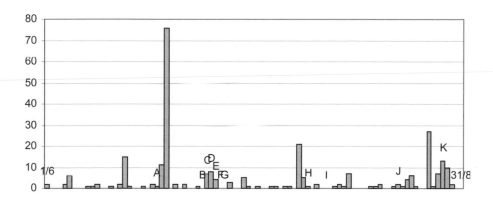

Figure 6.46. *Number of defacements of .jp domain sites*
(from June 1st to August 31st 2009)

More hackers seem to be active during the riot week. Is this still a mere coincidence of dates? Probably yes, because no defacement over this period was directly linked to the Xinjiang crisis by the content of its slogans.

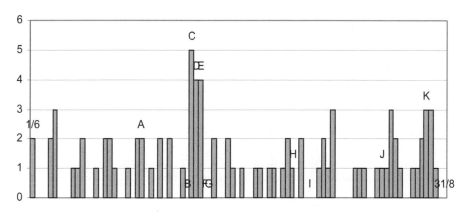

Figure 6.47. *Number of signatures on defacements of .jp domain sites*
(from June 1st to August 31st 2009)

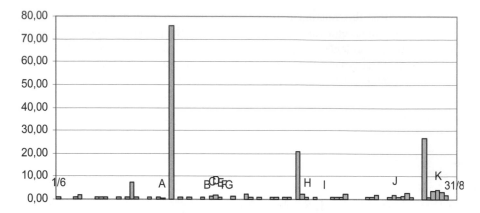

Figure 6.48. *Number of sites defaced by signature on .jp domain sites (from June 1ˢᵗ to August 31ˢᵗ 2009)*

6.3.3.7. *Defacements on the .au domain*

Australia, a country whose defacements on their Film Festival website and the consequences were highly mediatized, was not subjected to waves of massive attacks and government sites did not see a renewed intensity of their attacks. The number of hackers involved in the defacements had no noticeable increase, no more than their individual effectiveness.

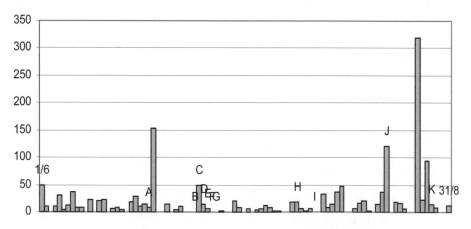

Figure 6.49. *Number of defacements on .au domain sites (from June 1ˢᵗ to August 31ˢᵗ 2009)*

One single attack seems to be linked to the Xinjiang crisis. Therefore, it seems that the Film Festival was an isolated incident, and a case coming out of a bigger mass of attacks.

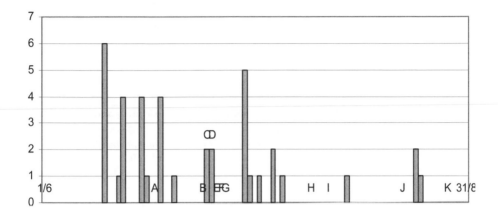

Figure 6.50. *Number of defacements on gov.au domain sites (from June 1st to August 31st 2009)*

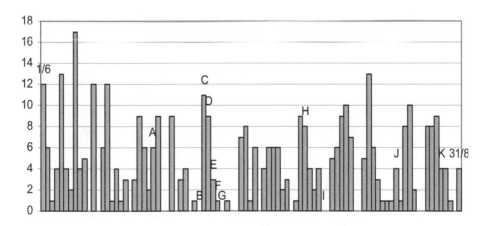

Figure 6.51. *Number of signatures on defacements of .au domain sites (from June 1st to August 31st 2009)*

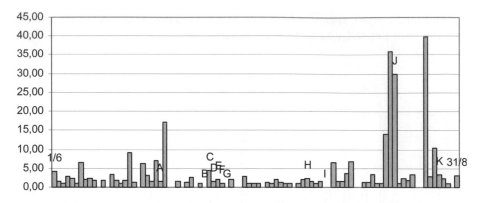

Figure 6.52. *Average number of sites defaced by hackers on .au domain sites, daily average (from June 1ˢᵗ to August 31ˢᵗ 2009)*

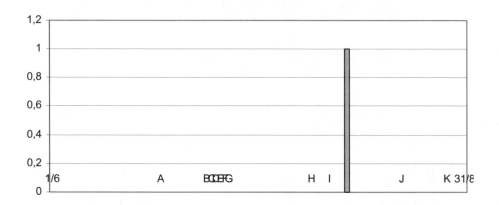

Figure 6.53. *Number of defacements with direct content on the .au (daily average from June 1ˢᵗ to August 31ˢᵗ 2009)*

6.3.3.8. *Involved hacktivists*

The attacks on the .cn sites were claimed by 311 signatures during the period studied (from June 1ˢᵗ – August 31ˢᵗ 2009). In fact, we should speak about "signatures" and not "hackers", because a signature may represent a group of individuals, distributed over several territories and working as a network.

Out of the 311 signatures, the 62 most important ones (each one totaling the highest number of defacements for the period) total nearly 90% of the defacements on the .cn domain during the trimester. 20% of the signatures have nearly all the defacements to their credit. This trend was checked on the other ccTLD's.

Signature	Prize list			Attacks		
	Total	Single defacement	Mass defacement	Sites with direct content	Important sites with direct content	Date of attack on important site
1923Turk	50,932	14,893	36,039	11		
AKINCILAR	4,868	253	4,615	67	7	July 16th (3) July 29th (1) August 5th August 15th (2)
ALFONSO	622	110	512	1		
Eraycx	157	55	102	1		
HEXB00T3R	12,332	2,574	9,758	1		
Kanuni	923	130	793	19		
LegendTeaM	1	1	0	1	1	July 14th
NATURON	396	117	279	2		
PaS_hA	12	8	4	1		
PROTEST CHINA	1	1	0	1		
Qasim	391	140	251	1	1	July 20th
RevoLLe	429	96	333	1		
Sakab	1,183	299	884	2	2	July 15th July 17th
SALDIRAY& PC_MAN	1,769	787	982	1		
Swan	11,476	4,776	6,700	11	3	July 13th (2) July 30th (1)
The_CiLqiN	1,100	181	919	8	1	July 31
	86,592	24,421	62,171	129	15	

Table 6.4. *Hacktivists attacks on .cn domain sites*

Out of this set, 16 signatures were identified as carriers of messages directly linked to the Xinjiang crisis, hardly more than 5% of the signatures involved against the .cn domain during the trimester.

We cannot speak of a "wave" of cyberattacks on Chinese sites which are directly linked to the crisis. The conclusions drawn rely solely on the data taken from the zone-h database, but it is likely that a real wave of target attacks would have been more visible if they had taken place, despite the non-exhaustivity of the reference base.

In the Tables 6.4 and 6.5 the "prize list" column shows the total number of sites defaced appearing in the hunting table for each signature, which thus means that we can consider the relative important of the source of the attack.

With regard to the content directly linked to the crisis, the .hk domain was only hit by 2 signatures.

Signature	Prize list			Attacks		
	Total	Single defacement	Mass defacement	Sites with direct content	Important sites with direct contents	Date of attack on important site
AKINCILAR	4,868	253	4,615	1	0	0
ClienCode	189	175	14	1	0	0

Table 6.5. *Hacktivists attacks on .hk domain sites*

The content directly linked to the crisis affecting .tw domain sites only involved 4 signatures.

Signature	Prize list			Attacks		
	Total	Single defacement	Mass defacement	Site with direct content	Important sites with direct content	Data of attack on important site
EL_MuHaMMeD	12,152	3,458	8,694	1	0	0
eraycx	157	55	102	1	0	0
islamordusu.org	24	4	20	1	0	0
M0µ34d	15,390	530	14,860	9	0	0

Table 6.6. *Hacktivists attacks on .tw domain sites*

On the .mo extension, only 2 signatures were recorded for this period, and without any direct content linked to the Xinjiang crisis.

Signature	Prize list			Attacks		
	Total	Single defacement	Mass defaccment	Site with direct content	Important sites with direct content	Data of attack on important site
SEXY_KUALA	126	103	23	0	0	0
1923Turk	50,977	14,902	36,075	0	0	0

Table 6.7. *Hacktivists attacks on .mo domain sites*

Signature	Prize list			Attacks		
	Total	Single defacement	Mass defacement	Site with direct content	Important sites with direct content	Date of attack on important site
The_CiLqiN	1,100	181	919	1	0	-
Ruzgarin_oglu	84	49	35	1	0	-
STARTURK	2,824	1,258	1,566	1	1	14/07/09
	4,008	1,488	2,520	3	1	

Table 6.8. *Hacktivists attacks on .tr domain sites*

Out of the attacks on the .tr extension, only 3 of them have direct content. Only 1 out of these 3 hit an important site. There has been no defacement with direct content recorded in the zone-h database. This does not mean, however, that there were no defacements.

A single direct content attack on the .au extension should be listed. The signature is *ClienCode*, a small-scale hacker since he/she only totals up 189 defacements[59].

Signature	Prize list			Attacks		
	Total	Single defacement	Mass defacement	Sites with direct content	Important sites with direct content	Date of attack on important site
ClienCode	189	175	14	1	0	0

Table 6.9. *Hacktivists attacks on .au domain sites*

	.cn	.hk	.tw	.mo	.tr	.jp	.au
Signatures	311	40	87	2	258	61	180
Defaced sites	4,960	77	684	2	1,167	281	1,595
20% of the signatures on the extension	62	8	17		51	12	36
20% of the signatures totaling n defacements (x%) on the extension	4,431 (89.3%)	38 (49.3%)	572 (83.6%)		823 (70.5%)	215 (76.5%)	1,331 (83.4%)

Table 6.10. *Statistics on signatures; a low number of actors can explain the majority of the attacks (from June 1st to August 31st 2009)*

---

59 According to data published on the zone-h.org base on January 19th 2010.

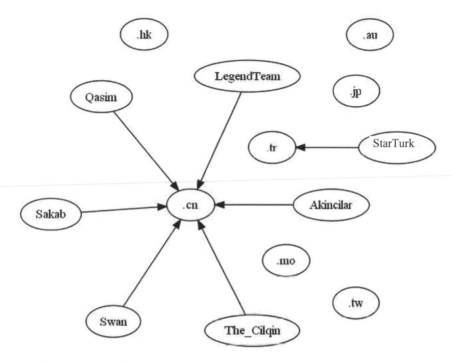

Figure 6.54. *Hacker signatures on important sites with content directly linked to the crisis (from June 1ˢᵗ to August 31ˢᵗ 2009)*

6.3.3.9. *Content of the claims*

In the following summary table we have shown the number of sites and important sites which were defaced by content directly linked to the crisis.

From this analysis we can see that:

– the .cn domain recorded the most defacements (4,962). It is followed by the .au extension (1,594), then .tr (1,172), .tw (685), .jp (281), .hk (77) and finally .mo (2);

– in absolute values, the content linked directly to the crisis firstly hit the .cn domain (129), then .tw (12) followed by .tr (3), and .hk (2). The other ccTLD's were not hit by targeted attacked on the theme of the Xinjiang crisis;

– in frequency, the most hit ccTLD's by directly related content to the crisis are .cn (0.025), .hk (0.025), .tw (0.017), .tr (0.0025) and finally .au (0.0006) .mo and .jp are worth 0.

Content	.cn	.hk	.tw	.mo	.tr	.jp	.au
Direct content (linked to Xinjiang events)	129 (4,962)	2 (77)	12 (685)	0,(2)	3 (1,172)	0 (281)	1 (1,594)
Frequency	0.025	0.025	0.017	0	0.0025	0	0.0006
Direct content attacks on important sites	15 (4,962)	0 (77)	0 (685)	0 (2)	1 (1,172)	0 (281)	0 (1,594)
Frequency	0.003	0	0	0	0.0008	0	0
Share of important sites out of the number of direct content attacks	15 (129)	0 (2)	0 (12)	0	1 (3)	0	0 (1)
Frequency	0.116	0	0	0	0.33	0	0

Table 6.11. *Summary of defacement content (January 1st to December 31st 2009). Shows the share of content directly linked or potentially linked to the Xinjiang crisis out of all the attacks*

The content of the slogans displayed on these defaced pages vary. Here are few examples:

– claims for identity, political claims: "for East Turkestan" (signed Kanuni, Turkish hacker, attacking a .cn site), "attack until you are free" (signed Sakab, attacking a .cn site, claiming to be a hacker from Saudi Arabia), "Damn China, Free Urumqi" (signed Pas_ha, attacking a .cn site);

– insults, provocations, claims, accusations: "Fuck off from East Turkestan lans, long life to Independent Uyghuristan... This map indicates the stolen lands of Uyghurs, Tibetians and Mongolians who are systematically being oppressed and massacred by terrorist China" (signed 1923Turk.biz, attacking a .cn site). The defense of more global causes takes over the Uyghur cause and assimilates it to the same cause as for the Palestinians, and Muslims all over the world: "For Liban & Palestine & Iraq & Sudan...Uyghurs...Gaza...Iraq..." (signed M0£g34d on a .hk site);

– accusations of crime, genocide, in the tradition of the Turkish government's claims: "Terrorist China commits a new genocide in Sincan" (signed Palyo34 and 1923 Turk-Grup, attacking a .cn site), "fuck you killer China" (signed *Protest China*, a Turkish hacker attacking a .cn site), "murderer China we will not forget" (signed Saldiray, who even left, like many hackers, their email address teamturk@turk.tc);

– support: "Long Life to Rabiya Kadeer" (signed 1923Turk.biz, a Turkish hacker attacking a .cn site), "we are here for Uyghur support" (*ClienCode*, attack on a .hk site);

– threats: "fuck China do not kill muslims stop war you will pay the price" (signed *Sakab*, attacking a .cn site, claiming to be a hacker from Saudi Arabia).

6.4. Managing the "cyberspace" risk by the Chinese authorities

Crisis management, from the police, or from the military or political approach, for the quickest possible return to order very early on led to a series of operations in cyberspace, a dimension which is now impossible to ignore in crises and conflicts. Even if the Uyghur problem is a lot less portrayed in the media on an international scale than the Tibetan problem, it still remains as one of the major worries in the Chinese regime.

For instance, let us take the behavior of President Hu Jintao who chose to return to Beijing as matter of urgency in order to take this crisis into hand as an example. In such conditions, making the official voice heard, spreading official information, turned out to be vital. The authorities therefore put all the methods at their disposal into action, allowing them to better occupy the information space.

6.4.1. *Inaccessible sites*

In the 24 hours following the start of the Xinjiang riots, the authorities decided to block access to the Internet, cut off international communications and SMS's, as was confirmed by Yang Maofa, Director of the regional telecommunication administration [CUI 09]. These decisions were subjected to government decrees. These measures to block the Internet came at the same time as the ground actions led by the PAP forces[60].

---

60 *People's Armed Police*, paramilitary police structure which is in change of internal security, border security and since the law passed in August 2009, has the power of intervention during riots, terrorism matters, and other urgent situations. The PAP is different from the police forces, as it can be called to order by Beijing and not the regional government.

The restrictions on the Internet were preceded by other events. During the Shishou riots from the 19th to 21st June 2009, during which the population protested against the corruption of the city's authorities who tried to cover up an assassination as a suicide[61], the Internet had been cut off in order to neutralize the protester's activity and their means of organization using tools like Twitter. The site had already been blocked several times over the previous months, the night before the 20th anniversary of the Tiananmen protests (4th June 2009) [FOS 09], for instance. On this occasion, other sites bore the cost of the cuts: Flickr (image sharing site), Hotmail (email service), MSNSpaces, YouTube, Blogger and Typepad platforms[62], or even Bing.com, Microsoft's new search engine. The measures to control and restrict had already been applied in a coordinated fashion from 5pm onwards on June 2nd 2009 [FOS 09].

The blocking process seemed well under way. As soon as the Xinjiang riots began, many sites could not be accessed from other large Chinese cities or from abroad: press sites such as the *Xinjiang Daily*[63], *Xinjiang Metropolis Daily*[64], the *Xinjiang Legal Daily*[65], the *Morning Post*[66], and information gateways such as iYaxin[67], Tianshan[68], the *Xinjiang Television Station*[69], which is the region's main television channel, the *Urumqi People's Broadcasting Station*[70] channel, the local television channel *Urumqi UTV Station*[71], and even the government's site for the city of Urumqi[72].

When the authorities chose to cut off the internet, the objective was also to stop the enemy occupying the screen: the strategy aims to keep its control over the

---

The PAP is mainly placed under the authority of the Ministry of Defense (Central Military Commission, CMC), and some of its services also come under the service of the Ministry of Public Security. The PAP can be called upon to exert missions of external defense in situations of war, in support of the PLA. The PAP officers are dressed in olive green, and the public police officers have blue uniforms.

61 en.wikipedia.org/wiki/2009,_Shishou_riot.
62 *China's internet crackdown ahead of Tiananmen anniversary*, June 4th 2009, blogs.telegraph.co.uk/news/demotix/9953443/Chinas_internet_crackdown_ahead_of_Tianamen _anniversary/, (site consutled on January 16th 2010).
63 www.xjdaily.com/.
64 www.epaper.xjts.cn/.
65 www.xjfzb.com/xjfzbindex.asp.
66 www.epaper.168cb.com/.
67 www.iyaxin.com/.
68 www.tianshannet.com/.
69 www.xjtvs.com.cn/.
70 www.ucatv.com.cn.
71 www.utv.soxj.com.
72 www.urumqi.gov.cn.

visible[73]. "When the representation of violence is managed with as much care as the very violence itself, then the conflict involves controlling the flow of images[74]", and therefore controlling the vectors of these images.

From August onwards, internet users in Xinjiang could access approximately 100 regional gateways (banks, regional administration services). During the blackout months, some sites and services were operational, but others were not. Visibly, internet users from the region themselves found it hard to know what could go in and what could come out. Internet users living in Xinjiang were able to maintain blogs, which demonstrates that the blackout was not a *total* blackout[75]. It seems that the only truly blocked sites were those hosted outside the Xinjiang province[76]: only the local government sites were visible – sites from Beijing and Shanghai, national information sites such as CCTV and foreign media were inaccessible, and auction site Taobao (equivalent to eBay) could only be used on a regional scale.

On December 29th 2009 [CUI 09], internet users in the region of Xinjiang had access to two new sites: xinhuanet.com and people.com.cn. This gradual re-opening marked a return to a certain sense of normality, at any rate, the end of a period where some were living as though in a "return to the stone age[77]". But the renewal of the Internet announced at the end of December was only partial and progressive, since users of xinhuanet.com and people.com.cn were limited, with the Xinjiang users not actually able to leave comments, or to access the site's forums. This decision to re-open the Internet gradually was formed by the regional government, and then approved by the central government. Regulating the Internet clearly comes under the responsibility of national authorities. The choice to re-establish Internet access only came about when the region's situation was said to have improved and was more stabilized. Some users were able to over turn restrictive measures by going to other cities (to Dunhuang, for instance, the neighboring province to Gansu),

---

73 *Quand l'ennemi occupe l'écran. La Maîtrise du visible* is the title of the first section of the book (When the enemy takes over the screen. Controlling the visible)[HUY 02].
74 [HUY 02], p. 17.
75 *The Truth about Xinjiang's Internet Situation*, December 7th 2009. "How much information is really getting into and out of Xinjiang? Is the internet completely cut or just partially? If so, how am I updating this blog while still living in Xinjiang?" www.farwestchina.com/2009/12/truth-about-xinjiangs-internet.html (site consulted on January 15th 2010). The writer of these posts is presented as a 26 year old American living in Xinjiang with his wife for 3 years.
76 Idem.
77 Idem: "Today marks five long months since communication was severely cut here in the province of Xinjiang. With the exception of two short trips outside the province during this time, my wife and I have had to sit here and endure a frustrating feeling that we are now living in the stone ages".

to find Internet access. When we know the major role played by information systems in our modern society, then taking away a society's connection is like denying it the ability to hear, speak, trade...the society is silenced and punished.

Besides the information from the press or blogs, it is interesting to visualize the impact of such measures to block the Internet on a graph. The information available on the site for the American project "Herdict"[78], which lists the claims of inaccessibility to sites world-wide, makes it possible to analyze the trends of incidents or censoring country by country. We will look at two sites here: YouTube and Twitter. The analysis of claims of inaccessibility from China with regard to YouTube highlights an important peak in March 2009, which is probably related to the Tibet crisis. The authorities took measures to restrict access to YouTube in this anniversary period.

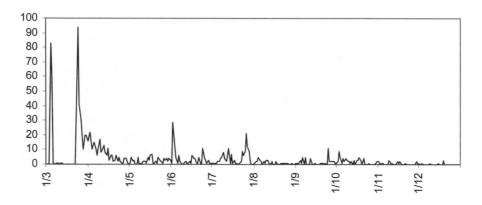

Figure 6.55. *Changes in claims of inaccessibility to YouTube in China. Using data taken from the Herdict base (March 1ˢᵗ to December 31ˢᵗ 2009, no data before March 1ˢᵗ)*

But comparatively, very few declarations of inaccessibility were recorded in China during the Xinjiang riots. A close-up on the June-August 2009 period, however, shows an initial rise at the beginning of June which coincides with the 20ᵗʰ anniversary of the Tiananmen massacres, followed by an increase during the Shaoguan incidents, and also during the Xinjiang riot week.

78 Herdict is a project from the *Berkamn Center for Internet & Society*, from Harvard University [www.herdict.org/web/]. This project suggests listing inaccessible sites in the world, with the information provided by internet users themselves. The database offers a search per country and the data is classified in chronological order. The internet users who run into difficulties with accessing sites are asked to feed the database. The objective is to try to chart different phenomena and to understand what is happening when sites are inaccessible.

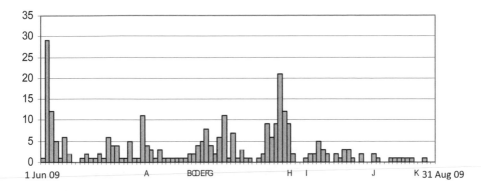

Figure 6.56. *Changes in claims of inaccessibility to YouTube in China.*
Using data from the Herdict base (June 1ˢᵗ to August 31ˢᵗ 2009)

The histogram showing the inaccessibility to Twitter in China shows two important rises: one coincides with the 20th Tiananmen anniversary, and the second which is even more important, coincides with the Xinjiang riots. Once again we will note, as was the case for the statistics taken from Google Trends and Alexa.com, that the phenomena are precise, and not followed by serious effects in the short, medium and long term. The close up on the June-August 2009 period confirms this trend.

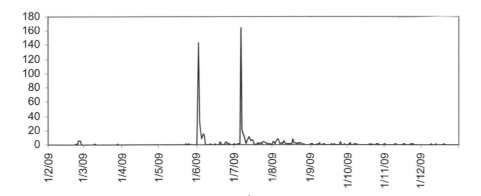

Figure 6.57. *Changes in the claims of inaccessibility to Twitter in China. Using data taken*
from the Herdict base (February 1ˢᵗ to December 31ˢᵗ 2009)

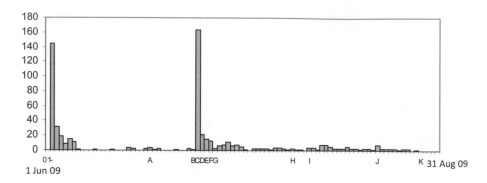

Figure 6.58. *Changes in the claims of inaccessibility to Twitter in China.*
Using data taken from the Herdict base (February 1ˢᵗ to December 31ˢᵗ 2009)

The statistics based on internet users' claim must, of course, be used carefully. Are these claims checked by the heads at Herdict? Are the internet users more inclined to state certain phenomena in a time of crisis? The graphs presented here seem to demonstrate that actions are operated on sites during important events.

6.4.2. *Cutting off telephone communications*

As with Internet access, international telephone communications and SMS messaging were cut off in the region in the 24 hours after the riots started. The Chinese cell phone provider *China Mobile* suspended its services in the region, to help with a return to peace and to prevent the incident spreading out of control. *China Unicom* did not interrupt its services in Xinjiang.

Users tried to overcome the difficulties caused by the blackout: with calls direct to Xinjiang from abroad being impossible, they were initially forwarded on to contacts in China, which transferred them to Xinjiang. But this method was quickly rendered ineffectual by further measures taken by the authorities.

The blackout carried on for several months; as long as the blackout on the Internet. When the authorities announced the gradual re-establishment of Internet access at the end of December 2009, there was no schedule given with regard to re-opening international telephone lines, or SMS's.

6.4.3. *The risks of cyberspace*

There were several opposing forces in these events: populations, authorities (national and regional government, police forces, army, the law), pro-Uyghur, anti-Uyghur, pro-Han, anti-Han, pro-Muslim, anti-Muslim parties, etc.

Each group, on its own level, was able to find a suitable, or threatening, tool in cyberspace. The Chinese authorities, which used information space and cyberspace as an instrument of power, opted for a radical cut of some communication channels which were likely to slip out of their control, to the benefit of those which could be controlled.

The blackout, which paralyzed Internet communications and telephone services at the same time, officially sought several objectives:

– to isolate insurgent rebels, denying them any possibility to communicate with other groups, either inside or outside of China;

– to prevent the blaze from continuing to burn, stopping the voices encouraging the riots from being heard;

– limit the violence from spreading as much as possible, preventing the revolt from rooting even further and from spreading outside the main cities which were already hit, spreading like wild fire outside the region;

– prohibiting all kinds of information from being spread (real, fake, twisted), coming from those observing the situation, witnesses, rebels themselves or their partisans, who favored the game of violence.

Censoring is a proven method in China, but the results are often temporary. During the first half of the 1980s "with the censor which fell onto Xinjiang (…) the situation seemed to calm down until the agitation started again, this time in the universities" [KUM 98].

There is a high temptation to censor the Internet, because this space presents many risks for the authorities. Firstly, it represents the vector for rumors, which could destabilize society.

Ilham Tohti, Professor of Economy at the University of Minzu in Beijing and of Uyghur race, was arrested[79] for criticizing the Xinjiang government, because his

---

79 en.wikipedia.org/wiki/Ilham_Tohti.

website *Uyghur Online*[80], was one of the channels for separatist discourse and had helped to organize riots by spreading rumors[81].

It is also via the Internet that the fake information regarding the attack on a Chinese female worker by other Uyghur workers was spread[82], in Shaoguan. Yet, "starting a rumor on the Internet is like throwing a bottle into the ocean: very symbolic, but not very useful"; "rumors do not blossom on the Internet randomly. On the one hand, they are deeply rooted in a folklore which has been analyzed by ethnologists for a long time. On the other, they use networks, any networks, to spread them. Thus, we must protect ourselves from isolating the electronic support of other media formats" [FRO 02].

Can we still presume that a simple post, several even, published on some sites or forums, were able to trigger off waves of violence such as in Shaoguan? This seems unlikely. In fact, how many workers were literate, how many were even *connected*? There were certainly other channels for spreading information; the rumors on the Internet were just a part of the bigger puzzle. The Internet and its numerous applications (Twitter, YouTube etc.) and cells phones are carriers of information, misinformation and rumors. Rumors could become a useful for social destabilization. Furthermore, let us use the example of the rumor which was started in the city of Kaifeng, in the Henan province, posted on the Tianya site on July 10th 2009, according to which radioactive leaks were spreading across the city. This was started by the local media which the authorities had to deny during a press conference on July 12th.

This rumor stemmed from a real incident, but which was not as serious as the one posted on the site. On July 17th, new posts were published confirming that a highly radioactive product would explode at 4pm in the city of Kaifeng. Gripped with panic, the population prepared to leave the city to destinations more than 20 km away as the information on the Internet had indicated. Those who were not convinced by the rumor were, perhaps, then convinced by the population's movement [SHE 09]. This rumor[83], once more, restricted the authorities from organizing themselves and adopting reactive behavior.

---

80 www.uyghuronline.com/ (site consulted on January 10th 2010).
81 *Outspoken Economist Presumed Held*, 8th July 2009, www.rfa.org/english/news/uyghur/ Tohti-07082009151608.html.
82 *Rumor-mongers express remorse over fabrications about factory brawl*, July 10th 2009, www.newsgd.com/news/guangdong1/content/2009-07/10/content_5352496.htm, (article consulted on January 15th 2010).
83 See the following works on the subject of rumors from psychologist [FRO 02a] and [ALL 47].

The *People's Daily* accused the USA of using the Internet for spreading rumors and leading operations of information warfare in this vein, in countries where they wanted to intervene, such as Iran during the 2009 elections[84].

The Internet is also a potential channel of misinformation. The use of images and videos taken out of their original context, either because no one took the time to check and validate the sources, or because the manipulation was intentional, looks to demonize an enemy through any means, and to attract sympathy towards the victims, etc.

The objective sought by the Uyghurs (and those in support) when they use images taken from the original context may be to attract sympathy for their cause, but also (China's interpretation) to create a feeling of animosity and repulsion amongst the Chinese against the West which is always held responsible, indirectly, for the Xinjiang massacres. In fact, the riots were the direct consequence of the American intervention in Afghanistan, with the West's intervention in the region only leading to disruptions in China [CHA 09].

A high proportion of the media used images taken out of context. A photo taken during the Shishou riots[85] (in 2009), initially published on June 27th by the *Southern Metropolis Weekly*, was used by Reuters, the *Daily Telegraph* and the WUC[86] to denounce police violence in Urumqi.

On July 28th, an internet user who was presumed to be an important member of the WUC was accused of broadcasting a video called *Uyghur woman beaten to death*, but which was actually a CNN video filmed in Mosul in Iraq on April 7th 2007[87]. The WUC broadcast a photo of violent incidents in Urumqi on its website[88], from the AFP and which only showed a simple car accident. Reuters showed the image of a seriously mutilated body but did not take the time to check the source and had to withdraw the image[89]. But once the images had been broadcast, they were scattered across the Internet, their creators having lost control over them, and they could be used for any causes and any arguments.

---

84 *China Paper Slams US for Cyber Role in Iran Unrest*, January 24th 2010, www.newsdaily.com/stories/tre60n0v3-us-china-us-internet/.

85 en.wikipedia.org/wiki/2009_Shishou.

86 See the video from CCTV9 on YouTube www.youtube.com/watch?v=ab8Vqns6uYk (video consulted on January 11th 2010).

87 *Rumormongers of Urumqi Riots Arrested*, April 6th 2009, www.chinadaily.com.cn/china/ 2009 xinjiangriot/ 2009-08/06/content_8536276.htm.

88 www.youtube.com/watch?v=ab8Vqns6uYk.

89 [BLA 09].

The Internet is now seen, in the age of Web 2.0, as a tool for organizing protests, riots and revolts. Authorities confirm that the riots were organized and led from abroad, using the Internet in particular as a channel for communication. "The *World Uyghur Congress* caused the disruptions by using the Internet in between other methods, calling upon those living outside the law to be brave and do something big[90]".

Twitter is in the authorities' line of vision because it is perceived as a revolution enabler (capabilities to enable exchanges in real time, rally up crowds), or even a tool for interfering in the internal affairs of countries, or a diplomacy tool by networks.

The Twitter phenomenon has won over the world, and questions have even affected the Pentagon[91].

But if the questions are winning over the US world of defense and security, it is also because (as the statistics show) some of these applications are essentially used in the USA. Figures published by the Sysomos organization[92] in January 2010 shows that American users made up 51% of the world's Twitter users (and 56% of all "Tweets"), followed by the Brazilians (8%), and France coming in at 13th place with just 1%. The evidence shows that there is a particular concentration of this application on the American continent. China is not in the top 20 (report[93] published in January 2010), but it was 17th in the report published in June 2009[94] with 0.49% of the world's Twitter users. Would such a low concentration of those using this tool allow us to describe it as a tool for facilitating mass mobilization in China?

According to the *New York Times*, Chinese experts studied the "colored revolutions" and maintained that the Internet and mobile telecommunication tools were allowing demonstrators to get organized and hit the world [WIN 09]. Chinese experts also kept the methods used by governments to counter such uses.

Finally, the Internet is a tool of expression which is not exempt from danger. The internet user is an improvised citizen/journalist, citizen/reporter. It is no longer just a tool for displaying our private lives, our ideas, but to account for events. This

---

90 *Civilians, Officer Killed in Urumqi Unrest,* July 6th 2009, "The World Uyghur Congress has recently been instigating an unrest *via* the Internet among other means, calling on the outlaws to be braver" and "to do something big", www.chinadaily.cn/china/2009-07/06/content_8379985.htm.
91 tech.yahoo.com/news/ap/20090810/ap_on_hi_te/us_pentagon_twitter_tracking.
92 www.sysomos.com/.
93 *Exploring the use of Twitter around the world*, January 2010, www.sysomos.com/insidetwitter/geography.
94 *Inside Twitter*, www.sysomos.com/docs/Inside-Twitter-BySysomos.pdf, report, June 2009.

information broadcasting process is slipping out of the authorities' control. The information which is published on certain Chinese sites is immediately copied by internet users somewhere else in the world, in order to "preserve" [DOR 09] the content. Of course, there are videos posted on YouTube. There are foreign sites like [drop.io/urumqi] which collect all the information and documents regarding incidents. It is a matter of "saving" the documents which are presented as proof.

The means of communication were cut off. The content[95] on blog and searches in search engines were filtered (a search for keywords such as "Urumqi" or "Xinjiang" sent back no results on Fanfou.com, but this censoring was not specifically linked to the Xinjiang crisis. We know that this type of filtering on terms judged as "sensitive" has been practiced for a long time in China[96]". Comments posted by Internet users were replaced with a terse "there are no comments at this time" or "this posting does not exist" [BLA 09]. The authorities also attempted to prevent photos of injured, mutilated bodies being published. These measures were rapidly over turned: photos, videos and comments were spread through China and across the whole world, particular via foreign sites, over which the Chinese authorities had no power at all.

Anti-censoring is opposed to censoring. The Web 2.0 tools authorize the spreading of ideas, communication, allow actors to express themselves, direct witnesses or simple opinion relays[97]. The websites hosted abroad are natural relays of these opinions. The Eastturkestan.net[98] site plays this card of denouncing the violence and oppression of the Chinese invader, the demonization of the occupier and images in support of this until the end (showing victims, blood, tears, and Uyghur victims). This method reminds us, for instance, of the methods used on Chechen websites denouncing the violence of the Russian occupation, and those methods used on pro-Palestinian sites denouncing violence in Israel.

In China, despite content filtering, dissenting voices could be heard on the web[99]: calls to punish Uyghur protesters[100], accusations of separatism, calls for

---

95 The censoring is called "harmonization".
96 Particularly aiming to prevent the spread of inter-ethnic resentment and to avoid subjects regarding government politics on China's minorities.
97 *Chine: Twitter et Youtube, médias anticensure face aux violences du Xinjiang*, July 6th 2009; www.net-stream.fr/Net/Acteurs-du-Net/Chine-Twitter-et-YouTube-medias-anticensure -face-aux-violences-du-Xinjiang_21_201__70960.html.
98 www.eastturkestan.net.
99 *Chinese Go Online to Vent Ire at Xinjiang Unrest*, July 7th 2009, www.reuters.com/ article/technologyNews/idUSTRE5651K420090707?sp=true.
100 Anonymous post on blog: www.sina.com.cn.

vengeance[101], internet user's interrogations, surprised that the police had let the riots reach such an extreme level[102], etc. Bloggers called upon the mindset of Wang Zhen, a Chinese general who, in 1949, planted seeds of terror within the Uyghur community when he led communist troops into repression in the Xinjiang region, to take it into the New People's Republic of China.

The Xinjiang riots are not the first incidents to be offered to citizen-reporters for observation. During the violent protests in Weng'an, Zhou Shuguang, a Chinese citizen as a self-proclaimed journalist and identified in the Chinese blogosphere under the username *Zola*[103], carried out a personal survey, interviewed the family of the young dead teenage girl, and broadcast reports on MSN, QQ, Twitter and on his personal page.

During the Weng'an incidents, internet users were able to support the protesters by using platforms such as Tianya.cn, Kdnet, Strong Nation, Sina.com, Netese, QQ, which offer chat rooms for bloggers. The official medium *Xinhua* even offered a space for internet users to express themselves, their anger, and their support for the protestors. This chat room recorded 200,000 connections on the day of June 29th and 2,000 comments[104]. These spaces are no less controlled, and some are censored by active mediators which delete the posts as they arrive.

Seen from outside China, such initiatives taken by citizens provide the opportunity of a different vision to the one offered by the official media. But the fact that the information comes from the citizens themselves does not mean that there is any more truth in it. This does not mean either that it is forced to contradict the official version in order to reflect on the events.

To what extent are the videos published on the Internet the work of simple citizen reporters? They do not have entire control over the use of blogs, chat rooms and others such as YouTube or Twitter. The Chinese government therefore paid to have one-by-one "censors" (the "50-cent-ers" because they were paid 50 cents per censored post), responsible for filtering and cutting content, but also responsible for taking part in forums, chats and spreading information in social networks[105].

---

101 "The blood debt will be repaid. Han compatriots unite and rise up" writes Jason on www.baidu.com.
102 See blog posted by "zfc883919" on the Xinjiang gateway, www.tianya.cn.
103 zuola.com.
104 en.wikipedia.org/wiki/2008_Weng'an_riot#cite_note-12 (site consulted on January 11th 2010).
105 www.danwei.org/the_thomas_crampton_channel/chinas_50cent_twitter_censors.php.

For instance, what should we make of the origin of the videos broadcast on YouTube[106] or LiveLeak[107] at the start of September 2009, which were filmed by a hospital's surveillance systems, and show several individuals massacring a man on the floor (Uyghurs attacking a Chinese Han, it was said). Who divulged these videos? The police authorities? The hospital staff? And regarding the authorities, why did they broadcast them: for propaganda reasons? Or was it to reinforce the anti-Uyghur sentiment in the public, national or international opinion, or to strengthen China's security measures[108]?

6.4.4. *Dealing with the media and information content*

Faced with the practically inevitable permeability of information space, and faced with this impossibility of absolute control, the authorities seem to have chosen a kind of opening and have centered part of their activity on communication (information operations).

Li Wanhui, member of the Xinjiang regional government, told the BBC: "let the facts speak for themselves" [HOG 09].

The BBC article underlines the opening, in terms of communication, of the Chinese authorities who are more accustomed to tighter control. But should we really see a more open attitude to communication in the Chinese attitude?

Evidently, journalists were able to get to the ground quickly, but in the mean time telephone communications had been blocked, the Internet had been partially blocked, a journalist from al-Jazeera had pointed out that the only place in the city which had an Internet connection was the Hoi Tak hotel where the press room had been set up for the foreign media (the journalists had no other choice but to converge towards this communication point). The official version of the events was given on a local, regional, national, and international level, to some extent taking back up some of the arguments developed at the beginning of the year 2000. This was a period when the Chinese authorities launched a communication campaign in and about Xinjiang which aimed to transmit several messages: imputing disturbances in the region to attempts from other countries to not only destabilize the region, but the whole of China, and linking the Uyghur opposition to Islamist terrorism, particularly al-Qaeda. The Chinese media sent out information in the Xinjiang province which boasted ethnic harmony and the success of the Chinese

---

106 www.youtube.com/user/xjwlmq (site consulted on January 15th 2010).
107 www.liveleak.com/view?i=76b_1252064524.
108 See questions on France 24, in a post called *Video Surveillance Footage: Beaten to Death by Uighurs*, from 10/09/2009, www.observers.france24.com/en/content/20090910-video-surveillance-footage-beaten-death-uighurs-china (site consulted January 15th 2010).

political system, and also warned against three demonizing forces, namely terrorism, separatism and extremism[109]. The violent acts perpetrated by the Uyghurs were presented in the beginning as an act of terrorism caused by the WUC which was based in the USA.

The BBC article confirms that the Chinese authorities have held on to the lesson learned from the crisis management in Tibet, where foreign journalists had been denied access: the lack of information and communication, and the total blackout had conveyed a negative image, giving the impression that the powers in control wanted to hide something. This perception was, then, taken into consideration in the Xinjiang crisis management: it would be more beneficial to communicate, to say, to speak, to see, rather than to silence and deny. If China is worried about this perception, then it demonstrates that the Xinjiang crisis was not dealt with as a purely internal matter. They must show the rest of the world that the national unity has not been jeopardized due to the Xinjiang riots, the separatist movements, or an ethnic clash, and that the Han people are in fact the victims (by giving journalists the opportunity to visit injured people in hospital, we can see that the Han people make up the majority of the victims). It is also a matter of giving the rest of the world the proof that their claims on China have been taken into account: maintaining crisis management, respecting minorities, respecting human rights, respecting Muslim worship.

Other observers and commentators (such as Zhou Bing for instance, political journalist from Hong Kong [HOG 09]), observed that this opening up to communication was self-imposed and actually demonstrated the lack of control over information and the situation by the Beijing authorities. Is it, then, a question of being more aware of the impossibility to totally control information space?

The choice of opening up to the foreign press, for an all over communication but which is the only official source of communication, also makes it possible to better manage the scheduling, to tell a story that we want to be heard: "several Uyghurs felt that the media, controlled by the State, only showed one story to the national and international community" [UNP 09]. The key to the strategy consists of giving the official scoop on events, before any others (and particularly foreign media) do so.

The principle lies in the speed: if the foreign media is not heard first, then the authorities will therefore be on the defensive from the beginning. In this crisis, as with any conflict from now on, thought of belligerence and the audience[110]. The authorities are not the only ones to have attempted to occupy the field of

109 *Chinese Muslims Target of Propaganda Effort*, July 15th 2009, (article consulted on 30/12/2009), www.msnbc.msn.com/id/31927269.
110 [HUY 02], p. 46.

information, and played the card of communication. Have not some attackers willingly chosen to kill right in front of the surveillance cameras so as to "produce maximum surprise on maximum points of visibility"[111]?

6.4.5. *After the incidents: communication, reaction, control, legislation*

The government reinforced its communication in and on Xinjiang on a national and international scale. On August 27th, President Hu Jintao made an official visit to Xinjiang. On September 27th 2009, the government published a White Paper on ethnic policies, reminding of and confirming the respect for equality for all ethnic races in China: same freedoms, same rights, same duties. But faced with the appropriation of cyberspace by the opposing forces, particularly Uyghur diasporas, the Beijing authorities were forced to change their communication strategy. "It is increasingly more difficult for the government to maintain, both internally and externally, the fantasy of stability in Xinjiang" [KUM 98].

On the international front, diplomatic tensions arose from the Chinese government's reaction to countries which, like Japan, Australia or Taiwan, welcomed (or planned to do so) Rebiya Kadeer.

The authorities' management crisis also led to new measures for regulation and control being applied. Thus, on September 27th the Xinjiang authorities voted on a law (the Information Promotion Bill) which makes any separatist discourse on the Internet illegal. The access providers are asked to control their users and to inform the authorities of any violation of the law.

Let us remember, however, that the ban on using the Internet to incite a division within the country, to bring a conflict to national unity, to incite discrimination between nationalities, to spread rumors, to incite violence and terrorism, is already part of Chinese law (particularly regarding a regulation written on December 11th 1997 on computer networks, security, and Internet protection and management), and in the acts of making people aware and the restrictions which weigh heavily on the content providers who are held responsible for what is published[112]. In December 2009, new measures were also put into place, aiming to better control site content, particularly pornographic sites. These measures were presented by the foreign press as a new tool for controlling and censoring, entering into the logic of Chinese politics.

---

111 [HUY 02], p. 39.
112 *State Council Order*, no. 292, September 2000.

354 Cyberwar and Information Warfare

This idea of tightening up the control was a consequence from the events in Xinjiang in July 2009. Under a pretext of controlling pornographic content, the authorities not only aimed to reinforce control over content, but also on sites and businesses which have the right to exist on the Chinese Internet. New rules for recording and validation are being planned, which could even be applied to foreign businesses. Have the Xinjiang events led to an acceleration in the process of tightening up the law?

6.5. Chinese information warfare through the Xinjiang crisis

With China not being at war, its army has no ground for applying and validating its doctrines on information warfare. We do not possess either, in terms of quality of the observers, data which enlightens us sufficiently on the capabilities of state-governed devices and the Chinese military.

Indeed, if we consider that the waves of cyberattacks whose victims are the governments, agencies, ministries, and companies everywhere in the world come from China, then we may conclude that in the end, this country has the means to intrude information systems, that it is in the process of charting cyberspace and the potentials of each space, and that it is leading espionage operations (the latter being a convention – or usual – operation) which are not, of course, this single nation's prerogative, even if the methods are slightly too aggressive in the eyes of the victims.

The analysis of large internal crises which the authorities must face up to is, perhaps, an interesting source of information which reveals or confirms certain aspects of the modern Chinese philosophy on information warfare.

The country is committed to the informationization[113] of its armies; a vital transformation to turn them into a force in these modern times. Informationization and the development of cyberwar capabilities is even, from now one, one of the criteria for measuring the army's qualitative evolution. The objective is very clear: to be capable of winning wars led by information (information warfare) from now until the middle of the 21st Century. The real objectives are undoubtedly fixed on a shorter scale. Chinese information warfare is still the heart of computerized war[114].

The aggressive, defensive and offensive use of information and information systems which operated during this period by actors involved on both sides in the

---

113 The term *informationization* must be taken as a synonym for *cyberization*, *information* as an equivalent to *cyber*. *Information attack* means *cyberattack*, if we refer to references in [GUA 05].
114 Yuan Banggen, 1999.

crisis, authorizes us to say that we are indeed in the presence of information warfare operations. What authorizes this even further is the authorities' control over resolving the crisis, the manipulation of information space on power directives, and the implications of military actors (PAP) on the ground, those key actors of information warfare.

6.5.1. *Xinjiang, land of information warfare*

In 2005, Martin Andrew, officer of the Australian Air Army and specialist in Chinese military affairs, said that Beijing was preparing for armed insurgencies in the two regions of Tibet and Xinjiang [GER 05].

He also underlined that the region would be the first test center for Chinese information warfare: "Xinjiang is not only important as a high altitude training area. The Xinjiang Military Region, and not the Nanjing Military District, has now become the premier information warfare test center for the PLA. Secondly, it is the training area for large-scale operational level developments. Because of its isolation and varied terrain, it has become the premier training area for developing the new "informatized" warfare that the Chinese military is striving for.

China can develop its idea of information warfare in a relatively free airspace and ground environment enabling the use of offensive electronic warfare and large scale maneuvers away from prying eyes and without interfering with commercial activities. The Xinjiang military region recently saw a series of exercises in the Taklimakan Desert where it incorporated a C4I LAN into a division in an area 1,000 km long that integrated intelligence, command and control, automated artillery fire support, airspace surveillance and control and logistics resupply. Units in Xinjiang have been commended by the PLA hierarchy as leading the way in the field of C4I. This also means that if a series of insurgent incidents were to occur simultaneously in different parts of Xinjiang, security forces already have the infrastructure and means to rapidly respond to them. The Chinese have conducted an information war campaign against the Uighurs in international forums by labeling them terrorists and producing a white paper and briefings outlining their crimes against China" [AND 05].

The region also houses communication interception sites (SIGINT – signal intelligence) in several cities: in Kitai and Korla[115] (these listening stations were developed at the beginning of the 1980s, build under the CIA with equipment provided by the NSA, then jointly managed for around 10 years) [SHI 02], in Kashi,

---

115 Code names: *Saugus* and *Saucepan*.

Lop Nor, Dingyuanchen (station tuned to Russia) or even Changli (interception of satellite communications) [FAL 08].

6.5.2. *Chinese information warfare in the prism of Xinjiang management crisis approaches*

Chinese information warfare displays the following characteristics:

– technological superiority does not guarantee success in all situations; the strategy remains as the most important factor;

– cyberwar is an important action, making it possible to manage network control. This control is a major aspect in the Chinese information operations theory. Whoever has control over the network can lead preemptive actions, either in a war of propaganda, or in real confrontations[116];

– information warfare remains an essentially military concept, a power tool. The crisis management in Xinjiang was military[117], and involved the highest ranks of power;

– according to the known doctrine [GUA 06], information operations notably consist of blocking communication channels whilst guaranteeing the security of its own information flows. It is a matter of taking control over the enemy's information flows and establishing information control, a prerequisite for gaining advantage in other domains. This approach is common to the information warfare philosophies everywhere in the world;

– the military doctrine plans to damage networks in a preemptive way, to stop the enemy from collecting, processing or spreading information or accessing information necessary to support combat operations, which would allow armed forces to reach their operational objectives (deploying their troops, etc.). The method consists of making the enemy blind and mute;

– information control is also, via information operations, manipulation of the press;

– cyberwar is becoming a central theme. "For a long time now, cyberwar has stopped being a question of science fiction", "the war of the computer network age

---

116 *Nation State Cyber Strategies: Example from China and Russia*, by Timothy L. Thomas. p. 467, [NDU 09].

117 Thousands of men from the PAP (*People's Armed Police*) were deployed in the streets of the region's capital, long, armed-vehicle convoys surrounded and occupied the streets, and military helicopters flew over the city leaving pamplets asking the population to stay at home and stop fighting [FOR 09].

is becoming a basic combat style, who effects may be stronger than bullets". "The Internet will become the place of an inevitable arms race"[118].

6.5.2.1. *Speed and reactivity*

The OODA loop concept (observe, orient, decide, act) claims that victory falls to the side who gains the advantage in this chain of action. Speed has achieved top ranking in the age of information and computerization. The Chinese cannot escape from the importance of such speed. "The soldier's reaction speed has always been the most important aspect of war. Today, with the informationization of war, we must focus more on this reaction speed"[119]. "Time [...] is the showcase of war. With the informationization of war, time is more important than before, and this is especially the case when one of the enemies has the means to share information, giving him an advantage over the other"[120].

In the crisis resolution, it also involved having the advantage by controlling information (and therefore information systems), it involved guaranteeing this control quickly or rather, taking back this control because a conclusion was being established: if the riots were able to blow out of control, then it is probably due to the loss of control in information space. Superiority is supposed to process useful data first, to have it when necessary, to know how to process it, and to give it to C2.

Had Chinese security not seen the premises of the riots? The same authorities confirm that the separatists had been organized through the Internet, and confirm to have intercepted WUC communication, specifically from Rebiya Kadeer, demonstrating the implication of the diaspora in the riots. According to the mayor of Urumqi, the July 5th protest had been organized online via services such as the QQ Groups[121]. If this is really the case, then we must conclude that the communications were not intercepted early enough, or maybe not at all. Or perhaps they were intercepted but not interpreted or analyzed, or not identified as coming from those preparing for riots. Whatever the case may be, many messages traveled through cyberspace and nobody intercepted them or paid heed to them. The result is the same: the authorities were taken by surprise, the rioters acted quicker than the authorities, and they were overwhelmed in a defensive position from the beginning,

---

118 Repeated in an article published on July 14th 2009, remark from Colonel Dai Qingming, Air Army, 戴旭:中国必须警惕丧失网络战规则制定权[图] mil.eastday.com/m/20090714/u1a 4504541.html.
119 Published on January 8th 2009, www.news.xinhuanet.com/mil/2009-01/08/ content_10623910. htm, 打赢信息化条件下局部战争是军队核心任务 (consulted on January 8th 2010).
120 Published on February 5th 2009, www. news.xinhuanet.com/mil/2009-02/05/ content_ 10765624. htm, 军报：数据链作战网络将颠覆传统战争理念.
121 www.news.cctv.com/china/20090707/105812.shtml, July 7th 2009 (Video in Chinese).

358 Cyberwar and Information Warfare

in a reactive situation. These riots also signify the failure of the intelligence services to control the entire flow of information entering and leaving a country and region as big as this one.

Thus, it is a question of acting quickly, but not in an initial advantage situation. It was important to catch up lost time. Reaction and speed were the two key elements in the crisis management, combined with the control over information space.

Just a few hours. This is the time that would have been needed for information space to be involved in the regulation measures, in order to proceed to blocking the Internet, to cutting off telecommunication systems (extreme measures if any). These *few hours* meant that the authorities were relatively prepared to react to such a situation, because the communications in an entire region cannot be cut off without the Beijing authorities authorizing it.

By cutting off the enemy's communication flow, the authorities were trying to prevent interactions between the real and virtual world, or in other words, the material space and the information space. Early on in the crisis the real world could be controlled by managing the virtual space. It was not foreseeable to leave this control to the enemy. Leaving him this control would be the same as offering him a chance at success, at least providing him with new opportunities to draw out the confrontation. Cyberspace was quickly dealt with by Beijing for this reason.

The region is well equipped with interception sites, the Internet is monitored, separatist sites and actors are observed in particular, intelligence is organized, and the constantly tense region is part of a particular vigilant regime. Could the authorities have been informed and let it happen due to the inability to react, or to anticipate?

If the authorities were not, or just badly, informed, then this is demonstrated by the impossibility of controlling all the information flowing in cyberspace.

At least (and this is the last hypothesis here) the Chinese system for controlling and regulating cyberspace is not less effective, structured and coordinated than we generally imagine it to be. This could mean that the Chinese intelligence systems are not less infallible than the Western services, and that the Chinese have no more means for absolute control over cyberspace than the rest of the West. This also means that the authorities would be condemned to only being able to exert the reactive element of security in cyberspace.

6.5.2.2. *The public national opinion as a sensitive system*

We know of the importance given by governments to their public opinion. This may even be understood as being a vital infrastructure. It is possible to aim to destabilize a country by hitting its energy distribution systems, its transport systems and its communications systems, but also, of course, its ideas, its public opinions, its way of thinking and its culture.

Influence operations, whose content will be conveyed in cyberspace, are the potential threats on State stability. Social networks (Twitter, Facebook, etc.) have entered the national and international political scene.

From a Chinese point of view, there are several different criteria which define these networks today[122]. They are, for instance:

– a new arrow in the quiver (a new resource, a new weapon);

– a subversion tool;

– a powerful political tool;

– a tool for spreading rumors;

– a tool for concealment;

– used for political and cultural infiltration in a country.

They enable groups or governments to conceal their involvement via the offered anonymity.

6.5.2.3. *Cyberspace permeability: ultimate control impossible?*

Concealing information coming from outside States which harbor dissenters, members of hostile diasporas, and movements which are considered as terrorist movements by China, seems impossible to control. On the other hand, no real pressure seems to be possible against these States.

Information cannot be contained in a more long-lasting way within China's geographical/political borders, and not even within Xinjiang's borders. If networks can be temporarily cut off from the rest of the world, if the censors and police can watch and monitor, then the individuals themselves are mobile, they can travel, and imagine solutions to overcome the restrictive and controlling measures.

---

122 He we take a summary of these criteria in an article published on 9th August 2009 on the Cenews site (*Central European News in Chinese*), www.cenews.eu/?p=16453 陈虎点兵：数据链作战网络与信息化战争武器平台 (site consulted on January 11th 2010).

In their blackout mentality, the authorities seem to be asking themselves the following question: what is, then, the smallest security unit that we can consider? That which may be described as a perfect fortress, where no subversive idea can pass through, and from which no information which is prejudiced against such security can leave?

The permeability of cyberspace has made States even easier to penetrate, and this is taking into account this permeability that the States must defend their sovereignty from.

We can put forward a few conclusions and hypotheses here:

– the control over information space, of cyberspace, even in China, and even with the means to control and censor that we give it, is still inaccessible[123];

– the Chinese authorities do not really have control over information space on a national level, as they are overwhelmed by various phenomena, which questions the asymmetrical relationships between the belligerents;

– perhaps, simply, we must conclude that controlling information space is not useful in all crisis and conflict contexts? Controlling cyberspace or information space by US armed forces has not brought them a crowning victory in recent wars;

– are the ISR and CNE more directed to outside of China than inside?

– are the Chinese intelligence services sufficiently equipped to put all their efforts into detected strong signals?

– are they not strained by a growing number of defeats that they must confront head on? "A country's security conditions are becoming complex. More and more we are being confronted with threats to security, both traditional and untraditional. The strategic competitors, who are ever increasingly more intense around China, between the world's more powerful countries, and the neighboring countries which have no stable political situation, count for all the potential problems for the region's security. The separatist movements are endemic. We are being confronted with new challenges"[124];

– would the Chinese intelligence services also be the victims of a clash of interests, and would information have difficulties flowing between the services on its way to the decision-makers?

---

123 "Bloggers and other Web sources are rapidly supplanting Communist-controlled news outlets. Cyberprotests have managed to bring about an important constitutional change. And ordinary Chinese citizens can circumvent the Great Firewall and evade other forms of police observation with surprising ease" [AUG 07].
124 Published on February 6th 2009, news.xinhuanet.com/mil/2009-02/06/content 10771342.htm, 陈虎点兵：数据链作战网络与信息化战争武器平台.

– the Chinese State's sensitivity to information has been confirmed. The choice to cut off the channels of communication was extreme (cutting communication means also makes it possible to avoid disagreements of a far too thick fog of information) but it demonstrates the lack of effective counterattack, of alternative solutions. By cutting off the communication, the authorities, perhaps, pointed the finger at their own center of gravity.

6.6. Conclusion

The essential element of managing the Xinjiang crisis lies in the primacy given to perception management, whose target is cognitive processes, behavior, able to convey a genuine description of the situation [AND 09], rather than trying to present misinformation. The objective was not strictly internal. The authorities had to monitor the promotion of national objectives: defending the national unity, the sovereignty, the legitimization of repressive actions, but also to aim to affect the way in which other nations see China. Beyond these objectives, was it really in China's best interests to throw an entire region into an almost total blackout for more than 6 months? This break in communication probably hid other, deeper, problems or issues than just controlling the problem linked to the Uyghur cause. China, like other modern nations, greatly relies on information technologies for its development. Thus, how can we explain that an entire region in China was taken out of the game that two days of bloody rioting cannot justify?

It is, then, appropriate to question this choice, which is one of the major aspects of this crisis, and to form a few hypotheses on the reasons for this drawn out blackout:

– opening up cyberspace to Xinjiang represents a danger for the State, in the region or beyond it. But, what are the authorities so afraid of? Are they not in a position to manage cyberspace to their advantage?

– by forcing the movements opposed to Xinjiang to communicate via other means, they were forced to use other more material/physical means, that the authorities are capable of controlling better;

– the authorities could control information flow in cyberspace, but the cost of this control is far too high. According to the principle of asymmetry, the weak have an advantage over their relationship with the strong, since they can use means which are less costly, forcing the strong to make large investments to counter this use;

– the Chinese authorities, no more than the US or other nations, cannot completely control information flow: too much information, too quickly, and important information is becoming imperceptible, technology is a ruse, a threat for those who let themselves get caught up in it;

– with regard to the stakes that the control over cyberspace presents us with, the blackout over the region served as a test: a place to observe the population's reactions, the structures and infrastructures in a new context, a space of controlled cyberspace where the data flows unilaterally, sparingly; but also a place to observe the consequences on the economy, on the populations, on the capabilities to be resilient in a situation of social lives with reduced information. Could an unconnected society today live, grow, and continue its development?

– the theory of information warfare or information operations is based on two objectives: use, intercept, exploit, disturb, alter and destroy the enemy's information and information systems, and protecting its information and information systems from the same operations led by the enemy. But, in this setting of internal crisis, the information and information systems belong to China. It does not involve attacking information and outside systems which are identified as belonging to the enemy. The theory of information warfare and information operations had not registered the limitations of scuttling, which is possible when the enemy is within our lines. The binary theory (actions on an enemy, protecting our own camps, the two are separated by a demarcation line, were it virtual) is no longer relevant in this situation. The target is, here, in the fortress. A scuttling which, in the speed needed for the reaction, opposes the duration, an action limited in time, and which is prolonged;

– the Internet is a vulnerable weapon system. This sentiment is shared globally and explains in particular the pressure exerted by the USA who want to maintain their position of power over cyberspace. This was a pressure which was strengthened the day after the New York attacks, a period of war against terrorism and inside enemies justifying attacks on rights to private lives and exceptional regimes which, finally, materialized. The prolonged denial of communication stems from this logic: a justification through the war on terrorism, the fight against an inside enemy, attacks on essential rights which must bend to claims from superior security; a temporary measure to last and become the rule. When censoring alone is no longer enough, when cyberspace absorbs too many security forces and concentrates too many potential threats, then the information highways will be temporarily, and then forever, closed;

– the blackout in Xinjiang is perhaps not just in Beijing's interests: the region is, remember, bordering a country at war. Faced with the impossibility of managing cyberspace, the authorities have no other solution than to take measures as extreme as the blackout. But the impact of such a decision is also negative with regard to the international community which only sees the strictness of the Chinese political system, and its strategies for censoring and denying fundamental human rights (freedom of expression, communication). Is cyberspace the center of gravity for China's enemy, or actually China itself? We maintain that the nation's security would be of a far higher interest than technology, were it an essential choice.

Forming a sort of conclusion, the summarizing table below identifies a few elements of the information operations which may have been put into place during the various stages of the Xinjiang crisis.

Date	Facts	Element
25-26th June	Rumors lead to confrontations between Uyghurs and Han in the Early Light International toy factory in Shaoguan, Canton province	Opinion manipulation (Psyops, deception)
	Preparing and organizing riots (if not spontaneous) via communication tools like Twitter?	C2 Uyghur
July 6th	In the 24 hours after the riots started, telephone communication and a part of the Internet were cut off	C2 (disrupting riots, cutting off relations between leaders and troops), perception management (Psyops)
	Communication the official version of the facts, not allowing the opposing force to speak	Perception management
	Speed of the reaction (speed of the Internet blackout, of telecommunication block)	Reactive measure. Shows weaknesses in the ISR, CNE and EW which had not prevented or anticipated
	Attacks on Chinese/pro-Chinese, Turk/pro-Turk sites, etc.	Hacktivism, no proven CNA, no proven hacker war
	Across China: blog content controlled, along with websites and forums	Perception management (blocking cyberactivist messages)
	Cyberactivism through diasporas: influencing Chinese and foreign authorities, rallying for the Uyghur cause, finding an opinion relay, looking for political effects	Psyops, perception management
	Video broadcasts (riot violence)	Perception management, Pysops, misinformation, deception
	Use of images taken out of context	Psyops, deception, misinformation, perception management
July 8th	Hu Jintao who was supposed to participate in the 35th G8 summit in Italy, cuts his stay short and returns to China due to the situation in Xinjiang	C2 (re-establishing the link between the highest command and actors on the ground)
July 9th	Chinese authorities confirm proof of the WUC's implication in the riot organization: interception of Internet content and telephone messages	ISR, CNE, EW

July 13th	Turkish Embassy in Beijing's website defaced	Hacktivism, no CNA proven, no hacker war proven
July 28th	Rebiya Kadeer arrives in Japan. Chinese authorities react	Perception management
July 28th	Authorities send SMSs to the Xinjiang population, telling them not to believe in the rumors. Users cannot send SMS's	IO, Psyops, perception management
August 1st	The site for Melbourne's International Film Festival attacked: anti-Kadeer slogans and Chinese flag displayed	*Hacking*, no proven CNA, no proven hacker war
August 7th	Melbourne Film Festival site hacked	*Hacking*, no proven CNA, no proven hacker war
August 17th	Rumors circulate about needle attacks in the streets of Urumqi	Misinformation, rumors (Psyops, deception)
August 27th	Hu Jintao visits Xinjiang	Psyops, perception management
September 8th	Taiwan Film Festival organizer's blog hacked	*Hacking*, no proven CNA, no proven hacker war
September 27th	Chinese government publishes White Paper on ethnic policy which confirms that all ethnic groups are to be treated equally in China: same freedoms, same rights	Psyops, perception management
End of December	Announcement of the progressive reopening of the Internet in Xinjiang, with restrictions	Perception management

Table 6.12. *Elements of information warfare in the 2009 Xinjiang crisis. These elements were activated by various actors on the different sides of the confrontation*

6.7. Bibliography

[ALL 06] ALLES E., "Usages de la frontière: le cas du Xinjiang (XIXe – XXe centuries)", *Extrême Orient – Extrême Occident*, 28, 2006.

[ALL 47] ALLPORT G., *The Psychology of Rumor*, Henry Holt & Company, New York, USA, 1947.

[AND 05] ANDREW M., *Beijing's Growing Security Dilemma in Xinjiang*, The Jamestown Foundation, www.jamestown.org/single/?no_cache=1&tx_ttnews%5Btt_news%5D=3869, 2005.

[AND 09] ANDERSON E., ENGSTROM J.G., *China's use of Perception Management and Strategic Deception*, Science Applications International Corporation, November 2009.

[AUG 07] AUGUST O., "The great firewall: China's misguided – and futile – attempt to control what happens online", *Wired Magazine*, www.wired.com/politics/security/magazine/15-11/ff_chinafirewall, 23rd October 2007.

[BLA 09] BLANCHARD B., *China Tightens Web Screws After Xinjiang Riots*, www.itbusinessnet. com/articles/viewarticle.jsp?id=791423, 6 July 2009.

[BOR 09] BORK E., "US must help Uyghurs", *Los Angeles Times-Washington Post*, gulfnews.com/opinions/columnists/us-must-help-uighurs-1.492192, 11th July 2009.

[CAS 03] CASTETS R., "Le nationalisme ouïghour au Xinjiang: expressions identitaires et politiques d'un mal-être", Perspectives chinoises, perspectiveschinoises.revues.org/ document156.html, no. 78, 2003.

[CAS 04] CASTETS R., *Opposition politique, nationalisme et islam chez les Ouïghours du Xinjiang*, Les études du CERI, no. 110, October 2004.

[CHAO 09] CHAOFAN W., *Urumqi Riots Part of Plan to Help Al-Qaida*, www.chinadaily.com. cn/opinion/2009-07/16/content_8434355.htm, 16th July 2009.

[CUI 09] CUI J., *Net Access Being Restored in Xinjiang*, www.chinadaily.com.cn/china/2009-12/30/content_9244023.html, 30th December 2009.

[DOR 09] DORAN D., *Savvy Internet Users Defy China's Censors on Riot*, www.google.com/ hostednews/afp/article/ALeqM5jlMPMzVRIgHQFdLL_ShBYw_af3Vw., by D'Arcy, AFP, 6th July 2009.

[FAL 08] FALIGOT R., *Les services secrets chinois de Mao aux JO*, ch. 12, Nouveau Monde, Paris, France, 2008.

[FOR 09] FOREMAN W., *Chinese Troops Flood Streets After Riots*, www.breitbart.com/ article.php?id=D99AF7UG0&show_article=1, 8th July 2009.

[FOS 09] FOSTER P., *China Begins Internet "Blackout" Ahead of Tiananmen Anniversary*, www.telegraph.co.uk/news/worldnews/asia/china/5429152/China-begins-internet-blackout -ahead-of-Tiananmen-anniversary.html, 2nd June 2009.

[FRO 02] FROISSART P., "Rumeurs sur Internet", *Les Cahiers de médiologie*, no. 13, Gallimard, Paris, France, 2002.

[FRO 02a] FROISSART P., *La rumeur. Histoire et fantasmes*, Editions Belin, Paris, France, 2002.

[GER 05] GERTZ B., *China's Western Woes*, Inside the Ring, www.gertzfile.com/ gertzfile/ring081905.html, 19th August 2005.

[GUA 05] GUAGQIANG P., YOUZHI Y., *The Science of Military Strategy*, Military Science Publishing House, Beijing, China, 2005.

[HOG 09] HOGG CH., "China seeks control through openness", *BBC News*, news.bbc.co.uk/2/hi/asia-pacific/8140901.stm, Beijing, 8th July 2009.

[HOU 00] HOUQIN GW., XINGYE ZH., *The Science of Campaigns*, National Defence University Press, Beijing, China, May 2000.

[HUY 02] HUYGHE F.B., *Ecran / Ennemi. Terrorismes et guerres de l'information*, www.huyghe.fr/dyndoc_actu/424eb3aed503a.pdf, Editions 00h00, Paris, France, 2002.

[KRE 09] KREKEL B., "Capability of the People's Republic of China to conduct cyber warfare and computer network exploitation", *Northrop Grumman Corporation*, 9th October 2009.

[KUM 98] KUMUL A., "Le 'séparatisme' ouïgour au XXe siècle: histoire et actualité", cemoti.revues.org/document54.html, *Les Ouïgours au vingtième siècle, Cahiers d'Etudes sur la Méditerranée Orientale*, no. 25, 1998.

[KRA 09] KRAMER F.D., STARR S.H., WENTZ L.K., *Cyberpower and National Security, Center for Technology and National Security Policy*, National Defence University, Washington, USA, 2009.

[RAM 09] RAMAN B., *China's Largest Ever Long Range Military Exercise*, www.southasiaanalysis.org/%5Cpapers34%5Cpaper3354.html, 13th August 2009.

[RIC 07] RICE R., *Uyghur Ethnicity and Human Rights Discourse in Post 9/11 China*, vcas.wlu.edu/VRAS/2007/Rice.pdf, University of Tennessee, Knoxville, USA, 2007.

[SEY 00] SEYTOFF A., *Urumqi Explosion: Military Accident or Act of Uyghur Terrorism?* www.cacianalyst.org/?q=node/264, 27th September 2000.

[SHE 09] SHEN S.L., *Chinese Trust Rumors More than Officials*, www.upiasia.com/ Politics/2009/07/23/chinese_trust_rumors_more_than_officials/1499/, UPI Asia.com, 23rd July 2009.

[SHI 02] SHICHOR Y., *Pacifying the West: Confidence Building Measures between China and Central Asia*, University of Haifa, Israel, 2002.

[SHI 09] SHICHOR Y., *Ethno-diplomacy: the Uyghur Hitch in Sino-Turkish Relations*, www.eastwestcenter.org/fileadmin/stored/pdfs/ps053.pdf, Policy Studies 53, East-West Center, 2009.

[UHR 09] UYGHUR HUMAN RIGHTS, *Separate and Unequal: the Status of Development in East Turkestan*, report of Uyghur Human Rights Project, www.uyghurcongress.org/en/wp -content/uploads/28-09-2009-Status-of-Development.pdf, Washington, USA, 28th September 2009.

[UNP 09] UNPO, "Repression in China. Roots and repercussions of the Urumqi unrest", www.unpo.org/images/reports/repression_in_china_roots_and_repercussions_of_the_urumqi _unrest_unpo_november_2009.pdf, Unrepresented Nations and People Organization, November 2009.

[USL 09] USLU E., "Are China's Uyghurs operating an al-Qaeda network in Turkey? Ankara and Beijing Discuss Cooperation against Terrorism", *The Jamestown Foundation, Terrorism Monitor*, www.jamestown.org/single/?no_cache=1&tx_ttnews%5Btt_news%5 D=35564, vol. 7, n° 30, 1st October 2009.

[VEN 07] VENTRE D., *La guerre de l'information*, Hermès, Paris, France, 2007.

[VEN 09] VENTRE D., *Information Warfare*, ISTE Ltd, London and John Wiley & Sons, New York, 2009.

[WIN 09] WINES M., "In latest upheaval, China applies new strategies to control flow of information", *The New-York Times*, www.nytimes.com/2009/07/08/world/asia/08beijing .html?_r=2, 7th July 2009.

Chapter 7

Special Territories

7.1. Hong Kong: intermediate zone

Hong Kong is the only territory of its kind in relation to its geographical position, its political status, its culture, and its history. This territory represents the special cases of States or zones in the world which find themselves at a crossroads between two worlds, marking a boundary between cultures and civilizations. These places are the center of attention, and have become major issues. If Hong Kong is a step towards China for both businesses and also tourists, then it is also a rallying point for those against the Beijing regime, because what is forbidden in China is still often authorized or tolerated in Hong Kong. The opposition's claims can therefore be voiced there. Naturally, cyberspace will be a tool through which these tensions, crises or confrontations will be expressed.

7.1.1. *Strategic and political situation in Hong Kong*

Since 1997, the special administrative region of Hong Kong has returned to China. The principle of "one country, two systems", proposed in 1984 by Deng Xiaoping during negotiations with the UK on the retrocession of Hong Kong to China, rules the territory. Conforming to this principle, Hong Kong will be able to pursue its activities with a high level of autonomy until 2047 (50 years after

---

Chapter written by Daniel VENTRE.

retrocession to China in 1997). The principles governing Hong Kong are written into the *Basic Law*[1], the constitutional document promulgated by China in 1990.

Well before 1997, Hong Kong had already turned towards mainland China, taking advantage of their economy opening up to the rest of the world. Chinese presence in Hong Kong has been confirming itself ever since. In 2004, there were some 2000 Chinese businesses in Honk Kong [WAI 10]. The increased influx of financial transactions between China and the rest of the world via Hong Kong went alongside transactions of goods, services and people.

The "border" between Hong Kong and mainland China has become an area of strategic crossing. The territory welcomed in 223 million visitors in 2009, out of which 170 million had come in through mainland China[2]. 49,000 Chinese people from the continent had also moved into Hong Kong in the same year. The authorities favor this movement of people: an electronic border control system (*e-Channel*) has been installed at the borders between Hong Kong and mainland China in order to alleviate control procedures and to facilitate movement of the Hong Kong residents.

This movement of people bears witness to the importance given to Hong Kong by China as much as by the West, both seeking to preserve the precise character of Honk Kong. For the West, Hong Kong – both international and Chinese – is a bridge over to China, and in the same way for China, it is a gateway opening up the rest of the world.

From a political point of view, the *Basic Law* ensures the autonomy of the Hong Kong government in relation to Beijing. But the impact of Beijing can still, nonetheless, be strongly felt. The numerous political demonstrations and demands for more autonomy, and democratic elections are proof of this. There is, then, an ambiguous blend of autonomy, freedom[3] and discreet yet definite pressure coming from Beijing, which power struggles are playing in favor of. The Hong Kong population is holding on to the slogan "one country, two systems", but this principle is based on a fine balance. In February 2010, the press was moved by the story of a

---

1 This document is comprised of 9 chapters and 160 articles.

2 www.yearbook.gov.hk/2009/en/pdf/C20.pdf

3 The freedom of expression, protest, and the media. We can even say that Hong Kong is one of the best informed countries in the world, with around 700 daily newspapers and periodicals spread across the territory. Hong Kong is, from a media point of view, an international platform used as a regional base by a large proportion of headlines in the foreign press. Figures are provided by The Hong Kong Yearbook 2009, Chapter 17, www.yearbook.gov.hk/2009/en/pdf/C17.pdf. Freedom of expression can also be seen through the presence of Falun Gong in Hong Kong, punished in China. But it is not rare to see placards and other signs of protest close to train stations and in the middle of the city in Hong Kong, denouncing the violence inflicted on him in China.

Chinese dissident who had entered Hong Kong illegally using a fake passport, and who was also supposed to be trialed in Hong Kong, yet who was handed over to Chinese authorities. Brought to trial in China for a crime committed in Hong Kong, he was condemned to nearly 10 years imprisonment[4].

Conforming to *Basic Law*, Hong Kong's defense is guaranteed by the Chinese army[5] since the retrocession in 1997. The building housing the Chinese army is located in the middle of Hong Kong, in Central[6]. If the armed forces know how to be very discreet, the number of soldiers is still high: we do not know the exact amount, but the military is estimated to hold between 4,000 and 6,000 individuals from the Chinese land, marine and air army. Giving no specific figures, the Chinese army states that the number of officers based in Hong Kong is high enough to guarantee Hong Kong's security [TSA 10]. The forces are distributed according to direct command from Beijing, and administrative control from the military region of Guangzhou.

We can see that Hong Kong is clearly in a transitional phase (over 50 years), but that it is also a geographical and political middle-ground between two worlds. If it is a place of cooperation, opening up and favoring exchanges, then it is primarily a place of tension because this balance must be maintained. And so those against the Beijing regime have a privileged doorway to the mainland.

7.1.2. *Hong Kong's cyberspace*

Hong Kong has greatly benefited from both China's economic contribution from 1978 and the region's telecommunications boom, setting itself up as the telecommunication hub between China and the rest of the world. "Today, Hong Kong is a telecommunications hub in the Pacific Asia region, and a bridge towards mainland China", wrote Rita Lau, secretary for economic and commercial development in CAHK's annual report in 2009[7]. 400,000 kilometers of optic fiber was deployed in Hong Kong. With the country playing the role of a "hub", it is also a passing point for a significant number of submarine cables.

One of the advantages of Hong Kong's ICTs industries would reside in its profound knowledge of Chinese and Western cultures. This has transformed Hong Kong into an ideal bridge between mainland China and international businesses trying to extend their activity into this area of the world. A legal framework has

---

4 "A stain on "two systems" that won't go away", *South China Morning Post*, 6th February 2010.
5 *People's Liberation Army Hong Kong Garrison.*
6 *Liberation Army Forces Hong Kong Building.*
7 www.cahk.hk/Publication/OfficialGuide2009/Message/Mrs.Rita%20Lau.pdf

come into play to reinforce the position of this territory in relation to China, such as the CEPA (Closer Economic Partnership Agreement), a convention which offers Hong Kong based businesses privileged access to the mainland China market. Hong Kong, strong in this position, has become one of the most developed markets in the Asian ITC sector [LAM 07].

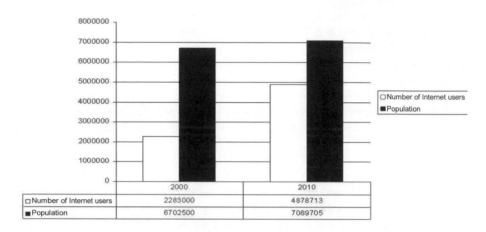

	2000	2010
□ Number of Internet users	2283000	4878713
■ Population	6702500	7089705

Figure 7.1. *Population of internet users in Hong Kong. From 2000-2010. Table generated using data from www.internetworldstats.com/asia.htm*

Honk Kong has also been able to take advantage of its highly concentrated population (the majority of some 7,000,000 inhabitants inhabiting a surface area of just 40 km^2)[8] in order to develop high-tech telecommunication infrastructures (telephones, the Internet). Hong Kong was the first city in the world to have entirely digitalized telecommunication systems. Today, 80% of homes are connected to broadband networks, and the penetration rate of cell phones has reached 170%. Wi-Fi is everywhere: in villages, mountains, buses, etc. The island has excellent telecommunications networks, particularly supporting its financial systems. In 2010, Hong Kong had a population of 7,086,705 inhabitants[9], 4,878,713 internet users[10] (a penetration rate of nearly 70%), and 3,587,080 Facebook users[11].

---

8 According to the statistics published in the *Hong Kong Yearbook 2009*, www.yearbook.gov.hk/2009/en/pdf/C20.pdf.
9 Statistics taken from www.internetworldstats.com/asia.htm.
10 February 2010.
11 August 2010.

Figure 7.2. *Antennas pointed towards communication satellites (Hong Kong, Tai Po)*

7.1.3. *A framework suited to crises*

In Hong Kong, all the ingredients needed for us to imagine scenarios of confrontation within cyberspace are brought together:

– a territory which is used as a privileged place of exchanges between two worlds, and is therefore a strategic area;

– a special political situation;

– all the actors are brought together on the same, smaller territory;

– an extremely well connected territory;

– high-tech telecommunication businesses (networks, satellites, etc.);

– high level research centers, likely to be victims of espionage operations or providing high-tech solutions in the ICT sector;

– a discreet yet present Chinese army primarily active on a strategic territory. The first Chinese Military Intelligence Bureau focuses on HUMINT (HUMan INTelligence) type operations on Hong Kong (as well as Taiwan and Macao) [DUM 10], aiming to collect technological information which could be useful for the development of the Chinese army. Besides human intelligence operations, intelligence through data collection, communication interception and signal intelligence (SIGINT) are clearly just as easy (coming under the missions from the third bureau of the Chinese army, whose communication stations are located in Shenzhen, just opposite Hong Kong)[12];

---

12 www.globalsecurity.org/intell/world/china/pla-dept_3.htm.

– generations growing with computers, hackers on Hong Kong soil;

– activists use the territory as a base to launch operations on mainland China, for instance, during precise events such as the commemoration of the Tiananmen massacre on June 4th. "Group hopes to penetrate mainland's firewall with live radio broadcast of June 4 vigil", was the title of an article published by journalist Fox Yi Hu in the Honk Kong daily *South China Morning Post*, on June 3rd 2010[13].

– a group of Hong Kong people, led by Yang Kuang[14], tried to broadcast live on the Internet, on an online radio site, the June 4th 2010 vigil organized at Victoria Park (Hong Kong). The previous year, an identical attempt by Green Radio had failed, with the operation only based on a single server that the Chinese authorities had quickly localized and blocked. But in 2010, these 40 servers were used with different IP addresses. Activists, being militants for the Hong Kong free elections, also rallied up pirate radios, which were shut down and then reopened again. The radio stations were relayed by Internet websites. Local radios were raided by the police, but the sites stayed active. Citizen's Radio was among one of these stations, with the location being moved from Mong Kok to Chai Wan (in 2009), and five activists were arrested[15];

– reasons for social protests generating actions in cyberspace by citizens: protesting against problems of housing, education, racial discrimination, public health, public freedom, expression, political rights, environment, security, etc.;

– a situation of closeness and sharing a single space which primarily creates conditions favoring information and information systems exploitation (is it not easier to steal a laptop, to carry out social engineering to get into data systems when we share the same spaces on a daily basis? Is it not easier for China to incept the data from all those communication from or to Hong Kong?

The border between Hong Kong and China is not one of these impenetrable, hermetically sealed barriers, as may be the case for some States. On the contrary, with Hong Kong having reintegrated China, the crossings have been made much easier. But for those against the system, forbidden to stay in mainland China, the border may remain as an obstacle, a challenge, an object or systems whose resistance must be put to the test.

---

13 p. A3 of the paper.

14 Who was also a memeber of Citizen's Radio and was one of the activists condemned a few months earlier in Hong Kong for having started a radio station without a license.

15 Namely Leung Kwok-Hung, Tsang Kin-Shing, Tik Chi-Yuen, Spooky Chan, Wong Chun-Kwok. Information published in the daily paper *South China Morning Post* on 12th March 2010.

7.1.4. *Hong Kong's vulnerable cyberspace*

Hong Kong's internet has been the victim of regular attacks and is, then, no different to the rest of the world in this respect.

The high increase in the number of sites hit over 2010 is particularly noticeable. The annual average over the 11 previous years is 300 defaced sites, with the first 10 months of 2010 recording 1,125 defacements, nearly four times the annual average.

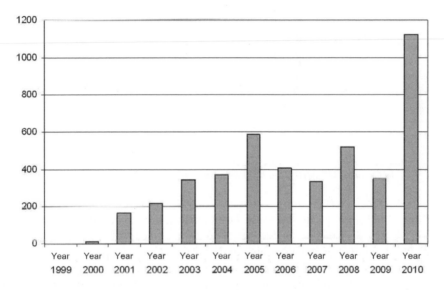

Figure 7.3. *Defacement statistics for .hk sites from January 1st 1999 to October 30th 2010, taken from data published on zone-h.org*

The statistical evolution of the first ten months of 2010 is presented in Figure 7.4.

The graph peaks have no direct or indirect relation with events linked to Hong Kong political life. The event on June 4th caused no specific events. Of course, these are only defacements listed on the zone-h site, which does not claim to be exhaustive. Other attacks not included in the defacement category perhaps occur at peak times but are not listed.

Many site defacements are listed on the site zone-h.org, but not in a significant quantity. The reason for this is either that the database is not exhaustive, or that hackers are aiming directly at China rather than Hong Kong.

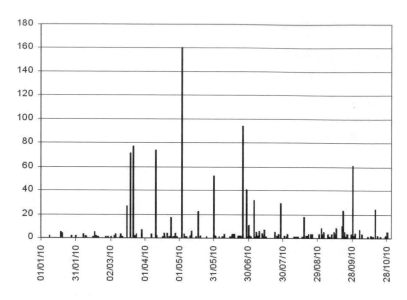

Figure 7.4. *Histogram showing defacements on .hk domain sites, from 1st January to October 31st 2010, data from from statistics published on zone-h.org*

Hong Kong, through its precise position as an interface between China and the rest of the world, could be, as Stephen Coonts imagines in his novel *Hong Kong* [COO 00], the target of attacks aiming to destabilize Chinese power. In this novel, a group of five people working in the telecommunications company *Third Planet Communications*, attacks one of the city's vital infrastructures: its electric network. The aim of this attack is to destabilize the authorities, an action which is written into a revolutionary project with the aim of taking over power in China, by bringing down the Communist government. "Revolutions are about control – which is the essence of power. We must take control away from the Communists"[16]. Attack is a given. "One of the female engineers began typing. In seconds a complex diagram appeared in the screen. Everyone watching knew what it was: the Hong Kong power grid. 'Now we will see if the people of China will be slaves or free men,' Wu said. Months of preparation had gone into this moment. If the revolutionaries could control China's electrical power grids, they had the key to the country […]. The engineer at the computer used one finger to click the mouse. The lights in the room went off [….]. The lights in Hong Kong were *off!*"[17]. In this story we find the conventional figure of the all-powerful individual who just needs to press a key to cause a major event. Here it is a question of targeting the city's vital infrastructures. Radars in the airport were temporarily out of service. "the emergency generators

---

16 [COO 00], p. 107.
17 [COO 00], p. 104-105.

were online in three minutes and the radars sweeping the skies in three and a half"[18]. Even if the major infrastructures have relatively quick means of starting up again, the aggressor has a freedom of action time. Cutting off the electricity sowed the seeds of chaos in information systems: "When the controllers finally got one of the computers online, the hard drive refused to accept new data via modem. Manually inputted data was changed in random ways – flight numbers were transposed, altitude data were incorrect, way points were dropped or added, and the data kept changing. It was almost as if the computer had had a lobotomy"[19]. There is prolonged chaos in the port of Hong Kong where the management system is also paralyzed. "The technicians in the Hong Kong harbormaster's office were also having problems. The radars that kept track of the myriad of ships, barges, tugs and boats of every kind and description in Victoria Harbor and the strait were working, but the computer that processed the information and presented it to the harbor controller was no longer able to identify or track targets. When the technicians tried the backup computer, they found it had a similar disease"[20]. This attack marks the beginning of a revolution: "The revolution has begun!"[21]

In this novel, Hong Kong is chosen as a platform from which attacks on Chinese authorities are launched.

The novel recalls precisely just how Hong Kong, following the example of Singapore, is dependent on its harbor infrastructure and its financial system, which thus constitute the territory's most vulnerable, vital infrastructures. CAHK's 2007 report drew up a list of the communication infrastructures developed in Hong Kong, which may especially be considered as vital infrastructures: the public transport system Octopus, the airport's management system, the harbor's management system and the banking system.

Hong Kong organizes its own security system. By taking part in cyberattack simulations, as was the case in 2008 in the APCERT Drill framework, or still on July 16th 2009 when the Hong Kong CERT led a large-scale exercise, covering the entire territory and aiming to review the level of preparation of the Internet's entire infrastructure[22]. Many cyberattack scenarios were carried out. This exercise was implemented after an increased number of cyberattacks was recorded in Hong Kong (455 incidents involving cybersecurity during the first semester of 2009, meaning a rise of 12% in related to the same period from the previous year).

---

18 [COO 00], p. 105.
19 [COO 00], p. 106.
20 [COO 00], p. 107.
21 [COO 00], p. 108.
22 *HKCERT Conducts Hong Kong 1st Cyber Security Drill*, July 16th 2009, www.info. gov.hk/digital21/eng/press/press_releases_200907162000.htm.

In terms of network security, the figures shown by HKCERT seem reassuring. Only 219 security alerts in 2009 were published on the site, compared to 138 in 2001, which does not indicate any major increase. A total of 1,631 alerts were published over the 2001 period – third trimester of 2010. No virus alert has been published on the site since 2008, and only 89 over the 2001-2010 period. 8,158 safety incident reports were also recorded during the same period, as well as 9,144 virus attack reports.

Just like everywhere else in the world, hackers have been arrested over the last few years in Hong Kong. Let us use the example of Choi-Kong Lam, a young hacker only 19 years old, condemned to 6 months' imprisonment in December 2000 for interfering with the operation of a local Internet access provider (HKT, of cable and wireless). In the same period, a group from the Hong Kong government proposed increasing the penalty for cybercrimes and, in particular, to bring the maximum prison sentence for computer hacking from 5 to 14 years.

Hong Kong is no less affected by events impacting its information space due to the vulnerabilities specific to cyberspace than any other nation in the world.

Across a territory with a small surface area such as Hong Kong, scandals hitting celebrities from show business or politics, in the form of attacks on their private lives, may cause large problems within society and the political and economic sector. In this sense, the Internet may prove to have a fearful efficiency of impacting individuals and, through them, groups and social networks.

We have been able to note how the role of rumors might be important in China, as anywhere, and how the Internet and its new applications make it possible for this phenomenon to be played out with more efficiency than before. These last months, a number of riots and working class uprisings have found their origins in China, based on information or rumors spread on the net and its new applications (Twitter, Myspace, etc.) [VEN 10].

Hong Kong has not been spared from the use of the Internet for means of destabilizing individuals and groups of individuals.

The Edison Chen affair illustrates this. This was a scandal which scattered across the Hong Kong celebrity environment. In January 2008, hundreds of photos revealing the actor's sexual exploits with famous stars were published on the Internet. Publications were spread over several days. The scandal involved well-known actresses and stars, such as Gilian Chung, Bobo Chan, Cecilia Chung, Mandy Chen, etc. Edison Chen preferred to leave Hong Kong.

Nearly 3 years after the publication of these photos, a number of them are still available on the Internet today. Edison Chen had saved photos and films of his sexual encounters on his cell phone. The data had been stolen from his cell when it was being repaired. The story drew a wave of attention in Hong Kong and whoever had put the photos online that had been downloaded elsewhere would be liable to go to prison.

In Hong Kong, sensitive and nominative data has also been stolen:

– within the police force (for instance, data from 20,000 plaintiffs was stolen in March 2006);

– in the financial sector (theft of nominative data in the Hong Kong and Shanghai Banking Cooperation, in 2008).

Without a doubt, Hong Kong is a target. But it might also be a place where attacks originate. The famous hacker group, the "Blondes" had a base in Hong Kong, where they launched thousands of attacks on neighboring China.

7.1.5. *The Google affair*

In December 2009, Google and many other American companies were victims of computer hacking. These companies reacted, with Google acting as a spearhead and immediately accusing China of its lack of intervention and complicity. For Google, this was officially going too far. It had been the victim of China's pressure, of these hackers and its authorities which had been imposing censoring constraints for years too many times. Google threatened to stop censoring its search engine in China, and to come out of China.

By being based in Hong Kong, in spite of everything Google chose to stay in China (one country, even if there are two systems), at the same time distancing away from Beijing (two systems, even if there is only single country). But nothing could guarantee that the company was safer in Hong Kong than in Beijing from the potential intrusions made by Chinese hackers.

A stretch of ocean separates the island of Hong Kong from mainland China, and on the mainland on the other side of the border, stretches Shenzhen, with those intimidating industrial centers where we also find high-tech businesses clustered together whose development is supported by Beijing. China is omnipresent in Hong Kong, in Times Square, as anywhere else. Companies live in the lion's den in Hong Kong as much as they do in Shenzhen or Beijing. Google's action is therefore placed on a more symbolic scale.

2000	Google develops interface in Chinese for its site Google.com
2002	Google.com is temporarily accessible in China
2006	Google.cn is launched
2008	Free music downloading is launched, for compete with Baidu
March 2009	Authorities block access to YouTube
June 2009	Google is accused of broadcasting obscene content. Google.com and Gmail cannot be accessed in China
September 2009	Lee Kai-Fu, head of Google China, resigns to start up his own company
October 2009	A group of Chinese writers accuse Google of violating copyrights
January 2010	Google announces that it no longer wants to censor content in China and thus triggers its possible withdrawal from China

Table 7.1. *History of Google in China*

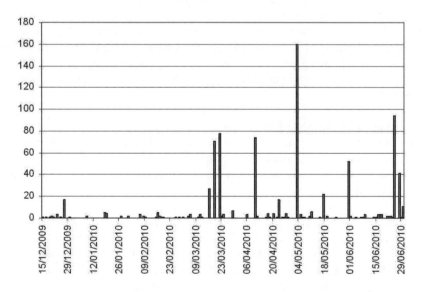

Figure 7.5. *Site defacements during the Google affair (December 15th 2009 to June 30th 2010). Graph generated using data published on site zone-h.org*

Google was then set up in Times Square, a symbolic place also chosen by students and activists to erect the Goddess of Liberty, a few days before the commemorations on June 4th 2010[23].

According to a survey led by the *Global Times*, branch of *People's Daily*, to the question "what do you think of Google's withdrawal from China?" more than 84% of participants (27,000 people) answered that it was not important to them[24]. If Google wants to leave, whether it does or not, we can simply go back to Baidu, we can live without Google, an anonymous person had written on the Xinmin.cn portal.

But the Chinese authorities who had been relatively indifferent up until then to Google's fate and choices, reacted rather firmly to the official announcement of the end of Google's censoring: "Google violated its written promise" declared a Chinese official, "and made a mistake by stopping the censor of search engine results in Chinese, as well as accusing China of computer hacking[25]. China was said to have opposed the political involvement of business affairs. The Foreign Affairs minister, however, confirmed that the Google affair had no impact on Sino-American relations. From a business point of view, Google's position worried Chinese partners who had signed publicity contracts, thus demanding compensation if Google came to close the Chinese portal[26].

At the same time, a company managed by Huang Jiangxuan created a "copy" of Google, *Goojje*, and obtained funds to get up and running (more than 10 million Yuans). The company was set up in the high-tech industrial park in Shenzhen. It was not the multiple attacks on the site that discouraged its founder, or the letters from Google demanding that Goojje stop its activity, whose logo happens to be similar to Google's[27].

7.2. North Korea: unknown figure of asymmetrical threat

North Korea is a particularly interesting study case from many different angles: the country is not well known, very little verifiable information comes from it, no one can draw an accurate image of the country's situation, particularly regarding its communication infrastructures (telephones, Internet), and no one is in a position to say whether North Korea actually represents a cyber threat alone, i.e. without the

---

23 The symbolic structure was confiscated by the police and put in the Victoria park. A statue was erected in the *Chinese University*.
24 "Web users express indifference and uncertainty over Google exit", *South China Morning Post*, p. 4, March 23th 2010.
25 *South China Morning Post*, March 24th 2010.
26 *Shenzhen Daily*, p. 9, March 18th 2010.
27 *Shenzhen Daily*, p. 2, March 1st 2010.

help of its Chinese neighbor. What are the capabilities of North Korea? Would it be able to launch large scale, destabilizing operation or only intelligence operations? Can this country, whose Internet infrastructures are so small, play with the big kids when it comes to cyberwar?

The North Korean Internet was designed as an Intranet that its citizens could use on a national scale in 2000. The accessible content was designed strictly in the same country. A few elitists, particularly political and military [HAS 04], can however access the global Internet, via connections at China Netcom and through satellites. The first cell phone network was created in 2002 by the company Loxley Pacific and the North-Korean government. Residents in Pyongyang and a few other cities in the country can now use cell phones, without, however, being able to access direct international communications, with restrictions on communicating with foreign residents[28].

Over the last few months, North Korea seems to be progressing towards more Internet services, and looking for national solutions to develop its information systems:

– on June 11th 2010, the *New York Times* reported that 1,024 IP addresses were recorded by North Korea via a company registered in Pyongyang. Might this be one of the first moves on behalf of the North Korean Republic towards the global Internet?

– North Korea uses servers located abroad (in China or Japan, for instance) to broadcast official information: the *Korean Central News Agency* site (www.kcna.co.jp) is hosted in Tokyo, and the *Pyongyang Times* site (www.times.dprkorea.com) is hosted in Beijing;

– the country has developed its own operating system[29], the *Red Star Operating System*, based on Linux[30];

– in August 2010, the official site Uriminzokkiri[31] was put onto Twitter as well as Flickr and YouTube. The North Koreans have no access to these pages which are intended for international usage.

---

28 *US pushes North Korea on Twitter Freedom*, August 17th 2010, http://news.yahoo.com/s/pcworld/20100818/tc_pcworld/uspushesnorthkoreaontwitterfreedom (site consulted on August 18th 2010).
29 *North Korea's "Secret Cyberweapon": Brand New Red Star OS*, 1[er] March 2010, http://rt.com/Top_News/2010-03-01/north-korea-cyber-weapon.html.
30 http://ashen-rus.livejournal.com/4300.html.
31 www.uriminzokkiri.com/2010/index.php.

Figure 7.6. *Red Star Operating System*[32]

North Korea launched a program aiming to catch up on its delay in terms of new information technologies: teaching programs were developed across the whole country, and industry developments are encouraged there. The Pyongyang authorities clearly displayed their desire to base the country's economic development on the ICT sector [KIN 04].

7.2.1. *Cyberattacks blamed on North Korea*

According to a report published in October 2005, the South Korean army confirmed North Korean intrusions into 33 out of 80 wireless military communication networks, used by units during military exercises with the USA (Ulchi-Focus Lens Exercise).

The South Korean army also confirmed that Pyongyang used 26 websites, upheld directly by the government or other pro-Pyongyang organizations, to ensure the regime's development and to lead propaganda operations. Through these sites, the North Korean authorities spread information headed towards their spies abroad.

According to Bruce Klinger, an analyst for the *Heritage Foundation's Asian Studies Center*, North Korean hackers attempted to get into American and South Korean military systems in 2006.

In July 2006, Unit 121 penetrated South Korean and the US DoD servers and caused damages [SIN 09].

---

32 Other images are available on the website: http://pics.livejournal.com/ashen_rus/pic/0003fcpe/

In October 2007, North Korea tested logical bombs: the information worried the United Nations Security Council, who voted for a solution to forbid computers being imported into North Korea.

In September 2008, authorities in the capital city of Seoul accused North Korea of leading cyberespionage operations against its armies by sending Trojan horses into email inboxes belonging to South Korean soldiers [CON 08].

The South Korean National Intelligence Service (NIS) informed the Prime Minster that since 2004, 130,000 government documents have been hacked (without specifying the number of documents hacked by the North Koreans). As is customary in these situations, the authorities hastened to specify that the stolen documents contained no highly confidential content.

In March 2009, a colonel from the South Korean army received an infected document via email, which was blamed on North Korea. The North Korean army hacked the South Korean's army command systems and stole passwords to enter the National Institute of Environmental Research site[33]. Regarding this incident, the South Korean military systems were therefore not secure enough when faced with North Korean (or elsewhere) hacker attempts. Hackers stole confidential information on the CARIS site (Chemical Accident Response Information System), upheld by the NIER. Nearly 2,000 pieces of secret information were stolen, with the names of 700 manufacturers of toxic chemical products revealed.

On April 7th, 2009, Pyongyang warned the United Nations Security Council that it would act firmly if the council took measures following the launch of a long range missile three days prior[34] (launched April 5th, officially condemned on April 13th by Security Council). Each person sees an act of provocation in the acts of others. Following the condemnations and hardening up of the American position, North Korea declared themselves ready to react: "There is no limit to the strike to be made by the revolutionary armed forces of the DPRK"[35]. Can cyberattacks be, for Pyongyang, measures and responses in proportion to the matter at hand? For which case can we build a relationship with between the "condemnations of the international community" and the potential "responses via cyberattack". In this case, the favored targets are, of course, South Korea, but also the 15 countries making up the Security Council. This means that those responsible for the security of the vital systems in particular must show themselves to be vigilant towards the political

---

33 *Military Admits N. Korean Hacker Attack*, November 4th 2009. http://english.chosun.com/ site/data/html_dir/2009/11/04/2009110400775.html.
34 *North Korea Poised for Cyber Salvo*, April 20th 2009. http://defensetech.org/2009/04/ 20/north-korea-poised-for-cyber-salvo/.
35 *North Korea Poised for Cyber Salvo*, April 20th 2009. http://defensetech.org/2009/04/ 20/north-korea-poised-for-cyber-salvo/.

action led by their own authorities on the international front, because it is likely to increase system insecurity.

In June 2009, Pyongyang accused South Korea of wanting to take part in the cybersecurity exercise "Cyber Storm"[36], considering this participation to be a provocation[37]. North Korea accused the USA of using this exercise to prepare preemptive attacks on anti-American and independent countries. This threat against Seoul was interpreted as proof of Pyongyang's involvement in the July 2009 cyberattacks.

From July 4th to 8th sites belonging to financial institutions, businesses, American (US Department of the Treasury, intelligence services) and South Korean governmental administrations and services (Prime Minister's Cabinet, parliament, Ministry of Defense, Ministry of Foreign Affairs) were paralyzed by cyberattacks. The majority of the Korean sites attacked belonged to conservative organizations.

www.auction.co.kr
www.chosun.com
www.hannara.or.kr
ebank.keb.co.kr
ezbank.shinhan.com
banking.nonghyup.com
www.assembly.go.kr
www.mofat.go.kr
www.mnd.go.kr
www.president.go.kr

Table 7.2. *List of South Korean sites hit (according to Panlabs, July 8th 2009)*[38]

Prime suspect: North Korea [PAR 09] or a pro-North Korea aggressor. A few days after the attacks, the British hackers were called up [SCH 09]. According to the South Korean intelligence services, the attack could not have come from isolated individuals. This was a DDoS attack. The machines used to launch the attacks were

---

36 Exercise organized by the United States Department of Homeland Security in 2009 and which aims to simulate a federal response to a major cyberattack.
37 *South Korea Hit by More Cyber Attacks*, July 9th 2009. www.foxnews.com/story/ 0,2933,530900,00.html.
38 List of sites attacked dating back to July 8th 2009, published on http://pandalabs. pandasecurity.com/ddos-attacking-us-and-south-korea-government-sites/.

located in 5 countries: Germany, Austria, Georgia, South Korea and the USA[39]. According to the NIS, 12,000 computers in South Korea and 8,000 in the rest of the world were used for the attack[40]. Other reports listed 167,000 machines compromised in the 74 countries used for the attack[41], others with 50,000 machines[42]. The aim of the attack was to test the information security systems and to test the USA and South Korea's resistance to these provocations. The aggressor benefits from these incidents, testing security systems or simply interferes with the systems' operation. The victims also benefit from these incidents. They give sustenance to North-American discourses on the necessary reformulation of security and defense policies. The incidents finally contribute to holding the South Korean discourse on the threats from the North, and to underline the belligerent nature of the relationship, due to the behavior of Pyongyang. South Korea also warns against Chinese and North Korean espionage attempts, and denounces intrusion attempts (more than 95,000 per day) in military networks[43]. These cyberattacks are part of the extended provocative maneuvers from Pyongyang against Seoul and the USA (nuclear tests in October 2006, May 2009 and ballistic missile launch in July 2009).

The North Korean cyber threat is linked to the Chinese cyber threat, where Pyongyang finds the resources it is lacking in there. We therefore have a power struggle in cyberspace which is similar to the one we already have in the geopolitical domain: USA/South Korea against China/North Korea. In between both of them, we have Japan.

In December 2009, the daily paper *Chosun Ilbo* published an article revealing that North Korean hackers had stolen an American war plan [MCC 09], namely a document with a codename of Oplan 5027, showing a strategy devised by Seoul and Washington in a war situation on North Korea. As is customary, official declarations stated that the stolen documents contained no sensitive information. According to Chosun Ilbo, it is extremely worrying to see North Korean hackers able to penetrate the Defense's information systems so easily. It was carried out with such ease that questions are now being asked as to the level of utility of the defense which is currently positioned all along the border separating the two countries. North Korea seems to be turning cyberspace into one of its favored operation grounds for espionage, and knows how to use it efficiently.

---

39 *North Korea Army, Lab 110, Suspected over Cyber Attacks*, July 11th 2009, www.huffingtonpost.com/2009/07/11/north-korea-army-lab-110-_n_229986.html.
40 *North Korea May Be Behind Wave of Cyber Attacks*, July 8th 2009, www.foxnews.com/story/0,2933,530645,00.html.
41 According to the Vietnamese business BKis, who also confirmed that the host server was in the UK.
42 According to an estimate by Joe Stewart from SecureWorks.
43 *South Korea Hit by More Cyber Attacks*, July 9th 2009, www.foxnews.com/story/0,2933,530900,00.html.

But the question raised by the paper is not specific to the Korea based army. All over the world, armies are relatively sensitive to enemy cyberoperations, when the information leaks are not coming from the soldiers themselves.

In August 2010 the press revealed a similar incident occurring between January and March 2010. Sensitive data was again stolen from South Korean soldier computers. Malwares were sent to the computers of 13 South Korean officers in order to steal secret information[44].

On October 16th 2010, more incidents were revealed to have taken place over the year, striking the Ministry of Foreign Affairs and the South Korean Ministry of Defense. Confidential documents were hacked. This time, China was accused[45]. But the documents concerned included information on China's relations with Pyongyang or Kim Jong-Il's visit to China.

In November 2010, a few days before the G20 summit in Seoul, cyberattacks blamed on North Korea were increasing. The daily paper Chosun Ilbo confirmed that the North Korea hackers were in China. Would it not simply be a question of Chinese hackers?

7.2.2. North Korea's capability in cyberwar

If the assessment of the real capabilities in information warfare or cyberwar is a difficult exercise when we are dealing with a country who makes no secrets of their policies, strategies and objectives on the matter (the USA, for instance), then it seems clear that any attempts to measure the capabilities of a country as closed as North Korea would not give any satisfying results. However, information and figures have been put forward:

– articles spread across the Internet suspect North Korea of the creation of "cyberwarrior" units, dating back to the end of the 1990s, notably within the army itself;

– the regime might have taken on between 500 and 1000 pirates to attack foreign countries[46], made up of a single information warfare unit within the army [KIM 09] and acting on government orders. The group of hackers working for the North Korean army is given the codename Lab 110 [KIM 09]. On June 7th 2009, the group

---

44 *Hackers Steal Army Secrets from South Korea*, August 27th 2010, http://techinfo.co.in/ wordpress/hackers-steal-army-secrets-from-south-korea.
45 *Chinese Hackers Seized SK Defense Secrets*, October 26th 2010, http://techinfo.co.in/ wordpress/chinese-hackers-seized-sk-defense-secrets.
46 *N. Korea's Powerful Hacker Army*, July 10th 2009. http://english.chosun.com/site/ data/html_dir/2009/07/10/2009071000588.html?FORM=ZZNR3.

received the government order to attack and destroy South Korean networks[47]. The existence of a unit known as "121" was also called upon, created in 1998, whose mission was to increase military capacity by developing asymmetrical war and cyberwar means;

– in 2004, articles listed 600 hackers in North Korea [LEE 04];

– in February 2006, an article talks of the existence of a hacker school in North Korea [MCW 03];

– apparently in 1997 North Korea created the Moranbong University to train cyberespionage experts[48];

– other analysts listed 12,000 hackers and a budget of more than $56 million (US), when at the same time the Yonhap News agency listed 100 hackers and no more than 1,000 within the 121 unit. Whatever the case, what we do know is that nobody knows anything which is set in stone;

– American observers have estimated that these hacker units are in a position to paralyze the US Pacific Command and cause damage to US networks (stealing documents, spreading viruses). The idea was put forward in 2005 during a conference in Seoul on security[49], organized by Byun Jaejung, Agency researcher for development of the Defense. These conclusions would be the fruit of the simulations (for which no information could be provided). According to Jaejung, North Korea was starting to create hackers in 1981, at the Mirim college;

– the skills learned in hacking came from the country's main universities: Pyongyang Automation University (Mirim University) which belongs to the army, Kim Chaek University of Technology, Pyongyang University of Computer Technology;

– North Korea might have been behind the CIA in terms of hacking capability[50];

– in 2009, North Korea came in at 8th place in the global threat matrix in terms of cyber capabilities [COL 09]. It developed specific skills, proved important experience in attacking South Korean or North American sites, developed capabilities for cyberespionage and had the potential to develop cyber weapons;

---

47 *N. Korean Hackers Ordered to "Destroy" S. Korean Computer Networks*, July 11th 2009, www.foxnews.com/story/0,2933,531637,00.html.
48 *South Korea is at War*, January 18th 2010, www.strategypage.com/htmw/htiw/articles/20100118.aspx.
49 *N.K. Hacking Ability Matches that of CIA, Analyst Says*, June 3rd 2005. www.asiamedia.ucla.edu/article.asp?parentid=25233.
50 *N. Korea's Powerful Hacker Army*, July 10th 2009. http://english.chosun.com/site/data/html_dir/2009/07/10/2009071000588.html?FORM=ZZNR3.

– the accusations and information published are often based on revelations from the South Korean National Intelligence Agency (NIA)[51]. These capabilities are estimates which come from South Korea, but which the USA cannot confirm [MCW 03];

– the information and declarations most often come from unidentified[52] or uncertain sources;

– North Korea develops its communications capabilities with the help of the international community. South Korea also provides its northern neighbor with fiber optics (45 km of fibers delivered during 2009, 37 km of copper cables had been sent between 2002 and 2007), in terminal equipment for fiber optic networks and measurement instruments. But these fiber optics were used to develop army networks and made the task of the South Korean NIS more difficult[53]. North Korea asked for new deliveries, delayed in Seoul (2010).

In the cyber threats matrix weighing down on the USA, China comes in first place with Russia, both known as being a "very high threat", North Korea, along with Iran, is judged as being a "high" threat.

Faced with the cruel lack of information regarding North Korea's real capabilities, it is clear that allegations, hypotheses and fantasies can keep gathering momentum.

It is also interesting to see how a State which has no Internet network infrastructure or decent telecommunication infrastructures compared to developed countries is presumed to be in a position to launch large scale operation against South Korea, the USA and other adversaries, including Japan. One of the explanations will be the use of Chinese infrastructures and capabilities.

This demonstrates a strategy, or at least a useful tactic of the weak to strong, and shows that a population with a very low penetration rate and for the Internet and any

51 *N. Korean Hackers ordered to "destroy" S. Korean Computer Networks*, July 11th 2009, www.foxnews.com/story/0,2933,531637,00.html (site consulted June 2010).
52 *N. Korean Hackers ordered to "destroy" S. Korean Computer Networks*, July 11th 2009, www.foxnews.com/story/0,2933,531637,00.html. "The paper, citing unidentified members of parliament's intelligence committee, said the institute, known as Lab 110, specializes in hacking and spreading malicious programs. The Ministry of People's Armed Forces is the secretive nation's defense ministry. The NIS — South Korea's main spy agency — said it couldn't confirm the report… The agency, however, issued a statement…saying it has 'various evidence' of North Korean involvement".
53 *Seoul Hampered its Own Ability to Spy on North Korea*, April 14th 2010, http://english. chosun.com/site/data/html_dir/2010/04/14/2010041400876.html.

form of telecommunication may present itself as a major challenge or an adversary in a context of information warfare, and particularly in cyberwar.

Western or South Korean investments in the gradual development of quality network infrastructures in North Korea are clearly in their own interests. An "existing infrastructure", indeed signifies a "an attackable target". At the current time there are not many of them.

7.2.3. *The Cheonan affair*

North Korea is accused of having torpedoed a South Korean warship on March 26th 2010, the Cheonan, leaving 46 South Korean victims. This major incident revealed tensions and power struggles between the two Koreas. The incident mobilized the international community.

The incidents which occurred in Summer 2010 between South and North Korea are not isolated facts. Tensions have been rising between the two countries for decades and have resulted in armed confrontations many times. For example, let us cite the destruction of a North Korean semi-submersible in 1998 by South Korean forces. In 1999, South Korean troops opened fire on North Korean patrol crafts which penetrated a debated fishing zone. In 2002, a South Korean patrol craft was sunk. In 2009, shots were fired on a North Korean patrol craft. Finally, we saw the destruction of the South Korean corvette, Cheonan, in 2010. These incidents are only one of the methods taken by the permanent confrontation between the two Koreas.

This incident is interesting because it demonstrates the scheme of accusation/alliance/denial in the attacks which are difficult to attribute to a particular country (we either lack undeniable proof, or the accusation has negative consequences on a scale we cannot control), and accusations which are systematically denied by the accused. This scheme is, in fact, what can be found within the framework of cyberattacks, and also attacks whose origin is difficult to pinpoint, which generally start by accusations (against China, Russia, etc.) based on indices or convictions, that the accused parties systematically deny.

In the Cheonan case, as in the case of cyberattacks, we find that:

– multiple actors are involved;

– actors, have their own interests to defend, interests which condition their arguments, interpretations, analyses;

– power struggles may change with events.

An interesting article published in the Hong Kong daily *South China Morning Post* [CHI 10] goes back to the analysis proposed by North Korea itself via its Ministry of Foreign Affairs. North Korea is known more for its threats than for its political analyses, remarks the article. The actors are accompanied by their reputation. This reputation can be highly influential, or even determine the opinions that we form of it, the images that we have of it. South Korea denied the accusations. However, denial does not make the culprit. The role of denial, to refute accusations is a recurring practice in international relations. China, accused of cyberattacks, systematically denies the facts for which they are reproached. According to the North Korean ministry, it is easy to find the culprit: we simply need to ask the question: "who benefits from the crime?" But the crime does not always benefit the creator, and the culprit is not necessarily the direct creator.

The difficulty of finding a guilty party is not just related to cyberspace. This problem is often finger pointed as being limited to cyberspace, and has advanced as one of the major cogs in implementing retaliations, and political or military reactions. In the "real" world, this responsibility might seem an easier exercise, when we have incriminating evidence and material elements making it possible to judge, but it is not necessarily any easier.

The problematic issue here is the way of using the accusation. Should we accuse the first person, even if it means doing so without having identified or blamed, thus putting the opponent party in a defensive situation? Or is it better to favor some thinking time to, perhaps, have a more sound blame?

The attack took place in a marine setting. Another major incident on sea space took place in summer 2010 when Israeli soldier attacked a Turk ship. In both cases, the incidents took place at sea. If we refer to existing comparisons between cybernetic space and sea space, then it is possible to see similarities with violent acts led at sea and in cyberspace. In the Cheonan case, the attack was unstoppable, and even if the backdrop of permanent tension which reigns between North and South Korea calls upon the forces of both States to remain in permanent alert mode, then the attacks still take their victims by surprise. Attacks led in cyberspace share this characteristic: with the awareness of threats being high, as well as security measures against these threats, then cyberattacks may still be prepared with the utmost discretion, circumventing defenses, and finally attacking by surprise. The second point that we will maintain here will be the strategic characteristic of operations led in both these dimensions. The oceans are a place for States to express their power through acts of violence, and this is the same for cyberspace.

7.2.3.1. *The cybernetic dimension of the Cheonan affair*

On May 20th 2010, an international survey concluded on the North Korean attack of the Cheonan. In the following weeks, according to South Korean intelligence,

North Korean hackers had stolen usernames[54] to post rumors on South Korean blogs, notably accusing authorities in Seoul of creating out nothing proof accusing Pyongyang[55]. The post content was the same as the official statement made by the North Korea National Defense Commission, posted on the official site, Uriminzokkiri. The website Free North Korea Radio (based in Seoul) recorded a high peak in the number of messages describing the Cheonan incident as a "construction made out of nothing".

But we do not know how to distance ourselves from the assumption that the interrogations on the official version from the Seoul authorities actually comes from South Korean citizens, and that there are not as many North Korean hackers as we would have it believed in this case. Protesters handed out leaflets in the streets of Seoul. It was, of course, not a case of North Korean protesters but only activists of the Northern regime or those against the Southern regime (which is very different, because being opposed to Seoul does not necessarily mean being pro-Pyongyang[56]).

In South Korea, as with anywhere else in the world, the protesters now know how to use the Internet and cell phones to get organized (as was the case in 2008 when protests were organized against the importation of American beef). The Twitter phenomenon has won over Asia.

A DDoS attack launched from 120 servers in China is listed around June 2008[57], and linked to the Cheonan affair. A website belonging to the South Korean government was also attacked [SHI 10]. Perhaps other attacks were identified, but in the absence of claims, it is still difficult to link a cyberattack to a given context.

7.2.4. In the face of North Korea: the capabilities of South Korea

South Korea is one of the most technologically developed countries in the world, particularly in the ITC domain. The TCP/IP network started up on May 15th 1982; one of the earliest developments of the Internet in the world. The first connection linked a computer from the Computer Sciences department at the National University of Seoul, to a computer from the Korean Institute of Electronic Technologies (now the ERTI), in Gumi. In January 1983, a third computer was connected to the KAIST (Korea Advanced Institute of Science and Technology),

---

54 *N. Korea in Clandestine Web Campaign Over Cheonan*, June 2nd 2010. http://english.chosun.com/site/data/html_dir/2010/06/02/2010060200550.html.
55 *North Hackers steal IDs to Post Cheonan Rumors*, June 2nd 2010, http://joongangdaily.joins.com/article/view.asp?aid=2921288.
56 The law forbids the spreading of messages favoring North Korea.
57 *Hackers Attack South Korea Government Website*, June 10th 2010, www.earthtimes.org/articles/news/328218,south-korea-government-website.html.

thus forming the beginnings of a real network. In July 1986, the first IP addresses for Korea were allocated.

In 2010, the annual survey led by Rutgers put the city of Seoul at the top of its category for municipalities at the height of electronic administration (*e-government*)[58]. The city also came out on top in 2003, 2005 and 2007. In June 2010, South Korea had 39,440,000 internet users, meaning 81.1% of its population (48,636,068 inhabitants according to the National Census Agency)[59].

On Figure 7.7, we notice that the number of internet users has not stopped growing over these last 10 years: this represents slightly less than 40% of the population in 2000 and 81% in 2010. But in usage, we see large differences according to age bands: 95% in the 6-29 year olds connect daily, against only 27% of the 50+. 70% of those in the city connect to the internet, versus only 46% of rural populations.

Evidently, the potential number of hackers, of hackers acting independently in the defense of the nation's interest, is higher in South Korea.

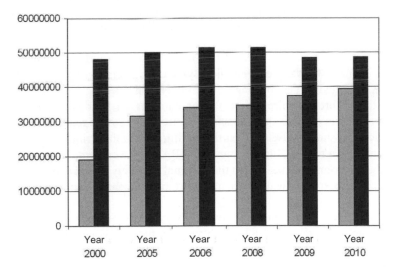

Figure 7.7. *In black, the South Korean population, in gray the number of South Korean internet users. Adapted from statistics published on www.internetworldstats.com/asia/kr.htm*

---

58 July 13th 2010. http://news.rutgers.edu/mcdrel/news-releases/2010/07/seoul-and-prague-ach-20100713.
59 www.internetworldstats.com/asia/kr.htm.

What is missing here are the North Korean targets. Hacktivists can only attack sites in South Korea or abroad, which might have common interests with the North.

The NCSC (*National Cyber Security Center*)[60] is a platform created in February 2004 which coordinates the public and private, and civil and military sectors in the fight against cyber threats. This authority is working alongside the National Intelligence Service, NIS.

In January 2010, South Korea put a new cyberwar unit on its feet [LEY 10], responsible for countering attacks most often coming from China and North Korea, and particularly the some 95,000 daily attacks listed against military networks.

Seoul has never hidden its strategy to develop information warfare and cyberwar capabilities. The 2000 report from the South Korean ministry of Defense revealed that the army had 177 computer training centers. One of the questions that we must ask is with regard to the level of accepted interoperability by the USA and South Korea in this domain.

These developments in capabilities constitute an argument for Pyongyang: if the South develops its cyberwar abilities, then the North must follow suit. Each actor with the same reasoning will find his justification for the arms race.

Faced with the persistent threats from the North concerning cyberattacks as well as conventional attacks, Seoul is deploying new defense methods. After the bombings led against Yeonpyeong Island on November 23rd 2010, the authorities decided to reinforce the firepower of their cannons on their island and reinforce tanks protection in case of a land attack, and threatened severe retaliation. Following cyberattacks in July 2009, and partly giving in to the temptation of fanciful protection using a fortress, digital "bunkers" [PAU 10] were temporarily deployed to protect the government's means and the national economy from DDoS attacks. Each incident is a pretext for new deployment and reinforcement of their capabilities.

The permanent provocations between North and South Korea, resulting in military attacks and tens of deaths each year on both sides, are an example of the level of violence that both States are to accept before moving on to a higher stage. In this context, we may ask ourselves about the position of cyberattacks in this confrontation: nothing will confirm that at least one of the States gives cyberoperations a strategic role which is either equal to or higher than operations led in conventional spaces. Could a cyberattack justify breaking a ceasefire?

---

60 www.ncsc.go.kr.

7.3. Bibliography

[CHI 10] CHING F., "The unlikely winner", *South China Morning Post*, p. A13, June 2010.

[COL 09] COLEMAN K., *North Korea Poised for Cyber Salvo*, http://defensetech.org/2009/04/20/north-korea-poised-for-cyber-salvo/, 20th April 2009.

[CON 08] CONSTANTIN L., *South Korean Military Equipment Development Secrets Compromised by Hackers*, http://news.softpedia.com/news/South-Korean-Military-Equipment-Development-Secrets-Compromised-by-Hackers-94876.shtml, October 2008.

[COO 00] COONTS S., *Hong Kong*, Orion, London, UK, 2000.

[DUM 10] DUMITRESCU O., *Considerations About the Chinese Intelligence Services*, www.worldsecuritynetwork.com/showArticle3.cfm?article_id=18347&topicID=53, 16th July 2010.

[HAS 04] HASSIG K.O., *North Korean Policy Elites*, IDA Paper P-3903, www.brookings.edu/views/papers/fellows/oh20040601.pdf, June 2004.

[KIM 04] KIM Y.H., "North Korea's Cyberpath", *Asian Perspective*, vol. 28, no. 3, p. 191-209, www.asianperspective.org/articles/v28n3-h.pdf, 2004.

[KIM 09] KIM H.J., *North Korea Army, Lab 110, Suspected Over Cyber Attacks*, www.huffingtonpost.com/2009/07/11/north-korea-army-lab-110-_n_229986.html, 2009.

[LAM 07] LAM F., "Message from the Executive Director", *Official Guide to Communications in Hong Kong*, Communications Association of Hong Kong, Hong Kong Trade Development Council, p. 14, 2007.

[LEY 10] LEYDEN J., *South Korea Sets up a Cyberwarfare Unit to Repel NORK Hackers*, www.theregister.co.uk/2010/01/12/korea_cybcrwarfare_unit/, 12 janvier 2010.

[MCC 09] MCCURRY J., "North Korean hackers may have stolen US war plans", *The Guardian*, www.guardian.co.uk/world/2009/dec/18/north-southkorea-hackers, 18 December 2009.

[MCW 03] MCWILLIAMS B., "North Korea's school for hackers", *Wired*, www.wired.com/politics/law/news/2003/06/59043, February 2006.

[PAR 09] PARRY R.L., "North Korea launches massive cyber attack on Seoul", *The Sunday Times*, www.timesonline.co.uk/tol/news/world/asia/article6667440.ece, 9th July 2009.

[PAU 10] PAULI D., "South Korea builds digital 'bunkers' against DDoS attacks", *ZDNet Australia*, www.zdnet.co.uk/news/security-management/2010/11/18/south-korea-builds-digital-bunkers-against-ddos-attacks-40090902/, 18 November 2010.

[SCH 09] SCHOFIELD J., "British hackers claimed to be behind us and Korean attacks", *The Guardian*, www.guardian.co.uk/technology/2009/jul/15/hackers-internetattack, 15th July 2009.

[SHI 10] SHIN S., RICHARDSON B., *South Korea Says Cyber Attacks Came from China Sites*, www.businessweek.com/news/2010-06-10/south-korea-says-cyber-attackscame-from-china-sites-update1-.html, 10th June 2010.

[SIN 09] SIN S., *Cyber Threat Posed by North Korea and China to South Korea and US Forces*, www.scribd.com/doc/15078953/Cyber-Threat-Posed-by-North-Korea-and-China-to-South-Korea-and-US-Forces-Korea, May 2009.

[TSA 10] TSANG P., "PLA personnel stay away from recreation club", *South China Morning Post*, p. A3, 4 mars 2010.

[VEN 10] VENTRE D., CHAUVANCY F., HUYGHE F.B., FILLIOL E., HENROTIN J., *Cyberguerre et guerre de l'information. Stratégies, règles, enjeux*, Hermès-Lavoisier, Paris, France, 2010.

[WAI 10] WAI-MAN L., LUEN-TIM LUI P., WONG W., HOLLIDAY I., *Contemporary Hong Kong Politics. Governance in the Post-1997 Era*, Hong Kong University Press, Hong Kong, 2010.

Conclusion

As we come to the end of this reflective work, we offer our readers a summary of the major themes, principles and questions which run through these 7 chapters. Our analysis, centered on the themes of information warfare and cyberwar, has allowed us to put forward a few main ideas. The distinction between *classic war* and *modern war* (in the sense of "cyber" or "technological"), is not entirely relevant. Strategic laws, however, remain relevant, even if the ways of applying force are evolving.

Thus, the role of the "strategy" in the information realm is confirmed as being a key aspect. Strategy is the only component which can give a meaning to the actions we take, and to give the operations force. In the absence of a strategy, attacks only have limited impact because they are non-exploitable. It is not enough, then, to have cursors ready to be sent to action (individuals mastering technology, targets to be aimed at), or a cyberarsenal (viruses, intrusion methods, concealment). Moreover, we must fix more superior objectives, include them in a comprehensive political system, and finally, write scenarios which can reach the objectives defined by the strategies. Therefore, in order to understand the current cyberattacks (the real ones, and the ones we invent), it is fundamentally important to focus on the strategy construction which may guide them, whilst avoiding focusing on the information that started the incident itself.

If strategy maintains its first place position, then for us it is, above all, an ability to anticipate, an action strategy, a proactive attitude and not a response strategy, a reaction strategy or a strategy for a total lack of reaction (is the "do nothing" approach possible? A question asked even by Martin Libicki in his recent major report *Cyberdeterrence and Cyberwar* published by the Rand Corporation in 2009) [LIB 09].

Conclusion written by Daniel VENTRE.

In a conflict context, it is not so much the speed (even if the OODA loop principle is still effective) or the capacity to anticipate one action before another, even when it is combined with an important striking power (strategic surprise is not a guarantee for victory) as the capacity to see thoroughly and build a strategy which can ensure success.

The concepts of *combination* and *complementarity* are essential here. There can be no strategic surprise without complex combinations, and no useful and effective cybernetic attack without operations accompanying it in other dimensions:

– if information warfare and cyberwar can disrupt the use of force, they do not substitute it;

– information warfare and cyberwar are not exclusive of the other dimensions of conflict;

– further still, actions led in cyberspace are not enough alone to produce important effects on the real world. When China manages a situation of crisis in cyberspace, it uses combinations of abilities and methods. When it manages the cybernetic and information dimension of the crisis, then it is done by a combination with the other dimensions;

– the methods must be combined together, but the elements within each combination must also be combined;

– cyberwar is already the art of combination: we must act simultaneously on its three dimensions (physical, syntactical and semantic);

– the difficulty that strategy is confronted with however remains as the assessment of the impact of using these combinations, of the influence between these dimensions, and the definition of the best combinations to reach a given objective.

Do we dare say that we are still in a period of observation, of testing (scale test), and of learning in this field?

All the problems related to aggressive operations lie in the ability to turn information "powerful", so it has an immediately useable "impact"; the information's power will come from the target choice, from the ways of using this information (or data), and from the most effective combination that we can set in motion (information, cybernetic and other dimensions). The speed of the operations materialized will also be a primary factor. The attacks must not only be directed towards systems.

Information warfare and cyberwar are not part of cybercriminality, both in terms of their motivation and nature.

But, information warfare and cyberwar are "wars" which are not really wars. They are not self-controlled; they are built into a strategy, and the characteristics of their manifestation seem to forbid descriptions such as "act of war" at the current time.

Inaccuracy (outlines, borders), uncertainty (origin of the attacks, possibilities, impacts, effects of the combinations, interactions, controlling abilities), fog (too much information, lack of visibility), lack of fixed situation (the space will evolve), impossibilities (of defense, imputability, recourse) persistent doubt, suspicions, and invisibility of the enemy all characterize the negative aspect of information and cybernetic space.

These "negative" characteristics (or positive, depending on the point of view: attacker or attacked?) are at the source of the sentiment of risk expressed by those connected with the information and cybernetic dimension. This perception has a major impact on our action. This risk forces us to engage in methods of resisting the psychological pressure that forms the cybernetic attacks, whether real or potential. If investing in cyberspace security guarantees no protection against this risk, then not investing will guarantee exposure to this risk. Therefore, Western developed countries who are dependent on their information environment are engaged in a sort of head-on race.

The set of uncertainties, inaccuracies and impossibilities to be defined and controlled opens the channel up to representations, to building a reality whose somewhat fictional, stereotyped character is, perhaps, not without its consequences on the representation that the actors themselves have of security and defense, and therefore on the very methods of conflict in progress or to come. Thus, we are handing the weak the power to fight the powerful (cyberspace as a tool for justice, the hacktivist as the sworn enemy of political and social injustice), to break through the protective walls of security (getting through firewalls, breaking down the Pentagon's or the NSA's software barriers), we are granting technology with a power which is harmful for society (if the technological systems fall, the society model which depends on it will collapse, as technology can conflict with citizen rights) and to those who use it, we are giving them disreputable intentions (wanting to attack, wanting to spy, wanting to destabilize). In this context of representation, generating the image of the enemy is also a key element of the cyberwar/information warfare problem. The technique tells us that it is difficult, if not impossible, to impute a cyberattack with certainty. We also know that the ability to use lines of code does not make an actor (whether this is an individual or a State) a criminal or a belligerent. The mere ability is not proof. And so, today, putting a face and name to these attackers hidden away in the shadows is a challenge. This is, then, left to the imagination, to interpretation, to construction, to hypothesis. These things will perhaps coincide exactly with the reality of it all. But, then again, perhaps not.

So who is the aggressor? There is no state-governed enemy so long as no State recognizes an attack. There is no possible enemy so long as we cannot impute with certainty, and above all, there is no enemy if the operation is only a matter of criminality. But this argument opens up the door to paranoia. Recognizing that there is no particular enemy is a bit like admitting that they are potentially everywhere. It is also a bit like admitting that the enemy is inside our own speakers. This is a slippery road which we will not go down here. However, the methods of discrimination allow us to classify real and potential problems, to limit the range of our own adversaries, competitors, potential enemies, that we do not, perhaps, share with our neighbors or allies.

Faced with all the uncertainties and impossibilities, we will also question the effectiveness of a security approach such as the "fortress" type or the "Maginot line", conditioned by a relatively dichotomous vision of the environment (targets and aggressors, good and evil) which clearly lends itself badly to information environments which are relatively fuzzy, to the permeability of systems, especially as "skirting" is a major art of attack in this dimension.

Finally, let us remember that man is (re)placed in the center of the technological structure that is the cybernetic dimension, and of course, the information dimension in its entirety:

– conflicts, crises and confrontations make individuals act, target individuals and societies. Information space and cyberspace are a place for expression, for conflicts to play out, a channel for action, but man comes in and out of the system;

– the human being is the arm, the brain, and the target of these wars (of information and cybernetic wars);

– information and cybernetic weapons are not satisfied with disrupting the technical systems, and are not confined to disturbances in the electromagnetic spectrum;

– the human brain is the target which suffers, as much as the technical systems, Denial of Service attacks, and saturation due to too much information, remaining as one of the main difficulties in situations of risk;

– information warfare and cyberwar are instruments of power: strengthening or weakening human power to the benefit or detriment of other humans.

Using information warfare or cyberwar is equivalent to displaying a will for power. We must think about their usage according to concepts such as power, influence, and strategy, which our model of society has at its disposal for defending its fundamental values. But what power do these methods of war really impart?

It is not a question of absolute or total power. Computer attacks alone probably have more of a power to harm, to disrupt, to influence than massive, decisive, irreversible destruction. The adversary's power is also born out of our own weaknesses that he will research and exploit, without looking to impose any spectacular "cyberarsenal": the attacker tries to exploit his target's weaknesses, to work on his flaws, his software and hardware, his human, psychological, strategic, tactical and political failures. The weakness may still be due to a lack of knowledge of his own environment and context. In the relationship between belligerents, it is the other's weakness which must be sought out, and not our own power.

The control over information space and cyberspace necessarily includes control over the building blocks which construct its base system. Europe must take the intervening measures in order to try to deal with technologies, standards and infrastructures. Taking China as a model in this field, which is trying to develop its *own* Internet, and to ensure control over it in the pursuit of its own interests (that we will not discuss here), and is striving to free itself from the grips of international standards by creating its IPv9, or achieving autonomy in the production of its own operating systems. This does not mean building a citadel which is cut off from the world and impenetrable, but rather managing its own environment better, freeing itself from the hold that others may have over its mentalities, on *our* model of society. Our weaknesses might also be born out of our insufficient use of the capacities of information space and cyberspace on an international scale, to the benefit of the defense of our fundamental values.

Bibliography

[LIB 09] LIBICKI M., *Cyberdeterrence and Cyberwar,* www.rand.org/pubs/monographs/ 2009/RAND_MG877.pdf., Rand Corporation, Santa Monica, USA, 2009.

List of Authors

François CHAUVANCY
CICDE
Ecole Militaire
Ministry of Defence
Paris
France

Eric FILIOL
$(C + V)^O$
ESIEA
Laval
France

Joseph HENROTIN
CAPRI
Paris
France

François-Bernard HUYGHE
IRIS
Paris
France

Daniel VENTRE
CESDIP
CNRS
Guyancourt
France

Index